A Biography of

Madeleine Korbel Albright

Ann Blackman

A LISA DREW BOOK

SCRIBNER

Seasons *of* Her Life

A LISA DREW BOOK/SCRIBNER
1230 Avenue of the Americas
New York, NY 10020

SCRIBNER and design are
trademarks of Simon & Schuster Inc.

Set in Perpetua
Designed by Brooke Zimmer
Manufactured in the United States of America

3 5 7 9 10 8 6 4 2

Library of Congress Cataloging-in-Publication Data
Blackman, Ann.
Seasons of her life : a biography of Madeleine Korbel
Albright / Ann Blackman.
p.   cm.
"A Lisa Drew Book."
Includes bibliographical references and index.
1. Albright, Madeleine Korbel. 2. Women cabinet
officers—United States—Biography. 3. Cabinet officers—United
States—Biography. 4. United Nations—Officials and
employees—Biography. 5. Ambassadors—United
States—Biography. I. Title.
E840.8.A37B53   1998
327.73'0092—dc21
[B]   98-28124
CIP

ISBN 0-684-84564-4

To Mike
and
Leila and Christof
With love

Contents

PART III PROFESSOR ALBRIGHT

PART IV MADAME SECRETARY

Author's Note

Seasons of Her Life is based on interviews with almost two hundred friends and acquaintances of Madeleine Albright and her family. Many individuals were interviewed numerous times. Because people's memories differ, I tried to rely on several sources for each anecdote. In many instances, I read quotes and passages back to the source, even if the person was not named, to check for accuracy and nuance. Where memories differed, I footnoted the disparity.

When quotation marks are used to recount conversations at which I was not present, at least one participant in the dialogue repeated the words to me as verbatim. In rare instances when information came from interviews conducted on "deep background"—meaning the source refused to be identified in any way—it is reported without attribution, but in every case the source was in a position to know the facts described.

In weighing information provided by officials in the Clinton administration, I tried to consider the motives and biases that are part of every political culture: of those who worked for Albright, wanted to work for her, did not get a job with her, had a spouse working for her, had a spouse who did not get a job with her, or, in some cases, of individuals who wanted the jobs Albright got.

Any errors that remain, either in fact or analysis, are mine.

Introduction

GEORGETOWN. New Year's Eve, 1996. At the corner of 30th and N Street, inside the redbrick Federal mansion that Abraham Lincoln's son Robert Todd once called home, a fire crackles softly at either end of the long, rose-colored living room. Tiny colored lights on the Christmas tree sparkle and dance off the eighteen-foot ceiling, and the silky voice of Ella Fitzgerald floats through the hallway. Guests are shoulder to shoulder, politicians and journalists, elegantly turned out in diamonds and black tie, toasting each other with clever, irreverent one-liners, clinking fluted, crystal champagne glasses shimmering with well-iced Moët & Chandon Brut. In the kitchen, Ernesto Cadima, crisp in his white jacket and chef's toque, is tossing a ham hock and sautéed onions into the pan of black-eyed peas.[1]

By 9:45, the annual party of Washington media stars Sally Quinn and Ben Bradlee is well under way. Hollywood diva Lauren Bacall—"Betty" to her friends—has arrived. Colin Powell and Al Gore are en route. Their entrance will be noted, casually, of course. No elbowing and finger-pointing. Most of those in the room have met them before.

Just after 10:00 P.M., a 1992 bulletproof black Cadillac Fleetwood limousine, equipped with a "secure" telephone for conversations with the president, pulls up to the curb, followed by a black Chevrolet Suburban "war wagon" carrying four security agents. Out steps Madeleine Albright, the newly nominated secretary of state, radiant in black silk. As she enters the pine-decked hallway, all heads turn. Even before the butler whisks away her black velvet wrap, she is quickly embraced with hugs, kisses, and shrieks of joy.

Albright had not intended to come this evening. In fact, she had not accepted the highly coveted invitation until that very morning,[2] when a friend persuaded her to put away her black briefing books for a few hours, that it was *important* to be seen at places like this, to do a drop-by. Albright mulled it over. She had no other plans, but something rubbed her the wrong way. It was so damned typical of Washington, a city obsessed with power, fickle to the core, a climate where who's up and who's down changes faster than the weather. She had lived right here in Georgetown, only a few blocks away, for more than thirty years. Yet this was the first time that Sally and Ben had invited her to their fete, the first time she was thought of as part of their A-list. Albright told friends that she was not sure that she wanted to attend. This was the uptown crowd. Would she fit in?

The irony was delicious.

When Madeleine Korbel Albright became secretary of state on January 23, 1997, the white male establishment that has long dominated American foreign policy was taken aback. It was one thing to entertain the notion of a woman in charge, to put a woman's name on the "short list" to placate the feminists. It was quite another for a woman to actually move into the spacious, seventh-floor office at the State Department, where even the secretary's private clothes closet had been outfitted with a sock drawer for men.[3]

Clinton made a dramatic statement when he chose Albright for the number one cabinet position. Although women have made considerable progress in breaking into middle- and upper-management, very few make it to the top. Of the Fortune 500 companies, only two have women CEOs.[4] Female executives hold high-level jobs, but all too frequently they are in departments that do not lead to advancement. There was another, more subtle irony to Clinton's choice. For a significant number of middle-aged male WASPs, who consider American foreign policy their private province, the day Madeleine Albright became secretary of state will go down in history for one reason: It was the day they were beaten by a girl.

Despite criticism that Albright is not a visionary like Thomas Jefferson, the country's first secretary of state, or a strategist like Dean Acheson in the Truman administration,[5] she was, in other ways, more than qualified for the job. She had earned a Ph.D. in political science and international relations, worked on Capitol Hill, served in the Carter White House as a staff member on the National Security Council, taught foreign policy at Georgetown University's School of Foreign Service, and represented the United States as the American ambassador to the United Nations. She had established herself as an outspoken advocate of human rights, an issue of growing importance in the United States' delicate relationship with China. And, having fled both Nazism and communism in her native Czechoslovakia, she understood the dangers of living in an oppressed society. "She knows what it means when the powerful decide about the less powerful, and that when they divide spheres of interest among themselves, this always leads to wars and misfortune," says Václav Havel, president of the Czech Republic and a friend of Albright since they met in 1990.[6]

It is this visceral understanding of modern European history that distinguishes her from most American leaders. "This is what Madeleine experienced personally," Havel says. "So she is aware of the meaning of symbols like Munich, symbols of division that never lead to peace and stability. She knows all about appeasement, about democracy making concessions to a dictator." Albright knows firsthand what happens to a country when dictators raise their swords, tyranny reigns, and everyone in the apartment building heads for the air raid shelter.

Just as important to her selection, however, was the fact that Albright was the candidate with whom the Clintons—both Bill and Hillary—felt most comfortable. President Clinton realized that he had in her a dazzling speaker with unquestioned loyalty to the people she served, a natural politico who could handle the press while giving him credit for American foreign policy decisions and not seek acclaim herself, as Henry Kissinger had done under Richard Nixon. "She was tough and strong on the issues that I thought were important, especially on Bosnia," President Clinton says. "She supported what I did on Haiti. When we had to do difficult things that didn't have a lot of popular support in the beginning, she on principle agreed with me. I could see she was willing to take . . . risks."[7]

Perhaps Albright's greatest skill is her understanding of American politics, a game that requires a sharp eye, a well-tuned ear, and, inevitably, a sizable dollop of good luck. Too often in the past, foreign policy decisions were made by politicians with no experience or feel for diplomacy. Or diplomats shaped policy with little understanding of the wishes or culture of those people in whose name the policy was formulated. Albright is a rarity among our national leaders, a person who understands both American politics and foreign policy and how one affects the other. In this delicate operetta that combines the two, Albright is a master, the crystalline voice of justice and common sense. "I thought she would be the person most likely to connect with the American people, to bring the message of our foreign policy home," Clinton said.[8]

This is not a book that analyzes Albright's approach to American foreign policy. Rather, it is the life story of a woman whose climb to the top rung of American politics was as unanticipated as it was unconventional. While any serious biography about a secretary of state cannot ignore foreign policy, I leave it to others with far more expertise in world affairs to assess the official impact of her tenure. My mission was to follow the path Albright walked to shatter the glass ceiling and become the first female secretary of state; to understand how, in a society that treats abandoned first wives like driftwood, Albright blossomed after her divorce. Who is this woman? Where did she come from? How does she think? What makes her, among all the other brilliant men and women in America, stand out?

I began this book with no road map except the desire to trace Albright's life, which I already knew had far more texture than that of most public officials. I first met her when I was covering the vice presidential campaign of Geraldine M. Ferraro, to whom Albright was foreign policy adviser. I interviewed her in my capacity as a *Time* magazine reporter when she was the U.S. ambassador to the United Nations. She was once my guest at a White House correspondents dinner, and we have numerous friends in common.

My goal has been to show how the life of this secretary of state was shaped: growing up in wartime Europe, coming of age in 1950s America, marrying into a family with more money than compassion, and spending her working years, like countless mothers for whom she blazed the trail, trying to master the precarious dance between family and job, vocation and avocation.

Albright has had a complete life—husband, children, dog—what Zorba the Greek called "the full catastrophe." She has known the security of loving parents, the comfort and rhythm of married life, the joy and challenge of raising children, the penetrating sadness of a stillbirth, the gnawing emptiness of her parents' deaths, the pain and anger of divorce. Ironically, the divorce liberated her, firing a fierce ambition that propelled her to the top echelon of American government.

This is the story of a woman who cares deeply for her daughters and family, a generous friend who regularly opens her home, whether to a friend needing respite from a messy marriage or someone simply stopping overnight in the city. It is the story of a homemaker turned politician turned diplomat who thrives on friendships with women and enjoys the company of men.

Like many successful and driven people, Albright places great confidence in her skills and ability to get things done, but she is also a woman of abiding insecurities who needs constant reassurance. Offstage, friends find her surprisingly vulnerable, convinced that someone or something out there is going to bring her down. She is more obsessed with her image than almost anyone on the public stage today.

This need to prove that she is just as smart as men at the bargaining table is one shared by many professional women. "Prominent men are considered smart until they are proven stupid," says Deborah Tannen, professor of linguistics at Georgetown University. "Women tend to be considered stupid until proven smart. The suspicion is that they do not deserve to be there."

Shortly after I started my research, Michael Dobbs, a veteran correspondent for the *Washington Post* and a onetime colleague of mine in Moscow, reported that Albright's parents had been born Jewish and that three of her grandparents had died in the Holocaust.

The story created tremendous controversy. Albright was raised in the Roman Catholic Church, so the fact that she might have a Jewish heritage was interesting but not remarkable. What was astonishing was that she claimed ignorance of her ethnic history. The Czech-born secretary of state, who had spent her career studying the history of Eastern Europe, insisted that she had only recently learned that her parents might have been Jewish, that she knew her grandparents died in World War II, but that she had never asked how. Nor, she said, had her Czech-born father, Josef Korbel, ever discussed his own family history with his children, even though he spent the first part of his career as a diplomat in service to the Czechoslovak government and the latter part teaching and writing about Eastern European history. Albright's assertion of ignorance stretched the imagination. It appeared that she was either extraordinarily naive or evading the truth. For a leader who had been in office less than two weeks, neither thought was reassuring.

Dobbs' reporting opened new avenues as I tried to understand the family history and experiences that have shaped Albright's life. As I traced her life from Prague to London, back to Prague and Belgrade, to Long Island, Denver, Wellesley, New York, Chicago, and Washington—from Georgetown to Capitol Hill, the White House to, eventually, Foggy Bottom—I found very few people who believe she was truly ignorant of her family heritage. In interviews in London and Prague with a dozen friends and colleagues of the Korbel family, not one thought it possible.

Yet almost to a person, those who knew and worked with Albright's father say that, at every turn, he distanced himself from his Jewish heritage, that he was an ambitious, pragmatic man who thought that being labeled a

Jew would be an obstacle to his career and his children's future. "The Czech government was not anti-Semitic, but it didn't help to be a Jew in the Ministry of Foreign Affairs," said the late Lev Braun, a BBC announcer and a Czech translator who worked with Korbel during World War II.[9]

Albright's love and admiration for her father are well known. At her swearing in as secretary of state, she cited him as one "who taught me to love freedom."[10] But there is more to Körbel's history than his daughter has discussed in public, hues of gray in a complex portrait of warring political ideals that she has painted more in black and white.

To understand Albright, one must understand Josef Korbel. Intellectually and emotionally, they are very much alike. As well as being an intelligent, gregarious, and witty diplomat who spoke six languages and had a reading knowledge of two more,[11] Korbel had an uncanny instinct for survival, an instinct that caused him to surrender his name, his citizenship, and his politics, and to bury his religious heritage.

Korbel seemed to want to forget not only his roots but even the Holocaust itself. While he wrote five scholarly books about modern Eastern European history, he barely mentioned the fate of Jews in World War II, the most horrific chapter in the period of his expertise. In his 1977 book, *Twentieth-Century Czechoslovakia, the Meanings of Its History,* published almost thirty years after he arrived in America, Korbel notes the existence of concentration camps almost as an aside and makes less than a dozen minor references to the Czechoslovak Jewish population that was virtually wiped out by Adolf Hitler. His longest reference is three sentences.[12]

In his later life, Korbel became a professor of international studies at the University of Denver, teaching European history and mentoring scores of students. He could not have had a more attentive pupil than his daughter Madeleine. It was Josef Korbel who taught her that a leader must articulate foreign policy in ways ordinary people can understand, that in times of crisis, citizens will not rally to the cause if they do not understand the impact it will have on their daily lives. Korbel was a loyal aide to Czechoslovak president Eduard Beneš and Foreign Minister Jan Masaryk, but he was critical of their handling of the Munich accord because they did not explain it clearly to the Czech people. Korbel also thought Beneš would have been a more effective leader had he spruced up his appearance and looked more distinctive. "His unprepossessing appearance deprived him of physical charisma," Korbel wrote.[13]

Consciously or unconsciously, Madeleine Albright absorbed these lessons well. Her father's analysis of what happened at Munich became the essence of the kitchen-table politics she takes to America's heartland at every opportunity. Her ability to reduce complex foreign policy issues to bumper-sticker slogans is one of her most celebrated qualities.

And unlike Beneš, Albright looks like a leader. Although short of stature and hardly svelte, she has learned to cultivate a distinctive look, using her signature jewel brooches, patriotic silk scarves, and a black Texas Stetson to make her presence known—and felt. Unlike Pamela Harriman, the late ambassador to France and doyenne of Democratic politics, who conquered a host of prominent and wealthy men in her bedroom before she invited them into her salon, Albright is not a femme fatale. Raised in an Eastern European tradition by parents who taught her that a woman can be both intelligent *and* delightful, she uses coquettish charm to elicit support from men without alienating other women.

Most important, Albright personifies values that we all celebrate. She is the immigrant who works harder than the rest of us to succeed, the physical embodiment of steely American patriotism. Despite her lifetime in Democratic politics and a reputation for bluntness, it is that patriotism, combined with her wartime experiences, that makes Albright acceptable to conservatives on Capitol Hill.

At the same time, Albright is the perpetual outsider: the Czech-born child in wartime London; the daughter of privileged diplomats in postwar Eastern Europe; the eleven-year-old refugee girl arriving in New York; one of only a handful of foreigners at a fancy private school in Denver; the scholarship student and self-styled Democrat among well-heeled Republicans and Yankees at Wellesley College; the daughter-in-law of a prominent and wealthy newspaper family that never really accepted her, even after she converted from Roman Catholicism to Episcopalianism to please them.

A sense of separation and distinction, and a striving for legitimacy, stretched through her life. In the sixties, when young mothers were expected to stay home to raise their families, Albright enrolled in graduate school to learn, of all things, the Russian language. As a young woman looking for a career, she did not choose teaching or nursing or art history, occupations deemed "appropriate" for women of her generation, but the arcane field of foreign policy, long the domain of Ivy League–educated men. In the early seventies, members of the Woman's National Democratic Club asked her to advise them as to how to have more of an impact on national policy, yet they rarely invited her to join them after the meetings for an informal lunch with the girls.

*   *   *

In many ways, Albright has been and is a bridge, spanning generations, cultures, and party politics as few before her have been able to do. As a child, she was eager to meld her family's Czech background with her new life in America; as a young mother on the board of Washington's exclusive Beauvoir School, the National Cathedral Elementary School, she worked to improve communication between school officials and parents; as a career woman in the White House, she became a friendly link between her warring Polish mentors—Zbigniew Brzezinski, her boss at the National Security Council, and Secretary of State Edmund S. Muskie, who had given Albright her first job on Capitol Hill. Now, as secretary of state, she has developed an unlikely and remarkable rapport with the conservative chairman of the Senate Foreign Relations Committee, Jesse Helms, whose cooperation, or intransigence, could spell success or failure for foreign policy in the Clinton administration. As she moved from country to country, culture to culture, language to language, war zone to war zone, school to school, marriage to divorce, academia to politics, slowly climbing the political ladder rung by rung, Albright reached out, eager to make friends, generous in sharing her wealth and contacts, all the while remaining enormously ambitious and focused on success.

Many people ask if Albright cooperated with me as I researched her life. The answer is no, and yes. When I began reporting in January 1997, Albright's friends reacted with enthusiasm. But several weeks later, when the *Washington Post* published its story about her Jewish roots, Albright issued an edict that she, her family, and her closest staff members would not cooperate with any of those writing books about her. Hoping to change her mind, I wrote Albright, as well as her brother, sister, and two closest staff members. I asked them to reconsider, arguing that those who know her best would be the most likely to paint the most compelling portrait of who she is. For nine months, I received no response.

Yet as I began interviewing Albright's friends and associates, it was clear that the secretary was monitoring my progress with an interested eye. On several occasions, her press secretary, James P. "Jamie" Rubin, told me Albright's staff was "reevaluating" her decision not to cooperate with biographers, implying that if I wrote favorable stories about her for my employer, *Time* magazine, they might be more compelled to cooperate. I told Rubin that I had never written a news story for what it would get me or the person in the news, and I would not write a book that way.[14]

As time went on, Albright's team began to soften. When I was putting finishing touches on the manuscript, they provided me with an extraordinary document, an eleven-page, single-spaced letter, penned in longhand by Albright's mother, Mandula Korbel. The essay offers personal details of the

Korbels' married life, as well as details of their escape from the Nazis. Written in hesitant English, with many phrases crossed out, it is a poignant love letter to her deceased husband, a wife's attempt to preserve on paper details of a life long since etched into her heart. Because women of this generation leave so few papers, their view of the world often goes unnoticed. Mandula Korbel's essay makes it clear that the couple struggled harder than they ever let on to deal with the horror of what they left behind. Yet in the eleven pages, it is never suggested that one reason they left Czechoslovakia was because they were Jewish.

In the end, less than a week before the manuscript was due, I had three sessions with Albright, totaling about six hours. The first was on Saturday morning, February 7, at her house. The black Chevy "war wagon" with four security agents was parked outside. When an agent unlocked the front door to let me in, the secretary of state was on her knees in front of the fireplace, fanning logs until they flamed. A second session the following week took place in her inner sanctum at the State Department.

In each interview, Albright was enormously forthcoming and open about her life, eager to recount stories and determined that I get the facts straight. She was also aggressive, as well as dismissive of individuals who she suspected had said something negative about her. As my mom used to say, she is *not* breast of chicken. At one point, when I advanced a theory about men and women with which she took umbrage, she implored, "Don't write about yourself or other women. Write about me." When I repeated to her what innumerable aides have said—that if a story is 99 percent positive, she will focus on the other one percent—she looked me in the eyes and said without apology: "So eliminate the one percent."

Albright had no opportunity to approve or reject any material used in the book. It contains disclosures she will dislike and judgments with which she will disagree. In the name of accuracy and at her request, I went over with her the facts of what she calls "the Jewish business."

Six months after Albright became secretary of state, she visited her native Prague and, for the first time, confronted the raw proof of her family's Jewish heritage. As she stood outside the Jewish Town Hall, her eyes filled with tears as she explained what it meant to her to see her grandparents' names among the 77,297 Holocaust victims painted in red and black on the walls of the Pinkas Synagogue. "Identity is a complex compilation of influences and experiences—past and present," she said. "I have always felt that my life has been strengthened and enriched by my heritage and my past. And I have always felt that my life story is also the story of the evil of totalitarianism and the turbulence of twentieth-century Europe."[15]

While the statement is a bit grandiose, it is also correct. And Albright has reason to be enormously proud of her personal history. She is part of a generation of immigrants, many of them optimistic, idealistic, and hard-working self-starters like herself, who are changing the face of America as it heads into the twenty-first century.

Hers is also the story of a woman who dared to dream, whose curiosity, ambition, and determination to master the rules of the game and explore new challenges distinguished her from her peers from childhood through middle age. She is an individual with a deep reservoir of intelligence, savoir faire, and common sense; a woman who takes advantage of the seasons of her life, decade by decade.

PART ONE

 ——————*Madlenka*

1

Bohemian Spring

"There were so many possibilities in the newly developed Czechoslovakia for talented young people who wanted to be a part of building the real democracy under [the country's founder, Tomáš G.] Masaryk and [its foreign minister, Eduard] Beneš. Joe wanted very much to be one of them."

—Mandula Korbel, personal essay

BOHEMIA, the ancient seat of kings, is splendid in springtime. Creamy white blossoms of towering chestnut trees stand proud and tall, straight as toy soldiers. Yellow flames of forsythia and lacy bushes of fragrant, violet lilacs line well-worn roadways that wind from village to village through sugar beet and rapeseed fields. Storks making their trip north from central Africa dot the skyline, and ravens begin repairing their twisted nests in church belfries.

By early June, bright red poppies and delicate strands of Queen Anne's lace fleck the rolling countryside as far as the eye can see. Along the paths that lead through the low mountain range dividing Bohemia from Moravia, purple and yellow irises flutter in the wind like miniature flags raised to celebrate another winter gone by. The network of roads, in place since the thirteenth century, is lined with flowering trees: cherry, pear, walnut, and apricot—all originally planted in the eighteenth century by Austrian empress Maria Theresa. She also ordered a fish pond built in every village square, along with a bell, in case of fire.

On June 7, 1878, Arnošt Körbel, Madeleine Albright's paternal grandfather, was born in the small country village of Kunčice, outside the town of Kýšperk, now called Letohrad. It is a centuries-old farming community, set in a pass between the Eagle Mountains and the Bohemian-Moravian Uplands, some ninety miles east of Prague.

Arnošt married Olga Ptáčková[1] from the nearby town of Kostelec nad Orlicí. The couple had three children: a daughter named Markéta, the oldest; a son, Jan, who followed his father into the building materials business; and Josef, the youngest and most intellectual of the three. Born September 20, 1909, Josef was described on his birth certificate as "Jewish and legitimate."[2] He was also left-handed.[3]

Josef was nine years old when World War I ended. On October 28, 1918, the Republic of Czechoslovakia grew out of the remnants of the Austro-Hungarian empire, and with it came the dreams of a nation for democratic rule. Witnessing the birth of democracy had a momentous effect on young Josef, who would identify himself with the national spirit of Czechoslovakia throughout his life.

The Körbels were prominent and hard-working, one of only about a dozen Jewish families in the town that, at the time, was home to about three thousand inhabitants. The umlaut over the *o* in their name, which was pronounced "KUR-bel," suggests a German origin. Arnošt Körbel owned a neat, three-story row house that stood across the street from the Kýšperk railway station at No. 305 Tyršová.[4] Built in 1909, the year Josef was born, it was one of only two houses on the street, which was lined with sturdy maples. A sign painted on the front advertised wares sold by the family business: tile, mortar, caulk, and sand. It was written entirely in Czech, which was unusual and showed that the family was fully assimilated into Czechoslovak society. A quarter of the population was German, and most Jewish merchants advertised in both languages.

Arnošt Körbel was a tall, outgoing chap with wide-set eyes, a straight nose, and a dimpled chin. He was a prosperous businessman who provided timber to Jan Reinelt's match factory, the principal industry in the area. In back of his house, Körbel had a stable where he kept two teams of horses that he used to haul cartloads of wood from the railway station to the factory. Körbel was astute at marketing, and by working together, he and Reinelt sold matches as far away as Prague.[5] Körbel and Reinelt were close friends as well as business partners. They sat frequently in the early evenings in Reinelt's dining room, going over their books, which they kept in a long wooden chest. Carefully crafted from local oak, the chest still stands in the same place today.[6]

Věra Ruprechtová, Reinelt's granddaughter, a chirpy, excitable woman with soft, curly hair and tiny, cornflower-blue eyes, still lives in the family homestead, where Körbel spent many hours discussing business. It is a large, ochre-colored house with high ceilings and long windows covered with bobbin lace curtains that hang from intricately carved wooden valances. The kitchen, heated with a small woodstove, also serves as Věra's bedroom. In the dining room she keeps a table filled with family pictures, a shrine to days gone by. There is an aging photo of Arnošt, wearing a double-breasted suit and fedora, sitting in a wooden cart parked next to the house.[7] Outside, an overfed brown bulldog named Dingo, friendly and outgoing like Věra, patrols the fence line, keeping watch over the family property. The house and chest are important to Věra, a touchstone with her family's history.[8]

Clearly enjoying the momentary fame that comes with having known the Körbels, Věra Ruprechtová holds court in her kitchen, her thoughts tumbling out in no particular order as she lays out plates full of powdery Czech cookies called *koláče*. As she talks, she peels hot boiled potatoes to serve with stewed chicken legs and big bowls of creamy, sliced cucumbers. As was common in the war years, she insists on sending visitors back to the city with fresh country eggs.

Arnošt Körbel, she says, was like a member of her family. He was a thoughtful employer whose workers were grateful for the more than a hundred jobs he provided in the area.[9] Religion did not appear to figure strongly in the Körbel family life, she says. Körbel celebrated the Christian holidays with the rest of the community, singing Christmas carols with his workers and accepting the loaves of Christmas bread they gave him as gifts. Věra did not know Körbel was born Jewish and did not think his workers did either. "If he were Jewish, they wouldn't have liked him as much," she says with a crisp conviction that suggests she feels the same way. "There was nothing Jewish about him."[10]

Arnošt Körbel was insistent that his children get a good education. Josef's fifth-grade report card for the school year 1919–20 shows that he was a fine student, getting all 1s and 2s in his subjects, on a scale of 5. His best subjects that year were the Czech language, civics, math, religion, and music. He was also a conscientious student. The report card shows that he missed only two days of school. It lists his religion as Jewish.[11]

There was no secondary school in Letohrad, so at the age of twelve Josef Körbel began attending classes in the nearby town of Kostelec nad Orlicí, a prosperous community where he boarded. A serious student, Körbel was active in the cultural and political life of the school. He belonged to its theater group and, even at his young age, aspired to be a diplomat, newspaperman, or politician.

It was here that he fell in love with Anna Spiegelová, a student in the same school.[12] She came from a comfortable family. Her father, Alfred Spiegel, owned a general store. Her mother, Růžena Spiegelová, had given birth to Anna in 1910, at the age of twenty-three.[13] They called their daughter by the

Czech diminutive, Andula. The daughter of assimilated Jews, Andula was a pretty young woman, about five feet tall with brown hair and green eyes. She was energetic, a bit offbeat, quick to laugh at jokes made by those around her but not one to tell them herself.[14] She was the kind of person who said exactly what she thought. When Josef once called Andula "the most talkative woman in eastern Czechoslovakia," she slapped him. Andula was bright. When she was a teenager, her family sent her to study business secretarial skills at a school called Les Hirondelles (The Swallows) in Geneva, Switzerland, where Andula learned to speak French.[15] Les Hirondelles was a family-run finishing school for girls from "good families" that wanted their daughters to become cultured brides for husbands of great promise. Situated in a residential part of Geneva overlooking the old town, the school encouraged the girls to have an active, but protected social life. Courses included languages, art history, music, world history, and letter writing. Good table manners and proper dress were encouraged. Students came from all of Europe, North and South America, England, and the "Colonies." They were expected to get to know the world through friendship.[16]

In 1928, when Arnošt Körbel became the director of a building materials company,[17] the family moved to Litice, which was five train stops from Letohrad. Josef, who by that time had completed secondary school, went to Paris for a year, where he studied French and liberal arts at the Sorbonne.[18] On his return to Prague in 1929, Körbel began his training for life as a diplomat, studying international law and economics at the prestigious Charles University, one of the oldest schools in Central Europe. Because he knew that foreign languages would be an important tool for a diplomat, he studied German and French with private tutors during his vacations. He also made a point of spending time in the Sudetenland section of Czechoslovakia, where he could practice speaking German.[19] He completed his doctorate in May 1933, then spent two months working for a law firm in Prague.[20] After obligatory military service as a lieutenant in the Czechoslovak army, Körbel worked briefly in another law firm. He also used this time to study English and Russian. On November 22, 1934, Körbel joined the Czechoslovak Ministry of Foreign Affairs.[21] He was twenty-five years old.

Josef Körbel was a handsome man. He stood five feet nine inches and had thick chestnut hair. His jaw was square, like his father's, with the same distinctive, dimpled chin. Körbel dressed like a gentleman, usually wearing a suit and dark tie, and he carried himself with his shoulders high. Women found him attractive.

On April 20, 1935, seven years after they met, Körbel married Andula, his high school sweetheart. The ceremony took place in Prague. On their marriage certificate, there was a blank to be filled in for each partner's religion. Both gave the same answer: *bez vyznání,* or, roughly translated, "without denomination"[22] or "without confession." Josef called his bride Mandula—Má Andula, "My Andula"—a diminutive she kept throughout her life. She called him Jožka. The late Jan Stránský, a lifelong friend of the Körbels, who lived in Connecticut, called theirs "an ideal marriage."[23] Mandula must have agreed. "He was certainly a man worth waiting for," she penned more than four decades later, after her husband died. "Very often I was wondering what I admired most in his personality. Was it his perseverance, which he probably inherited from his father . . . or did I love him because of his big heart, gentleness, unselfishness and loyalty to his family which he inherited from his lovely mother?"[24]

After they were married, the Körbels lived in an art nouveau apartment in Prague, where they had lots of friends. Josef was a junior diplomat with the Czechoslovak Ministry of Foreign Affairs, which kept him working long days at the office. Mandula spent her time keeping house and enjoying the city's buoyant café society. Josef was the more intellectual of the two, but he appreciated his wife's intuitive sense of people. She was not just compassionate, she was also street smart, and he depended on her.[25]

In January 1937, Josef Körbel was assigned to the Czechoslovak embassy in Belgrade as a junior press attaché. It was a relatively minor position, but the exposure to the inner workings of a key embassy was good training for a young, ambitious diplomat. Mandula, who was six months pregnant, went with him. She and Josef began learning Serbian, the predominant language of the Balkans.

Shortly before she was due to give birth, Mandula returned to Prague, where her family could help care for the new baby. On Saturday, May 15, 1937, Marie Jana Körbelová was born in Prague's Smíchov Hospital, not far from the Bertrámka homestead where, a century and a half before in a valley of vineyards, Mozart completed his famous opera *Don Giovanni.* It was a warm day, interrupted by an occasional rain shower. In the distance, still audible over the din of a lively quarter of the city, the silver melody of church bells rang on the hour from the towers of St. Václav Church. On their daughter's birth certificate the Körbels again marked *bez vyznání* in the space reserved for religion.[26] The first child of Mandula and Josef Körbel was named after Mandula's sister, Marie. Her grandmother called the baby "Madla," which soon became "Madlenka." Although the world would later know her as Madeleine Korbel Albright, she would be called "Madlenka" throughout her childhood.

Despite growing restiveness in the neighboring countries of Eastern

Europe,[27] daily life in Prague was relatively cosmopolitan. The local cinemas featured Laurel and Hardy and *Snow White and the Seven Dwarfs,* as well as Gary Cooper in *Desire* and *Anna Karenina* with Greta Garbo and Fredric March. Newspaper headlines trumpeted the civil war in Spain and political trials in the Soviet Union. On a lighter bent, there was a national contest to choose the first Czechoslovak airline stewardess.[28]

When Madlenka arrived home from the hospital, her presence created the kind of excitement and attentiveness that usually surrounds the birth of a first child, "the biggest addition to our happiness, not only to us, but to both our parents," her mother wrote years later. Madlenka was a good baby,[29] a healthy embodiment of all their hopes and dreams for a happy and successful future. Visitors were chosen carefully and asked to keep their stays short so as not to tire the proud new mother.[30]

One of the first to arrive was Madlenka's nine-year-old cousin Dagmar, known to the family as "Dáša."[31] She was the daughter of Josef Körbel's sister, Markéta. Dagmar's grandmother Olga Körbel brought Dagmar to the apartment. Peering into a bassinet, they saw a tiny baby tightly wrapped in soft white blankets with only her face and hands peeking through. "She was like a little doll," the elder cousin said. Not surprisingly, Dagmar was disappointed that she was not permitted to hold the new baby in her arms. "We were allowed to have a look and then we had to go next door," she said.[32]

Dagmar attended primary school in Strakonice, a town about 80 miles (120 km) south of Prague, where her family lived before the war. For one hour a week she studied religion. "I went to the Jewish class, and the local rabbi, whom I loved, had a row with my father," Dagmar said. "I had invited him to come see our lovely Christmas tree, and he [became] furious with my father."[33] Dagmar said that on several occasions, her grandfather and grandmother joined her family for the holidays in Strakonice. "I knew we were Jewish, but we always celebrated Christmas," Dagmar said.[34]

For centuries, Jews played an important role in Prague and the kingdom of Bohemia. The earliest records of Jewish history show a well-informed Jewish adviser to the caliph of Cordoba, Ibrahim ibn Jacob, who traveled throughout western and central Europe and visited the Czech principality. In the ninth century, one of the most important trading routes crossed through central Europe, leading from the west and the Frankish river Rhone to Kiev. For the merchants, among them Frankish Jews, the journey lasted eighteen months. By the tenth century, they shortened the trip by establishing a central meeting place. Frequently, they chose Prague.

In this era, Jews enjoyed the same rights and privileges as the Roman and

German merchants. They were free to settle along trading routes or near marketplaces where they dealt in furs, grain, wool, fabrics, tin, and wax, as well as horses, cattle, and slaves. They imported exotic commodities: expensive textiles, jewels, weapons, salt, wine, and oriental spices. The most educated worked as office clerks and physicians.

Yet in 1096, when the Christian soldiers of the first crusade traveled through Prague, a pogrom was staged, an act unheard of until that time. By 1215, community life had become increasingly difficult. Jews were proclaimed prisoners and slaves of the Holy Roman Empire, the property of rulers whom they paid to protect them. The Hussite revolution in the fifteenth century made it possible for Jews to acquire some professional skills. But when they cooperated with the Hussites, they were expelled from Austria and Bavaria. In 1454, they were banned from all royal towns in Moravia, a banishment that lasted four hundred years.

By the sixteenth century conditions had improved. One of the great scholars of the time, Rabbi Löw, was a friend of Rudolf II. Another Jew, Mordechai Maisel, was the king's banker. But by 1745, five years after Maria Theresa ascended the throne, Jews were banished from Prague for their support of the Russian army. It was only with the reign of her son, Joseph II, that they gained more rights. In 1786, Jews were permitted to settle outside the ghetto walls. And in 1848, they were permitted to buy land and employ Christians. The constitution of 1867 proclaimed full civil and political emancipation for Jews in the Austro-Hungarian monarchy.

By 1890, there were 95,000 Jews living in Bohemia, 45,000 in Moravia. The majority considered the Czech language their official tongue. Yet German was the preferred language of the multilingual monarchy, and some of the most celebrated authors of German literature were Jewish: Franz Kafka, Franz Werfel, Max Brod, Oskar Baum, and Ludwig Winder, among many others. The Jewish intellectuals were a catalyst that linked the German and Czech communities, and they often acted as interpreters. The assimilation process continued and intensified after the declaration of the Czechoslovak Republic under the democratic leadership of President Tomáš G. Masaryk.[35]

By the 1920s and 1930s, the Czechoslovak countryside was generally a comfortable place for Jews to live. There was little anti-Semitism. "You couldn't tell a Christian family from a Jewish one," says Hana Hanšlová, who was born in 1912 in Náchod, some thirty miles from Kýšperk, to a family that was half-Jewish.[36] Oldřich Šafář, the town historian for thirty-five years, says that while 8 percent of the Náchod population at this time was Jewish, there was only one Orthodox family.[37] In fact, there were so few practicing Jews that local rabbis had trouble getting ten men together for a minyan, the quorum required by Jewish law to say certain prayers.[38] If families in the Körbels' village of Kýšperk wanted to attend religious services, they had to go to the Jewish community of Žamberk, four miles away, which was the site of the closest synagogue. A small Jewish cemetery, set on a hillside overlooking the main street, served the chain of country villages.[39]

Even in the major cities, many Jews had no attachment to the culture and ritual of the Jewish religion.[40] Like the Körbels, many shared in Christmas celebrations with friends, not so much for the religious symbolism but for the joyous tradition. "I was the only Jew in my elementary school," says Michael Kraus, an architect in Cambridge, Massachusetts, who was born in Eastern Bohemia in 1930. "We had servants who were not Jews, and we had a Christmas tree for them." Kraus, whose father was a local physician, says his family also ate the traditional Christmas carp at holiday time: "I remember it swimming around in the laundry pail before it was slaughtered." Although his father was not an observant Jew and did not attend synagogue, young Michael never had any question that he was born Jewish. "Your religion was marked on all your documents," he says, "even the school report cards you got every six months with your grades." Another reason was that all Czechoslovak students were required to have an hour a week of religious education, and the program of study depended on the family's religion. Occasionally, a student would mark *bez vyznání,* but it was unusual because it stigmatized them. The others called them the "*bez vyznánís.*"[41]

When Madlenka was old enough to travel, Mandula returned to Belgrade to be with Josef. With a promising career ahead and a healthy new baby at home, Körbel's future looked bright. "Because we were young and happy, we . . . sometimes ignored the dark clouds which were forming on the political sky around us," Mandula wrote later. "We all were aware of it, but were hoping that somehow it [would] pass without catastrophe."[42] Her husband was well-educated, and his parents had done everything possible to prepare him for the tumultuous years that lay ahead. Yet who could know the choices the young diplomat would face in the ten dramatic years between 1938 and 1948, years that sealed Czechoslovakia's fate for half a century? The pathways were muddled, the stars unaligned. His would not be a world of black and white, but a panoply of grays, a constant tug between head and heart, where democracy and the balance of power pitched and yawed precariously like a sailboat running before the wind.

2

The Escape

"Unfortunately, the time of our personal happiness was all too short. Hitler was
too strong and too aggressive, and the Western Democracies at that time too weak,
and so the little Democratic Republic Czechoslovakia was the first to suffer, and
with it, millions of innocent people."

—Mandula Korbel, personal essay

As a young diplomat on his first assignment in Yugoslavia, Josef Körbel
was considered ambitious, a hard worker who took every assignment seriously. As a junior press attaché, his job was to organize lectures about
Czechoslovak history and literature and to arrange the showing of Czech
cultural films. Körbel was responsible also for coordinating secret meetings
with Serbian and Balkan leaders of the democratic opposition, a sensitive
task that he enjoyed.[1] But most enjoyable were the evening soirées of prewar Belgrade, where influential members of the international diplomatic
corps would exchange news and gossip over cocktails and dinner at the various embassies around town.

Körbel was a popular guest on the diplomatic social circuit. While Mandula tended to defer to her husband in public, Josef was gregarious, flirtatious with women, and brilliantly witty. "He had many friends here,
especially artists," says Jara Ribnikar, whose husband, Vlado, was editor in
chief of *Politika,* Serbia's leading newspaper. "Oh, because he was press
attaché, there were always journalists around, of course, but also painters,
sculptors, writers. He was a man of culture. Many people liked him. That I
can tell you because I was often with him."[2]

Jara Ribnikar's friendship with Körbel started before the war. "There
would be an official reception and then the official people would go, and we

would stay and sing songs," she said. "Everybody had to sing. Körbel had a good voice and knew many songs, even Serbian ones." She and Vlado often met Körbel at receptions or dinners at the French embassy. "That was the place where he danced," she said. Körbel had a magnetic personality, but he was not, according to Ribnikar, a ladies' man. "He was charming and everyone liked him," Ribnikar said, "but he was not a Don Juan, not at all."

That Körbel was Jewish was not a secret in the diplomatic community. "Everybody knew," Ribnikar said. "Before the war to be Jewish was very normal. Nobody thought about it as something special. He was a Czech, and we knew he was Jewish. It didn't interest us. The atmosphere was like that at the time."[3]

The atmosphere was about to change. The shadow of Nazi Germany loomed over Czechoslovakia. When Adolf Hitler became chancellor of the German Reich on January 30, 1933, he set in motion a plan for European domination that called for the destruction of the Czechoslovak state.

Hitler and the Nazi Party rose to power in Germany in part by tapping into the German people's sense of anger and humiliation over the German defeat in World War I and the terms of peace dictated at Versailles. Yet Hitler also appealed to Germans by embodying a set of values long thought to be rooted in the German psyche. He preached nationalism, strong leadership, will, force, and race, and, in doing so, struck a mystic chord in German cultural and political consciousness. In effect, Hitler viewed life as a struggle for racial survival and hegemony, believing that the survival of the German race demanded territorial domination and complete victory over the Eastern European states. He envisioned German glory under the "thousand-year Reich." In order to attain that goal, he set his eyes upon the vast territory that stretched from the North Sea to the Ural Mountains for the living space—*Lebensraum*—necessary to sustain it. *Lebensraum* required war, and war, in Hitler's view, would provide the true measure of the German race.[4]

The small countries of Eastern Europe, which already had strong cultural and economic ties to Germany, were natural targets of Hitler's aggression. For five years, Hitler focused his attention on Czechoslovakia, which, under the rule of President Tomáš Masaryk, was the most industrialized, most democratic, and most prosperous country in Eastern Europe.[5]

As American correspondent Max Putzel wrote from Prague in April 1938, "Without guilt of prejudice one can fairly admit that the political system the Czechs have created within the short space of 20 years is far and away superior to any other in Central Europe . . . , a democracy in some respects obviously superior to that of the United States, which is the oldest in the world."

The Czechoslovak state rose from the ruins of the Austrian empire. At the end of World War I, the Allied powers agreed to the formation of an independent state from the three "historic provinces" of the Bohemian king-dom (Bohemia, Moravia, and Southern Silesia), the primarily Slovak terri-tory of northern Hungary, and Carpathian Ukraine.[6] The creation of any nation-state from the remnants of a vast empire, however much based on historical precedent, is an imperfect and, to some degree, arbitrary one. The new Czechoslovak state included peoples of varying ethnic backgrounds and historical traditions.[7] The largest minority group consisted of more than three million ethnic Germans, slightly less than one quarter of the new nation's total population.[8] German majorities existed in the Sudetenland in western, northern, and southern Bohemia; the areas of former Austrian Silesia; and northern Moravia.[9] With time, the blanket term *Sudeten* was applied to all Germans living within the former Austrian provinces.[10] Part of the majority during the reign of the Austrian empire, the Sudeten Ger-mans now found themselves in the minority among Czechs and Slovaks.[11] Decades of antagonism between the Czechs and Germans could not be papered over by the construction of a new country, and the conflict between the new Czechoslovak state and its German minority, often angling for autonomy within Czechoslovakia or independence from it, was a con-tentious issue that would play a crucial role in the prelude to World War II.

Hitler exploited the large presence of Germans in the Sudetenland by using them as a pretext for German involvement in Czech affairs. Masking his true intention—"to smash Czechoslovakia by military action"[12]—Hitler hoped to establish just cause for German intervention in Czechoslovakia by framing the Sudeten issue as a case of Czech repression of an abused Ger-man minority.[13] And though Sudeten Germans were, by and large, treated quite well by the Czech government, particularly in comparison with other minorities across the world, Hitler's rise and the emergence of a powerful Germany nonetheless offered the Sudeten Germans an alternative to the cultural antagonisms that consumed Czechoslovakia. The presence of a revi-talized Germany on its border transformed the fledgling nation's Sudeten minority problem from a merely disruptive and contentious issue into a point of real danger.[14] For Czechoslovak leaders, the question would increasingly become how best to meet Sudeten demands without sacrificing the Republic. For Hitler, the question was always how to exploit Sudeten grievances to destroy Czechoslovakia.[15]

With Germany's occupation of Austria, and Hitler's declaration of Anschluss—the political union of Austria and Germany—on March 12, 1938, the Führer turned his attention to the occupation and total dismemberment of Czechoslovakia.[16] As it turned out, Britain and France assisted him in this matter. For even in the wake of Anschluss and the reality that the geopolitics of central Europe had shifted dramatically, Britain refused either to guarantee Czechoslovakia's borders or support France in the fulfillment of her obligations to support Czechoslovakia against foreign aggression as outlined in the Locarno Pact of 1925.[17] From Britain's perspective, war over Czechoslovakia was unthinkable. Prime Minister Neville Chamberlain's primary concern was the preservation of the British Empire and European peace, and if that could be achieved by ceding the Sudetenland to Germany, then that was the proper thing to do.[18] As Chamberlain declared in a radio broadcast in late September 1938, "How horrible, fantastic, incredible it is that we should be digging trenches and trying on gas masks here because of a quarrel in a far-away country between people of whom we know nothing."[19]

Britain was under no formal obligations to Czechoslovakia other than those outlined generally in the Covenant of the League of Nations. Still, both Britain and France shared some responsibility for the creation of Czechoslovakia (however imperfect that construction might have been) at Versailles twenty years before, and therefore both bore some moral responsibility for its territorial integrity. This is to say nothing of France's formal pledge to aid Czechoslovakia should the state come under attack.[20] Given France's reliance upon Britain in its relations with Germany, however, Chamberlain's commitment to staying out of war effectively left Czechoslovakia with no security against German aggression.[21] In fact, through the duration of the Sudeten crisis, France willingly followed Chamberlain's lead and, while paying lip service to Czechoslovakia, secretly welcomed the opportunity to wiggle out of its obligations.[22] Unwilling to go to war, Britain and France assumed the lead in pressing Czechoslovakia into accepting Germany's demands. In a telling communiqué to the German Foreign Office in May 1938, British officials stated that if the Germans would "confidentially" indicate their demands, the British "would exert such pressure in Prague that the Czechoslovak government would be forced to accept the German wishes."[23]

Such concessions were, in the end, meaningless, for Germany desired nothing short of war and had no intention of achieving a diplomatic resolution. The Sudeten question was a subterfuge. In fact, in late March 1938, Hitler instructed Konrad Henlein, political leader of the Sudeten German

Party, the heart of German nationalist sentiments,[24] that "demands should be made that are unacceptable to the Czechs."[25]

As the Sudeten crisis intensified, Chamberlain enlisted the aid of Italian dictator Benito Mussolini in an attempt to prevent war. Mussolini persuaded Hitler to agree to a summit between Britain, France, Germany, and Italy. Meeting in Munich on September 29, the four powers formally agreed to the cession of the Sudetenland to Germany. Czechoslovakia was given no voice. The agreement allowed German troops to begin occupying predominantly German areas by October 1.[26]

The Munich Agreement created a crisis in Czechoslovakia. "Munich was the final crushing blow," Korbel later wrote. "But it was also the moment of truth. The anguished days of watching, imploring, cajoling; the disbelief at the perfidy of friends and the betrayal of allies; the desperate hoping and then the loss of hope—all were finally over, and Czechoslovakia faced the enemy, alone. The nation's independence was in grave jeopardy, indeed, it was all but lost."[27] President Beneš met with his generals at Hradčany Castle on the morning of September 30, but all present knew that the risk of military resistance now, when it was clear that Czechoslovakia would be going it alone, left the government with few options. Later that day, the government issued a statement declaring that it accepted the terms of the Munich Agreement. However, it added that the "Czechoslovak Government at the same time registers its protest before the world against this decision which was taken unilaterally and without its participation." In a radio broadcast later that day, Prime Minister Jan Syrový issued a proclamation: "We were deserted. We stand alone."[28]

News of Munich left Czech soldiers and civilians devastated and demoralized. Some soldiers wept as they withdrew from bunkers in anticipation of German occupation.[29] Citizens rioted in the Czech provinces.[30] "Enthusiasm and determination were in fruitless conflict with utter depression and despair," Korbel wrote later.[31] Throughout the spring and summer of 1938, Czech morale had remained buoyant and optimistic. Some Czech people, faced with the prospect of war or capitulation, had rallied enthusiastically to the defense of their country. When, on September 21, Beneš reluctantly accepted terms reached by Chamberlain and Hitler at a meeting in Berchtesgaden (which did not, as it turned out, differ all that much from those worked out eight days later at Munich), somber, angry crowds gathered in the streets of Prague to register their protest. "Give us arms," they shouted.[32] On September 23, when talks in Bad Godesberg between Chamberlain and Hitler seemed on the verge of breaking down (in light of increased Nazi demands), and British officials warned Beneš that Britain could no longer in good faith advise against Czechoslovak military mobilization, Czechoslovak citizens were electrified by a surge of communal energy.[33]

That energy had spread quickly throughout Czechoslovakia. Able-bodied men joined the military. Körbel, himself a reserve officer in the Czechoslovak army, left Mandula and Madlenka in Belgrade and reported to his regiment.[34] All military installations were activated, including fortifications constructed along the border with Germany. The country was virtually 100 percent mobilized by the time the Munich conference took place. "I remember visiting my grandparents in Eastern Bohemia in the summer of 1938," says Jan M. Stránský of London, a grandnephew of Jaroslav Stránský, a renowned minister in the Czechoslovak government. "They lived near the German [now Polish] border. My uncle, Frank Kraus, had joined his military unit and commanded an armored train. In the woods and hillsides behind their house was one of the concrete bunkers. During the prelude to the mobilization, my friends and I would go up the hill to visit the soldiers. I brought them jams and fruit preserves that my grandmother had made."[35]

For the civilian population, mobilization meant that people had to take part in air raid and gas raid drills in cities and towns throughout the country. "I remember going to school in Prague with my own gas mask tucked into a canvas case that I wore over my shoulder," Stránský says. "I walked through a park on the way to school where there were trenches dug for people to take shelter in case of air raids."[36] Civilians were evacuated from areas along the German border and often took shelter with friends and family members who lived in the interior of the country. People stored emergency food and other rations in their homes, and in some cases, parents even packed their children's clothes in anticipation of evacuation to Russia, considered the only real friend Czechoslovakia had left.[37]

By late September 1938, Czechoslovaks were prepared for war. "Czechs Defiant," read the page-one headline in the *New York Daily Mirror* on September 26, 1938. When word of Britain and France's acquiescence to German demands at Munich spread throughout Prague, Czechoslovaks felt betrayed.[38] They had to face the painful truth that the Western democracies had abandoned them, a reality that sapped their faith in the integrity and reliability of the West.[39]

But Czechoslovaks also had to confront the reality that their own leaders had capitulated. Many of Beneš' political and military advisers had implored him to reject the terms reached at Munich. "It is true that others have betrayed us, but now we alone are betraying ourselves," one adviser said.[40] Körbel, too, was disappointed in Beneš and foreign minister Jan Masaryk for their lack of leadership in the crisis. "During the critical months preceding Munich, [the] leaders had made only perfunctory remarks about national self-reliance and the country's military strength," Korbel wrote later. "No psychological preparation had been even explored should the eventuality of facing the enemy alone ever arise. Even in the last days, when it became clear that France was desperately determined to extricate herself from her treaty obligations, the government concealed the real situation from the people."[41]

Körbel recognized that in times of crisis, a leader must reduce complicated foreign policy issues to understandable terms that people can relate to their own lives if he expects them to support the leadership's position. The diplomat thought the occasion demanded strong, charismatic leadership to rally and energize the common people. "It was one of those moments when the pendulum of history may swing one way or the other, depending on the will of a nation's leaders," he wrote. "In Czechoslovakia in 1938, the pendulum swung to capitulation."[42]

Munich sounded the death knell for Czechoslovakia. Although Britain and France pledged in the agreement to defend "the new boundaries of the Czechoslovak State against unprovoked aggression,"[43] both powers would, in the end, manage to skirt their commitments. Poland and Hungary quickly seized the opportunity to make good on historical claims to lands within the Czechoslovak state. In October, Polish forces occupied Těšín in northern Moravia and Hungary gained lands in southern Slovakia and southern Ruthenia. In the same month, Prague granted Slovak and Ruthenian autonomy, splitting up the country.[44] Four months later, on March 15, 1939, Hitler forced the new Czech president, Emil Hácha, to sign a declaration delivering the truncated Czechoslovak Republic into the protective hands of the Reich.[45]

That same day, German forces marched into Prague. Temperatures were below zero. "The people of Prague, their faces grim, their arms raised and threatening, watched the German soldiers shivering in the tank turrets and the open trucks that rumbled through the streets of the desolate city,"[46] Körbel wrote later. Hitler entered Prague the next day and celebrated his triumph by sleeping at Hradčany Castle. He immediately proclaimed Bohemia-Moravia a German protectorate. On March 23, he signed an alliance with newly independent Slovakia.[47] With the reality of occupation, Korbel wrote, "[t]he ultimate meaning of Munich was at last completely clear."[48]

Munich would become the twentieth century's most salient symbol of appeasement. Today, it is synonymous with diplomatic cowardice. In London shortly after Munich, Jan Masaryk spoke for a bereft country. "I have repeated lately that my little country has paid almost the supreme price in trying to preserve European democracy," he said. "And I say to you that if it is for peace that my country has been butchered up in this unprecedented manner I am glad of it. If it isn't, may God have mercy on our souls."[49] Given the path history would take, Masaryk's words cast a haunting shadow over the whole affair.

Two months after Munich, in November 1938, the Yugoslav prime minister, who had frowned on Körbel's penchant for meeting with leaders of the democratic opposition, demanded that he be recalled to Prague. Körbel had been attacked by Prague fascist papers as a "man of Beneš."[50] Soon afterward, the new Czechoslovak government, little more than a puppet of the Nazi regime, replaced Körbel, as well as others in the Foreign Ministry, with Nazi sympathizers.[51]

Beneš, who resigned the presidency on October 5, 1938, spent the winter and spring of 1939 in London and the United States protesting the destruction of Czechoslovakia. In Paris, his supporters and staff put together an Endangered Persons list of forty-eight people, of various ranks and backgrounds, whose government position or religion would put their lives in jeopardy. Its purpose was to form a cadre of individuals who would become a government-in-exile. The list was to be relayed to friendly governments with the hope that they would issue visas. Körbel was identified on the Endangered Persons list as a "ministerial councilor."[52]

Upon his return to Prague, Körbel understood that his life was on the line on two counts. First, he was a Beneš protégé. Second, he had been born a Jew. If he hoped to save his family, Körbel knew he would have to flee his homeland. According to Mandula Korbel's recollections, Josef thought he might be able to use his contacts in Yugoslavia to land a job as a London-based reporter for a Yugoslav newspaper, a move that would both get the family out of Czechoslovakia and place him close to Beneš and other political figures in the planned government-in-exile. He traveled to France and England to contact key figures in the Czechoslovak exile resistance, returning to Prague just days before German forces overran what was left of the Czechoslovak state in March 1939.[53]

Leaving Czechoslovakia immediately after the German occupation was impossible. "There was complete chaos in Prague," Mandula Korbel wrote afterward. "Communication was stopped for awhile. Banks were closed. Friends were arrested. We learned from competent sources that Joe's name [was] also on some list of people who should be arrested."[54]

Escape was risky. Exit visas were hard to obtain, and gates to the West were closing. Körbel's first thought was to go back to Belgrade. "My first thought for safety went to Yugoslavia," he wrote in his book *Tito's Communism*.[55] He knew the country. He had Yugoslav friends, and he was not alone in his plight. His plan would have to be made with much secrecy. He knew that if he did not get out as soon as possible, he would never make it—a situation that befell many Czechoslovak Jews.

The days were tense. Josef and Mandula sent Madlenka, barely a toddler, to the town of Poděbrady, about forty miles from Prague, to stay with her maternal grandmother.[56] The Körbels moved out of their apartment and spent the days before their escape literally walking the streets of the city, hoping to remain undetected until they could obtain the necessary papers to flee.[57] They stopped occasionally to rest in cafés and restaurants, making sure they were always in public places, where arrests were less likely to occur.[58] At night, which is when the Gestapo usually grabbed its victims, they were hidden in various houses around the city. "With all the possible and impossible planning, and with the help of some good friends, lots of luck and a little bribery, the last plan worked," Mandula Korbel wrote.[59]

On March 25, 1939, ten days after Hitler occupied their homeland, the Körbels were handed fake diplomatic papers, written in Czech and looking very official, stating that they had permission to leave the country.[60] That was approximately 5:00 P.M. By eleven o'clock that same night, they boarded a train to Belgrade, carrying only little Madlenka and two small suitcases, hurriedly packed, holding a few possessions. It was, Mandula wrote afterward, "the last time we saw our parents alive."[61]

It had to be wrenching for Josef and Mandula Körbel to bid farewell to parents they held dear, to embrace them, undoubtedly wondering if this time would be the last. Such sorrow can be overwhelming, leaving a raw emptiness that never completely fades. In their case, the parting was all the more final because all communication between Czechoslovakia and the West would all but be severed. Such tragic farewell scenes were repeated throughout Europe.

When the Körbels arrived in Belgrade, they needed a place to stay. They immediately turned to their old friends the Ribnikars, who had been close to Körbel during his term as press attaché. But Yugoslavia's government had sided with the Germans, and even old friends dealt carefully with each other. In the four months since Körbel had been recalled from Belgrade, the situation in Europe had become ominous, and the Ribnikars feared associating with the Körbels. Plans of escape were discussed in absolute secrecy. Only those who needed to know the details were informed. "Times were very, very dangerous then, and no one told you anything," says Jara Ribnikar. "I only knew my husband helped them, but I don't know how he did it. It was very difficult, because at that time no one asked questions. But I knew he helped them. He told me." But that was all she knew.[62] It would not have dawned on her to inquire about the Körbels' escape route.

The Körbels spent two weeks in Belgrade. Josef took care of several practical matters, including the transfer of family money to England and arranging meetings with Yugoslav newspapers. With plans in place, the family traveled from Belgrade to Greece, and from there made their way to Britain. It was the beginning of May when they arrived.[63]

Josef Körbel's older brother, Jan, was already in London. Fearing Nazi repression, he had managed to escape from Czechoslovakia a few months earlier with his family. Jan Körbel had remained in the building business with his grandfather and hoped to establish a new family business in England.[64]

It was early spring 1939. The Körbels did not have much time to pull their lives together and acclimate themselves to English culture. By September, barely five months after they arrived in London, Germany invaded Poland, pulling France and Great Britain into the war. For the Körbels and thousands of refugees like them, life would never be the same. Madlenka, a jolly, fat child who would soon begin to talk,[65] was not yet two years old.

3

Battlefronts

"So our life for six years was very temporary. We were living in other people['s] furniture and moved [a] couple [of] times from one place to another for many different reasons. It was sometimes for financial reasons or safety reasons or more comfort."

—Mandula Korbel, personal essay

THE KÖRBELS' FIRST WEEKS in London were depressing. They moved into a small, dreary boardinghouse, unimpressive by any standard, but one they were grateful to afford. With thousands of Eastern Europeans flooding the city, there were few jobs. Mandula spoke no English. Simply finding a park where Madlenka could be amused was a daily struggle.[1]

Körbel soon made contact with colleagues from the Czechoslovak foreign office. Within a few weeks, they had set up a temporary office in quarters rented by Foreign Minister Jan Masaryk. Mandula was pleased that her husband had an opportunity to start rebuilding his professional life away from their sad surroundings. "It was nice for Joe that he at least had a place to [go to] leave this depressing boardinghouse and start to establish some contact," she wrote.[2]

Soon the Körbels moved to 25 Prince's Gate Court, a redbrick, eight-story apartment building shared by other émigré families, not far from Hyde Park.[3] Little Madlenka had her own bedroom. Her parents slept on a Murphy bed, which stores vertically and pulls down from the wall. They lived on money they had secreted from Czechoslovakia, a small savings from the sale of Arnošt Körbel's business in Prague in 1938, when he retired.[4] They also had access to a special trust fund established by the British government for Czechoslovak refugees,[5] many of whom served in the Czechoslovak government-in-exile.

Josef Körbel doted on his daughter. As a result of spending so much time with adults, Madlenka was a grown-up little girl and did not have many playmates. Körbel sometimes took her with him to the office and introduced her to whoever was there.[6] One of those who remembers Madlenka at the time is Pavel Tigrid, a colleague of her father in London. "I wasn't very interested [in children], frankly," Tigrid says. "But I remember her as everywhere, terribly intelligent, a doer. Madlenka had to be noticed."[7]

One day Körbel took his little girl to a parade to see a detachment of Czech soldiers that was going off to serve with the British Royal Air Force as they squared off against the Germans. One of the soldiers picked up Madlenka, and a local newspaper photographer snapped a photo. It ran with a caption that read: "Father saying good-by to his daughter." Körbel was furious. When Madlenka saw the picture, she asked, "Who was the other father?"[8]

Although the Körbels were living in a foreign country, they spent most of the time with Czechs. They were, however, friendly with two Swiss women, one of whom had been Mandula's teacher when she studied in Geneva. The Körbels stayed in the women's country house occasionally, always insisting that they be paying guests. "We could only observe the English people and their reactions to the difficult situations from a distant [sic]," Mandula wrote, "more as observers than good friends. . . . It took me a long time before I could understand some of their way of life and was feeling comfortable in their midst."[9]

The leading force behind the government-in-exile was Eduard Beneš. After fleeing Czechoslovakia in October 1938, Beneš went to London. Bitter and indignant over Munich and the circumstances that led to his resignation, he continued to regard himself as the legitimate Czechoslovak leader and to sound a voice against the injustice that had been perpetrated. He was lecturing at the University of Chicago when German forces rolled into Prague in March 1939, and he immediately sent messages to British, French, Soviet, and American leaders to register his protest against the violation of the Munich Agreement. He returned to London in July 1939, in anticipation of the outbreak of world war,[10] wanting to be close to the action and hoping that, with a rapid Allied victory, he and the other leaders might restore the Czechoslovak state to its pre-Munich form.[11]

Shortly after the war started in September 1939, Beneš and his fellow exiles in London established the Czechoslovak National Committee, which in time gained recognition as the official political body of Czechoslovak emigration. The organization's ultimate goal, however, was to be recognized as the official Czechoslovak government. In July 1940, Beneš notified the British foreign secretary, Lord Halifax, that the National Committee had decided to establish a provisional Czechoslovak government in Great Britain. The British agreed, and Beneš was elated. He considered British recognition of the government-in-exile tantamount to recognition of Czechoslovakia as it had been constituted before Munich. He quickly passed word to Czechs living under German occupation that their state had been given a new life, and that after the war he would return as their president.[12]

After serving as a correspondent to two Yugoslav newspapers, Körbel helped organize the government-in-exile's information service. In 1940, he was named head of its broadcasting department, a position that put him in charge of programs sent over the BBC.[13] Czechoslovak statesman Prokop Drtina described the programs as "radio propaganda," explaining that they were "an extremely important part of our connection with home."[14] When three-year-old Madlenka heard her father's voice come out of the radio, she could not understand how he got inside.[15]

Körbel did not actually work for the BBC. The broadcasting company allowed the Czechoslovak government-in-exile to run an independent news service and to use BBC airwaves to send war news and morale-building messages to their people back home.[16] Located on George Street, not far from Marble Arch, the government-in-exile began broadcasting on September 8, 1939, five days after the outbreak of war with Germany. The first speaker was Jan Masaryk, then a private person living in London, soon to be foreign minister in the Czech government-in-exile.

The Czechoslovak broadcasts were irregular at first, but by the end of 1940, there were two broadcasts a week. In 1943, the BBC gave the Czechoslovak government two programs daily, each 15 minutes long. One was at 7:15 A.M., the other at 8:45 P.M. By the end of the war, there were eleven broadcasts to Czechoslovakia a day—a full 145 minutes—that Körbel orchestrated.[17] "Körbel was a very good boss, very severe," says Pavel Tigrid, who was working for the BBC when Körbel tapped him to come to work for his broadcasting division. "It wasn't easy. Everyone who had a voice, however stupid or intelligent, wanted to talk back home over the BBC. There were stupid generals and intelligent writers, and [at first] Körbel had only a half hour a day. Körbel's biggest problem was deciding how to allocate these fifteen-minute programs."[18] Twice a week, Körbel hosted a program with Jan Stránský, private secretary to the prime minister of the Czechoslovak government-in-exile, and journalist Ivo Ducháček. Titled "The Three Friends," it was meant to be a conversation workers might have at a pub over a beer. "We were very critical of the Germans," Stránský says (adding they did not drink beer during the show).[19]

Tigrid says Körbel's job required someone who could manage the massive egos of the government leaders. Jan Masaryk, by now foreign minister of the Czech government-in-exile, was one of the most popular diplomats in the West. The son of the nation's founder, Tomáš G. Masaryk, and Charlotte Garrigue, an American born in Brooklyn, New York, Jan was a playboy, not nearly as serious as his scholarly father. Jan had emigrated to the United States in 1906 when he was still a child, but in 1919, after the creation of the Czechoslovak Republic, he returned to Prague to serve as ambassador to Britain, a post he held for thirteen years. A brilliant linguist and conversationalist, Jan was a charming man much in demand on the embassy social scene. His radio addresses were especially popular.[20] "There was a certain hierarchy," Tigrid said. "President Beneš spoke on state occasions and whenever he wanted to. Ministers and members of the government, especially Jan Masaryk, were popular. Masaryk was certainly number one. He spoke weekly, on Wednesdays, and others were jealous. Körbel simply had to have the courage and backing to tell those who wanted access to the airwaves, 'No, impossible.' Of course, the pressure was tremendous. Many went to the president or [ministry state secretary] Hubert Ripka to denounce him, but he did very well and resisted. On top of it, he had the courage to give the younger ones of us who were twenty-five and twenty-six a chance as well. Occasionally I introduced speakers and, from time to time, I had the opportunity to write a short commentary. So this is to say Körbel was in a difficult position and did very well." Tigrid remembers Körbel as a kind man, very witty, sarcastic when necessary, and a good diplomat. Emphasizing Körbel's insistence on fairness when he dealt with colleagues, Tigrid says, "Those who were refused had to be told why."[21]

Eduard Goldstücker, an acquaintance of Körbel in London and later a professor of German literature at Charles University in Prague, says Körbel was popular with those who worked for him. While addicted to his work and very industrious, "he had a great talent for pulling together people from various camps and various political shades, Goldstücker says. "Politically, he followed the Beneš Democratic line very consistently."[22]

Körbel was a pragmatist. At one point, the Czechoslovak government lacked good Slovak speakers, so he hit on the idea of hiring Vladimír Clementis, a highly intelligent and talented speaker, a Communist who was not on good terms with the Czechoslovak Communists in London. Körbel consulted with Václav Nosek, later the minister of interior of the postwar Communist government in Prague, who said that while he and his colleagues would not recommend the appointment of Clementis, they would not withdraw their collaboration with the broadcast department if he got the assignment.[23] Clementis accepted the assignment and worked closely with Körbel.[24]

Körbel was so respected by his colleagues for his ability to work with demanding personalities representing different voices in government that many took for granted that he would have a long, successful career in the Czech foreign service. "I think he was the most gifted among the young Czech diplomats in that period," says Avigdon Dagan, who was in charge of cultural propaganda for the Czech government-in-exile. "Had the country taken a different turn, I think he would have been one of the leading people in the Czech Foreign Ministry. He may have become foreign minister."[25]

There was, however, one aspect of Körbel's personality that grated on Dagan. While Körbel was not affiliated with any religion, he tended to try and conceal his Jewish origin. "Everyone knew it," Dagan says. "It was no secret, but he tried to hide it. Since I was a Zionist, this went against my grain." Dagan, who now lives in Israel, says that whenever he tried to approach Körbel to discuss what was happening to the Jews, his friend refused to listen. "He was never ready to admit he was a Jew," Dagan says. "Whenever you started to talk about Jewish matters, he clammed up. He was like a closed shutter. Or he would start talking about something else. For me, this was very difficult to swallow."

Dagan found Körbel's refusal to acknowledge his heritage especially grating in light of the plight of millions of Jews throughout Europe. "In 1942, we knew what was happening in the concentration camps, that there were already gas chambers," he said. "He probably knew better than I because he was getting BBC material. But this didn't really seem to influence him, to change his mind."[26]

In truth, details of how the Jews were being persecuted spread earlier. On September 18, 1941, Hubert Ripka, the minister of state with the Czech government-in-exile, used the BBC to send a message entitled "We Think of You" to Czech Jews. "It was not sufficient for these [Nazi] barbarians to rob and plunder the Jews, cruelly to persecute them and sadistically to torture them," Ripka said. "We here abroad are well informed about everything that is happening at home. . . . We know that they are driving you out of your towns, that they are restoring the ghetto, that they imprison you in concentration camps and torture you there to death, we know what happens in the so-called labor camps at Německý Brod, Terezín near Choceň and elsewhere where even the older and invalid Jews are driven and where they must work eleven hours a day under the most shameful food and lodging conditions."[27]

The BBC's first broadcast describing the actual use of gas against Jews was on its 6:00 P.M. Home News Bulletin on July 9, 1942. "Jews are regularly killed by machine-gun fire, hand grenades—and even poisoned by gas," the bulletin stated. The 9:00 P.M. bulletin mentioned the use of "mobile gas chambers." Avigdon Dagan said he tried to talk to Körbel about the situation, "but it was impossible. He was afraid of touching any Jewish subject. He was a very ambitious man. He wanted to make a career. And he did, after all."

Another man who worked with Körbel had a similar view of him. "Körbel wanted to distance himself from his Jewishness because of the memories it brought him," says Ctibor Rybár, who worked in the Czechoslovak Ministry of Foreign Affairs and spent two years in prison in Hungary for being involved in the Slovak national resistance movement. "Some wanted to forget more or less. Körbel wanted to forget absolutely." Rybár, a former Communist who was later to become editor in chief of the Olympic Publishing House, said Körbel set himself apart from other Jews: "He didn't like to rub shoulders with us." Rybár says it took him a long time to tell his own children that his entire family went to the gas chambers. "I told them gradually, step by step," he says. "Today the kids blame me for not leading them to their Jewish heritage. They had to work through it by themselves."[28]

Although there was no doubt that Körbel was ambitious, one could argue that he was not denying his Jewish heritage but simply not interested in it, that he was an un-Jewish Jew, a nonbeliever who took no part in any aspect of Jewish life, whether it was religious, educational, or cultural.[29] At the same time, it is impossible to put aside the fact that Körbel's parents were ethnic Jews, that when Josef Körbel took his family to London, Arnošt and Olga Körbel had stayed behind in Czechoslovakia, left in the hands of Nazis, where—as the BBC reported under Körbel's direction—thousands of Czech Jews were being sent by boxcar to concentration camps.

The Körbels shared their Christmas and Easter holidays in England with Dagmar Deimlová, the daughter of Josef's sister, Markéta, and her husband, Rudolf Deiml, a family doctor. When the Germans occupied Czechoslovakia in March 1939, the Deimls had hoped to flee. But unlike Josef Körbel, Rudolf Deiml did not have diplomatic connections. Permission to leave was tightly controlled by the Germans, and exit visas were hard to obtain. Deiml had been offered a medical position in the United States, but he could not secure a visa in time to escape.[30]

Facing an uncertain future, Markéta and Rudolf Deiml made a traumatic decision. Hoping to spare the lives of their two daughters, eleven-year-old

Dagmar and six-year-old Milena, they booked passage for the girls on a children's train sponsored by an English stockbroker named Nicholas Winton, who was organizing refugee efforts for Czechoslovak and Jewish children. But despite their careful plan, fate intervened. Only days before the girls were to leave, Milena fell and broke her arm.[31]

Whether the Deimls thought Milena was not well enough to travel, or perhaps because they could not bear to send both children away—Dagmar is not sure which—Milena stayed with her parents. Dagmar boarded the train to London alone on July 1, 1939, two months before the outbreak of war.[32] It was one of the trains run by ČEDOK, the Czechoslovak National Tourist Agency, that took more than six hundred child refugees to England. Dagmar, who was not on the first train, was assigned the number 298. It was written on her trunk in white paint.[33]

She remembers the day with perfect clarity: "There were 241 children on that train, all Jewish," Dagmar says, "Some of them were very small. Most of them cried. I sat alone and kept saying to myself, 'Mummy wouldn't like to see me crying. Mummy wouldn't like to see me crying.' I sort of huddled in the seat. I remember looking forward to crossing the English Channel because I had never seen the sea before. But we crossed at night, so I didn't see it at all."[34] Like an aging actress recalling a particularly poignant scene that she spent years trying to understand, she tells her tale in a low, desolate monotone, a smoky voice that seems to flow from a deep well of sadness, sometimes falling silent when she comes to a moment or a choice or a question that defies words.

The train traveled from Prague to Holland, where the children boarded a ferry for the port of Harwich on the North Sea coast. Then they continued by train to London, where they were met by potential foster parents. Josef Körbel met Dagmar at the Liverpool Street Station. It was early evening.[35] "He embraced me, and I remember the first thing I told him was that I had a message for him," Dagmar says. "It was a letter from my mother." Körbel took the letter, but he did not read it right away. The atmosphere was chaotic, a cacophony of tired children wandering around, searching for British families who had promised to sponsor them. Instead, Körbel put the letter in his pocket and told Dagmar he would read it later. She never learned what it said.[36]

Dagmar's other uncle, Jan Körbel, had also established his family in London, and Dagmar spent her years in wartime England traveling between the two families. The Körbels enrolled her in the Berkhamsted School for Girls in Hertfordshire, a small, private school that was popular among prominent families who wanted to ensure a proper education for their daughters.

Clementine Churchill, the wife of Winston Churchill, and her sister, Nellie, were alumnae. The Körbel family sometimes visited Dagmar at school, and she would often baby-sit for her younger cousin. "Madlenka always knew her mind," Dagmar says today. "I looked after her. I loved her. I loved all the cousins."[37]

As the winter of 1940 faded, the war in mainland Europe intensified. On the night of April 9, 1940, Hitler's armies invaded Norway and Denmark, which had hoped to remain neutral. A month later, on the morning of May 10, Germany swept into Belgium and the Netherlands, and the Nazi southern column drove west across northern France. On June 17, France fell. Britain braced itself for a German invasion. On August 15, after weeks of waiting through the "Phony War," wave after wave of Nazi planes swept over England in the opening assault of the Battle of Britain.[38]

At summer's end, terrifying night raids began. September 7 was the beginning of a savage bombing campaign against Britain's major cities that would continue for thirteen consecutive nights. The damage to London was catastrophic. One bomb fell on Buckingham Palace. Others hit the British Museum and the Houses of Parliament.[39]

Each night when the bombing started, the Körbel family retreated to the basement of their apartment building. They often took bedclothes with them; if the raids were not too intense, the children could be made comfortable and get some sleep. "I remember sleeping on bunk beds and seeing lots of pipes around," Madeleine Albright says.[40] Dagmar remembers holding Madlenka on her lap. Once, when a bomb landed but did not detonate, all the houses in the area were evacuated and a bomb-disposal crew arrived. "They told us afterward that it would never have exploded," Dagmar says. "When they opened it, they found a message from the Czech workers who had made the bomb but sabotaged it: 'Don't be afraid. The bombs we make will never explode.'"[41]

In his memoirs, Prokop Drtina, minister of justice in the postwar government, writes that he enjoyed living two stories below the Körbels in London, because he and Josef were able to spend practically all their waking hours together discussing their broadcasts and the unfolding politics of the war. "This was rather joyful work despite the rather bizarre conditions we found ourselves in," he wrote. "We were working quite often with the whiz and detonation of Nazi bombs, and sometimes amid a never-ending cannonade of the British anti-aircraft artillery. But we were absolutely devoted to our jobs which, framed in an adventurous and dramatic setting, became not only our love but our passion."[42]

The apartment neighbors, who included an interesting array of intellectuals and politically sophisticated diplomats and military officers, spent many hours in shelters, drinking tea prepared by the air raid wardens and eating dark rye bread they spread with pork fat and salt.[43] Drtina remembers the Körbels' daughter fondly from those days. "Madlenka Körbelová, a four-year-old charming child, was a pleasure and an entertainment for all those in the air raid shelter who became close and friendly quickly in the dramatic conditions," he wrote. When the bombing ended, the families often climbed to the flat roof of the apartment building; from here they could see the houses burning around them.[44] Then they would retreat again to the shelter. "We slept down there practically every night," Madeleine Albright remembers. "We'd come up in the morning. Then I would go around with my parents and see what had been bombed."[45] The Red Cross made a movie to show what life was like in the air raid shelters, featuring Madlenka as the child. Her payment was a pink, stuffed rabbit with long, soft ears.[46]

Most Londoners sought refuge from the air raids in apartment basements, in makeshift shelters, or in the Underground, London's extensive subway system. A poll taken at the time indicated that when darkness fell and air raid sirens sounded, roughly 44 percent of the city's residents scrambled into public shelters, 44 percent remained in their homes or in personally built shelters, and 12 percent stayed with friends or roamed the streets.[47] More often than not, public shelters were located in subway stations — the British government had not developed the spacious, deep shelters necessary to house and protect thousands of people—and each night individuals and families hunkered down on the platforms with food, drink, books, suitcases, and blankets.[48] Official efforts to stop people from using the subway stations proved futile.[49] With scores of people cramped together, and with the accompanying sights, sounds, and smells, some people naturally found the shelters intolerable. One woman recorded her reaction in a diary: "Seeing every corridor and platform in every station all along the line crowded with people huddled three-deep, I was too appalled for words. The misery of that wretched mass of humanity sleeping like worms packed in a tin—the heat and smell, the dirt, the endless crying of the poor bloody babies, the haggard white-faced women nursing children against them, the children cramped and twitching in their noisy sleep. . . . Why, if I wanted to torture my worst enemy, I could think of no better Procrustean bed for the purpose."[50]

Yet despite the obvious dangers and fears, despite the inescapable discomforts of being packed together with hundreds of strangers, the nightly stay in the Underground took on a festive air for many Londoners. People passed the time reading, singing, playing cards, or listening to buskers, street performers who brought their acts underground each night.[51] At the heart of the theater district in Aldwych, renowned performers like Laurence Olivier, Vivien Leigh, and Ivor Novello would on occasion drop by the Underground station after performances and entertain the people with a few songs or sketches.[52]

In time, the government officially sanctioned the use of subway stations for shelter and helped to improve conditions by providing extra toilets, sanitation units, first-aid supplies, and food provisions.[53] Groups such as the Women's Volunteer Service lent a hand staffing canteens and assisting with first-aid work.[54]

All in all, people tried to make the best of a frightening situation. "It was not unpleasant," says Anna Stránský Sonnek, daughter of Jaroslav Stránský, niece of Jaroslav and Antonia Císař, and a close friend of the Körbel family during the war. She says that she and the Körbels usually retreated to the apartment basement when the air raids started, and the atmosphere often took on the air of a social occasion. "We chatted and chatted," she says. "When a nice quiet moment came, we would go to the street for fresh air and get a cigarette. That's when I started to smoke. It was like a big party."[55] Sonnek says that on Christmas Eve, families put up decorations, almost as if they were defying Hitler to spoil their holiday celebrations: "People would play mouth organs, and couples would dance. It was a Merry Christmas that year. During the Blitz, we refused to let Hitler knock out our way of life."[56]

One night during the Blitz, Prokop Drtina and Körbel were working on a radio broadcast together when the sirens sounded. Mandula Körbel, with Madlenka in tow, had retreated earlier to the air raid shelter. But the men were preoccupied with their work and decided to stay in the apartment, which was quieter than the crowded shelters. They knew they were risking their safety, but they had important work to finish by morning. Their decision turned out to be a bad one. According to Drtina:

> We were entirely mistaken this time. Our London quarter was obviously a direct target of the German raid that day and so the whiz of the bombs was unusually penetrating, and the bombs were apparently falling in the vicinity of our neighbourhood, because the shakes were extraordinarily strong. Our eight-floor apartment house staggered several times so that we had the feeling of a strong rocking. And once, a whiz bomb and the whistling of a flying bomb was so piercing that we both cowered instinctively. Dr. Körbel almost darted under a table. The fall of the bomb was deafening, and our house was rocking so much that it reminded me of a ship on a high

sea. I would never have believed a huge iron and concrete building could tremble so much and still not lose its stability and its coherence. When Dr. Körbel got on the floor, we were out of danger anyway and despite our fear, we could not resist a laugh of relief. But again, more bombs started whizzing through the air and further blows blasted. Our tragic-comic experience led us to the conclusion that this was no time for fooling around, and we rode down to the basement to join our wives.[57]

As hard as they worked on their radio broadcasts, Körbel and Drtina could be distracted occasionally. Living near Körbel on the eighth floor was a striking Canadian woman about whom they knew little "but whose beauty we admired secretly."[58] Körbel and Drtina, both married men, would sneak glances at the young innocent, laughing and joking with each other about whether they would see her in the shelter that night. Sadly, the woman did not survive the war. "Agitated by the air raids, she ended her life one day by jumping out the window," Drtina writes.[59]

There was an intensity in the London air, an electricity that kept people alert to signs of danger, even as they tried to carry on with the everyday pattern of normal life. "The Germans always came at dusk when we would be sitting down to dinner," says Jiřina Tondr, another Czech refugee who lived near the Körbels in London and worked as a secretary for the Czech government-in-exile. "You'd appear at work in the morning, and everyone was so glad to see you. Mr. Körbel would always make a joke. It was wonderful. Everyone was so together. Stop into any house, and you would be offered a cup of tea." Tondr remembers seeing Mandula Körbel walking in the mornings, holding little Madlenka by the hand as they shopped and went to the park. It was a sweet scene, one that brings a smile to her face almost sixty years later.[60]

German night raids continued through the autumn and early winter of 1940. Poor weather conditions limited German bombings in January and February 1941, but in late February, the weather improved and Germany accelerated the pace of attacks throughout England.[61] The storm of air attacks on London and other English cities in the spring of 1941 was not a prelude to a German invasion of England, though the British were meant to believe it was. Hitler had, in fact, effectively tabled plans for an invasion in mid-September 1940, when it became apparent that German efforts to obliterate England by air were not sustainable as the Royal Air Force brought down more and more Luftwaffe bombers. Hitler instead turned his attention to an invasion of the Soviet Union. But fearing that the transfer of German airpower to the east would invite the British to step up their attacks on German cities, Hitler ordered attacks on English cities in the spring of 1941, as a reminder to the British of the horrors they could expect should they launch a massive air assault on Germany.[62]

On March 19, a new round of air strikes hit London, inflicting the worst carnage in that city to date, claiming some 750 civilian lives. A month later, the intensity of raids reached a new plateau when German bombers hit London on two separate nights, each time dropping more payload than ever before. The toll of the two night raids on British citizens was severe: Roughly 2,000 people died, and 148,000 houses were destroyed. The Germans planned the largest attack for May 10.[63]

Between 11:30 P.M., Saturday, May 10, and 5:37 A.M., Sunday, May 11, some 507 German bombers dropped a massive 708 tons of bombs—including incendiaries, high explosives, and land mines—on the streets of London.[64] The bombs devastated the city, causing the worst damage of the war. While previous attacks had targeted the East End and the City of London, no section of the city was spared this time.[65] Incendiary bombs started more than 2,000 fires that at one point consumed 700 acres of London, an area one and a half times the reach of the Great Fire of London in 1666. The British Museum, Tower of London, Westminster Abbey, and the Houses of Parliament all suffered direct hits. Bombs gutted the House of Commons and scarred Big Ben.[66] In all, the rain of bombs killed 1,436 Londoners and seriously injured 1,800 more.[67] "That's when my parents decided they had to get out of London," Madeleine Albright says.[68]

As bombing raids intensified and the city became even more unlivable, the Körbels moved to the British countryside, where they shared a seven-room, sixteenth-century farmhouse owned by Josef's brother, Jan, and his family,[69] who had purchased it for £5,000. The house was located on Bank Mill Lane in Berkhamsted, the same quiet country town, some twenty miles northwest of London, where Dagmar was enrolled in school. "My parents were clearly the second-class citizens of that operation," Madeleine Albright says. "The truth is, my uncle and my father did not get along."[70]

With a clay peg-tile roof, hand-hewn beam ceilings, a fireplace big enough to sit in,[71] and a long, narrow kitchen with small, leaded windows that looked out over the courtyard to a barn and stables, the house offered a cozy respite from the war-ravaged city. In June, pale lavender wisteria blossoms covered one side of the house, and tangled, thorny branches of a climbing yellow rose circled the front door.[72] A tiny sign over the portal read "The Old Cottage." A large English garden led to the Grand Union canal, which flows high enough above the house that the Körbels worried that if a bomb broke the canal wall, the house would be flooded. There were pleasant wooded areas nearby where the families often walked, and a central market in town sold fresh vegetables.[73]

During the week, Josef and his brother, Jan, commuted by train to London for work. On weekends, the Körbels' home became a retreat for Czech friends. "It was like going to heaven because we could be fairly sure there would be no bombing or air raids," says Anna Sonnek, who visited often. "We would bring food because it was a time of rationing."[74] Wartime allocations were meager. Each week a local Berkhamsted resident was permitted one egg, two ounces of butter, and two ounces of cheese. Many country people kept rabbits and chickens to supplement their food supply.[75] "We cooked goulash more than anything else because you could stretch it," Sonnek says.[76] They would add whatever pieces of pork or beef they could find to a thick sauce, heavily spiced with onions, tomatoes, peppers, and pungent red paprika. Served over potatoes or steamed dumplings, it was a tasty, inexpensive dish that could serve a crowd.

At Berkhamsted, the Körbels converted to Roman Catholicism. Josef, Mandula, Madlenka, and Josef's brother were all baptized on May 31, 1941, in a private afternoon ceremony at Berkhamsted's Sacred Heart Church,[77] located on a steep hill called Park View Drive. Madlenka had just turned four years old. The Reverend Anselmus Špaček, a Franciscan Czech priest distinguished by a white stole that he wore over a flowing brown habit, traveled from London to Berkhamsted to perform the ceremony.[78] Standing on a stool in the back of the church near the doorway, little Madlenka put her head forward for the priest to anoint her with three scoopfuls of holy water. Raising his hands in prayer and speaking in Latin, he baptized her "Maria Joanna, in the name of the Father, Son, and Holy Spirit." Antonia Čísařová, a family friend, served as godmother to Madlenka and her mother.[79] Jaroslav Stránský, a Czechoslovak minister, who was close to both President Beneš and Foreign Minister Jan Masaryk, became godfather to Josef Körbel and his brother, Jan. Madeleine Albright has no memory of her baptism. She was surprised to learn from this author that her parents had been baptized as Roman Catholics at the same time she was.[80]

The Körbels had a party the night before the baptism. The guests had arrived by train. "My uncle had a couple of bottles of wine, which was rare during the war," says Anna Sonnek. "Towards midnight the priest looked at his watch and said he must stop eating and drinking if he is to perform a mass and baptism the next day. My uncle, an astronomer, offered a theory that because of the summer changing time, they had an extra hour so it would do no harm if they opened the other bottle of wine." The story would be told many times among the Stránskýs.[81]

It was not all that common for Jews to convert to Catholicism, even during the war. "During this time, it was done only when people thought it would save their lives," says Tomáš Kraus, a leader of the Jewish Community in Prague.[82] The majority of the Czech population at the time was Roman Catholic.[83] Yet according to the late Lev Braun, a BBC colleague of Josef Körbel, his conversion surprised Jan Masaryk, the Protestant Czechoslovak foreign minister, who wondered aloud: "How could this coward do this?" In Braun's view, Masaryk's comment reflected his own horror of the atrocities being waged against the Jews in other parts of Europe. "One doesn't do such a thing in a time of persecution," Braun said.[84]

Eduard Goldstücker, a fellow Czechoslovak who became a lifelong friend of the Körbel family, talked to Körbel about his conversion to Catholicism. Goldstücker says that in May 1943, two years after the baptism, Körbel explained that he and Mandula had converted to make life easier. "They told us they did it especially and above all for the children's sake, that they didn't want their children's lives to be complicated by their Jewishness or by an explanation of why they changed religions," Goldstücker says. "Madlenka was a small girl also, so why should they tell her? That was their attitude." Goldstücker says one of those influential in persuading the Körbels to convert to Catholicism was Jaroslav Stránský's wife, Milada, an ardent Catholic and a distinguished, soft-spoken woman.

Goldstücker, a Jew and a member of the Communist Party, lived during the war with his family in Oxford, where he did postgraduate work in German literature. In February 1943, he was offered a job in the education department of the Czechoslovak government-in-exile. Körbel asked if Goldstücker and his family would be interested in sharing a rented house with the Körbels twenty-eight miles southwest of London in a little town called Walton-on-Thames, a farming community that offered temporary refuge from wartime London. Goldstücker agreed. The address was 22 Stompond Lane, a curving country road a half-mile from the railroad station. Built in the early 1930s, the house had four bedrooms and a long kitchen that overlooked a huge backyard. "I moved in with my wife and my child, who was sixteen months," he says. "Madlenka was six, and her little sister, Kathy, was still in a perambulator. It was a very pleasant life. In the middle of the war, that was a blessing. We woke up every morning, and we went together to the railway station to catch the train to our work."[85]

Madlenka often accompanied her father on his way to the station on her little bicycle. He would leave her at school, and then she rode her bike home when the school day ended. She often spent afternoons playing field hockey on the grassy lot across from her house. Occasionally she visited neighbors for high tea, which she did by climbing through a hedge that separated the properties.[86]

The Körbels kept chickens in the backyard to supplement their wartime food supply. One day Mandula Körbel asked Madlenka to give them a drink. The child filled a milk bottle halfway with water. But instead of pouring it into a pan, she simply left the bottle outside. "How do you think the chickens are going to drink the water?" Mandula asked her daughter. "They have long necks," Madlenka replied.[87]

On Sundays, Czech friends came to the countryside to unwind. The men would pace up and down the long backyard deep in conversation, their hands clasped behind their backs. After lunch, they would play Mariáš, a popular Czech card game.[88] Madlenka amused herself by playing priest. She had an altar, candles, and a little silver cup and would use the cup to put out the flame on the candles. "I was a very serious little Catholic girl," Madeleine Albright says today. "I went to confession all the time."[89]

In summer, the Körbels went to the beach at Lyme Regis, a coastal town in Dorset, known for its windswept nights and snug inns. On the beach were antitank obstacles known as Dragon's Teeth, concrete cubes, carefully placed four feet apart to slow an enemy invasion.[90] Madlenka thought it was a jungle gym.[91]

Kathy Körbel, called "Káča" by her family, was born on October 7, 1942, in a hospital in Beaconsfield, not far from Walton-on-Thames. Madlenka, who was just learning to read, visited her mother and sister in the maternity ward before they came home.[92] A new child in the family meant that Mandula Körbel was busier than ever. "She was my live doll," says her cousin Dagmar, who was fourteen when Kathy was born.[93]

Madlenka started first grade at the Ingomar School, located at the corner of Ashley Rise and Station Avenue. The school's motto was "Play the Game." Summer uniforms for girls consisted of pale-brown-and-white-striped cotton dresses, a brown blazer, and a Panama hat. Mandula Körbel enjoyed meeting her daughter after school because it gave her a chance to meet other parents with small children, even though it was always on a superficial level.[94]

During the war, each child carried a gas mask in a tin painted with the school colors. The children kept the kits with them all the time, even when they left the classroom. "You came home now and again to find hot shrapnel on the pavement," says Diana Ely, who was a pupil at Ingomar during the war. "I remember waiting in the gym when the air raid siren went off and we would be sent to the shelter below ground."[95]

Josef Körbel was an air raid warden in the community. One night during a blackout, he was walking down his driveway and bumped into one of the brick pillars that mark the entrance, cutting his eye and shattering his glasses. Because people were not permitted to turn on lights, the family could not see how badly he was hurt. Luckily, it was not serious.[96] When they were forced to retreat to air raid shelters at night, Madlenka passed the time by singing "A Hundred Green Bottles Hanging on the Wall."[97]

Goldstücker remembers Mandula Körbel as a lovable woman, who kept her husband's best interests at heart. "We had a typical English house with the bedrooms upstairs," he says. "The door of my bedroom and the door of Josef's bedroom were next to each other. One morning Körbel was leaving his bedroom smiling. I knew Mrs. Körbel was ill with influenza, and I asked him why he was laughing. 'I have to laugh,' Körbel told me. 'I went to see Mandula to console her, and she's convinced she is going to die. She was giving orders on who I should marry after her death.'"

Not all of their encounters were so amusing. Körbel and Goldstücker had a narrow escape one day in 1944, when their train, which was running three minutes late, arrived at the Waterloo station in London only seconds after a bomb exploded. They climbed down from the train to find passengers lying on the platform, covered with blood. The episode left them badly shaken, but luckily neither was hurt.[98]

All in all, Goldstücker and his family lived quite happily with the Körbels at Walton-on-Thames from May 1943 to the end of June 1944, when the German bombing intensified. Then came new terror. "The Nazi rockets started flying over our heads on their way to London," Goldstücker says. "Some of them fell in the village."[99]

The worst damage, however, was in London. The pilotless V-1 flying bombs, known as Doodlebugs, started on June 12, 1944. One bomb fell right outside Bush House, the headquarters of the BBC in London. It destroyed the building's partitions, windows, clocks, and all the material prepared for that day's Czechoslovak broadcast. The English secretary was badly wounded, as were two announcers who were on duty. The bomb exploded seven minutes before the midday broadcast was to begin, yet both announcers managed to transmit their program with only a few minutes' delay. One announcer had his trousers blown off, but that did not deter him from reading the news straight from the English text, translating as he went.[100]

By the end of the month, some 50 V-1s were hitting London daily, killing

6,184 civilians.[101] "The air raids started as soon as evening was approaching," Goldstücker said. "There would be an air raid siren and the air raids would last all night." Goldstücker said he and Körbel had purchased a table with thick steel plates that was known as a Morrison Shelter, named after Baron Herbert Stanley Morrison, the minister of home security. It was shaped like a dining room table and kept in the dining room, and the families sat around it to eat their meals and dove underneath when the air raids started. Six feet long, four feet wide, thirty inches high, and fitted with wide, heavy steel legs, the table was not much bigger than a single bed.[102] "There was a mattress meant for a family of four, maximum, two parents and two children," said Goldstücker. "When we were afraid that the danger was very acute, we just crawled on it and huddled together, two sets of parents and three children. When nothing happened, we would get out."

Years later, Mandula Körbel reflected on her time in London. "It is difficult to say about those six long years, if [they] were very unhappy or rather happy," she wrote. "There were years of hope and mainly we were young and the horrible news about suffering of so many people in Czechoslovakia reached us much, much later. During the war, we were with millions of others fighting the danger of bombing, but somehow got used to it and survive[d]. But we had the hope and determination to survive."[103]

4

A Living Hell

"When we went to Terezín, we thought it was for two months. Nobody ever thought it would take longer. A person somehow can get used to anything. We had seen dead people around. It somehow didn't affect us anymore."
— Irena Ravel, Theresienstadt survivor, June 14, 1997, Prague

---

THE GERMAN ARMY moved into Bohemia and Moravia in a blinding snowstorm in March 1939. If there was any silver lining in the Munich capitulation, it was that the new protectorate was spared heavy bombing. "Bohemia has retained its muddy villages, its geese, its beer, its earthy fertility," wrote George Kennan, when he arrived in Czechoslovakia as secretary of the U.S. legation. "And the city of Prague, to which Italian and Austrian architects long ago gave a grace and harmony unrivaled in central and northern Europe, has lost none of its charm."[1]

Outward appearances, however, masked the true character of the German occupation. As a protectorate of the Third Reich, Bohemia and Moravia were placed under the strict control of a Reich Protector, who assumed dictatorial powers.[2] German officials filled cabinet posts, while local administrative offices were set up across Bohemia and Moravia.[3] President Emil Hácha's government was little more than a front for German rule.[4]

If Bohemia and Moravia retained their aesthetic beauty, the German invasion exacted a heavy toll on the Czech people. In the first months following the occupation of Prague, Nazi rule was marked by relative restraint and moderation. The German police force, the Gestapo, targeted primarily political figures and intellectuals.[5]

Czech resistance sparked a harsh backlash. In time, political and cultural expression was all but snuffed out. Universities and theaters were closed, political parties banned, and the people—particularly the intelligentsia and Jews—mercilessly persecuted.[6] Losses from political persecution and deaths in concentration camps during World War II ranged anywhere from 36,000 to 55,000 lives. The Czech Jewish community was almost wiped out. More than 70,000 Bohemian and Moravian Jews were murdered.[7]

Czechs also paid a price in material and economic terms. Hitler was determined to channel Czech resources—labor, industry, military equipment—to serve the German war effort. German forces assumed control of military equipment (it was a bitter irony of Munich that England and France sold Hitler weapons that would later be turned against them) and industrial facilities consigned Czechs to work in coal mines, iron and steel works, and armament production facilities. Some Czechs were even transferred to Germany.[8]

Following the occupation of Prague, the tapestry of daily life for Jews began to unravel. One by one, the routines and pleasures that made up a normal society were placed out of reach, forbidden or simply removed. The Germans introduced strict laws requiring Czech Jews to register property. A September 1, 1941, decree stipulated that every Jew appearing in public must wear a yellow star of David, inscribed with "Jude." "There were many orders given at this time," recalls Irena Ravel, a survivor of the concentration camp known as Theresienstadt. "First of all, the banks were closed, and Jews couldn't draw out money. Our shops were taken away, then factories and businesses. Children were thrown out of school, professional people out of professions. Jewelry had to be handed over, as did cars, motorcycles, bicycles, silver, musical instruments, and small animals. Everything had to be given away. Radios, ski things, fur coats. Slowly everything went. The theater, the cinemas, the parks, swimming pools, restaurants, slowly everything was forbidden."[9]

The same decree that required Jews to wear a yellow star of David forbade them to move from one city to another, from town to town, from village to village. "That meant families couldn't see each other anymore, and friends couldn't see each other," says Ravel. "Then ration cards were given. The Germans were already hungry, and they took everything they could. The Jewish people got ration cards, but they could go shopping only in the afternoon when nothing was to be gotten anymore. So slowly it went, order after order. . . . Mostly people were afraid. People were absolutely thrown out of normal society. This is how it was."[10]

Czech intransigence prompted the Reich to adopt a more radical policy in the fall of 1941. Hitler replaced the "moderate" Reich Protector, Baron

Konstantin von Neurath, with Reinhard Heydrich, the head of the SS. Von Neurath had revealed an extensive network of Czech resistance groups, and Heydrich immediately set out to destroy them. On September 28, 1941, the day after he assumed power, Heydrich declared martial law, launched wholesale arrests, and executed suspected resisters en masse. The wave of terror was numbing.[11]

Heydrich's arrival was especially ominous for Jews. He set in motion the process of deportation of Jews to Auschwitz and other concentration camps in the East. As part of that program, Hitler's "final solution," Heydrich mandated that Jews be required to live in the fortress town of Terezín, some forty miles north of Prague. He established a Jewish camp there on November 24, 1941. It was called by its German name: Theresienstadt.[12]

Theresienstadt was a living hell. In 1942, the town's 7,000 non-Jewish residents were sent away, leaving the Jews—German, Dutch, Danish as well as Czech—totally isolated. Some 144,000 Jews were sent to Theresienstadt between 1941 and 1945. They were literally packed into the camp. For tens of thousands of Western Jews, it was merely a way station on the path to Auschwitz or other death camps in the East. Victims arrived by freight train outside the ghetto,[13] at a station called Bohušovice, and marched, luggage in hand, to the town two miles away. Conditions were brutal. Approximately 33,000 died there of starvation, malnutrition, or typhoid, while 88,000 were sent on to Poland's Auschwitz or other camps. Only 19,000 lived to see the end of the war.[14]

In August 1942, more than 50,000 people were crowded into twelve barracks and several houses. "Every corner, every corridor, every house attic . . . was full of people," writes author Ctibor Rybár in his book *Jewish Prague*. Each person was allotted 0.6 square meters,[15] hardly enough room to turn around in. During some periods, 90,000 people lived in an area that had once been home to only 7,000. There was little food, and what meals Jews had consisted of watery soup. Hunger was an unshakable companion. The death rate reached such high levels—15,891 Jews died in 1942 alone—that the Germans constructed a crematorium capable of incinerating 190 bodies a day.[16]

Many Jews who arrived at Theresienstadt had absolutely no idea what life would be like for them. Some thought there would be social occasions and brought their finest clothes. Others paid for their transportation and, hoping to be as comfortable as possible, requested quarters facing south.[17]

Some were part of the Czech, German, and Austrian intelligentsia: artists, scientists, politicians, and professors who happened to be Jewish. Amid the squalor of Theresienstadt, residents did their best to foster a vibrant community, full of culture and sophistication, hoping to hold on to at least a modicum of everyday life. The camp had a library that offered more than sixty thousand books for circulation. Orchestral and theatrical performances provided rich entertainment. Lecturers offered spiritual guidance. During the day, artists painted scenes acceptable to the Nazis. By night, they drew forbidden pictures of the ghetto as it really was—and hid them.[18]

Adults worked on average eighty to a hundred hours a week. Although school lessons were prohibited, children were often taught in secret. With pencils and crayons, the little ones painted poignant scenes of hunger, sickness, and death. Today these pictures hang in galleries at Theresienstadt and in Prague—searing testimony to the horrors they endured. Of the fifteen thousand children who passed through the camp, only a few hundred survived.[19]

In the fall of 1943, the Nazis sent 456 Danish Jews to Theresienstadt, and the Danish government demanded that the Red Cross visit the camp to survey the conditions. Using the visit as an opportunity to counter rumors that they were running death camps, the Nazis orchestrated an elaborate ruse. Before the visit took place, the Germans sent many Jews to other camps. They planted flower gardens and added fresh coats of paint to houses, scrubbed sidewalks, and laid turf on the green. They established a concert hall, social center, and a synagogue. Paul Epstein, head of the Jewish Council of Elders, welcomed the Red Cross visitors wearing a black suit and top hat. A band played. Children performed the opera *Brundibar,* and customers patronized a café built for the visit. The hoax was so successful that the Nazis produced a propaganda film showing how wonderfully they were treating the Jews. Afterward, they deported most of the performers, including the children, to Auschwitz.[20]

It was in the awful conditions at Theresienstadt that Josef Körbel's father died. Arnošt and Olga Körbel, Josef's parents, arrived at Theresienstadt on July 30, 1942. They had been packed into a freight train along with 936 other Jews back in Prague.[21] Arnošt died six weeks later, on September 17, 1942, most likely from typhoid fever, which had swept the camp. On October 23, 1944, Olga Körbel was sent to Auschwitz on the second transport from Terezín. She went directly to the gas chamber.[22]

Cousin Dagmar's parents arrived at Theresienstadt in October 1942, four months after Arnošt and Olga. Milena, the little girl who had broken her arm only days before she would have escaped on the Children's Train with her sister, was with them.[23] Dagmar's mother, Markéta—Josef Körbel's sister—died February 15, 1943, a victim of a typhoid fever. Milena died at Auschwitz in 1944. She was twelve years old.[24] On June 12, 1942,

Madlenka's maternal grandmother, Růžena Spiegelová, arrived in Trawniki, a concentration camp in Poland.[25]

Word of mass executions began to spread late in the war. In June 1944, two Jews escaped from Auschwitz and reported that four thousand Czech Jews had been executed in gas chambers and that the Nazis planned to gas three thousand more. On June 19, 1944, four months before Olga Körbel was gassed at Auschwitz, the BBC's Czech service broadcast a denunciation of the reported mass execution. "This new crime of the Nazis is incredible in its inhumane horror," the statement declared. "Those who took part in carrying out such bestialities will not escape justice." There is little question but that Josef Körbel, in his capacity as director of the government-in-exile's broadcasts, would have known about this broadcast. What we will never know is how it affected him, whether he had any way to know the fate of his own parents, what he and Mandula talked about while their daughter slept.[26]

Allied forces were pushing Germany toward defeat. In the spring of 1945, the liberation of Prague was imminent. The question of who would do the liberating, Soviet or American forces, carried tremendous implications for Czechs and Slovaks. Beneš' hopes for a democratic Czechoslovakia in its pre-Munich form hung in the balance. Different military decisions and outcomes at the end of the war could have appreciably altered the course of Czechoslovak history.[27]

That same spring, Soviet troops crossed the Carpathians and entered Slovakia. American forces pushed eastward across Germany. On April 18, 1945, American troops, led by General George S. Patton, entered western Bohemia. "Thank God, thank God," Beneš exclaimed when he heard the news. He immediately sent word of congratulations to Patton. With Americans troops only sixty miles from Prague, and Soviet troops almost twice that distance to the East, the people of Prague joyously anticipated liberation at the hands of democratic forces.[28]

However, after an exchange of messages between General Dwight D. Eisenhower and Commander General Aleksey I. Antonov of the Soviet forces, the American army's advance toward Prague was stopped at the Karlsbad-Pilsen-Budweis line.[29] On May 5, the Soviets asked General Eisenhower not to proceed. A group of American tanks had advanced to within ten miles of Prague but were ordered to withdraw. Four days later, on May 9, Soviet tanks reached the outskirts of the city.[30]

Thousands of lives would have been saved if the Americans had been allowed to come in. But in the end, it was the Red Army that liberated

Prague. Allied leaders were loath to set limits on their forces, particularly in light of what appeared to be Soviet attempts to liberate, in addition to Prague, every Central European capital. In this case, however, it has been suggested that Eisenhower effectively traded Allied acceptance of the Soviet effort to liberate Prague for Soviet approval of Allied plans to liberate Denmark. Though Denmark and Prague were not necessarily mutually exclusive for the Allies, and despite the obvious advantages of having a Western army liberate the Czech capital, cession of Prague guaranteed an unspoken quid pro quo for Soviet acceptance of a Western liberation of Denmark.[31]

Beneš and his government returned to Prague but faced dim prospects for a democratic future.[32] Josef Körbel later summed up the atmosphere of the day. "No politically mature citizen could misunderstand the implication of the military strategy of those last days," he wrote in *Twentieth-Century Czechoslovakia*. "The West was not interested in Czechoslovak democracy; its fate was left to the Communist and Soviet forces. This realization had a shattering effect on the morale and psychology of the Czechoslovak people: after six years of agony, as in a kind of nightmare, they watched something like Munich happening once again."[33]

The Czechoslovak people, barely freed from the grips of one totalitarian state, found themselves facing an uncertain future within the orbit of another. Once again, they were victims of Western indifference.

5

Lists That Lie

"I remember the flight very well. I never wanted to go on a plane again."
—Madeleine Albright, February 7, 1998

WITH THE WAR OVER, Josef Körbel returned home before the rest of his family, arriving on the first plane from London to liberated Czechoslovakia with triumphant members of the government-in-exile. The elegant city of Prague, with its Gothic spires and street after street of pastel Renaissance and Baroque facades, had been spared heavy damage.

Mandula Körbel flew back to Prague in July, bringing with her eight-year-old Madlenka, three-year-old Kathy, and Cousin Dagmar, who was seventeen. The flight was horrendous. The plane, which held about forty people, was crowded. Mandula was dreadfully airsick. Passengers huddled together on hard seats in the bays that once cradled bombs. "I sat with Auntie, and we had the two children between us," Dagmar says. "There were so many people sick. I crawled up, and the pilot allowed me to come to the cockpit for a while. We were just flying above Germany, and he said, 'Do you want to see what we did to Dresden?' And I said, 'Yes, I would.' He duck-dived and went up again, and all the people screamed. That was the first time I saw Dresden."[1]

Dresden was, simply put, a picture of hell. In running bomb raids over the city on February 13, 14, and 15, more than 1,400 British and American bombers had dropped their payloads in a 36-hour period. Firestorms swept through large parts of the city, lighting the skies for miles around. Some fires burned for days, leaving blocks of buildings gutted. The attacks exacted horrific carnage, "officially" killing some 39,773 people, while another 20,000 were lost in the ruins or incinerated beyond human recognition.[2]

Distant glimpses of war's destruction from miles above Dresden could not prepare Dagmar for the personal tragedy that awaited her. After spending the last year studying at the Czechoslovak School in Great Britain, located in Northern Wales, she was going home with a mixture of sadness and excitement. The International Red Cross had sent lists of war victims to her school—a List of Survivors, a List of the Missing, and a List of the Dead. "We all looked through the lists, and I found my mother's name on the List of the Dead," she says. "My grandfather Arnošt was also on the List of the Dead. My grandmother, my father, and my sister were on the List of Survivors."

Dagmar hoped to find her father when she arrived in Prague. But as she stepped off the plane with Mandula and the girls and looked around eagerly, she saw no sign of him. "There was only Uncle Josef, no one else from the family," she recalls. The realization sunk in. The International Red Cross lists were not accurate. Along with her mother and grandfather, Dagmar's grandmother, father, and sister had all perished.[3]

Josef Körbel drove his family and Dagmar to Hradčany Square, a small, hilltop park shaded by tall acacia trees, just a few steps from the castle. He had leased a large, five-room apartment with a big fireplace and separate maid's quarters on the second floor of a large, seventeenth-century house that had been built for local gentry.[4] Intricate Baroque friezes highlighted the windows, and an arched wooden doorway opened to a quiet, cobbled courtyard, where long strands of ivy twisted amid the balconies. A romantic little country restaurant, decorated with pink and white geraniums, did a brisk business on the ground floor. From their apartment, Mandula could peer through windows looking over the courtyard to keep an eye on Madlenka playing below.

With her parents dead and no where else to go, Cousin Dagmar moved in with the Körbels, since Josef Körbel had been appointed her guardian when she was in London.[5] Although the family was living through the trauma of learning that many of their closest relatives had been murdered by the Nazis, there was little discussion of it within the house. "My family did everything they could to make life as normal as possible for us," Madeleine Albright says. "I think they were glad to be back in Prague, but what blows my mind is that they were the ages that my children are today."[6]

Dagmar thinks Josef Körbel must have learned of the fate of his parents from lists provided by the International Red Cross, just as she had. But she cannot be sure. He never discussed it with her afterward. "I was told I had to brace myself and do as best I could," she says. "My uncle said you must take things as they are." Dagmar says that the Körbels offered modest emotional support, telling her "I could always rely on them if I needed anything." Still, she says, she tried to keep out of their way, finding solace among school friends whose families had met the same fate. "We met, and we held each other," she explains.[7]

Josef Körbel, by now thirty-five, was in line for a key position in the new government. Like many of his colleagues, he was eager to fit into the new Czechoslovak society. One way he did this was to drop the umlaut in his last name, shifting the pronunciation from "KUR-bel" to the more Czech-sounding "KOR-bel." Pavel Tigrid, Korbel's friend from their BBC days, had been born Shonfeld and changed his name to Tigrid for the same reason.[8] A few years later, when she was a preteenager living in America, Madeleine found an old document that belonged to her father, spelling their family name with the umlaut. She asked him why the two little dots were there. Her father explained that the umlaut made the name sound German and that there was not an English typewriter with that key on it.[9]

The postwar-political climate was far different from the one Korbel knew before the war. Throughout the period between the end of World War I and the start of World War II, Czechoslovakia's foreign policy had been oriented toward strengthening ties with the Western democracies, rather than building relations with the Soviet Union. Munich, however, destroyed Czechoslovakia's faith in the West. Consequently, throughout the war, Beneš committed the government-in-exile to engaging the Soviet Union and looking to them to guard against future German aggression.[10] In December 1943, Beneš signed a friendship treaty with the Soviets. The treaty provided for the reconstruction of Czechoslovakia in its pre-Munich form, free of Soviet interference. But in a stipulation that spoke volumes about the postwar balance of power in Eastern Europe and in Czechoslovakia itself, the treaty also dictated that the new Czechoslovak government would have to readily incorporate Czechoslovak Communists into its political system.[11]

The anticipation of a strong Communist presence in postwar Czechoslovakia had been a driving force behind Beneš' foreign policy. The Czech leader hoped that by fostering warm relations with the Soviets, he might dissuade Joseph Stalin from encouraging a Communist coup in Czechoslovakia. Beneš took strides to include Communists in the government-in-exile in London, going so far as to offer important cabinet posts to

Czechoslovak Communists stationed in Moscow.[12] "From the middle of 1943 until the end of the war, I had secret meetings with the Beneš people to come up with a blueprint of how the government would look after the war," says Eduard Goldstücker.[13]

For its part, the Communist Party of Czechoslovakia—Komunistická Strana Československá (KSČ)—played a key role in Czechoslovak resistance efforts, particularly after the German invasion of the Soviet Union in June 1941.[14] Founded in 1921, the Czech Communist Party had been just one of many political parties during the war years, never gaining enough strength to be anything more than a negligible force within the democratic framework. Following Munich, KSČ leaders fled to Moscow, where they worked to expand the party's influence and power base once the war ended.[15]

Any question of where Beneš' policy of rapprochement with the Soviet Union and compromise with Czechoslovak Communists might lead was moot when Czechoslovakia fell into the Soviet's sphere of influence at the end of the war. A formidable Communist presence in a reconstructed Czechoslovakia was a reality that could not be ignored. More than that, however, many Czechoslovaks welcomed the Communist Party and the alliance with the Soviet Union. The joy stemming from liberation by Soviet forces and the disillusionment over Munich persuaded many that it would be in Czechoslovakia's best interests to build stronger ties with the Soviet Union.[16]

Such was the political atmosphere upon Beneš' return to Czechoslovakia in the spring of 1945. With the addition of the Communists, the new Czechoslovak government was almost completely reconstituted in its pre-Munich form. But the makeup of the provisional coalition government cast light on the postwar strength of the Communist Party. Communists assumed key posts, making it impossible for other parties to circumvent Communist elements in the new government.[17]

With virtually all of Czechoslovakia surrounded by countries occupied by Soviet forces, Beneš and other leaders had to proceed slowly, carefully reasserting their right to self-governance. The new government established a provisional National Assembly until elections could be held in May 1946. In October 1945, the National Assembly elected Beneš as president of Czechoslovakia. He then obtained promises from both the United States and the Soviet Union to evacuate their forces from Czechoslovakia in time for the May 1946 elections.[18]

Though Beneš worked with the Czech Communist Party during the war and after, he always believed that through normal democratic processes, democratic parties would gradually emerge as the dominant force in Czechoslovak politics. Furthermore, while he led efforts to complete an alliance with the Soviets in 1943, he hoped that a postwar Czechoslovakia would stand as a bridge between the Soviet Union and Western democracies. Czech Communist Party leaders, on the other hand, were committed to a gradual Communist takeover of the government through democratic means.[19]

Throughout the spring of 1945, Korbel worked hard to help the newly formed Czechoslovak government resettle in Prague. Exactly what position he held remains unclear. On his University of Denver curriculum vitae, Korbel says he was *chef de cabinet* to Czechoslovak foreign minister Jan Masaryk during this period.[20] After becoming secretary of state, Madeleine Albright described her father's position this way to several interviewers. However, when she used the term in a televised speech to Czech government leaders during her visit to Prague in July 1997, several of her father's colleagues who were listening said that it was not the post her father held. "He was not," says Antonin Sum, personal secretary to Masaryk. "I'm a little bit shocked."[21] Eduard Goldstücker, a lifelong friend of Korbel, insists that Korbel was *chef de cabinet* to Vladimír Clementis, a Communist who was deputy minister of foreign affairs. "I came home from Paris at the end of June 1945," Goldstücker says. "Clementis was in Yugoslavia on official business, and Korbel was sitting in Clementis' office as his *chef de cabinet*."[22]

Korbel's official Czech résumé, which lists his posts until December 12, 1948, including his various commissions and awards, states that after World War II, "he worked at the Ministry of Foreign Affairs again, and on September 1, 1945, he was put in charge of the administration of the Czechoslovak legation in Belgrade."[23] It does not list *chef de cabinet* to Masaryk as one of his posts. However, officials at the Czech Ministry of Foreign Affairs recently located one routine letter, dated May 22, 1945, and signed by Korbel, with his title typed at the bottom: "*přednosta kabinetu min. zahr. věci*," which translates to "director of the Cabinet of Foreign Affairs." The ministry also produced a short article from the Yugoslav newspaper *Politika,* dated September 29, 1945, the day after Korbel's arrival in Belgrade. In the last sentence, it notes that since the end of the war, Korbel served as head of the cabinet of the Czechoslovak Foreign Ministry.[24]

Shown the letter and newspaper article, Eduard Goldstücker says that while he does not believe Korbel held the title, if he did, it was for a very brief period before he was sent to Yugoslavia as ambassador.[25] He and others suggested that when Korbel arrived in America, he sought to downplay his professional ties to Deputy Foreign Minister Vladimír Clementis, an ardent

Communist with whom he had worked for many years.[26] In an interview, Madeleine Albright conceded that her father held the interim position for only a short period. "This was not his longest assignment," she said.[27]

What is clear is that at the end of September 1945, Josef Korbel was appointed the top Czechoslovak envoy in Yugoslavia. One of those who supported his nomination for the job was Vladimír Clementis. The post was only a legation, a diplomatic mission headed by a minister. But when its status was upgraded to embassy in 1946, Korbel was named the first Czechoslovak ambassador to Yugoslavia. While the brutal struggle between communism and democracy would turn his diplomatic life into a nightmare of choices, this was a title he cited proudly for the rest of his life.

6

Brutal Choices

"The more I see the choices and sacrifices they had to make, the better I understand what they did. What they did was the basic instinct of parents: to protect their family and children and try to create a life for them that made sense."
—Madeleine Albright, February 7, 1998

ON SEPTEMBER 28, 1945, the Korbels flew into Belgrade aboard an old German Junker, a 1930s three-engine prop plane that had been used for both bombing and parachute drops. It had been left at the Prague airport when the Germans surrendered, and the Czechs had seized it. Only one official from the Yugoslav Foreign Ministry was there to meet them. It was, as Korbel would write later, "a modest welcome."[1]

As the Korbels drove into the city, they passed Serbian peasants walking slowly behind their wagons. The destruction from six years of war startled them. Where the railroad station had once stood, Josef Korbel wrote later, "now there were only piles of rubble; a temporary wooden roof tried unsuccessfully to conceal the ruins. The Military Academy was gone, and many other buildings had been destroyed by German and Allied bombs. There were wide, vacant areas where formerly small houses had been crowded together in the narrow streets. . . . Everywhere there were grass-covered heaps of bricks from destroyed houses."[2] Korbel was struck by how feverishly the people were working to rebuild the Yugoslav capital. Even children were helping to repave streets.[3]

Yugoslavia was an important posting for Korbel. As Beneš had hoped, Czechoslovakia had become a critical link between Soviet communism and democratic processes in the West. The Yugoslav Communists regarded Korbel and Czechoslovakia with a sense of wariness and uncertainty. The new Czechoslovak ambassador was caught in the ideological tug-of-war. He could observe how the Communists in Yugoslavia consolidated power by nationalizing factories, restricting the press, confiscating farms, and cracking down on opposition. Commuting between Prague and Belgrade, Korbel could see the same expansion of Communist influence in his native land. "During the time between the liberation and the February [1948] coup, Czechoslovakia tried to reestablish itself as a democratic country," says Eduard Goldstücker, his Communist friend who was working in the Ministry of Foreign Affairs in Prague. "Yugoslavia was already in the hands of radical Yugoslav Communists who looked on Czechoslovakia as a backward country. It was important to establish a good relationship between the two countries."[4]

Before leaving for Belgrade, Korbel had paid a visit to President Beneš. "Keep your eyes open," Beneš told him. "Personally, I have little confidence in [Yugoslav Marshal Josip Broz] Tito. He is, above all, a communist who succeeds in concealing his real aims by temporary nationalistic propaganda." Recognizing that his own fledgling government was riddled with Stalin partisans, Beneš instructed Korbel not to record or send home anything of a confidential nature. "The Soviet Embassy would have it the day after your report arrives in the [Czechoslovak] Ministry of Foreign Affairs," he said.[5]

Twenty minutes after arriving in Belgrade, Korbel placed a call to Vlado Ribnikar, his old friend who had helped his family escape to London in March 1939. Ribnikar never returned his call. Nor did Ribnikar's wife ever thank Korbel for a bouquet of flowers he sent to her when she was sick.[6] Undoubtedly Korbel understood their hesitancy to see him. But it also served as tacit proof of just how much the war had changed Eastern Europe.

Yet it was not until the new ambassador ran into the Ribnikars at a reception given by Tito that he realized how different Yugoslavia was under the Marshal's rule. "I was in the company of some Yugoslav generals when suddenly my former friend Ribnikar and his Czech wife passed," Korbel writes.[7] "This once elegant woman, who had used a good deal of make-up and had worn the most expensive dresses, looked shabby and weary. Her face was gray, her lips pale, her hair greasy. This time she could not avoid seeing me. Without giving a single word of welcome, she burst out, 'Don't count on me any more among Czechs, I have become a Yugoslav. The spirit of the Partisans has infiltrated me completely, and I have forgotten my Czech ancestors.'"[8]

Another aspect of the new Yugoslavia that saddened him was that the Communist government had outlawed the celebration of Christmas. "I felt deeply depressed during my first Christmas in Belgrade after the war," he wrote. "There was not a trace of Christmas in the capital. The streets, which looked joyful in prewar Christmas seasons, were no different now than on ordinary days. The shop windows were without Christmas decorations; people walking in the streets did not carry the customary parcels; only lighted candles in a window here and there disclosed that the Christmas tradition was still alive."[9]

On a Czechoslovak national holiday, Korbel hosted a reception at his embassy. Tito was among the guests. When the Marshal arrived with his own waiter, as well as his own sandwiches and wine, Mandula Korbel was furious. She thought that if the food was good enough for her guests, it was good enough for Tito. But when she asked the headwaiter to serve Tito some of her Czech hors d' oeuvres, the servant refused. Mandula picked up a tray and served him herself, suggesting little sausages that were a Czech specialty. Tito liked them so much, he had seconds. The waiter never spoke to the Korbels again.[10]

If the political climate of Belgrade was drab and confrontational, the Korbels' living quarters were quite grand. The family had a large, private apartment in the Czechoslovak embassy. On the second floor was a small ballroom with crystal chandeliers and brown marble walls.[11] The Korbels hosted concerts in it. A circular staircase led to the family's private quarters on the floor above.[12]

Madlenka's education became a subject of some concern. Because the Korbels did not want her in public school classrooms with the children of Yugoslav Communists, they brought a Czech governess to Belgrade.[13] She occupied a room next to Madlenka's and supervised her daily studies at home. Because Mandula Korbel called her daughter "Madlen," that is how the child signed her name. It was not until she was ten that she would learn otherwise.[14]

Life was lonely for Madlenka. With the exception of two children of another diplomatic family, both younger, she had few playmates and spent her spare time taking walks with the governess, who, at twenty, seemed much older. Summer vacation provided some relief. The family would spend a week at the beach on the Adriatic Sea in a resort called Opatija in what was then Northern Yugoslavia. They stayed at the Stalin Hotel. They spent another week in the mountains of Slovenia in Bled, a town with a big lake where Madlenka liked to swim.[15]

By the age of ten, Madlenka was academically ahead of other children in her age group. With few distractions at home and a private governess to supervise her, she excelled at her studies. However, because she was too young to qualify for the next grade level, her parents decided to send her to school in Switzerland. They chose the Prealpina School in Chexbres, a little town near Lake Geneva in the Swiss Alps. Madlenka was furious and told her parents she did not want to go.

She did not prevail. But because she had developed a skin rash, she arrived at the new school two weeks later than the other students. The fall semester had already begun. She did not speak French, and she did not know anyone there. The school also gave her a new name: Madeleine. Her world had turned upside down. "I hated it at first," Madeleine Albright says today. "And I didn't come home for Christmas that first year. My parents felt I should stay there." And what a dreary holiday it turned out to be. Most of the other girls did go home. Madeleine was sent to board at a nearby German school. "It was probably one of the worst Christmases I ever spent," she says. "I did not speak German. I was in this miserable place. And I had to stay in this horrible school."[16] That winter, Mandula Korbel gave birth in Belgrade to a son, Jan Josef. "It was the arrival of the prince," Albright says, with a mischievous smile of a resigned older sister. "He was a beautiful child with gorgeous blond curls. Everyone was thrilled."[17]

Back in Czechoslovakia, the Communists were extending their power base. Election results in May 1946 reflected the new balance of power in the country after the war. The Communists received 38 percent of the vote in national elections, the largest return for any single party. Klement Gottwald, the leader of the Communists, became prime minister. Beneš retained his post as president, while Jan Masaryk, the country's great champion of democracy, continued as foreign minister.[18] The Communist Party was proportionally the largest party in the National Assembly and the government, and though it still had to govern through a coalition, it nonetheless established itself as the most important power group in Czechoslovakia.[19] In fact, Communists assumed control of several important ministries that enabled them to lay the groundwork for a Communist takeover of the government.[20]

In September 1946, a year after the Korbels went to Belgrade, Cousin Dagmar faced exams necessary to enroll in Charles University in Prague. Dagmar says she never considered joining the Korbels permanently in Yugoslavia. At seventeen, she was eager to finish her schooling in Czechoslovakia. Although Korbel was listed on Dagmar's school records in Britain as her legal guardian and she was now orphaned, Dagmar says her uncle did not insist that she move to Belgrade with the family.

Madeleine Albright says she had always heard that Cousin Dagmar asked to join the Korbels in Belgrade with her boyfriend, but that Josef Korbel, a strict man, would not have his unmarried niece living under his roof with a man. "He would have had a fit," Albright says.[21] Dagmar says she did want her boyfriend to visit her in Belgrade, but that it was only for a few days during the summer when she was there on holiday. Her boyfriend, Vladimír Šíma, was planning to go to Yugoslavia on a student work project to build a railway, but when Dagmar asked her uncle if "Vláďa" could visit for a few days, he said no.[22]

Dagmar says that with no one else to look out for her in Prague, she moved in with a ninety-three-year-old great-aunt whom she had never met. It was an undesirable situation for Dagmar (and probably for the aunt as well), and it proved to be an arduous and lonely life for a young woman.

Although Prague had been spared extensive damage, the city was not a comfortable place in which to live. The winter of 1945 had been bitterly cold throughout Europe. Heating material was difficult to come by, making it hard to keep warm. "I didn't have a winter coat," Cousin Dagmar says. "I had clothes enough from England, but it's never so cold in England. The coats were not made for a Continental winter." As a result, in the summer of 1946, Dagmar went with a group of students to work in a mine in Northern Bohemia because the job afforded them extra rations of coal, food, and clothing. "Since we went to the mines, we got both the money and the extra ration cards, so I could dress myself properly for the next winter,"[23] she says.

While Dagmar was on her work detail, Korbel spent part of the summer of 1946 in France, one of twenty-four Czechoslovak delegates at the Paris Peace Conference. He wanted to take Madlenka with him on the trip, which he would make by air. But with memories of her bumpy plane ride from London to Prague after the war, the child refused to go.[24]

The purpose of the peace conference was to draft treaties between the victorious Allies and five of the vanquished nations that had thrown in their lot with Hitler: Italy, Rumania, Bulgaria, Hungary, and Finland. Germany was not invited.[25] In all, twenty-one nations took part.[26] Korbel's job was to chair the economic committee for the Balkan countries and Finland. He was considered qualified for the role because he had studied international economics in law school.[27]

The French were determined to be accommodating hosts. When a member of the Czechoslovak delegation expressed his wish to see the "real" Paris by night, not the Folies-Bergères or the Lido, which were for tourists, the French Foreign Ministry sent an official note to Czechoslovak foreign minister Jan Masaryk notifying the delegation that the visit to the brothels would take place starting at 9:00 P.M. on the following Wednesday evening. Many in the delegation, including a general in uniform, accepted the offer.

"Korbel refused to take part," says Ctibor Rybár, a member of the Czechoslovak mission secretariat.[28]

As at every such conference and meeting, there were many levels of politics at play—the obvious diplomatic discussions on one level, the more subtle jockeying for position on another. Rybár recalls that the delegation was divided into two groups. The most important group, headed by Masaryk and Clementis, occupied rooms in a fine hotel. The second group, to which Korbel was assigned, had rooms in far more modest quarters. "Korbel made a big fuss, so he got a better hotel room with the important delegation," recalls Rybár forty years later, still unamused. "I remember him as a self-important guy who wanted the best room with the ministers."[29] Korbel's proximity and persistence paid off. A year later, on June 17, 1947, the Czechoslovak government rewarded his hard work and dedication to Czechoslovakia by presenting him with "the military medal of First Grade as an act of his contribution to the liberation of the Czechoslovak Republic."[30]

The summer of 1947 was a turning point for postwar Czechoslovakia. In July, the Czechoslovak government, with Communist Party support, accepted an invitation from the Western powers to participate in opening meetings on the Marshall Plan—the U.S. program to rebuild the European economy. But Stalin quickly intervened and ordered the Communist Party leader, Prime Minister Klement Gottwald, to withdraw his support.[31] Both Beneš and Masaryk had thought that they could maintain an alliance with the USSR while functioning as a free parliamentary democracy. Stalin's intervention proved them wrong. That same month, Stalin summoned Masaryk to Moscow to spell out Russia's conditions for cooperation between the two states. Upon his return to Prague on July 12, Masaryk expressed the helplessness of Czechoslovakia's situation. "I left for Moscow as Minister of Foreign Affairs of a sovereign state," he said. "I am returning as Stalin's stooge."[32]

Through the rest of the year, the Czechoslovak Communists intensified their activities, ostensibly in preparation for the 1948 elections. In January 1948, Korbel returned to Prague from Belgrade to see Beneš and test the political climate. "The political battle between the democratic and Communist parties had reached its highest pitch," Korbel wrote later. "I had many political friends; they were in good spirits, confident of the forthcoming elections." Korbel wrote that because he had witnessed the violent politics of the Yugoslav Communists, "I conveyed to my friends my uneasy doubts about the certainty of the outcome of the struggle in Czechoslovakia, though I had shared their belief that one might cooperate with the Czech

Communists. They brushed my fears aside, saying that Gottwald was not a Tito and that Czechoslovak Communists were Czechs and Slovaks first, Communists second."[33]

Beneš received Korbel on January 12. The president spoke with difficulty, having suffered two strokes. Still, Korbel found him alert.[34] He told Korbel that he was confident about the internal situation in Czechoslovakia, that the elections would be held in the spring, and the Communists would lose. Korbel asked Beneš if the Communists might resort to a coup. "Don't be worried," Beneš replied. "The danger of a Communist putsch has passed. Return to Belgrade and carry on."[35]

These were Beneš' last words to Korbel, and he could not have been more wrong. Facing the prospect of losing power in the 1948 elections, the Communists took preemptive action. The party used its control over the Ministry of the Interior to purge non-Communists from the Czechoslovak security forces and replace them with party members. On February 20, a dozen non-Communist ministers resigned to protest the blatant misuse of security forces to suppress anti-Communist sentiment. They hoped their resignations would provoke new elections and a new balance of power with the Communists.[36] Five days later, however, Beneš was forced by internal pressures and the threat of Soviet intervention to accept the resignations and fill the vacancies with Communist appointments.[37] The democrats were shocked. The Communists had won in a bloodless coup d'état. The nation soon became a "people's democracy," a satellite of the Soviet Union. Once a beacon of democracy in Eastern Europe, Czechoslovakia was now a symbol of Soviet influence in the region.[38]

For the second time in ten years, democracy had been lost in Czechoslovakia. Except for a few hope-filled months during the "Prague Spring" in 1968, it would not resurface for forty years. On a broader scale, for Europe and the rest of the world, the events of February 25, 1948, sounded the battle cry of an ideological struggle between East and West that would dominate world politics for the next four decades. Korbel knew that the day signaled the end of Czechoslovak freedom and the end of Beneš' political life.

At some point in the winter or spring of 1948, the Czechoslovak government asked Korbel to represent Czechoslovakia as part of a special U.N. delegation. On January 20, 1948, the U.N. Security Council established a three-member commission to resolve the dispute between India and Pakistan—both newly independent countries—over the sovereignty of the state of Kashmir. Open fighting had broken out in the territory, and the

United Nations hoped to bring about a ceasefire and eventually create conditions for a plebiscite to determine whether Kashmir would become a part of India or Pakistan. The commission originally included the United States, Argentina, and Czechoslovakia, which, according to U.N. records, was nominated by India on February 10, 1948. On April 21, the Security Council added Belgium and Colombia. The delegation was called the United Nations Commission for India and Pakistan.[39] Jan Masaryk told Korbel that if he did not accept the commission post, a Communist would likely be appointed. Korbel discussed his decision with Philip John Noel-Baker, a noted British statesman and a member of the House of Commons.[40] When Korbel accepted the post, he was named chairman.

In his book *Danger in Kashmir,* Korbel maintained that he was assigned to the commission on February 5, 1948—almost three weeks *before* the Communist takeover in Prague on February 25, 1948.[41] He emphasized this point a year later in his request for political asylum in the United States, which he made when he got to New York. He repeated it in a statement he issued to the American press on February 14, 1949. "I was selected to serve on the Kashmir Commission before the Communist putsch took place in Prague," he wrote. "Minister Masaryk, and through him President Beneš as well, emphasized to me the international importance of the Kashmir dispute and attached a considerable significance to the fact that a democratic Czechoslovak representative could be of help to settle the dispute in a peaceful way and thus assist also to prevent the danger of spreading Communism in Asia."[42]

Korbel no doubt knew that this statement would play well with the American press. By stating that he accepted the position *prior* to the Communist coup, and by aligning himself with Beneš and Masaryk, symbols of Czechoslovak democracy, Korbel was portraying himself as a soldier fighting the noble fight against communism.

Korbel's official file at the Czechoslovak Ministry of Foreign Affairs, however, offers a different time frame. It states that Korbel was appointed to the commission on May 13, 1948, almost three full months *after* the Communist takeover. The distinction is important because it raises the question of whether Korbel willingly accepted a position from the Communist regime. Korbel had reason to shape the time frame to his liking, particularly after he had made the decision to flee to the United States. He was entering a postwar atmosphere in which, within a few years, red-baiting and McCarthyism would run rampant. It is understandable that he would try to bury any Communist ties. In his letter requesting asylum for himself and his family, Korbel presented his experiences with the U.N. commission as justification for political refuge in the United States, emphasizing the distance between himself and Czechoslovakia's Communist leaders.

If it is impossible to pinpoint when Korbel was named to the U.N. Commission for India and Pakistan, it is also difficult to discern when he decided to leave Czechoslovakia permanently and seek asylum in the United States. While it is known that he requested political asylum in February 1949, it is not clear whether Korbel made the decision to defect in the spring of 1948—when the Korbel family received visas to the United States, where the U.N. commission would continue its work—or later, when he and the rest of the family were already safely settled in the United States. But the fact that Korbel sought visas in May for his family would seem to indicate that he had decided to capitalize on the opportunity that the U.N. commission afforded his family and to escape Czechoslovakia sooner rather than later. His decision to continue to work on the U.N. commission for the Communist regime in Prague, however, complicated the story and made him vulnerable to criticism from those colleagues and friends who resigned from the government immediately after the Communist takeover.

Shortly after the February coup, Czechoslovaks suffered a loss that was as tragic for what it symbolized as for its practical consequences. On March 10, Czechoslovak foreign minister Jan Masaryk, son of Czechoslovakia's founder, Tomáš Masaryk, was found dead in the courtyard beneath the bathroom window of his private quarters in Czernin Palace, seat of the country's Foreign Ministry. Either someone had pushed him out of a second-floor window or he had jumped to his death. Whether it was murder or suicide remains a point of contention among Czechs today. But few would question that Masaryk's death, coming when it did, marked the loss of those freedoms and democratic principles for which his father and he had worked so hard and long.[43] Korbel and his wife flew from Belgrade to Prague for the funeral. Following the ceremony, they met with Cousin Dagmar in a hotel room. "That was the last time I saw them," Dagmar recalls.

Dagmar remembers Mandula telling her at the time that her uncle had received a U.N. appointment that would take him to Kashmir and that she would be living in London alone with the children. Dagmar says the Korbels never invited her to join them in the West.[44] Madeleine Albright disagrees with her cousin's version of events. Albright says that because her father was Dagmar's guardian during the war, he would certainly have asked his orphaned niece to come to England with his family. "There is no way in the world he would have left this young girl there if he had a choice about it," Albright says. "She was eighteen. She did not want to come with us."[45]

Whatever the case, Dagmar's recollection of when it was that she heard about Korbel's commission appointment bolsters Korbel's statements that he was appointed to the U.N. commission before the February 25 coup, or at least before the May 13 date specified in his official Foreign Ministry record. Also, the decision to send Mandula Korbel and her children to London suggests that Korbel decided fairly early in 1948 to flee to the United States. If he planned to travel to New York for the duration of the U.N. commission's work and then to return with the family to Prague, his wife and children could have remained in Eastern Europe at least until Korbel was ready to leave for the United States. We might reasonably conclude that Korbel sent his family to London in the summer of 1948 as a precaution, before the routes out of Czechoslovakia were closed down, as they had been when he made his escape from the Germans.

Although the United Nations Commission for India and Pakistan had been established on January 20, it was not convened and sent to the region until months later.[46] On June 15, the commission assembled for the first time in Geneva.[47] Korbel left Belgrade for Geneva in late May. Earlier that month, the Czechoslovak National Assembly had approved a new constitution that included many liberal and democratic provisions but, in reality, reflected the primacy of Communist power. Beneš refused to sign the document and, on June 7, resigned the presidency. Gottwald replaced him.[48]

Korbel's growing discomfort with the Communist government in Czechoslovakia became increasingly apparent to his friends. Eduard Goldstücker, himself a Communist Party member, remembers those days well. "The Communist Party took over the whole Czechoslovak government without anyone controlling it or sharing the power," he says. "That was a new development, and Korbel didn't feel at home or secure with the new regime."[49] At the same time, Korbel did not immediately sever ties with the Communist government. While many Czechoslovak officials resigned their posts in protest immediately following the February 25 coup, Korbel served the Czechoslovak Communist government for ten months. After finishing his term as ambassador to Yugoslavia, he served as the official Czechoslovak delegate to the U.N. Kashmir Commission until December 12.[50] While Korbel came under criticism for serving the Communist government as long as he did, there are indications that he saw working for the regime as his only opportunity to escape, and that his months of service gave him time to make the arrangements.

As he traveled, Korbel kept one eye on the political situation unfolding at home. Like many Czechoslovak diplomats, he was faced with a wrenching decision: to return to his homeland, where his safety, and that of his family, could not be assured, or to escape. It was a choice between the known and the unknown, of going back to his native country, where he understood the political landscape but where he and his family might be in personal danger if he refused to embrace communism, or giving up everything he had worked for to flee, virtually penniless, to the West.

Korbel knew his situation could become perilous, that the Communists were arresting, trying, and, in some cases, hanging former political leaders. He had to recognize that the U.N. post gave his family perhaps its only chance to flee. Some of Korbel's Czech colleagues believe that he made a secret agreement with another diplomat, probably British, to expedite the family's passage to America.[51] (Although it was common practice at the time for the newly formed Central Intelligence Agency to assist political dissidents in escaping from Eastern Europe, the agency refuses to confirm or deny that it helped Korbel reach the United States, insisting it is standard practice not to comment.)[52] Korbel was one of thousands who faced the question whether to stay or flee. Tens of thousands more did not have the luxury of choice. Finally, he made an agonizing decision. Korbel would forsake his dream of a democratically ruled Czechoslovakia and bid his native land farewell. Eduard Goldstücker put it starkly: "He decided not to go [home]."[53]

According to one account, Korbel had his personal secretary at the embassy in Belgrade hide some of the family's possessions in the embassy basement. He later sought to have them sent to the United States. (Many months later, the box that was supposed to hold the family valuables arrived at the Korbels' address in America. But when the family opened it, they discovered the secretary had sent the wrong box. This one was filled with the long red carpets used for ceremonial events at the embassy.)[54]

Once he had completed his escape plan, Korbel telephoned his wife in Belgrade and told her cryptically, "You're going on vacation. Take what you can."[55] On a blistering hot day in early summer, carrying only a few pieces of luggage, Mandula boarded a train in Belgrade with Kathy and John for another long, tiring journey. They stopped in Switzerland to see Madlenka, who was still in boarding school. As they walked around the city of Lausanne together, Madlenka introduced her young sister to the joys of bubble gum.[56]

In Lausanne, Mandula and her two younger children boarded a train for London. When they arrived, Mandula telephoned the Korbels' old friend Eduard Goldstücker, who was still there, serving his government. Josef Korbel had asked if his friend would provide his family with a place to stay. Goldstücker agreed. "When they arrived, they were exhausted," he remembers. "The children had not slept. They came to our house and slept very deeply for hours on end."

Goldstücker understood that had Korbel chosen to return to Czechoslovakia, his life would have been in grave danger. "As the years went by, everyone who was known in the West got into trouble," Goldstücker says matter-of-factly. "I evaded hanging just by a thread." He recognized that he and Korbel were better off not discussing the reasons behind his friend's decision to flee, that the safety of the Korbel family, and that of Goldstücker's family as well, rested on the appearance that this was just an ordinary visit by an old friend. "I didn't ask why," he says. "You see, I was a high Communist of the Communist regime, and he was evading the Communist regime. Nevertheless, he came to me, and I received him as a very dear friend." Goldstücker did not inquire about the Korbels' plans. He was quite sure his friend was headed for the United States, where the U.N. headquarters was located, but he realized that because they had parted company politically, it was better to leave such questions for another time.[57]

While the Czechoslovak government would eventually consider Korbel's actions treasonous, Goldstücker did not worry about the consequences of offering sanctuary to his friend. "I didn't think about whether it was dangerous or not," he says. "At that time we didn't think about being stamped as a traitor or anything of that sort. That came later, with the Soviet grip."[58]

Goldstücker and Korbel saw each other several times after that, both in London and in Denver. Each time they met, they had much to talk about: politics, their families, their experiences in the war. But there was one topic that was never raised. As close as they felt to each other and with all they had shared, the two friends never discussed the death of their families in the Holocaust. "We carried this horrible thing with us, but I don't remember talking about it," Goldstücker says. "It was a tragedy."[59]

It was all tragic. But the hardest part was about to begin.

7

The Defection

"I went to Yugoslavia in 1945 in the best of faith. This faith I lost."

—Josef Korbel, April 5, 1948

ONCE AGAIN, London offered the Korbels refuge from political turmoil at home. Within a few days of arriving back in the British capital, Mandula Korbel settled her family into a small basement flat on Earl's Court. It was a dark, dreary place, so small that the bathtub, with its gas-fired water heater, had to be in the kitchen. The family always worried that it would explode when they lighted it.[1]

Mandula kept herself busy taking care of Kathy, then six, and John, who was a year and a half. The U.N. commission planned to continue its work at its headquarters in Lake Success, New York. Quietly and efficiently, Korbel made arrangements to sail to America. When Madeleine's school term in Switzerland ended, she flew from Geneva to London to join the family.

As the summer progressed, Korbel's new position kept him in constant motion. On July 5, the commission left Geneva for Karachi, the capital of Pakistan.[2] Korbel spent much of the summer traveling between Karachi and New Delhi, the Indian capital, before spending several days in Srinagar in the Kashmir Valley.[3] The commission left Srinagar for Geneva on September 21 to prepare an interim report for the U.N. Security Council meeting in Paris.[4]

That fall, Madeleine enrolled in London's Lycée Français where all her classes were in French. "I used to take my books to school in a suitcase, because there were so many of them," she says. "It's the hardest single school I went to in my life."[5]

Mandula Korbel marked time until the family would again be reunited. Anna Sonnek remembers staying with Mandula for a few days in September 1948. Sonnek says that while the Korbels' flat was small, Mandula nevertheless offered to share it with her and her husband, Přemek, who had just arrived in London after a heart-stopping escape from Czechoslovakia. Having only recently gone through the emotional experience of fleeing Belgrade, made all the more difficult with children in tow, Mandula willingly opened her home to her Czech friends.

Anna and Přemek Sonnek had taken a train to Cheb, a small town in Western Bohemia, near the West German border. From there they drove to a house owned by a man who had promised to lead them across the border into West Germany. On this September afternoon, carrying a basket and pretending to be gathering mushrooms, the man showed the Sonneks into the nearby forest. After walking for about an hour in what they thought was Czechoslovakia, they crossed unknowingly into West Germany. A German border guard on a bicycle, who happened to be mushrooming with his girlfriend, spotted and held them. The Sonneks shouted and struggled long enough for their Czech guide to zigzag through the trees and escape back into Czechoslovakia. He was scheduled to escort Anna's parents across the border the next day. The Sonneks were put in a West German camp for Displaced Persons, where they stayed for two weeks before they made their way to London. Once there, they found the Korbel household not as joyful as it used to be. They were also waiting for their son to be escorted out so their own ordeal was not yet over. "During the war, the Korbels' household was usually noisy and cheery with the children playing around the grownups," Sonnek says. "But in September 1948, the atmosphere was not all that boisterous as it was before. This time we were waiting for our year-old son to be brought across the border to join us."[6]

The Sonneks escaped in 1948 because Anna Sonnek's father, Jaroslav Stránský, was politically unacceptable to the Communists. As minister of justice, and subsequently education, in the pre-1948 Czechoslovak government, he had been close to both President Beneš and Foreign Minister Masaryk. In February 1948, he was among the ministers who tendered their resignation to Beneš in the mistaken belief that by resigning they would force new elections and a new balance of power with the Communists in government.[7]

Anna Sonnek knew the Korbels well during the war years. She understood the family had a Jewish background, but it was not an issue they ever discussed. "I took it for granted they were Jewish," she says. "Of course, a fair number of people who escaped were Jewish. One expected it." What she did not know was that the Korbels planned to move to the United States.[8] Although they had received their visas in May, it appears that they did not disclose their plans to many people, including close friends. Korbel knew that his own political fate remained precarious.

Events moved quickly. On the evening of November 5, 1948, Mandula Korbel and her three children—Madeleine, Kathy, and John—boarded the SS *America* in Southampton, England. They carried twenty-one pieces of luggage. As the family of a diplomat, they traveled First Class.[9] The Korbels brought along a twenty-year-old Yugoslavian woman named S. Fanci Mencinger, who had been their maid at the embassy in Belgrade for two years.[10]

The ship made an easy, overnight sail across the English Channel to LeHavre. When passengers awakened in the morning, the port was calm, and the Korbels enjoyed a large breakfast in the First Class dining room. But the minute the ship set sail again, winter weather set in. The ocean turned wild. Mandula and Fanci were seasick for almost the entire six-day trip. They remained in their cabins while Madeleine cared for Kathy and John.[11] "I just tried to get through it," Madeleine Albright says today.[12] On November 11, Armistice Day, the ship arrived in New York.[13] The Korbels stood on deck as they sailed past the Statue of Liberty. Just ten days before, Madeleine and her family had listened to American election returns on the radio and cheered when Harry S Truman won an extraordinary, last-minute victory over New York governor Thomas E. Dewey. Truman would be her new country's president. This was the beginning of Madeleine Korbel's political consciousness.[14] She was eleven years old.

While his family was sailing for the United States, Korbel was in Paris with his U.N. commission. Vladimír Clementis, the longtime Communist who had worked with Korbel on broadcasts from the government-in-exile in London, was also there, heading the Czechoslovak delegation at the U.N. General Assembly. Since the Communist coup the previous February, he had risen to become deputy foreign minister. It was he who had recommended Korbel be posted to Yugoslavia as ambassador. Clementis liked Korbel and valued his loyalty.

Korbel and Clementis met briefly on November 8, while Korbel's family was aboard the SS *America,* three days out of Southampton en route to New York. Clementis asked Korbel for his opinion of the political changes in Czechoslovakia. Korbel replied that he was concerned because people were dissatisfied and that the economy was languishing.[15] He added that the Communist takeover of the Czechoslovak government in February had increased the danger of war between the Soviet Union and the United States, a situation he considered almost inevitable. Clementis disagreed. "The Russians will not start a war," he said, "and if the Americans did, the Russians would occupy the rest of Europe in a very short time." With that, the telephone rang. Clementis told Korbel he would see him when he returned from Prague.[16]

The two men met again on November 26. What unfolded next was an extraordinary conversation, a dialogue pitting two friendly colleagues against each other in an ideological tug-of-war that had already split their country open. In the end, it severed forever what had once been close personal and professional ties.

As Korbel later recounted the story, Clementis began by asking Korbel for his opinion of the new Czechoslovak government. Korbel replied, "Mr. Minister . . . you know that I am not a Communist, and therefore I cannot be but critical towards the events at home. . . . I shall tell you frankly that Communism and the Communist regime are unacceptable to me."

Korbel told Clementis that he had accepted the assignment as ambassador to Yugoslavia in 1945 "in the best of faith." But he added poignantly, "This faith, I lost." In the beginning of the assignment, Korbel said, he refused to accept critical remarks about the Communist government made by his Yugoslav friends, but was later persuaded they were right. "Communism cannot succeed but brings only hardships which people cannot and will not take," he said. "Step by step, I became critical, very critical." He went on to explain to Clementis why he did not think communism could succeed, that a government cannot compel people to work when they are driven by distrust, suspicion, and fear. "With a Communist regime are linked hardships which a fair man cannot swallow," Korbel said. "I am telling you, it is the end of freedom."

Clementis was not surprised, but his reply left no room for ambiguity: "That means that after the Kashmir commission is finished, you will not return home? Is that so?" Korbel had thought through his answer. "I would feel very unhappy," he said. "I would not enter into the Party . . . because I would not do what thousands of people did, that they joined the party for careers. . . . I don't see what I could do at home. Not only that I do not agree with Communism but, under the circumstances, I could not do any proper work. And above all, I could not take it politically because I would not know how to adapt myself and, at the end, this would be reproached to me."[17]

Clementis' reply was withering. "That means you are afraid," he said.

Korbel answered him evenly. "I have no reason to be afraid," he said. It was the psychological burden, he believed, that would be too much to bear. "And then," Korbel added, "one never knows of what I could be accused, one day. A Communist regime does not compromise." Korbel warned Clementis that even loyal Communists like himself might be in danger: "You criticized [the regime], Mr. Minister. . . . And this is a thing which is never forgotten." Clementis replied: "But I was right." That, said Korbel, did not matter. "It may return, one day, and be turned against you." Neither man could know how prescient those words would be.

Korbel told Clementis he did not think it possible to reverse the trend toward communism: "I think that it is necessary to have a progressive program but to conserve at the same time personal freedom without which there is no progress, and no endurable solution."

Finally, Korbel was blunt. "I cannot fight for Communism . . . ," he said. He had weighed the options. His mind was made up. "Whether to be loyal toward you, personally, or toward my conviction and conscience, you will understand that I cannot hesitate," he said. "This has been my opinion from the beginning when the change took place in our country."

Clementis confronted Korbel directly about his plans. "That means that you would not return if you had no work on the Commission?" he asked. "Where is your family?" Korbel replied that they were already in New York and that he planned to join them.

Clementis ended the conversation abruptly, telling Korbel what he knew intellectually but, as a dedicated Czech citizen, had to dread: He would be fired for disloyalty. There could be no turning back. "I shall, of course, strike you out of the list of Foreign Ministry officials," Clementis said. A few days later, Clementis left for Prague. The men never spoke again.[18]

The record of the discussion comes from an April 1949 memorandum, written by Korbel for a study group given by Dr. Philip Mosely of the Rockefeller Foundation in New York. The timing of Korbel's memorandum, however, raises questions. He wrote it just two months after requesting political asylum for himself and his family. Did he tailor it to portray himself as an ardent anti-Communist, eliminating any nuances or ambiguities in his true feelings about the political situation in Czechoslovakia? Any critical analysis of the dialogue must pose that question. On the other hand, Korbel's family, and the maid, had received visas for the United States the previous May and, as Korbel told Clementis, had already arrived in New York. This suggests that Korbel had decided to flee Communist Czechoslovakia months before he met with Clementis in Paris. Whether he planned to continue working for the commission in the United States or to defect right away is not clear.

In his conversation with Clementis, Korbel portrays himself as a staunch opponent of communism. Yet because he served under the Communist regime from the time of the February 1948 coup until his dismissal on December 12, some of his colleagues thought otherwise. Perhaps out of jealousy that he had been named to an ambassadorial post and then to a choice U.N. commission, perhaps because they suffered hardships and prison sentences that he did not, many of Korbel's wartime colleagues judged him harshly for keeping ties to the Czechoslovak Communist government as long as he did. "Everyone is different and everyone has to decide in a moment of crisis what to do," says Pavel Tigrid, the Czech statesman and writer, an old friend and BBC colleague of Korbel, who had spent many years in prison and in exile. "Some lines are broader than others. . . . If it were someone else, I would call him an opportunist. But Korbel was a loyal, hard-working civil servant who did what he was told to do, and it wasn't against his better judgment. He was a liberal who, in his heart, was critical of the hard Beneš line to the Soviet Union, but he never expressed it publicly, except among friends." The late Jan Stránský, son of Jaroslav Stránský, who witnessed Korbel's baptism and worked with him at the BBC, said Korbel balanced his political loyalties evenly. "He was a diplomat who served under Beneš," Stránský said shortly before he died. "He was not anti-Communist, but not pro-Communist either. He was in between."[19]

In Europe, where the political nuances of World War II are far better understood than in America, Korbel's view that the Soviets would save Czechoslovakia from Germany's clutches was shared by many people. After Munich, it was to the Soviets, not the West, that Czechoslovakia looked for its survival. "Basically, Beneš was marked for the rest of his life by Munich," Tigrid says. "He was obsessed by the idea of 'Never again Munich.' Therefore, he thought that the Soviet Union would be the decisive factor. He thought this was a good guarantee that Munich would never be repeated. But he was wrong for the simple reason that the notion that the West would go to the left towards the Social Democrats and the Soviet Union would open itself and move towards an open society and eventually to a democratic system was totally wrong, as we all know."[20]

With the clarity of hindsight, such judgments are easy to make. But at the time, by working with the Communists, Korbel was following his head, if not always his heart. "This policy called the Beneš policy was the rule and the law," says Tigrid. "Korbel [and others] subscribed to it wholeheartedly. I remember several times when . . . sometimes Korbel [was not] so sure, but that was the line, and we were the Beneš government. Beneš was the Czech policy. Period. Nobody else."

Some of Korbel's BBC colleagues so disliked what they considered the diplomat's pro-Soviet views that when Korbel returned to London for a visit in the early 1970s, some twenty-five years after the war ended, they refused to dine with him. Korbel appeared sad and surprised that people he considered friends found excuses not to see him. "He asked why no one wanted to talk to him," says Zdeněk Mastník, who started working for the BBC in 1948 in London, where he became a senior program assistant in charge of the Czech editorial board. "It was very painful for him. It was strange. There was such animosity, and he didn't understand it. For him it was a big shock."

Mastník says that his BBC colleagues pressed him to entertain the Korbels for dinner because he was the only person on the staff who had not worked personally with Korbel. Trying to be gracious, Mastník took Korbel and his wife to the restaurant at the Czechoslovak National House, London's unofficial club for Czech exiles, which even today retains its old-world flavor. Amid burgundy velvet drapes and a pungent aroma of goulash and cigarette smoke, patrons linger over such traditional Czechoslovak dishes as roast duck with dumplings and gravy served with sweet sauerkraut and caraway seeds, washed down with tall glasses of nutty Pilsner beer. When asked why, if he had worked so closely with Communists, Korbel had become such an anti-Communist when he moved to the United States, Mastník's face took on a look of someone who had just met the village idiot. "But what would you do?" he said. "What could he do in America? It was great he could get a job in a university. You do what you have to do to earn money."[21]

You do what you have to do. The staunch anti-Communist views that Korbel expressed when he arrived in the United States—those his daughter celebrates today—may well have been an attempt to distance himself as much as possible from his decision not to cut his ties to the Communist Czechoslovak government sooner than he did. Or they could be the testament of a man who has seen the devil and repents. His letter requesting political asylum in February 1949, and his April 1949 account of his conversation with Clementis, each portrays Korbel as a champion of democratic principles. He was seeking a new life in America at a moment when fear and suspicion of Communists were beginning to grip the nation he sought to adopt.

In Korbel's February 1949 statement to the press, which was excerpted by the *New York Times* on February 14, he claimed that he participated in the United Nations Commission for India and Pakistan as long as he did only to prevent a Communist from replacing him. Korbel's original statement concluded with a firm declaration: "I could not, of course, give any support to the Communist Government in Prague who is selling my country out to the Russian imperialists and driving the democratic and freedom-loving Czechoslovak nation into a complete slavery, economic proletarization, national and international degradation, alienating it from the traditional links with Western democracies and culture."[22] Such hyperbole no doubt served Korbel well in the United States, where the American press salivated over such a vitriolic attack against communism. It is little wonder that Korbel preferred that people think he worked as *chef de cabinet* to Jan Masaryk, a champion of democracy, rather than in the job his friend Eduard Gold-stücker insisted he held: chief of staff to Vladimír Clementis, a Communist.

There is no question that Korbel was a sincere democrat and legitimately disillusioned by communism. Perhaps it simply took him longer to come to grips with the choices he faced than it did some of his colleagues. Perhaps he was more acutely aware of the dangers that awaited him if he returned to Czechoslovakia. There is no doubt that the ten months he spent working for the Czechoslovak Communist government bought him time to plan an escape.

Korbel's writings suggest that along with Beneš and Masaryk, he felt deeply deceived by Stalin's repeated promises to stand up for Czechoslovak independence and not to interfere with the country's internal decisions. Like them, he, too, trusted the Communists and the Soviet Union for a time. Yet the strong anti-Communist sentiment he expressed in his later writings did not give the full picture. Rather than merely reflecting his disappointment with communism, he sought to bury any suggestion that he might have at one time believed that Communists and democrats would work together in Czechoslovakia.

On December 12, just over two weeks after Korbel's dramatic confrontation with Clementis, Korbel was officially dismissed from the Czechoslovak Ministry of Foreign Affairs. He was deprived of his citizenship, and all his property at home was confiscated.[23] Five days later, Korbel boarded the RMS *Queen Mary* in Southampton. Toting six pieces of luggage, he sailed for America in a First Class stateroom.[24]

Korbel's passage was paid for by the United Nations. By good fortune, the new Czechoslovak Communist government, like bureaucracies all over the world, was slow with its paperwork. Clementis sent a cable marked "urgent" to Dr. Vladimír Houdek, his government's representative to the United Nations, advising the international body of Korbel's dismissal and asking whether the United Nations would follow its lead and strip Korbel of his place on the Kashmir Commission. "Report whether according to [U.N. Secretary-General] Trygve Lie, the notification of this fact will automatically mean that he is losing his membership in the Kashmir Commission." But the cable was dated January 13, 1949—three weeks after Korbel was safely in America.[25]

The currents of history that swept over Europe in the decade between 1938 and 1948 forced Korbel to weigh his loyalties, to choose between a promising career, love for his homeland, and the safety of his family. In the end, love for his family and dedication to democratic ideals prevailed. His friends and colleagues did not always agree with the decisions he made as he negotiated a path to a safer world where his children and his grandchildren could prosper. But they had to appreciate his pragmatic instincts and skill as he wove through a maze of politics and propaganda. The wrong turn could have led to a closed door, prison, and death.

PART TWO

 Madeleine

8

Starting Over

"The part I think about most in my early background is that we were constantly going somewhere else. I had to make friends very easily. . . . The impression I always had was that I never felt like a child. I spent most of my time with adults. . . ."
—Madeleine Albright, February 6, 1997

AT THE AGE OF THIRTY-NINE, Josef Korbel started his life over in America. Although his status with the U.N. commission had yet to change, he knew that he would soon be stripped of all ties to the new Czechoslovak government. Korbel arrived in New York on December 22, 1948. Mandula, who spoke little English, was having trouble adjusting to her new world in an American suburb, and she was delighted when her husband joined the family. Christmas was only three days away. As always, they decorated a tree, thrilled to be together again.

The Korbels settled into a home just outside New York City. One of Josef Korbel's colleagues at the United Nations had helped the family rent a small gardener's cottage at 149 Station Road in a woodsy section of Great Neck, a prosperous and developing suburban community on Long Island's North Shore. In the 1920s, F. Scott Fitzgerald had used Great Neck as the model for West Egg in his novel *The Great Gatsby*. Before the Depression hit and the movie industry moved to Hollywood, Great Neck was the "in" place to live. Less than a half-hour train ride from Manhattan, it attracted entertainers and writers.

In Czechoslovakia, the Korbels had been a relatively affluent family. As diplomats, they lived in comfortable, sometimes luxurious quarters and had household help to take care of the daily chores. In Great Neck, for a time, they had Fanci Mencinger—"Fancika," as they called her—the Yugoslavian who had been their maid in Belgrade. A devout Catholic from Slovenia, she walked Madeleine to church every Sunday. Fancika left the family not long after the Korbels brought her to America, leaving Mandula to keep house.[1] "Mother used to tell stories of how she had to buy pots and pans but didn't know what to choose because she had never cooked, that she had no idea of what foods to purchase or in what quantity," says John Korbel. "They started a completely new life in 1949."[2]

Korbel chose the area because the United Nations' temporary headquarters was located in a building that once belonged to the Sperry gyroscope manufacturing company in Lake Success, one of the seven villages of Great Neck.[3] Korbel loved to walk the town's country roads, but it frustrated him that every few minutes, someone stopped to ask if he wanted a ride. "People in America are not used to walking," he told his family.[4]

The Korbels enrolled Madeleine and Kathy in Arrandale Elementary School on the corner of Middleneck Road and Arrandale Avenue, about a mile from the house. The school had a big playground. Across the street was a luncheonette where the children sometimes bought hot dogs for lunch.[5] The Korbels did not have television, so Madeleine watched *Howdy Doody* at the home of a neighbor. Mandula Korbel later discovered soap operas. She listened constantly for the end of the story, which never seemed to come.

At eleven, Madeleine was a pretty girl, slightly pudgy with soft blond curls and a wide, engaging smile. Like her father, she was already an accomplished linguist, fluent in three languages: Czech, which she would use at home with her parents throughout their lives; French, which she had first learned at the boarding school in Switzerland; and English, which she spoke with a British accent. Although Madeleine was the appropriate age for sixth grade, school officials thought initially that she should go into fifth grade because she was a foreigner unfamiliar with American ways. But when they tested her, they found that academically she qualified for seventh grade. Taking into account her age, background, and test scores, the officials decided to place her in sixth grade.

At first, Madeleine did not realize that she spoke differently from the other kids. One day in school, her class was learning a Thanksgiving song called "We Gather Together," and she heard one voice that did not blend in. Listening carefully, Madeleine recognized it as her own. That was the first time she realized she had a British accent, and she was determined to lose it.[6] A facile learner and a mimic, she tuned her ear to the American pronunciation.

Not only did Madeleine sound different from the other children, who thought her clipped consonants and nasal *A*s gave the impression that she had a mouth full of marbles, but she looked different as well, her coats a little too big or a little too small, dresses a little too short or too long—never quite right. Her schoolmates had the occasional boy-girl parties of early adolescence in which Spin the Bottle and Post Office were naughty attractions, but Madeleine rarely attended. Her parents frowned on the parties that American children took for granted. Also, they did not own a car. Just getting Madeleine to and from school events was a problem. "[My parents] were very strict," Madeleine Albright says today. "I could never do anything that the other kids did."[7]

Like most children who move to a new neighborhood, Madeleine wanted desperately to blend in. For years, she had always been different — the exiled child in war-torn London; the privileged daughter of the Czechoslovak ambassador in Belgrade; and now, the little refugee in America. "I always felt I was a foreigner," Albright says.[8] It was a self-image that she would live with throughout her childhood.

Although the Czechoslovak government had dismissed Korbel from the Ministry of Foreign Affairs, he continued to work for the United Nations Commission for India and Pakistan. The new Communist government in Prague did not know whether the United Nations would follow its example and remove Korbel from the commission. As noted, Clementis' January 13 cable to Vladimír Houdek asked if Korbel's dismissal from the Czechoslovak Foreign Ministry meant he automatically would lose his position on the Kashmir Commission.[9] Clementis sent another cable to Houdek four days later asking him to contact his Soviet counterpart to find out "whether the notification concerning Korbel's dismissal and his replacement by another person will be done without further delay."[10] Once again, the bureaucracy moved slowly. Two weeks later, Clementis sent a third cable to New York, saying that the matter had still not been resolved: "We are awaiting statement of the ambassador here who has requested instructions from New Delhi."[11] In the end, Korbel served the commission until it returned to the Indian subcontinent on February 1, 1949. Korbel said he learned about his termination from a U.N. press release, dated February 11, that included a published letter from Houdek.[12]

Josef Korbel moved immediately to make sure that he and his family could stay in America. On February 12, 1949, he wrote a letter to former senator Warren R. Austin, the U.S. representative to the United Nations, requesting asylum in the United States for himself, his family, and their twenty-year-old Yugoslav maid.[13]

In his letter, Korbel stressed that while he worked on the commission, he never reported back to the Czechoslovak government about the commission's work because he considered himself to be "a representative of the democratic and peace-loving Czechoslovak nation," rather than a servant of the Communist regime. The main text of the letter follows:

> Excellency:
>
> . . . I was selected to be Member of this Commission before the Communist putsch took place in Prague, on 25th February 1948. In agreement with my political friends in exile, I decided to stay on the Commission because I was of the opinion that I was helping the common cause of democracy and peace in preventing a Czechoslovak Communist to take my place. About this decision, I informed Mr. Lewis Douglas, the United States Ambassador in London, in June 1948.
>
> While on the Commission I refused to follow the policy of the Soviet bloc the representatives of which obstructed any positive work in the United Nations, its Commissions and other agencies. I did not send a single report to the Czechoslovak Communist Government about the Commission's activities considering myself to be a representative of the democratic and peace-loving Czechoslovak nation. Having this in mind I tried to contribute to the common cause of democracy and peace by working with other Members of the Commission in a spirit of mutual confidence. . . .
>
> . . . I cannot, of course, return to the Communist Czechoslovakia as I would be arrested for my faithful adherence to the ideals of democracy. I would be most obliged if you would kindly convey to his Excellency the Secretary of State [Dean Acheson] that I beg of him the right to stay in the United States, the same right to be given also to my wife and three children who came to the United States on the basis of my assignment to the United Nations. Their personal data are also enclosed. Miss F. Mencinger, the maid, has been employed by me almost two years, and I reliably know that she is a sincere democrat and a Yougoslav [*sic*] maid and a devoted Catholic. She is unable to return to Yugoslavia on account of the work she did for my family. . . .
>
> I am taking the liberty to enclose the text of a statement which I intend to give to the Press on 14th February.

Please accept, your Excellency, the expression of my highest consideration and deep thanks.

I am

Yours truly,

Josef Korbel[14]

Despite his protestation to the contrary, Korbel did send at least one report on the commission's activities to the Czechoslovak Communist government. According to documents in the files of the Czechoslovak Ministry of Foreign Affairs, Korbel sent a cable that he signed *internally* before it was signed officially at the end by the Czechoslovak ambassador to India, Jaroslav Šejnoha.[15] Dated July 17, 1948, and sent from New Delhi, the cable reads:

2756/B/1948
Re: Kashmir Commission

To: Minister Clementis

In regards to your No. 145.942, Korbel relates this: the Commission has developed activities in full. It convenes twice a day. It has established a military subcommission and is sending some members to Karachi right now. Its first goals is [sic] to stop the open fire. At the official places, I was told that they would welcome a trip to Kashmir. The Commission was accepted very well by the Indian government, and is constantly in contact with the executive minister of foreign affairs, Baipai (?) Presence of PKOPER (?) necessary. Otherwise, I cannot fully perform my duties. Please respond. Korbel.

ŠEJNOHA 1450[16]

State Department officials looking into Korbel's request for asylum contacted Thomas F. Power, Jr., an American official working at the United Nations, for more information on Korbel. Power, who had been at the founding of the United Nations in 1945 as a staff aide to Eleanor Roosevelt and who later became deputy secretary to the U.S. mission, sought out Jan Papánek, who had represented the Czechoslovak government-in-exile in the United States during World War II and later served as the first Czechoslovak ambassador to the United Nations.

With the Communist coup in February 1948, Papánek quit his post but remained in the United States, where he became involved with the American Fund for Czechoslovak Refugees. He toured refugee camps for several months in the fall of 1948, then returned to New York to urge the United Nations to mount a refugee relief effort.[17]

By coincidence, Papánek and Korbel were First Class passengers on the same crossing of the *Queen Mary* in December 1948, but there is no indication they met.[18] Papánek had publicly renounced the Czechoslovak Communist government, but Korbel had not. While there can be little doubt that they were aware of each other's presence aboard ship—everyone received a passenger list—they may well have avoided meeting. "Papánek probably didn't speak to Korbel on the ship because he didn't know where he stood," says Eduard Goldstücker, Korbel's old friend.[19] When Power asked Papánek for his assessment of Korbel, the former Czechoslovak diplomat expressed some reservations, in a decidedly mixed report. Power wrote:

> As requested, I asked Dr. Papánek on March 11 for his opinion of Korbel.
>
> Dr. Papánek said that he was not entirely sure what to think about him. He said that his firsthand acquaintanceship with Korbel had been rather brief. He knew that he had been of great assistance in making [Deputy Foreign Minister Vladimír] Clementis' political fortune by placing him on BBC during the war when Korbel was in charge of this work for the Czech Government-in-Exile.
>
> Papánek said there were some people who had a very strong opinion against Korbel for reasons which Papánek was not familiar. He said that other persons had alleged to him that Korbel as Ambassador to Belgrade had sent some of the best information regarding the real nature of Titoism to President Beneš and Prime [*sic*][20] Minister Masaryk through private channels. Papánek's understanding was that this information had been quite different from that which was being sent back officially along the party line. Papánek also heard it said that [British statesman Philip John] Noel-Baker had expressed the opinion in London last winter that Korbel had been very helpful to "our side" both while at Belgrade and while on the [United Nations Commission for India and Pakistan].
>
> Perhaps you could make a check with the British about Korbel in view of the quotation from Noel-Baker.[21]

What the "very strong opinion against Korbel" refers to is unclear. Some of Korbel's colleagues did resent his ties to the Communist regime (regardless of what their strength really was). Others disapproved of his apparent lack of interest in his Jewish heritage. No evidence was found that Papánek himself believed that Korbel was particularly sympathetic to the Communists.

Korbel spent the spring of 1949 writing a series of short essays on Eastern Europe, including his account of a conversation with Clementis in which Korbel denounced communism. Korbel wrote the papers for Philip Mosely, a respected diplomatic historian at Columbia University in New York and a member of the Rockefeller Foundation. Mosely was so impressed with Korbel's work that he wrote a letter to Ben M. Cherrington, recently retired chancellor of the University of Denver. Cherrington had founded the school's international relations program and headed its Social Science Foundation. Mosely knew that Cherrington wanted to expand the Social Science Foundation by infusing the faculty with foreign lecturers. Mosely proposed that Cherrington offer Korbel a one year job as a resident professor with a light teaching load that would permit him to expand his essays into a book about his experiences in Yugoslavia. Mosely suggested that the university and the Rockefeller Foundation split Korbel's $5,000 annual salary. Cherrington, who had done preliminary work in 1940 for what was to become the United Nations Educational, Scientific and Cultural Organization (UNESCO) in Franklin D. Roosevelt's State Department,[22] offered Korbel a job.

In early June, the Truman administration granted the Korbels' political asylum. Relieved, the ex-diplomat called friends at the United Nations to thank them for their support and told them that he had accepted a position as professor-in-residence at the University of Denver. He would be lecturing on international relations. Korbel also told them that he was substantially revising his book on his experiences as ambassador to Yugoslavia.[23]

Although they had converted to Catholicism, Josef and Mandula Korbel recognized the importance of finding other ways to assimilate into American society, particularly in light of the political and social climate in the late 1940s. Many European Jews immigrating to the United States found American Jews subdued and constrained by the prevailing white, Anglo-Saxon Protestant culture, which contained strong pockets of anti-Semitism. There was a quiet undercurrent of acquiescence, an unspoken understanding that it was easier for non-Jews to gain social acceptance and job opportunities that would allow them to attain the American dream. While some European Jews turned angry, many others chose to blend into their new environment by adopting the look, dress, and manners of the Gentiles. "Living as a Christian in the United States opened up new possibilities," writes Dr. George F.

Simor, a New York psychiatrist who grew up in Hungary in the 1930s and 1940s and came to America in 1956 at the age of twenty-seven. "To become part of this outwardly friendly, accommodating and politically privileged white American community (Protestant or Catholic) appeared as a very attractive alternative, and their perception was that in order to fully assimilate into this community, their Jewish identity had to be dropped."[24] The Korbels had dropped theirs eight years before.

As the 1940s ended, anti-Communist sentiment swept across America. In September 1949, President Truman revealed that Soviet spies had stolen the secret of the atom bomb. In January 1950, Alger Hiss was convicted of perjury amid allegations that he had spied for the Soviet Union while at the State Department in the 1930s. The next month, Senator Joseph R. McCarthy, an obscure Republican from Appleton, Wisconsin, claimed in a speech in Wheeling, West Virginia, to have a list of 205 State Department employees who were members of the Communist Party. Although McCarthy produced no evidence to support his allegations, the impressionable Washington press corps rushed to print his views without questioning their accuracy.[25] The McCarthy era had begun. Although McCarthy eventually was undone by his own excesses, the decade of the fifties would see thousands of patriotic Americans destroyed for some supposed or rumored disloyalty to the country. Even after the anti-Communist craze that catapulted Richard Nixon to national prominence died down in the 1960s, its afterglow continued to shape U.S. foreign policy for a generation.

As David Halberstam writes in his book *The Fifties,* McCarthy's charges of subversives in high places touched a raw nerve in the American people. "He had a wonderful sense of the resentments that exist just below the surface in ordinary people," Halberstam writes, "for he himself burned with those same resentments." The Communists-in-government theory rallied right-wingers, who accused the Democratic Party of being soft on communism. "Democrats would spend the next 30 years proving that they were not soft on communism, and that they would not lose a country to the Communists," Halberstam wrote.[26]

It was common practice after the war for the Central Intelligence Agency to help refugees from Communist countries settle into American life. In exchange for telling what they knew about the inner workings of the Communist regimes in their native countries, the CIA would offer refugees help in finding housing or a job. The CIA will neither confirm nor deny that it helped Josef Korbel. The agency rejected a Freedom of Information Act request by this author asking for any information showing whether Korbel had any connection with the agency, saying that if the agency did have information, it would be "classified for reasons of national security."[27] Yet many of Korbel's friends say they believe that he received assistance. "All diplomats who resigned after 1948 and went to the West sang like canaries," says Zdeněk Mastník, a former BBC official who met Korbel after he retired. "You wouldn't be admitted unless you were willing to."[28]

Meanwhile, the political situation in Czechoslovakia was deteriorating rapidly. Cousin Dagmar can pinpoint the day that her uncle defected because her own life immediately began to unravel. "I shall never forget that day," she says. "It was the sixth of December 1948 that he actually said he was quitting the Kashmir job. He didn't tell me, but I knew because events came in quick succession after that." First, she was expelled from the university. Then, while attending a Christmas party sponsored by the British Students Association, of which she was a member, she was approached by a man who had been one of her professors in Wales: "I asked him what he was doing here because he had never contacted us, and he said, 'Well, I was sent here to keep an eye on what you're doing.' So I knew he worked for the security."[29]

On January 3, 1949, Dagmar was called before a students' commission and saw the professor again. "He asked me, 'Where is your guardian?' And I replied, 'Probably in Kashmir.' And he said, 'No, since the sixth of December, he has been a deserter.'" Dagmar says she learned that the Korbels had moved to the United States "when they got there and wrote." She says that she knew also that they took a Yugoslavian maid with them, but it was not someone whose name she recognized: "They had so many maids, I don't know which one they took."[30]

Madeleine Albright says Dagmar did not want to leave her fiancé to join the Korbels in a faraway country. "I'm sure they had a fight about it," Albright says. "There is no way in the world [my father] would have left this young woman there if he had a choice about it. She was eighteen. She did not want to come with us. And as a result of not coming with us and as a result of my father defecting, she had a hard life. There is no question about it."[31]

Dagmar says that partially as a result of her uncle's defection, she was treated like a second-class citizen.[32] She could not find a job until the following October when she was told to report for work on a farm in the Sudetenland from which the Germans had been expelled. "It was terrible. I didn't want to go there," she says. "That was the worst thing that could have happened."[33]

Dagmar had been friendly for some time with a young man named Vladimír Šíma, whose mother and grandmother took a shine to her. They decided that Vladimír should marry Dagmar to keep her from being sent to the farm. While it was meant to be strictly a marriage of convenience, this one lasted. "We never parted," Dagmar says.

Cousin Dagmar tells a story that she says explains the character of her mother-in-law: "She was a widow. Her husband was a Russian legionnaire in the First World War, and he died when my husband was six weeks old. It was a very poor family, and she was a Communist Party member before the war [World War II]. When everyone was joining the party to save their jobs, she quit it. When my husband started his army service in October 1950, he went straight to a labor camp because his mother had left the Communist Party to protest the execution of Milada Horáková," an official with the National Socialist Party who was executed for treason.[34]

Albright recognizes the sadness of her cousin's story. Yet it angers her deeply that people question her father's motives. She says that even if Dagmar's mother-in-law was a Communist, Albright is not sure that would have affected her father's decision whether to ask Dagmar to go with his family to the West. "I doubt it, I doubt it," Albright said. "I do not know. I truly do not know. I do know that my father had taken responsibility for [Dagmar] during the war, and all I can do is judge what I knew about my father, who was the most humanistic person."[35]

Life was even harder for some of the colleagues Korbel left behind. Following a series of show trials based on what were most probably trumped-up charges, fourteen senior Czechoslovak government officials were condemned on the night of December 3, 1952. Of the twelve Jews among them, nine were hanged. Clementis, a descendant of an old Lutheran family and the Communist who worked with Korbel during and after the war, was among those hanged.[36]

Josef Korbel's earlier warning to Clementis that the Communist regime might one day turn against him proved right. The choice Korbel made almost certainly saved his life and his family. Once the Korbels had left Eastern Europe, it would not have been to Dagmar's advantage to keep in touch with them. The increasingly paranoid Communist regime distrusted citizens with contacts in the West, frequently subjected them to surveillance, and prevented them from attending the universities or holding positions of influence.

Perhaps Korbel did not take his niece because her boyfriend's mother had been a Communist. Dagmar strongly denies that she ever joined the Communist Party herself. And Albright insists that she has no idea what political views her cousin has held over the years. "It's sad," Albright says. "I'm sure when she looks at me and looks at my life and the fact that she has lived through this whole Communist regime . . ." Albright's voice trails off. It is a topic that pains her, partially because she cannot bear to see her father's motives challenged, partially because she is acutely aware of the disparity in the lives she and her cousin have lived.[37] But she does not think there is much she can do about it. "I can't make up to her her life," Albright says.[38]

At the end of her first school year in the United States, Madeleine's sixth-grade class graduated. As part of the program, the youngsters sang "School Days," "Take Me Out to the Ball Game," and "Whistle While You Work."[39] When graduation was over, the Korbels once again packed up their belongings. This time their destination was the American West.

9

The Teenager

"As I go back and tell you about my life, it seems pretty weird, but at the time, it didn't seem that weird. The only part I always felt was that I was a foreigner."

—Madeleine Albright, February 7, 1998

WITH THE PROMISE of a job and a new life lying ahead of them, the Korbels left Great Neck in June 1949, driving west in a new 1948 green Ford coupe purchased with the little money they had saved. It was a long trip, and the three children sat squeezed into the backseat, repeatedly asking, "When will we get there? When will we get there?" They spent the night in American motels, a novelty. The family was used to European hotels and had never stayed in a place where guests could park a car right outside the room.[1]

The Korbels had managed to retrieve some family furniture from Belgrade. A Mayflower moving van carted the load to Denver, leading Josef Korbel to joke: "Well, we can tell other people we also came over on the Mayflower."[2]

The Korbels were to remain in Denver, but they moved several times in the first few months. They lived for a few weeks in a house at 995 South Williams before moving in with another family. Then they found a house at 1045 South Gaylord, next door to a cemetery, which the children did not like.

Within six months, the family finally settled in a house in south Denver. The address was 2050 Race Street.[3] As John Korbel remembers it, their life was Spartan. They lived in modest university housing, a half block from the University of Denver football stadium and surrounded by parking lots;

whenever there was a game, the lots would fill up.[4] In her thick Czech accent, Mandula Korbel called it "this horrible dilapidated house." The parents' bedroom was in the basement, where Josef Korbel also had a small study. When it rained, the basement would get flooded, and they had to mop it up. Madlenka, as her parents still called her, had her own room upstairs, and Kathy and John shared a room.[5] Korbel, however, did not allow his modest means to dampen his spirit. He managed to find happiness in simple pleasures and good company, often inviting others from the university community to share dinner with the family. "Good conversation was to him the best of food and drink," said a friend.[6] Mandula entertained guests by reading their palms.[7]

Madeleine attended Morey Junior High School, which she loved. She had friends, enjoyed her studies, and was quickly becoming an Americanized teenager. She was responsible for her brother and sister, walking them to school in the morning before climbing on a bus to go to her own classes, taking the children to movies on weekends. To help make ends meet, Mandula Korbel took a series of clerical jobs, starting as a secretary in the Denver public schools, then working for a mutual fund business. It was uncommon for middle-class mothers in this era to work outside the home. But as Madeleine Albright explains fifty years later: "It was unusual to be poor."[8]

Mandula Korbel would arrive home from work exhausted and fix dinner. Afterward, she would stretch out on the sofa while Madeleine and her father washed the dishes. On Fridays, when school let out at 1:00 P.M., Josef Korbel and his children would put classical music on the record player— Mozart and operas were favorites—and clean house. Josef and Madeleine did the heavy chores. Kathy dusted the precious Czech crystal that they had brought with them. "I used to get so mad at my mother," Albright says. "I told her, 'I'm cleaning for your life, and I'm going to have to do it for my life, too.' "[9]

The University of Denver had one of the first programs in international relations in the United States. Korbel taught a class in that subject, as well as classes in Soviet and Eastern European politics. Soon he had a reputation as a popular instructor. "He was very concerned about his students and went out of his way to see people as individuals," says Joseph Szyliowicz, a professor whom Korbel hired at the university's Graduate School for International Relations.[10] One student remembered Korbel as a humble, compassionate man who "was so very generous with his time and cheerful in his guidance, always hoping to challenge those who felt themselves infallible and to encourage those who felt themselves inadequate."[11]

Having been granted asylum in the United States, Korbel wasted no time applying for American citizenship for himself and his family. On December 20, 1950, he wrote a letter to the chief of the State Department's South-Eastern Europe division, explaining that it would be difficult to comply with the application's requirement to submit a police report from Yugoslavia, where he had served as a diplomat, because he had enjoyed the customary diplomatic immunity. He added that even if he had a police record, Belgrade authorities would be unlikely to comply "because of my political attitude to the Communist Yugoslavia."[12]

Josef Korbel was a strict father. The children were not permitted to stay up late, and he would not stand for rudeness or disrespect. He expected them to dress properly and dressed formally himself, usually in a coat and tie.[13] "I don't think they had a dime," says Marion Gottesfeld, a University of Denver trustee who knew the Korbels. "I used to say, 'I bet he has one shirt,' and Mandula would see that shirt is washed and pressed every day because he comes to the university as 'the Professor.' "[14] Even when the family went skiing, Korbel could be formal. His children remember his flying down the side of a mountain, dressed in a topcoat and tie. But over the years, as turtlenecks and sport coats became popular, Josef grew a beard and sometimes appeared in public dressed more casually. He also became a top-notch fly fisherman. The hobby became his passion.[15]

Dinner was a formal occasion. The children were expected to be at the table on time. If someone was talking to a friend on the phone, he or she would have to hang up. "He was a strict, European parent," says John Korbel. "It never dawned on us not to respect our parents, and we were punished when we did something wrong. The most severe form of punishment was when our father wouldn't talk to us for a week."[16]

Madeleine took her Roman Catholic religion seriously. She went to catechism and confession regularly. She also made her First Communion in Denver. "I used to drag everybody to church," Madeleine Albright says. "I loved going." Unlike today, the service was in Latin. Half the prayer book was English, half in Latin. Madeleine, always precocious, says that she preferred the Latin.[17]

As the Korbels settled into Denver life, family routines were sacrosanct. Every Sunday when the weather was nice, the Korbels drove to the mountains for picnics and long walks, which Josef insisted they take together. He called it Family Solidarity. "That's when I felt foreign," Madeleine Albright says. "We had to be together all the time."[18] Mandula packed what Madeleine considered "a disgusting potato salad and meat-loafy hamburgers." Josef and Mandula picked mushrooms, which always prompted the children to joke that one day they would all be poisoned. No one ever was. The elder Korbels could tell a chanterelle from an amanita. They kept the Sunday ritual until the children were teenagers and complained that they would rather spend weekends with friends.[19]

At night, Josef Korbel helped his children write their history papers, always insisting that they work hard and get good grades. Madeleine did better than the rest, rarely getting lower than As. In the eighth grade, she won the Rocky Mountain Empire United Nations contest by reciting all the member countries in alphabetical order.

When Madeleine was ready for high school, her father told her that he wanted her to attend a small private academy, where she would get a better education than in the public system. The private school was offering scholarships, and Korbel thought his daughter would qualify for one. Madeleine was furious. For the first time in her life, she had friends, real friends, and she did not want to give them up. "It was the one truly big fight I had with my father in my life," she says today.[20]

Her father prevailed. Madeleine enrolled in the Kent School for Girls, one of the most prestigious private high schools in Colorado. It was located in a rural part of town, five miles from the center of Denver, and there were sixteen girls in her class. This was not a happy time. "I hated Kent when I got there," Albright says. "Everybody knew I was on scholarship. I was Catholic, and no one else was." The girls wore uniforms, so Madeleine was not embarrassed by her wardrobe. But that was little solace. "It took me a long time to get used to Kent," she says.[21]

Stephanie Allen, a classmate who arrived at the school a year later, says that Madeleine was well liked but did not quite fit in. "Madeleine was everybody's friend, but probably no one's best friend," Allen says.[22] Chester Alter, the chancellor emeritus for the University of Denver when Albright was named secretary of state, remembers that, as a young person, Madeleine was quiet and reserved. "There was nothing especially unique about [her]," he says, "except she was an excellent student and a hard worker."[23]

The Korbels' precarious financial status also made Madeleine feel like an outsider. "This was a school where people had money," says Stephanie Allen. "I didn't have money, and she didn't have money. But I was socially connected, and she wasn't. So we sort of had a half life together of being on the fringe of the social scene. We couldn't play the expensive games. We didn't go on fancy trips at spring vacation. We'd be home. The other kids would go to Aspen on skiing trips, but we couldn't afford to go. And they went places in the summer. We were home in the summer."

Allen says that she and Madeleine talked about these differences, but tried not to let the situation bother them. "We sort of watched it," she says. "We would observe that this is something we can't do." Madeleine, says Allen, was more independent than the others: "She was walking her own path. Sometimes it connected with us, and sometimes it didn't. I never felt she was the least bit envious."[24]

One of the few students from abroad to attend Kent with Madeleine was Julika Balajty Ambrose, whose parents were Hungarian. "We were foreigners," says Ambrose, now a dentist in Denver. "We both had accents. Our parents had huge accents. We were there because they wanted to have foreigners and to show they were broad-minded, which indeed they were."[25] The girls shared a bond, but Madeleine felt that even she and Julika had their differences. "Her parents had a lot of money, and mine did not," Albright says today.[26]

The Kent girls had potluck dinners every Friday night and took turns going to each other's houses. But they never went to dinner at the Korbels' home. "There was no way anybody would come over," Albright says. "Some of this probably was in my own head. But these were people who belonged to country clubs and were pretty. I think high school is hard for everybody, but I really did feel out of it."

Kent friends from those days paint a rosier picture of their high school days. "My first memory of Madeleine was that she was friendly," says Stephanie Allen. "She was the one who made an effort to make you feel a part of the school. I remember walking around the hockey field with her, talking as girls do, sort of pouring out your heart. I always felt I could tell Madeleine anything, that it would be held in confidence, and she would be appropriately sympathetic or amused."

Madeleine was a conscientious and serious student, who excelled in the classroom. "I was smart," she says. "There was only one person [at Kent] smarter than I was."[27] Stephanie Allen says Madeleine seemed more motivated than the other students. "She knew what she was going to do," Allen says. "She studied hard. It was a class of very bright girls. Madeleine was not the brightest girl in the class, but she was the most well-rounded person. She was a good friend. She could laugh and play with the rest of us. She did her studies, but she didn't rub it in."

Allen says that Madeleine, who sat in front of her in history class, once helped her with a paper on the Holocaust. "It was a terrifying thing to be exposed to at that age, and I remember how sympathetic she was. She didn't know anything about it. None of us did. We would sit around the lunch table and talk about how could anything so awful happen."

Madeleine, says Allen, "was very funny." She had a standard joke. "She would say she was a Czech, and she planned to marry a Czech, and they would have 'checkered' children. She wasn't a cutup or a clown, but she would always see the lighter side of things as well as the serious side."

Madeleine also had a gritty, aggressive edge to her that was especially pronounced when she took to the athletic fields.[28] "She was a good field hockey player," recalls Allen. "She'd come thundering down the field, and you wanted to get out of the way. She wasn't what I would call a superstar athlete, but she was competent and determined, and she played to win. But she was never mean-spirited or anything like that."[29]

Madeleine's determination and energy translated into action off the field as well. She served on the chapel committee and sang for the glee club. During her senior year, she was president of the student council.[30] And, in a move that showed that she truly was her father's daughter, Madeleine formed the Kent School for Girls' International Relations and Welfare Committee and appointed herself president.[31] "She was on the council and our most responsible, well-liked citizen," says Allen. "We didn't pooh-pooh her for being the council representative or head of those kinds of things. We'd say, 'Oh good, those are in Madeleine's hands. We can go do other things.'"[32]

For all of her interests and activities, Madeleine always found time for political discussion and debate. Like her father, she was becoming an avid Democrat. Although most of the families that enrolled their daughters at Kent were "I Like Ike" Republicans, the Korbels identified with the party of Harry S Truman. "Here was a school full of Republicans," says Allen. "We were a bunch of little rich girls, and then there were those of us who were on scholarship. Madeleine was on scholarship. Julika was on scholarship. I was on part-scholarship. Madeleine would come to school, and we would have formal debates on foreign policy issues and domestic policy issues, and she was always the champion for the Democratic side. She was one of the few who would articulate the Democratic point of view. It was like, you went to Kent and you were a Republican, but that didn't bother her at all."

That Madeleine gravitated toward liberal politics was not surprising. She lived under and admired her father's intellect and commitment to Democratic ideals. The ideas and convictions that took root during discussions around the family dinner table undoubtedly emerged during conversations and arguments with school friends. Allen remembers that Madeleine "was always up to her neck in political debates and conversations. She could hang around and talk girl talk and then turn around and debate the entire Republican school."[33]

For all of her tenacity, Madeleine never went through a rebellious stage in high school. After losing her battle to remain in public school, the only arguments she had with her family were over staying out late, but those never went beyond mild squabbles. In her last year of high school she tried smoking but gave it up. She did not like it. But her friends were smoking, so she wanted to try it. [34]

Eventually, Madeleine grew to appreciate Kent, but it never became a central part of her life. "I look back on that as a very weird period," Albright says today. "Girls are very nasty. We know that." She pauses for a moment and smiles. "They all love me now," she says. [35] Albright makes it clear that she understands the elusive nature of popularity and that the kind of power she enjoys today can affect the way people remember her.

The other Korbel children acquired an interest in history and international relations as well. "We grew up steeped in it," says Kathy. "It was just part of growing up in the family. We used to sit around the dinner table and talk about foreign policy all the time." There would be political discussions and historical debates. University professors were invited to the house to take part in these talks over cocktails and dinner. [36] Josef and Mandula Korbel also took pleasure in filling their small home with exuberant students. [37] "I remember having dinner there," says Julika Balajty Ambrose. "Most of the time at that age you giggle and talk, but around her table we had interesting discussions."

Korbel found he loved teaching. At one point, he even developed a lecture series for people in the community. Half the money they raised went to the university library. Korbel himself was a prolific speaker. During one nine-month period in 1951, he spoke before thirty-nine audiences. [38] Over the years, Josef Korbel traveled around the country giving lectures, which helped him develop a large network of academic and diplomatic friends. Not surprisingly, he was a man of strong opinions. His views on American politics were liberal, and he became a committed Democrat. "Our father was quite an intellectually imposing figure," says Kathy. The children were allowed to speak up, but mostly they listened. [39]

At the university, Korbel was a star. In 1959, he became dean of the university's Graduate School for International Studies, which he helped create, and director of the Social Science Foundation. He held both posts until 1969. [40] Ben Cherrington believed that hiring Korbel had been one of the best decisions he ever made. "Dr. Korbel and his wife, Mandula, had every excuse to become bitter about the events in their homeland," Cherrington wrote, "but with wisdom and rare courage, they determined that their three lovely children must have normal happy lives and the cruel experiences of the past must remain a closed chapter." [41] Others marveled at Korbel's ability as both scholar and teacher, an enviable combination in academia. He undertook the lonely, laborious task of producing six scholarly works, yet he remained fiercely devoted to his students, a teacher "par excellence."[42] One student recalled that Korbel's "academic loyalty was to honest scholarship and to hard-working students, both of which gained his lasting admiration."[43]

Korbel possessed an ability to spark a student's curiosity and to kindle the imagination and the desire to learn about the world.[44] Not surprisingly, his most attentive pupil and greatest admirer was his older daughter, Madeleine. She was more serious than her younger siblings, listened carefully to her father's discussions, and hung on his every word. It was under his tutelage that she absorbed the lessons of Munich.

Josef Korbel was a hero to all three children. "It was hard not to idolize him," says Kathy.[45] They saw him as a pillar of integrity, uncompromising in his beliefs, and very protective of his family. He was a proud man with a strong sense of himself. He had started over again and was on his way to building a fine reputation in the academic world. Korbel told his children that he loved Czechoslovakia and that the hardest decision he had ever made in his life was to leave. And he told them why: He refused to co-exist with communism.[46]

Madeleine Albright has much in common with her father, but she believes that she inherited qualities from her mother as well. "I'm like my mother in terms of my great loyalty and dedication to my family and my ability to work my way through practically any problem," she says. "My mother was an interesting woman who was adaptable. She grew up as somebody who had quite a lot. She came from a larger town than my father and was a belle and had a pretty good life. Then in London, we spent a lot of time in air raid shelters, and she did it with nothing. Then she became the wife of an ambassador, and she did really well at that. She liked that life. Then she came to the United States and started over again. Even though she didn't speak great English, she went to work as a secretary. I really thought that showed tremendous resilience."[47]

Mandula Korbel was a lively, warm, and caring mother, and as her children recall, very intuitive. But she worried constantly. Once when Madeleine was supposed to go out on a date after her parents had left the house for their own social occasion, her plans changed, and Madeleine ended up staying home and going to bed. Josef and Mandula returned thinking their daughter was still out with friends. They did not think to check her room. An hour passed. Mandula became more upset. Her husband was always slow to anger. But when his wife started to worry, the normally calm father became upset as well. Mandula paced up and down the living room. "It's eleven-thirty, how come Madeleine is not home?" she fretted. Finally, Madeleine woke up and walked out sleepily to the living room. Her mother got angry at her for making her worry so much.[48]

Mandula and Josef Korbel were highly protective of their children. When Madeleine was in tenth grade, a boy invited her to the high school prom. Josef Korbel did not want her to ride in the young man's car. Madeleine was furious, and she and her father reached a compromise. Madeleine was permitted to ride with her date, but her father followed them to the high school in his car. When the dance ended, he followed them home again. Madeleine was not happy about it, but she knew better than to argue with her father. All he had to do was give the children a firm look, and arguments ceased.[49]

In the fall of 1954, Madeleine applied to five colleges: Stanford University, the University of Pennsylvania, Mount Holyoke, the University of Denver, and Wellesley College. Kent officials were irritated that she cast her net so widely, but she knew she needed to be assured that at least one school would offer her a scholarship. Her father added more pressure. He told her that she would be expected to attend the school that offered the most money.[50]

Korbel had taken his daughter to see Wellesley the previous summer, when he was invited to give a lecture at the Massachusetts Institute of Technology in Cambridge. An English teacher at Kent named Marie Vallance, who had attended Wellesley, also sparked Madeleine's interest in the college. But Stanford had a wonderful reputation, and Madeleine thought that she might prefer a co-ed school in the West rather than a girls' school in the East.

A thick envelope from Stanford was the first to arrive. Madeleine was accepted for the fall's freshman class, but the letter did not mention a scholarship. Madeleine was hysterical. "I remember running out of the house," she says. "My father came after me and said, 'It will work out.'" As it turned out, Stanford did offer her a Rocky Mountain scholarship, but the letter did not arrive in the same mailing. "In those three or four days, I thought my life was over," Albright says.[51]

Within a week, she was accepted at all five schools. Wellesley College offered her a full scholarship, the largest of them all. But she was drawn to Stanford. "I remember trying to sort it out until the last weekend," she says. "I knew what I wanted to do. I wanted to be a political science major."[52] Wellesley won out. The Wellesley Club of Denver paid Madeleine's transportation to campus. "I feel responsible for that," says the University of

Denver's Marion Gottesfeld. "It cost her practically nothing to go to school."[53]

The Kent School for Girls 1955 yearbook pictures Madeleine with the short-cropped, curly hair style made popular a few years before by Hollywood star Elizabeth Taylor. The young graduate was wearing a string of pearls around her neck, part of the uniform of the day. Looking stylish, she could have been any young American girl graduating from high school.

After only seven years in America, Madeleine fit right in. The caption under her yearbook picture, set off by the logo for the International Relations and Welfare Committee, read: "International relations, Princeton, or any other topic brings forth a flood of comment from Madeleine, expert if on the first subject, and a bit incoherent if on the second. You will often find her taking a definite stand on matters, staunchly saying, 'You guys, this just proves it!' Her constant interest in anything she is doing, and the drive with which she does it, keep all interested in the activities of our 'emaciated' companion."[54]

So began the Americanization of Madeleine Korbel. Her character and interests were taking shape. The serious teenager was fast becoming a fun-loving, if serious, young woman.

10

Dust on Her Shoes

"The fact that I went to Wellesley seven years after I came to the United States I now find hard to believe. It did not occur to me that I was foreign. I was thoroughly American Madeleine."

—Madeleine Albright, February 7, 1998

WHEN MADELEINE ARRIVED at Wellesley College on Monday, September 19, 1955, she looked pretty much like the other arriving freshmen, with one exception. There was dust on her shoes, accumulated from the long and arduous trip from halfway across the country. The Wellesley girls, many of whom had come from wealthy Yankee families—the kind who named buildings after themselves—took note. One asked her if Denver had sidewalks. For most of the girls she would meet, the Colorado capital seemed as far away as Prague.

Wellesley, with its four hundred rolling acres bordering the western shore of Lake Waban and its Gothic-style buildings, was and still is one of the most beautiful campuses in America. Madeleine settled quickly into a corner, ground-floor room in Homestead, a small, gray, three-story house on the corner of College Road and Washington Street that once belonged to Wellesley's founder, Henry Fowle Durant. It had been converted into a dormitory for thirty-six freshmen. Her roommate, whom she would keep through her four years, was Mary Jane Durnford, a tall, quiet blonde from Windsor, Connecticut. The two often skipped dinner and went to the local "HoJo's," as the students called Howard Johnson's, for an ice cream cone. When the lake froze in winter, they sometimes got up at dawn to ice-skate.[1]

As the girls unpacked their trunks, they laughed at the similarity of their wardrobes. The yellow college handbook, mailed to prospective students, had instructed them to bring pedal pushers and blue jeans, although they were advised not to wear jeans in the village "in conformity with customs of the Town of Wellesley." For dates, "suits and wool dresses are the answer usually." They were told to bring a radio "if you like the morning news or take political science." And "a few unwritten rules" were carefully spelled out for them in writing:

- No curlers or bandannas in the dining room.
- You don't have to dress for dinner, although a skirt must be worn.
- Keep your room picked up, bed made, clothes away, books and socks off the floor—especially afore [*sic*] twice-a-week inspection.
- Be nice to the maids. Say "hello" in the morning and "thank you" for favors.
- Frowns unlimited for those who make whoopee after 10 PM.[2]

For the Class of '59, freshman-year tuition, room, and board was $1,850. The Korbel family had made sure that their elder daughter was outfitted with the co-ed uniform of the day: Bermuda shorts, matching knee socks, and the requisite camel-hair coat, though hers was noticeably too large. When she needed a new dress for the freshman prom, friends took her to Boston's famous discount store, Filene's Basement. A class photo shows her wearing her yellow freshman beanie and a sweater accented by a white dickie with a Peter Pan collar. In Miss Overacker's Poli. Sci. 101, Madeleine found herself sitting next to Winifred Shore, a classmate from Great Neck, whom she had not seen since her family moved to Denver. The girls lived in different dormitories, but their circles of friends would soon overlap.[3] They gave Madeleine a nickname that some still use but which she has always hated: Maddy.[4]

From the day she arrived on campus, Madeleine impressed her teachers with her serious nature and her determination to do well. "I was struck by her capacity to speak several European languages," says Edward Vose Gulick, who taught European diplomatic history at Wellesley and had Madeleine in class. "She was very serious."[5] In French class, however, Madeleine had a problem. Having lived in Switzerland and studied at a French school in London, she spoke French beautifully. But her grammar was that of a ten-year-old. The first paper she turned in came back with a letter grade of D. The teacher wrote in the margin: "*Vous avez massacré la grammaire.*"[6] Madeleine's roommate was good at French grammar, though she did not speak the language particularly well. The two young women made a deal: Mary Jane would correct Madeleine's papers, and Madeleine would help Mary Jane with her accent.[7]

The Wellesley College motto is *"Non Ministrari sed Ministrare"*—Not to be ministered unto, but to minister.[8] The school has a long tradition of "going out from Wellesley" to "make a difference to the world." Young Wellesley graduates were expected to be poised, self-confident, and well-spoken. As part of freshman orientation, each young woman was required to take a speech test to ensure that she spoke in carefully modulated tones. Barbara LeWin, a classmate from Buffalo, New York, was signed up for speech lessons because her voice was too deep and she had nasal *A*s. Another part of Madeleine's orientation: "posture pictures" required of all Ivy League and Seven Sister students between the 1940s and mid-1960s. Each person was lined up and photographed nude as part of a study of personal posture.[9] "It seemed ridiculous," Albright says today. "But nobody was outraged by anything. You just did what you were told."[10]

In many ways, the mid-1950s were gentle, simple years. Massachusetts' "blue laws" forbade companies from doing business, selling alcohol, or allowing entertainment on Sundays. Local movie theaters in Boston, twelve miles away, were featuring *Picnic, Giant, Guys and Dolls,* and Walt Disney's *Lady and the Tramp.* College students prided themselves on their collections of 33⅓ rpm long-playing albums of Nat King Cole, Miles Davis, or Bill Haley and the Comets.[11]

Madeleine was one of only five foreign students in the school. The others were from India, Hong Kong, Greece, and Poland. She was the only one who spoke perfect, American-style English. Clearly, she had already learned how to blend into the crowd. In fact, Madeleine was so socially at ease that her friends teased her about being a foreigner. When a U.S. Post Office notice appeared on campus declaring that "aliens" must register with local officials, her friends, led by Emily Cohen, dangled it from a light cord over her bed. "I remember coming back from the library and my friend Emily had completely trashed my room," Albright says.[12]

One day during the freshman fall semester, several women arrived at Homestead and explained to the dormitory monitor that they were taking the foreign students to downtown Boston to introduce them to the popular dress among American college students. They asked to see Madeleine. When she walked down the stairs, their eyes widened. In her plaid Bermuda shorts, tall socks, and Shetland sweater with a circle pin placed on the collar (as opposed to being worn in the middle, where it would signify she was not a virgin), Madeleine looked like a typical American teenager. When the women explained their mission, everyone had a good laugh.

Most Wellesley girls liked the school and appreciated being at such a prestigious institution, where their parents expected them to get a good education. "Madeleine was a very serious student," says Emily Cohen Mac-Farquhar, who has remained a lifelong friend. "She was not there to party and waste her time." MacFarquhar says that Madeleine often talked about her father, "whom she adored and who expected her to do great things. She was driven to achieve and to meet his high standards."[13]

The only course that all students were required to take was Biblical History, known as "Bible," which was taught for its literary and historical context rather than from any specific religious point of view. "We all groaned at the thought of taking it, but most of us found it to be one of the most memorable classes we took at Wellesley," says Barbara LeWin Luton.[14] Sophomores studied the Old Testament during the first semester, the New Testament in the second. Classmates say that Madeleine, raised Catholic, was very good at questioning what was generally considered a Protestant perspective. Madeleine's class met just before noon, and long discussions about theology often spilled over into lunch while the girls stood in line at the cafeteria. "I loved Bible," Albright says today. "It was taught as literature."[15]

To earn spending money, Madeleine had an on-campus job with the Pilgrim Laundry Company, which delivered fresh linens to the dorms each week. She would open bags of dirty sheets and pillow cases and count them to make sure that each girl left the right number. When she wrote to her parents what she was doing, they were aghast. "We may be poor, but you do not have to do other people's laundry," they wrote.[16]

The Wellesley Class of 1959 belonged to a bridge generation, a cohort of women wedged awkwardly between homemakers and careerists. Although young women attended the Seven Sisters schools in part to get a good education, another reason—and one more important for many—was to meet the brightest, most promising young men of the day at nearby Ivy League colleges. The young women defined themselves by their intelligence, but also by their looks and pedigrees, which were all-important if they were to marry well. The message was simple: Be smart, be successful, be married. No one, however, spelled out exactly how that should be done.

Within a few years, by the mid-1960s, the message would evolve, but not by much: A Wellesley woman was to write the Great American Novel while the kids were napping, but only after she had finished typing her husband's Ph.D. thesis. By the time young Hillary Rodham graduated from Wellesley a decade later, in Wellesley's Class of '69, and went off to Yale Law

School and Bill Clinton, so-called liberated women often decided to keep their maiden names and establish careers before settling down for marriage and children. For Madeleine's class, however, there was a conflict between the head and the heart, a tug-of-war between emotions and intellect that would take at least another decade to be addressed.

With the interest of Wellesley parents in mind, the college publications, like those of the other Seven Sisters schools, advised the young women how to meet eligible bachelors. A line from the *Wellesley College News* on why they should attend "mixers," the dances held regularly on fall weekends: "You may find a date for the next Harvard game or a future husband."[17]

For Madeleine, the college experience was much more intense than it was for most of the other girls. Having spent her childhood on the run in war-torn Europe, and her adolescence trying to become part of the American mainstream, she found Wellesley to be an oasis of intellectual and social delights. Just as she loved her adopted country and its freedoms, she loved Wellesley with an intensity that her friends recognized but did not totally understand. "We complained, but for Madeleine, it was wonderful," Mac-Farquhar says.[18] Almost forty years after she graduated, Albright's eyes well up with tears when she talks of her college days. "It was fabulous," she says. "I simply loved Wellesley."[19]

Madeleine impressed her friends with her interest in international affairs, but she also knew how to have fun. The school had only one television set, located in the Recreation Hall. The girls were avid bridge players, though Madeleine was not a regular. She thought the game endless. In winter, they would go "traying" on the snow, zipping down Severance Green on meal trays "liberated" from the cafeteria. Madeleine had a Princeton boyfriend, Elston Mayhew, a young man she knew from Denver who was a year ahead of her in school. She took delight in sporting a trophy, his orange and black Princeton scarf.[20]

Like virtually all girls' schools at the time, Wellesley's rules were strict. Curfew was 10:00 P.M. on weekdays, midnight on weekends. Students had to sign out listing the names of their escorts or chaperones, destinations, and hours of return. Each time their daughters planned to leave campus for the weekend, parents had to sign letters of permission. In the days before e-mail and fax machines, when long-distance calls were expensive, getting permission for an off-campus weekend required some serious advance work. On Friday and Saturday nights, couples would cluster in the dorm entrance halls in tight embraces, keeping one eye on the hands of the clock as they passionately kissed their dates until the stroke of midnight.

Men were not allowed above a dormitory's first floor, except between

2:00 and 5:00 P.M. on Sundays, when a couple was expected to leave the door ajar and keep three feet on the floor, a ludicrous rule which presumably would keep "good girls" (commonly understood to mean virgins) out of trouble. During the week, there would be late-night discussions about whether their dates had gotten to "first base," "second base," or "third." It was strictly taboo, but not unheard of, to "go all the way."

Cars were not allowed until the spring semester of senior year, and alcohol was strictly forbidden, though some girls kept sherry in their perfume bottles. The fiancé of one of Madeleine's friends once sneaked a bottle of wine on campus by sticking it up the arm of his sleeve, and poured it that way throughout dinner. Forty years later, the couples were still laughing about it.[21]

Madeleine worked on the *Wellesley College News,* a weekly that published on Thursdays and featured noncontroversial stories about campus life. Camel and L&M cigarettes were regular advertisers. Emily Cohen, who would later become one of the first in her class to join the working world, wrote a piece analyzing a campus poll: Of thirty Wellesley students surveyed, only seven were interested in postmarital careers. Another article in the same issue discussed the joys of married life: "The average housewife and mother of today is quite likely wedded to her house." To help Wellesley girls keep track of just who would reap these blessings, the paper had a regular page-two feature listing everyone who became engaged or was married. "We were all conformists in those days," says Winifred Shore Freund, who remains close to Albright. "Very few of us were not. We got pinned. We got engaged. We had a narrow vision of our future, compared to what our daughters have had."[22]

Like Emily, Madeleine aspired to become a journalist. Her first bylined story, written when she was a freshman and headlined "Hamburgers and Harvard, Diets and Dates," described low-calorie meals available in The Well, a popular campus eatery. "Calorie conscious?" Madeleine asked in her lead paragraph. "Hate liver and fish? The Well answers all these needs, according to Miss Aniela Gruszyska, supervisor."[23] In her sophomore year, when Madeleine was an associate reporter, she wrote a front-page story on the importance of American students learning foreign languages, quoting five Wellesley language teachers in one nine-paragraph article. Her awkward opener: "Need for more complete communication, higher rewards in academic pursuits, promotion of national interest and better international understanding in a shrinking world were cited as reasons why Americans should study foreign languages."[24]

In 1958, when she was associate news editor, Madeleine wrote a piece about John F. Kennedy, who was running for a second term in the U.S. Senate and was making a campaign stop at the Wellesley railroad station. By this time, Madeleine had learned the formula for a news story: the catchy lead, a few new facts to grab the readers' interest, and a memorable last paragraph, called the kicker. "No whistle blew and no train stopped, but Senator John F. Kennedy did saunter out on the platform of the Wellesley railroad station," Madeleine wrote. Her kicker: Kennedy was a half-hour late but signed a great many autographs, including "one for me, too."[25]

An avid student of American politics, Madeleine seemed to be modeling herself in her father's image. His interests had become her interests; only the countries of their expertise were different. Although the Wellesley campus in this era was more than 90 percent Republican, Madeleine, Wini Shore, and their school chum Emily Cohen had supported Adlai E. Stevenson, who tried unsuccessfully to unseat President Dwight D. Eisenhower in the 1956 presidential election. At one point, the three of them stood on a Boston street corner collecting "Dollars for Democrats," until they were threatened with arrest. Later they escorted Stevenson to the platform at a rally in Boston Garden.[26]

While their daughter was studying at Wellesley, Mandula and Josef Korbel plunged enthusiastically into life at the University of Denver, which was expanding its academic program to meet a growing enrollment. Josef Korbel was a valued professor, keen on starting a graduate school of international studies.

He was also eager to become an American. On March 25, 1957, more than eight years after they arrived as immigrants, Josef and Mandula Korbel became U.S. citizens in a ceremony in Denver's U.S. District Court. Madeleine, who barely had enough money for transportation home for Christmas vacation, could not afford to travel to Colorado for her parents' ceremony. She was granted citizenship that summer—August 14. In carefully rounded, schoolgirl script, she signed the certificate: Marie Jana Korbel.[27]

It was that summer of her sophomore year, when she was an intern at the *Denver Post,* that Madeleine met Joe Albright, a trim young man with dark hair and a rounded face, heir to his family's newspaper empire. She was working in the *Post*'s morgue, or library, filing clips and answering subscriber questions. When Joe arrived in the library one day to do some research, she noticed that he wore his class ring on his left ring finger and figured he was married. One day he struck up a conversation. "Do you go to school?" he asked. Used to explaining the location of her small liberal arts school to midwesterners, Madeleine replied, "I go to Wellesley College in

Wellesley, Massachusetts." Joe smiled. "I go to Williams College in Williamstown, Massachusetts," he said. It turned out that she had dated his best friend, who attended Harvard College.

At first, Madeleine had no inkling about Joe's background. When they went on dates, her mother insisted that Joe not always be the one to pay. After all, Mandula Korbel told her daughter, Joe was also a struggling student. Madeleine and Joe would go out "Dutch treat," as they said at the time, and split the cost of a date.[28]

Joe lived in a fraternity house two blocks from the Korbels', and Mandula Korbel, who liked the young man, took to inviting him to dinner. Madeleine was still dating Elston Mayhew, a Princeton beau who lived in Denver, and she found her mother's invitations to Joe awkward. But Joe had impressed the Albrights. Their house, though simple, was decorated with a lot of paintings. Most of the young men who came to see Madeleine took one look around and said something like, "Gee, you have a lot of paintings. Does your father paint?" Josef Korbel would mutter under his breath in Czech, "What a stupid boy. You can't go out with him anymore." When Joe Albright walked in, he said, "You have a lot of paintings. My father is a painter." Josef Korbel looked up. "This," he said to Madeleine in Czech, "is something new." Joe began talking to Madeleine's father about Harry Truman and made a critical comment. Korbel turned to his daughter and said, again in Czech, "*This* will not do." But as they talked more, Korbel was impressed. Joe was intelligent.[29]

Joe Albright was a serious young man, whose childhood was less peripatetic than Madeleine's but also difficult. He was born in New Orleans and, at the age of only one week, moved with his parents to Libertyville, Illinois. He was not born Joseph Albright, but Joseph Medill Patterson Reeve. Joe's biological father was Jay Fred Reeve, a respected partner in a powerful Chicago law firm that represented Joseph Medill Patterson, publisher of the *New York Daily News*. Patterson had two daughters, Alicia and Josephine. Josephine met Jay Reeve when she was working as a reporter for the *Chicago Daily News*. Reeve divorced his first wife and married Josephine in 1936. Joe was born the next year; his sister, Alice, three years later. In 1944, when Joe was seven, his parents divorced. Two years later, Josephine married Ivan Le Lorraine Albright, an artist who became famous for detailed pictures of death and decay. Ivan Albright adopted Joe and Alice and developed a relationship with them that Joe later called "ideal."[30]

Joe and Alice were favorites of their aunt Alicia Patterson, the grande dame of the family. Alicia was a gregarious and adventuresome woman who, with her husband, "Captain Harry" Guggenheim, owned and ran *Newsday,* a saucy, up-and-coming Long Island newspaper that they started in the show-room of a former Nassau County auto dealership.

With no children of her own, Alicia treated Joe like a son.[31] She was impressed that during the summer of his sophomore and junior years he had landed an internship at the *Denver Post* and started, as most cub reporters do, covering cops. When he returned to Williams, Joe was elected to Phi Beta Kappa and wrote his senior thesis in 1958 on the life of his grandfather, Joseph Medill Patterson, an account that remains the most scholarly work about the man.[32] Joe's mother, however, was infuriated by the dedication his son chose for the work: "To Madeleine, with whom . . ."[33]

Madeleine and Joe shared a love of politics and journalism. When Madeleine returned to Wellesley College for the fall of her junior year, she had a surprise for her friends. Six weeks after meeting Joe, she was "pinned," a step before engagement when a college man gives his steady girl his fraternity pin, to be worn over her heart, gold chain dangling just so. Madeleine arrived at Assembly Hall wearing a red Shetland sweater to show off Joe's Theta Delta Chi pin. Everyone swooned. Although a number of her friends were already engaged—marriage to the proper young man was, after all, one of the most important reasons for parents to send their daughters to a good college—some of Madeleine's friends were surprised. "I dropped my jaw," said Emily Cohen MacFarquhar.[34] "It had all happened over summer vacation." In fact, Joe had actually asked Madeleine to marry him. She decided pinning was a first step.[35]

One Wellesley classmate recalls Madeleine telling her how Joe prepared her for her first meeting with what he called his "rather different kind of family." Carefully, he told Madeleine what to expect: "They travel a lot and live in quite an international set." Madeleine replied, "Oh, my family is used to that. My father had a Guggenheim." Joe smiled. "My uncle *is* Guggenheim," he said.[36]

What did Madeleine's parents think when she announced that she had fallen in love and planned to marry, and that she would have to convert from Catholicism to Episcopalianism? What did they say to each other when they were alone, free to exchange their own private musings over where life had taken them and what might have been? Or had they blocked out memories of their own conversion so completely and irrevocably that they never discussed them at all?

In fact, the question of conversion did not come up right away. Josephine Albright, Joe's mother, would raise it later. And the Korbels were delighted with their daughter's choice in a young man. They loved Joe. It would be two years before the wedding would take place. They had plenty of time for reflection.

Madeleine once recalled that when she went to meet her future mother-in-law for the first time on Chicago's fashionable East Lake Shore Drive, she realized she had rather unsophisticated tastes for her fiancé's social circle. Josephine Albright told the young Wellesley graduate that she ought to be wearing a hat. "Then she took her to buy one," says Newton N. Minow, a Chicago lawyer to whom Madeleine recounted the story.[37]

On December 29, 1959, their engagement was announced in a three-paragraph story in the *New York Times.* It carried a picture of Madeleine with her hair still cropped stylishly short, just above her ears, showing off wide cheekbones and a pretty smile. The article noted that Madeleine's father, "a former member of the Czechoslovak diplomatic service, was ambassador to Yugoslavia from 1945 to 1947" and that he also served as "chairman of the Kashmir Commission for the United Nations." Joe's pedigree was duly noted: "Mr. Albright was graduated from Groton School and, with the class of '58, from Williams College where he was elected Phi Beta Kappa." The article noted that he was the grandson of the late Joseph Medill Patterson, publisher of the *New York Daily News,* and that Joe was already employed as a reporter at the *Chicago Sun-Times.*[38]

Joe, who graduated a year ahead of Madeleine, was living in Chicago. They visited each other once a month. Madeleine spent the spring her senior year planning their wedding and writing her senior thesis.

The thesis was an extraordinarily detailed and scathing account of the life of a left-wing Social Democrat in Czechoslovakia named Zdenek Fierlinger, a fellow traveler whose admiration for and devotion to the Soviet Union caused him to betray his country. Dedicated to her parents, "who taught me to speak Czechoslovakian," [sic] and "To Joe," to whom she had just become engaged, the 156-page thesis was titled *Zdenek Fierlinger's Role in the Communization of Czechoslovakia.* It draws heavily on writings and primary source material from her father and his wartime colleagues in the Czechoslovak government.

The report is impeccably researched, the work of countless hours reading books and documents in English and Czech in order to digest the complicated internal politics of her native country during and after World War II. With clarity and precision, Madeleine discussed the problems of the Czech government-in-exile, its negotiations with Czech Communists in Moscow, and the postwar feuds between the warring political parties, right up to the dramatic Communist takeover in February 1948, when Fierlinger was named minister of industry of the Communist government and her father was making the decision to renounce his own ties to the regime. "In the battle between Communists and democrats, fellow travelers not only exist but also prosper," she wrote. ". . . But Czechoslovakia was dead. A country whose cultural background had linked her to the West was anchored in the East. A people who had prided themselves on the individualism to which a democratic ideology is dedicated were forced into the mold which totalitarianism commands for its subjects. A little more than a decade has wrought its work, and Czechoslovakia is indistinguishable from any stereotype Soviet satellite."[39]

Clearly, Madeleine had spent many hours with her father discussing the political climate in which he had worked, the political loyalties of his various associates, and the reasons for President Beneš to look to Russia to save democracy in Czechoslovakia. "He understood that the Soviet Union would remain a major power in post-war Europe," she wrote, concluding that "Czechoslovakia must assure itself of Soviet friendship, its enmity would be disastrous."[40] In the preface, Madeleine acknowledged her father's contribution, formally offering "sincerest filial gratitude to Dr. Josef Korbel without whom this thesis would never have been written."

There was one fascinating similarity between her thesis and the books written by her father. While her treatise painted a vivid political picture of the death of democracy in Czechoslovakia, just as her father had in his writings, she made no mention of the personal tragedy that communism had inflicted on the Czechoslovak people or Hitler's treatment of the Jews. It was as if it were a topic that was off-limits, a subconscious decision to suppress the human aspects of the subject on every level, even the academic one.

On June 8, 1959, Madeleine was one of 364 seniors to receive her college diploma. Secretary of Defense Neil H. McElroy, the father of one of her classmates, was the featured commencement speaker. Young women educated at Wellesley, he said, "are given the ideal preparation to serve at the very heart of the home," that those who would become mothers were charged "to ignite the love and desire for education in their children." Not everyone was impressed. "I remember that stung, even then," recalls Winifred Shore Freund, or as she was listed in the '59 Wellesley college yearbook, "Mrs. Myron Freund," one of twenty-seven girls in the class who had married by graduation and taken their husbands' names. "It was before feminism, but I think a lot of us were offended by that. We thought we could do more with our education."[41]

Eventually, most of them would do much more with their Wellesley education, but not right away. Many women who came of age in the 1950s, married in their early twenties, and had children within a few years, found their image of the ideal marriage was shaken by the women's movement, which came along fifteen to twenty years later. When, eventually, the majority of the women in the Wellesley Class of '59 decided to go to work,[42] either by desire or necessity, their husbands often rebelled, leaving them caught with one foot firmly planted in one decade and the other foot in the next.

11

Love and Marriage

"I was married to someone I adored. I knew he would have an interesting life. I wanted to be a part of that, but also to do something that was interesting to me."
—Madeleine Albright, February 7, 1998

WITH A WELLESLEY DIPLOMA and a diamond ring, Madeleine's life sparkled. She had been a devoted daughter, who rewarded her parents for the sacrifices they had made to ensure that the lives of their children were more secure than their own. Her future seemed bright, filled with dreams of abundance and happiness.

Three days after graduating from Wellesley with honors, Madeleine married her Williams College sweetheart, Joseph Medill Patterson Albright. The formal ceremony took place on a Thursday, a day of hope in Czech tradition, at St. Andrew's Episcopal Church in the village of Wellesley. Madeleine looked like all young brides of the era, radiant in an elegant white wedding gown with a lace bodice, a single strand of white pearls at her neck, her hands gripping a bouquet of lilies of the valley and roses. Kathy Korbel, Madeleine's younger sister, was maid of honor. Alice Albright, sister of the groom, was bridesmaid. Sanford I. Hansell, a Williams classmate of Joe's, was best man and William H. Harter, another Williams classmate, an usher.[1]

It had been a difficult wedding to plan. Madeleine's family, who would traditionally pay for the wedding, was strapped financially. Joe's family was not only extremely wealthy, but "high society" as well. "The huge deal was that my family did not have money," Albright says today. "The question was how to have a nice wedding that fit in with this very complicated family."[2] Madeleine planned the event herself. By working in a campus eatery that sold doughnuts and orange juice, she had saved enough money to buy Joe a wedding present, a watch. She had enough left over to pay for a good portion of the wedding, including the pale green bridesmaid dresses, which she picked out at Priscilla's, Boston's premier shop for wedding apparel. The rehearsal dinner, paid for by the groom's family, was elaborate. The Albrights took the wedding party to Joseph's, one of the fanciest restaurants in Boston.

After the ceremony, there was a reception at the 1812 House in Framingham, Massachusetts. Most of Joe's relatives attended. As soon as it was over, Alice Albright made clear that she did not approve of her new sister-in-law's taste in clothes. She went into the bathroom, took off her bridesmaid's dress, and ripped it up. "She didn't like it," Madeleine Albright says today. "It was an ugly dress."[3]

But there was more to life than wedding finery. The newlyweds left for a weeklong honeymoon in the Caribbean, where they flew from island to island, enjoying the endless stretches of sandy white beaches.[4]

Adjusting to the idiosyncrasies and traditions of a spouse's family is never easy. Inevitably, the rhythms are different, the expectations too high or too low. Even for couples with similar backgrounds, the transition can be rocky. The Albrights were a complicated family, people for whom maids and mansions were as an accepted part of daily life as were the newspapers they ran. Madeleine found herself part of a circle that took its social position seriously. "It was not just the wealth, but that they were prominent," says a friend. "The Albrights were a very formidable family."[5]

Josephine Albright had not been eager to have her son marry a Catholic. In fact, it was Josephine who insisted that Madeleine convert. "It was a very hard family to be a part of," says a member of the extended clan. "Josephine was a rather mean alcoholic and acted very nasty to Madeleine. She would insult you. The general feeling was you weren't really wanted. She had a lot of anger in her that would focus on whoever happened to be around."[6]

On the other hand, the Korbels were very pleased that Madeleine was marrying an American from such a well-known, established lineage. "Josef told me that he was very proud that his daughter married into a prominent [newspaper] family," says the late Jan Stránský of Connecticut, an old and dear friend of the Korbels.[7]

Shortly after returning from his honeymoon, Joe Albright wrote an article about the economics of his new life for the *Chicago Sun-Times,* where he was getting experience on a paper owned by Chicago department store magnate Marshall Field, a friend of the Albright family. Readers could have been forgiven for thinking that Joe was just another struggling newlywed reporter hoping to make ends meet during a period of high interest rates and stubborn inflation. Dated June 16, 1959, the story carrying Joe's byline began:

> This is written by a 22-year-old cub reporter who became a husband only a week ago. . . . I doubt if I will ever make a step as important economically as when I promised to love, honor and cherish. Besides all the wonderful things that marriage is, it will also probably be an economic shock. . . . We entered into the venture of marriage with a considerable stockpile of resources—clothes, some money, wedding presents, health, education. In the few years we will both be working, we must acquire other assets of family life—furniture, rugs, pots and pans. It will be another 15 years before we can again afford such capital improvements. It seems out of the question for us to buy a house. . . . We will try to avoid installment plan buying. If there comes a choice between buying on time and not buying, chances are we will buy on time.

Joe went on to say that he owned a car, "one of the low-priced three," but kept it in storage for the previous year "because I loathe to buy license plates and pay insurance—and parking tickets." He wrote that to cushion inflation, he would invest in the stock market as a life insurance policy. Then he recounted a story of President Eisenhower, "one of my mentors in this department," who told business editors that he began making payments on an insurance policy shortly after he and Mamie Doud were married in 1916. But when the policy matured thirty years later, it was much too small for him to ask his wife to live on, even for six months.

Joe concluded the article on a misty note:

> But [Eisenhower's] early financial problems were not so bad, he said, because he was "young, and of course, very much in love."
>   And so am I.[8]

Joe signed up for the Army reserves, which began with a six-month stint at Fort Leonard Wood, Missouri, a base that became a temporary home for tens of thousands of GIs.[9] While Joe was in Army training, Madeleine moved back to Denver, where she lived at home. Because she arrived late in the summer season, she had trouble locating a temporary job. She finally found one at the Greyhound bus depot, booking reservations. She worked there for six weeks before moving to Missouri to join Joe.[10]

The couple found an apartment in Waynesville, right off Route 44, and Madeleine worked as a secretary in the local schools. Soon she landed a job as a reporter for a small newspaper called the *Rolla Daily News* in Rolla, Missouri, thirty-five miles away. She wrote obituaries, handled the social page, set type, took ads, and interviewed people who had seen UFOs. Her salary was $35 a week. "I loved it," she says.[11]

When Joe's tour was over, the Albrights moved back to Chicago, where Joe resumed his job at the *Sun-Times*. Madeleine, who had put in her time with a small newspaper, thought she might like to get a reporting job with one of the city's four newspapers. The idea did not sit well, however, with Joe's editors. Over dinner one night, one made his position clear. "Honey," he said, "you may want to be a reporter, but you can't be on a competing paper, and you can't be on the paper your husband works for, so why don't you find another career."[12] Madeleine Albright did not complain. "I understood," she says. "I went and got a different job. It's very different today."[13]

The remark was so typical of the time, an era when men held most jobs and wives were expected to follow their husbands dutifully and happily—or if not happily, certainly not in any way that would impede their husbands' careers. If a woman was resentful or angered by the situation, she had little choice but to swallow it and say nothing.

The job Madeleine did land was with the *Encyclopaedia Britannica,* which was owned by Bill Benton, a big financial backer of Democratic presidential candidate Adlai E. Stevenson of Illinois. Stevenson was a member of the *Britannica* board of directors and an intimate friend of Joe's aunt Alicia Patterson.[14] At the time, the *Britannica* offered coupons to those who bought a set of encyclopedias. The coupons entitled the buyer to send questions to be answered by *Britannica*. Madeleine was a researcher, a traditional spot for women, whose job was to find the answers to those questions.[15]

By the summer of 1960, Joe was established enough at the *Sun-Times* to be picked for the newspaper's team covering the Republican National Convention in Chicago. He wrote one front-page story about presidential nominee Richard Nixon holding a private meeting to tell Republican leaders why Henry Cabot Lodge should be the vice presidential candidate. When his colleagues heard that Joe got the scoop by hiding out in the bathroom of the hotel suite, they were impressed at his resourcefulness.[16]

Aunt Alicia was impressed as well, and soon she pressured Joe to move to her paper, *Newsday,* which was located in Melville, Long Island. Joe and Madeleine rented an apartment in nearby Garden City. It was 1961, and Joe was twenty-three. As he made the rounds of different departments of the paper, staff members regarded him as a decent guy and a diligent worker. At one point, when he was learning about the circulation department, he worked out of a district office in Nassau County's North End, where most of those around him drove station wagons. Joe arrived at work in a Mercedes-Benz.[17] Yet despite his wealth and family ties, his colleagues liked him. "Joe was a proper, straight-laced, and serious newspaperman," says Jim Toedtman, who served under Albright and later became *Newsday*'s Washington bureau chief. "He didn't have a whole lot of humor or flair, but he was very attentive to people's needs, and those who worked with him were very aware of his relationship with Alicia Patterson."[18]

In quick order, quicker in fact than his mother thought appropriate, Joe was given more responsibility. Soon he had a job on the copy desk as a rewrite man, the person who shapes reporters' stories before they go to press. "The staff thought him good and easy to work for," says Toedtman. "He was a good editor, but not a great editor, and he was nice to [young] reporters."[19]

Joe and Madeleine were also on their way to starting a family. Madeleine was pregnant. As she grew larger and larger, she began walking as a way to lose weight. She would walk five miles, stop for a cup of coffee, then turn around and walk home. She also started drinking a liquid diet meal popular at the time called Metracal. One day, walking to her doctor's office in the next town, she spotted a sign advertising Russian language lessons at Hofstra University in nearby Hempstead, New York.

Madeleine had always wanted to learn Russian, a tongue-twister of a language made all the more difficult by the necessity to learn the Cyrillic alphabet. It is hard enough to learn a new language in one's twenties, harder still when some letters in each word appear upside down or backwards. Madeleine had thought about taking Russian at Wellesley, but decided that because she knew Czech, which is similar, first-year Russian would be too easy. But she could not take second-year Russian before learning Cyrillic. The eight-hour-a-day Hofstra classes began in June and lasted eight weeks. The baby was due the first week in August. Madeleine calculated that if she started the course, she would not be able to finish it. "Too bad I can't do that," she thought as she walked to the doctor's office one day. When she arrived, the physician examined her. "I think you are having at least two," he said. Walking home, Madeleine contemplated what this new twist in her life would entail.

Six weeks later, June 17, 1961, Madeleine gave birth to twins. Anne was named after Madeleine's mother, whose official name was Anna; Alice, after her great-aunt Alicia Patterson. The girls were six weeks premature. Anne weighed three pounds, six ounces; Alice, three pounds, eight ounces. Both girls had collapsed lungs. The doctor told the Albrights that if the babies did not reinflate their lungs within forty-eight hours, they would not survive. If they did live, they could not leave the hospital until they weighed five pounds. Because they were extremely vulnerable to infection, even their mother was not allowed to touch them. "I was twenty-four years old and terrified," Madeleine Albright says. "There was nothing I could do. My husband was working. I didn't have a job. I couldn't go and [be with] my children. All I could do was look at them through the glass."[20]

To distract herself, Albright signed up for the Russian language class she had been thinking about earlier. "It occupied me," she says. "I'd go every morning." When her father took advantage of a university lecture and came East in July to see his first grandchildren, Madeleine greeted him in Russian. Her mother did not make the trip. The Korbels could not afford it.[21]

Despite Madeleine Albright's return to school, she had yet to set her sights on a career in politics. Her world was not dissimilar to that of most Long Island housewives. It revolved around her twins, whom she had to wake up to feed every two hours; her husband; and his career. "I went nuts that year," Albright says. "I kept thinking about what I would do." She had a freelance job with the *Encyclopaedia Britannica,* looking up odd facts that would appear in newspaper columns and bring attention to the company. She remembers one typical item: "Ostriches are voiceless, according to the *Encyclopaedia Britannica.*" But this kind of work was not satisfying to a woman with a Wellesley education. "I read, watched soap operas, fed the twins, washed bottles, took them for walks, and thought, 'I've got to do something,'" Albright says today. She also played a lot of tennis—the family had its own court in the backyard. And she hosted frequent dinner parties, often for Joe's co-workers at *Newsday.*[22] But the question nagged her: What was she going to do with her life? "I decided I should be a professor," Albright says. "It made sense. We were ultimately going to live on Long Island. Joe was going to be publisher of *Newsday.* I would have a job teaching at one of the Long Island universities. I wanted to get started."[23]

Within a few months, Joe Albright was rewarded with a transfer to Washington. It was his first long-term assignment at the paper, and he was to cover the State Department. Having worked in the various business departments of *Newsday,* he settled in to the addictive but often chaotic routine of news reporting, where he showed an aggressiveness that surprised and pleased his bosses in the home office. He had worked in all sections of the paper as he trained for the eventual job of publisher, but it was as a reporter that Joe excelled. He was better at digging up a story than writing it, which did not augur well for a young man expected to take over the family enterprise.

But the couple loved Washington. "It was incredible," Madeleine Albright says today. "Being a reporter in Washington was quite great. You are treated well even if you are only twenty-six years old."[24] Reporters see themselves as the lifeblood of news organizations, and there is no question that they have more fun. They may be temperamental, foul-mouthed, and woefully insecure, but they are far more entertaining than editors and publishers, curmudgeonly and miserly bastards who, unfortunately, have the real power.

The family lived in Georgetown in a narrow, red-framed house at 34th Street and R, just a few blocks from where Madeleine Albright lives today.[25] Danielle and Richard Gardner lived next door. Dick Gardner was only thirty-two, but he already had an impressive job at the State Department as an assistant secretary whose responsibilities included the United Nations.[26] "Dick was deputy assistant secretary of state for international organizations," Albright says. "I thought that was the highest level job I'd ever heard of."[27] Danielle Gardner had been born in Italy and, like Madeleine, she had taken pains to become as Americanized as possible, to lose her foreign accent, to modulate her voice. "Immigrants can get it to perfection if they have a good ear," Danielle Gardner says.[28] The two women were kindred spirits. Over the years, they would become close friends.

The Gardners' daughter, Nina, was a year old when the Albrights moved next door. The idea of twins confused her, and she referred to the girls as one, "Annealice," which she pronounced "Anne-aleece." The two couples even had Portuguese maids who were sisters. Felicia worked for the Albrights, Margarita for the Gardners. Felicia and Margo, as she was called, saw no need to telephone each other and would shout over the back fence to ask if it was time to take the children to the park.[29] It was a comfortable life, one that was fairly typical for the capital's upper crust at that time. Live-in help was a sign of social status as well as affluence. Housewives did little housework, but when Felicia and Margo had a day off, it fell to Danielle and Madeleine to take care of their three children by themselves. That included wielding the enormous stroller the Albrights had for the twins. "The maids' day off was no joke," Danielle Gardner says.[30]

The couples frequently had dinner together, and conversation usually centered on current events. Madeleine followed the latest twists and turns of whatever was happening overseas. Joe, always a newspaperman, would pump Dick Gardner for story leads. Danielle told Madeleine one day that she might like to work at the State Department; she thought it would be fun to be chief of protocol. No, said Madeleine, that was the job that she wanted.[31]

When the twins were six months old, the Albrights took them to Chicago for New Year's to visit Joe's family, including his sister, Alice, who was home on vacation from Radcliffe. An item announcing their visit ran in the social pages of the *Chicago Sun-Times*. Headlined "Albrights [*sic*] Housing Problem," the story read:

> Like many other grandparents, Mr. and Mrs. Ivan Albright are begin-
> ning to wonder how they are going to cope with housing arrange-
> ments when their children gather during the holidays. . . . With
> motels springing up in the area, the Albrights think it might be a
> good idea for them to take a quiet suite in one of them and let the
> young folks take over the house.[32]

Washington in the early 1960s was a period of soaring promise and patriotic ideals. On a sunny but freezing day in January 1961, John F. Kennedy, the youngest person ever elected president of the United States, assumed the mantle of power from Dwight D. Eisenhower, the oldest president up to that time. Ushering in a new generation of leadership, Kennedy promised to "pay any price, bear any burden" to assure the blessings of liberty throughout the world. His glamorous wife, Jackie, captivated the nation with her elegant clothes and stylish dinner parties.

It was also an era of endless fears and suspicions about the increasing power of the Soviet Union, a time when the possibility of nuclear war dominated the headlines, when families built crude bomb shelters in their basements and lined them with canned food in the vain hope that they might survive a nuclear attack. Schoolchildren practiced hiding under their desks to protect themselves from radioactive fallout.

It was a heady time for the Washington press corps. Unlike the combative relationship that evolved in the 1970s during the Watergate scandal that forced Richard Nixon to resign the presidency, the atmosphere between the Executive Branch and the Fourth Estate was much more symbiotic than it is today. Television was in its nascent stage. Walter Cronkite, Eric Sevareid, and David Brinkley were establishing themselves on the airwaves, but print reporters dominated, set the standards, led the pack. *New York Times* reporters James "Scotty" Reston and Tom Wicker, along with columnists Walter Lippmann and Joseph Alsop, were household names, the lions of the press corps whose back channels to the White House produced one scoop after another. "There was great excitement for people my age and

Madeleine's age and Joe's age being there during the Kennedy years," says James Hoge, who worked for the *Chicago Tribune* and would marry Joe's younger sister, Alice. "It was far nicer than it is today."[33]

The news itself was compelling. Issues of war and peace, even nuclear annihilation, captivated a nation that still had vivid memories of World War II and Korea. Nikita Khrushchev treated John Kennedy with contempt, baiting him with the threat of Soviet action to block all routes to Berlin if the United States did not sign a treaty guaranteeing Communist control of access to the city. Fearing that Khrushchev thought he lacked judgment and guts, Kennedy told Reston that he decided to impress the Soviet leader with the determination and firmness of the United States. He would do so in, of all places, Vietnam. "I don't think I swallowed my hat, but I was speechless," Reston wrote.[34]

As proof, Kennedy ordered another division of troops to Europe and tripled the number of U.S. advisers in Vietnam. After Vice President Lyndon B. Johnson returned from a fact-finding trip to the region and reported to Kennedy that the only way for the United States to win the war was to show more determination, Kennedy sent even more advisers to Southeast Asia.[35]

As often happens in Washington, the headlines of the day dominated conversation. Nowhere was it more evident than in the establishment circles frequented by Madeleine and Joe. The men making history lived in their neighborhood, worshiped at the same churches, sent their children to the same schools, dined in their house. "I used to cook and have dinner parties," Madeleine Albright says today. "I had these adorable year-old twins. . . . I loved it."[36]

Most Americans knew little about the Soviet Union, and very few spoke Russian. Madeleine Albright's childhood experiences in Eastern Europe, undoubtedly fueled by later conversations with her father, gave her more than just a visceral feeling for Russia. In this atmosphere, she made a decision that was most unusual for young mothers at the time: She started graduate work at the Johns Hopkins University's School of Advanced International Affairs in Washington. It was the fall of 1962, and her field was political science with an emphasis on international relations. "I wanted to get a Ph.D. there because I thought we would be here three or four years," Albright says.[37]

With a housekeeper to help out with the children, Madeleine signed up for a full academic load: four courses a semester, plus a year of foreign language. Again, she chose Russian. Her courses were daunting: The United States and the Changing World was required. Her electives included Development of the Soviet State, Comparative Legal Systems, States of Eastern Europe, and Mainland China.[38]

The year was difficult, and there were many times when friends asked

Madeleine if she was doing the right thing. Even with household help, she was under enormous pressure. The twins were just a year old; Joe had a demanding job covering the State Department; and Madeleine had thrown herself full time into her schoolwork. She was twenty-five years old. "I was motivated to have an interesting life and do something other than just be in the home," Albright says today. "I thought I could combine it all, and being a professor worked. But it was very odd because I found many people my own age were critical of what I was doing. The hardest part of this was finding my friends saying, 'Why are you choosing this form of life? Why are you spending so much time in school?'"[39]

As historian Doris Kearns Goodwin writes in her popular memoir about her childhood, *Wait 'Til Next Year,* ". . . it was the men who took the trains and went off each morning to make money and pursue careers while every woman in my neighborhood, without exception, was occupied solely in managing a household and caring for children."[40] Women were expected to be subservient to their husbands, to make themselves sexy and attractive. *Time* magazine published a cover story called "The Suburban Wife," whom it called "the key figure in all Suburbia, the thread that weaves between family and community—the keeper of the suburban dream." The housewife, said *Time,* was "breakfast getter ('You can't have ice cream for breakfast because I say you can't'), laundress, house cleaner, dishwasher, shopper, gardener, encyclopedia, arbitrator of children's disputes, policeman ('Tommy, didn't your mother ever tell you it's not nice to go into other people's houses and open the refrigerator?'). If she's not pregnant, she wonders if she is. She takes her peanut butter sandwich lunch while standing, thinks she looks a fright, watches her weight (periodically), jabbers over the short-distance telephone with the next door neighbor. . . . She paints her face for her husband's return before she wrestles with dinner."[41]

Not long after this, Betty Friedan published *The Feminine Mystique,* in which she argued that American society defines a woman only in terms of men— as housewife, sex object, mother—and never as an individual in her own right. Friedan wrote that this image was perpetuated by magazines, movies, and commercials and that it kept women passive and apart. She urged women "to see through the delusions of the feminine mystique" and understand "that neither her husband nor her children, nor the things in her house, nor sex, nor being like all the other women, can give her a self. . . ." Friedan emphasized another point: "Even a very young woman today must think of herself as a human being first, not as a mother with time on her hands, and make a life plan in terms of her own abilities, a commitment of her own to society, with which her commitments as wife and mother can be integrated."[42]

Friedan's message that women should find their inner voice to be complete individuals challenged the status quo, laying the seeds of a revolution that would change American society as few movements had before it. Of all the lives turned topsy-turvy by Friedan's thinking, none was affected as much as Madeleine Albright's generation, women who had grown up in the 1950s with a set of rules that would slowly crumble, marriage by marriage. "Who knows what women's intelligence will contribute when it can be nourished without denying love?" Friedan wrote. "Who knows of the possibilities of love when men and women share not only children, home and garden, not only the fulfillment of their biological roles, but the responsibilities and passions of the work that creates the human future and the full human knowledge of who they are? It has barely begun, the search of women for themselves."[43]

Unlike many of her Wellesley classmates, Madeleine Albright did not read Betty Friedan. "I think I was basically listening to some inner need," she says. "I wanted to do something interesting and useful with my life."[44] Her friend Wini Freund put it another way: "Madeleine and I felt we were independent women, partners with our husbands," she says. "We didn't need Betty Friedan to tell us that. We were feminists in a different kind of way."[45]

Joe Albright's world was about to undergo changes as well. On July 2, 1963, at the age of fifty-six, Alicia Patterson underwent surgery for a stomach ulcer and died of complications. Her strong-willed husband, known as "Captain Harry," controlled the business end of the paper and knew that he would need help from someone with experience on the editorial side. According to the book *Newsday,* his first move was to appoint Joe, who was only twenty-six, to be assistant to the publisher.

To all appearances, Joe was heir apparent. On July 19, 1963, Adlai Stevenson wrote a "Dear Joey" letter to Albright in which he said that Joe's sister, Alice, told him that Joe would be taking over *Newsday.* Stevenson was delighted at the prospect and said that he had had many talks with Joe's aunt Alicia Patterson about her plans for him and the paper. He ended with a gracious note: "Sometime if you and Madeleine are in town with nothing to do, I hope you'll do it with me."[46]

Joe and Madeleine Albright moved back to New York. Madeleine, who had taken the first tentative step outside the home, disrupted her graduate studies to follow her husband. Transferring credits was not easy, but she did not resent it. "I truly did not," she says today. "We loved Washington, but it was necessary to go back. I accepted it, kind of like my mother."[47]

The couple settled into a beautiful, nineteenth-century, white clapboard house with a circular drive. It was situated on five acres of a winding, wooded road called Remsen's Lane in Upper Brookville, a wealthy community on Oyster Bay in the middle of the Long Island horse country. Captain Harry Guggenheim lived in a mansion in Sands Point, not far away. With four bedrooms and a swimming pool in the backyard, the Albrights' life was considerably different from that of most young married couples, and certainly different from that of Madeleine's graduate school friends and other young *Newsday* staffers. But it was the perfect spot for a growing family. There was even a small gatehouse on the corner of the grounds.

Madeleine and Joe loved their home and kept it for years, even after they moved back to Washington and could only use it in the summer. They had a nanny for the children, but they tended the grounds themselves. The wide sweep of lawn was the scene of annual Easter egg hunts for friends' and neighbors' children, as well as regular scavenger hunts and barbecues.

While Joe plunged into learning the family business, Madeleine enrolled in Columbia University's Graduate School of Arts and Sciences to pursue the doctorate that she began at Johns Hopkins. It was September 1963, and she would take several courses each semester for the next two years.[48] Classes were held two and three times a week, and she drove the twenty-three miles from her home into New York City. When she wrote her dissertation, she often rose at 4:30 A.M. to write while her children were still asleep. "She was amazingly focused," says her ex-brother-in-law, Jim Hoge. "It took wells of energy to undertake raising a family, learning a language, and becoming an expert on foreign affairs."[49]

When she was not studying, Madeleine spent much of her time tending to the children, playing tennis, and giving dinner parties. Uncle Harry Guggenheim was a regular guest. Madeleine enjoyed cooking. At one point she and Wini Freund perfected a recipe for soft-shell crabs. (Their secret: a dash of Worcestershire sauce splashed into the butter used to sauté them.) "Neither she nor Joe spent lavishly," says Freund. "You would never have known that they were wealthy. I used to take Madeleine shopping at discount stores. She used to say that she had a scholarship mentality."[50]

The Albrights were also unfailingly generous with their friends. Over the years, countless people stayed with Madeleine and Joe, sometimes just for the night, often longer. Mort Abromowitz and his wife, Sheppie, stayed with them when they returned from an assignment in Thailand and were looking for a house.[51]

Marcia Burick was a regular visitor. Once she stopped at the Albrights' home on Long Island when she was on her way to Taiwan, where her then-husband, Steven Goldstein, was doing research. Marcia was nursing her four-week-old baby son, Danny, and Madeleine worried about Marcia because she hated to drink milk. To ensure that her friend would get enough calcium while she was overseas, Madeleine went to the grocery store and bought a cartload of Hunts Vanilla Pudding boxes, six to a pack. They filled an entire suitcase. Another time, during a rough patch in her marriage, Burick and her two little boys moved into the Albrights' Georgetown house for a week while Danny was being diagnosed with what turned out to be a condition that proved fatal. "I needed a place to get away and hide," Burick says.[52]

Madeleine and Joe not only opened their home to friends and families, they took them on regular family vacations. The Albrights had a house in Woodstock, Vermont, where they took friends to ski. For spring vacation, they often invited them to South Georgia, where Alicia Patterson had a hunting lodge on a plantation that stretched along the St. Mary's River. The adults would go quail hunting and hiking. The children would ride horseback on fat white Palominos and swim in the black waters of the river, which had its share of snakes. Marcia Burick was afraid of the reptiles. On one hiking trip, she said to Madeleine, "Why do you think God made snakes?" She was startled by Madeleine's quick reply: "Why do you think God made Germans?"[53] Burick understood immediately that Madeleine was referring to the Nazis.

Danielle and Dick Gardner were also frequent visitors. During one holiday, Madeleine and Danielle were on yet another diet. "I had just read about vinegar, and we were downing quantities of it before each meal," Danielle says. "Supposedly if you did that, the fat wouldn't accumulate."

Madeleine and Danielle Gardner had a lunch date at New York's University Club on November 22, 1963. While riding in a cab on her way to meet Danielle, just at the corner of Fifty-fifth and Fifth, Madeleine heard a news bulletin that President Kennedy had been shot. When she walked into the club, she and Danielle hugged each other. Several Irish waiters rushed into the dining room in tears. Madeleine went to the ladies' room, where she overheard a woman comment that Kennedy deserved it. "It was chilling," Albright says.[54] Like the rest of America, she spent the weekend at home in front of the television.

In 1966, five years after the twins were born, Madeleine learned that she was pregnant a second time. Her belly grew so large that doctors thought that, once again, she might be having twins. Madeleine joked to Marcia Burick that she was like Noah's ark, having children "by two, by twosey." There were no sonograms available at the time to monitor a baby's growth, but when she was six months' pregnant, doctors took an X-ray. They found Madeleine was not carrying twins but an undersized child. She had grown unusually big because she had contracted hydramnios, a condition in which the amniotic sac fills up with fluid. Madeleine asked the doctor a question. "What are the chances of the child being abnormal?" His reply: "Very good." Madeleine was not sure she heard correctly. "Let me ask you the question again," she said. His response was the same.

The twins had contracted measles during their mother's first few months of pregnancy. Mandula Korbel could not recall whether Madeleine ever had measles as a child, so doctors recommended a gamma globulin shot as a precaution. Madeleine was distraught. She went to a New York doctor to inquire about an abortion. "I had enough money and thought about going to Sweden," she says. The doctor told her she was too far along in the pregnancy, that an abortion would endanger her own life. "It's too late," he said. Madeleine had no choice but to wait for the baby to be born. "It was horrible, absolutely the worst time in my life," she says. "I started knitting an Irish sweater, one of those unbelievably complicated sweaters that you have to concentrate on constantly."

When Madeleine finally went into labor, the baby was stillborn. The Albrights were overwhelmingly sad, but Madeleine was also relieved. People wrote lovely sympathy letters, which helped, but she could not pretend to feel differently. "That's obviously why I think women need choice," Albright says today. She still has the Irish sweater.[55]

Joe was out of his depth as assistant to the publisher. In 1964, he was appointed editor of the new Saturday magazine, a job more suited to his talents. Then he became night city editor and a day editor in the Suffolk office, stressful jobs that require making snap decisions, balancing the competing talents of reporters with production deadlines, and making judgments on what stories should appear on page one.[56] "As an editor in New York, Joe wasn't overbearing, but he didn't join in the weekly softball games either," says Jim Toedtman. "We regarded Joe as tepid, not very aggressive."[57]

Captain Harry began looking for a strong person with a national reputation to run the paper, someone who would bring the kind of recognition and prestige he thought *Newsday* deserved. He decided on Bill Moyers, press secretary to President Lyndon Johnson. Moyers and Johnson had become estranged over the Vietnam war, and the lure of a top-level job in the world of journalism was too tantalizing for the ambitious Texan to turn down.

For Joe Albright, Moyers' appointment was a stomach-wrenching professional blow, the humiliation public, his disappointment acute. Even Joe's mother's reaction offered little comfort. "Naturally, I was disappointed that Joe seems to find himself off the ladder," Josephine Albright wrote to Harry Guggenheim. "However, the choice of Moyers seems to me brilliant and will add much luster to the paper. Some day I would like to talk to you about your ideas on Joe's future."[58]

Joe himself went to see Uncle Harry and asked if he should leave the paper. "You have temporarily been delayed in your rise on the editorial staff because you did not succeed in getting the best results when in charge of fairly large numbers of personnel," Harry wrote Joe afterward. "I have opened every door to you at *Newsday*. It would be unfair to *Newsday* and its stockholders, and to you in the long run, if I attempted to do more for you than this."[59] However, among *Newsday* staffers, no one was ready to write Joe off. "We thought an accommodation would be made for both of them," Toedtman says.[60]

Friends felt a certain sympathy for Joe. As a young man, he was under enormous pressure to succeed in the family business. He was a good reporter but never a whirlwind editor, which is where much of the power in a newspaper lies. While he worked in different sections of the paper, he was often pushed into jobs for which he was too young and had not had proper training, making it impossible for him to develop the leadership skills he would need to take over. Most important, he never proved his mettle to Captain Harry, who owned 51 percent of the paper.

Life was difficult on other fronts as well. Madeleine was still having trouble adjusting to life with the Albrights. Their family history of anti-Semitic and isolationist views stretched back to the nineteenth century when their ancestors emigrated to America from England. Aunt Cissy Patterson, Joseph Medill Patterson's sister, was, like her brother, from the Republican Midwest, and she prided herself on being an isolationist. Cissy, who owned the *Times-Herald* in Washington, had cheered when the Nazis invaded Czechoslovakia in 1939, forcing its partition. "Thank God for Munich," she wrote in an editorial.[61] She also criticized Franklin D. Roosevelt, who, by this time, had redoubled his efforts to help Jewish refugees escape from Germany.[62] Later she hinted broadly in editorials that persistent accounts of concentration camps and mass executions of Jews were being exaggerated by Jewish executives in the communications business. Her views cost the paper a considerable amount of advertising despite reminders from the *Times-Herald* business office that Cissy's second husband had been a Jew.[63] They were also totally at odds with the political issues and social values that Josef Korbel represented.

Ivan and Josephine Albright were more tolerant than some of their relatives, but nonetheless difficult. To dispel any idea that their son had married a poor little refugee, they played up Madeleine's European diplomatic background. "They thought of her as a Czech refugee," says a friend who knew them at the time. "I think they loved her and respected her mind, but they were always trying to make her into a classy Czech diplomat."[64] Recalling their early days in Denver when the family had trouble making ends meet, Madeleine would giggle and say, "If they only knew . . ."[65]

One of Madeleine Albright's friends insists that the elder Albrights had firm ideas about inheritance. In the event of Joe's death, his children and Madeleine could inherit his share of the family fortune, but she could not use the money to give financial assistance to her parents or siblings.[66]

To all appearances, however, the young Albrights' marriage was a good one. Even though many women of this generation kept silent about their desires to pursue their own dreams, friends say Madeleine and Joe understood each other. Madeleine counseled friends with marriage troubles, telling them she and Joe had discussed how important it was to present a united front. "They seemed so together on things like how to raise children," says Marcia Burick. "They had decided they could be a team."[67]

From the Wellesley Class of 1959 Record Book for 1964

Korbel, Madeleine Jane (Maddy) (Mrs. Joseph P. Albright)
Remsen's Lane, Upper Brookville, Oyster Bay,
Long Island, New York.

Graduate study—working for Ph.D. at the Russian Institute at
Columbia University.
Husband—Newspaperman; graduate of Williams.
Children—Anne Korbel and Alice Patterson, 3 year old twins

In the past five years have moved from Fort Leonard Wood, Missouri to Chicago to Garden City, Long Island to Washington, DC and back to Long Island. Only unusual accomplishment has been production of twins. . . .

12

The Korbel

"I certainly was upset during this trip. No question."
—Madeleine Albright, February 7, 1998

MADELEINE AND Joe Albright's family life was thriving. On March 5, 1967, Madeleine gave birth to Katie, their third daughter. Spring, always bountiful in upper Brookville, was just a few weeks away, and the twins would soon be playing under a fairyland of magnolia blossoms. Daffodils lined the curbsides of Remsen's Lane, cheering the arrival of warm weather. And dogwood, their pink and white petals delicate as a baby's cheek, were soon to open.

That summer, Madeleine and Joe decided to take a trip to Eastern Europe. Madeleine was eager to return to her native Prague. The Albrights were accompanied by Madeleine's fellow graduate student and good friend Steven Goldstein and his wife, Marcia Burick. Madeleine and Steve were classmates, students of Eastern Europe, and the trip provided a chance for firsthand research into the impact of Communist rule. For Madeleine and Marcia, both young mothers, a trip alone with their husbands was a treat. The Albrights' twins, Anne and Alice, by now six years old, and Katie, who was four months, stayed home with their nanny. Marcia and Steve left their two-year-old son, Kenny, with his grandparents. Madeleine was nervous about returning to Prague and had contacted the Czech embassy in Washington to make sure she would not be entrapped there.

It was an unusual trip, one of those vacations that provided delicious moments they laughed about for years. Not everyone spent a vacation visiting Communist Party museums. In the mid-sixties, Eastern Europe was hardly a garden spot for tourists. The hotels were third rate. Few had air-conditioning, and flies in the room were a constant irritant. The friends joked while driving from Romania to Bulgaria that they were making a tour of "pig villages." In Vienna, the foursome rented a Hertz car. Joe, Steve, and Madeleine shared the driving, while Marcia had a permanent space in the backseat. The group drove from Vienna to Budapest, then through Scolnicky in Eastern Hungary and on to Romania. As they drove through the Transylvanian mountains it started to rain, causing a hay thrasher to stall in the road. While waiting for a chance to pass, they made up newspaper headlines teasing Joe about his famous lineage: "Patterson Heir Reaped by Thrasher." Marcia wanted to stop for the night, but Madeleine refused. This, she said, was Dracula country. "I've read those books," she said: " 'Young Couple Stops In Castle, Never Seen Again.' "

In Bulgaria, the women had a mishap they would not soon forget. While visiting the tenth-century Rila Monastery, located in a mountainous resort area not far from Sofia, they stopped the car along the roadside for Madeleine and Marcia to make a quick trip into the woods. Not realizing what plants grew in the ground cover, each found herself sitting in a patch of poisonous nettles, prickly green plants that sting on contact. Startled, they ran out of the forest screaming. Spotting a fountain in the middle of the monastery grounds, they jumped into the basin and lowered themselves gingerly into the cold water. "Amazingly, it worked," Marcia said. "We called it 'the healing waters of Rila.'"

At another stop, they went to a house in Budapest set up for elderly victims of the Holocaust. These individuals, who all had numbers tattooed on their arms, had survived, but their children had died, so there was no one to care for them. Madeleine asked Joe to make a donation, and he left $100, a generous sum even by today's standards. Marcia joked about what Joseph Medill Patterson, Joe's grandfather and the conservative publisher of the *Daily News,* would say if he knew Joe was leaving part of the family fortune at such a place.[1]

As they crossed the Danube River from Romania into Bulgaria, the group stopped at a rest station for Marcia and Joe to visit the lavatory. But unable to read the Cyrillic alphabet, Marcia found herself in the men's room and Joe in the women's. They returned to the car giggling.

One afternoon in Bulgaria, while the Goldsteins and the Albrights had tea, their guide explained cultural differences in this region and expressed his opinion that "the Czechs are the Jews of Eastern Europe." When the two couples burst out laughing, the man was perplexed. He did not realize he had just insulted three of the four people at his table.[2]

When they crossed the border from Yugoslavia to Austria, Joe was the first to hand his passport to the border guard. "Joseph Medill Patterson Albright," the guard said in a voice filled with suspicion. "Four names?" Thinking that the guard was asking about documents for the rental car, Joe pointed to the wallet in his shirt pocket and said, "Hertz." The guard thought he said, "Herz," which means heart in German. Thinking Joe was having a heart attack, the guard opened the gate and waved them to a building marked "Red Cross" visible down the road. They drove through laughing.[3]

The trip had its funny moments, but there were poignant ones as well. In Belgrade, they walked around the outside of the Czechoslovak embassy, where Madeleine had lived with her parents when her father was the ambassador. Madeleine pointed out the balcony where she had stood as a little girl wearing a Czech national costume and holding flowers. Jokingly, she told Marcia that she should go to the basement to look for some of her childhood mementos that had been left behind in 1948 when the family escaped. They were never recovered.

The days passed quickly. After returning the rental car in Vienna, they boarded a train for Prague, which for Madeleine would be the most intense portion of the trip. As the train chugged along, she grew serious and wondered aloud whether she should draw attention to herself by speaking her native Czech in public. She worried also that they might be followed by the secret police. "She was very nervous, very quiet, and very tense," Burick says. "There was no joking around." While the others walked up and down the corridor of the train to pass the time, Madeleine never left the compartment.

When they arrived in the city, they found that ČEDOK, the central tourist agency, had booked them into a distant hotel. A hotel porter, who they suspected was a security agent, fingered their luggage tags, trying to read their names. "I went to Joe and said that I would stand next to the luggage," Marcia says. "Maybe we were overreacting, but it was at that point that Madeleine knew we were being watched." They decided Madeleine had no choice but to use her Czech to get them more convenient quarters where they would feel more at ease. By early evening, they were installed in the Alcron Hotel, just off Wenceslas Square, the center of Nové Město (New Town) and the focal point for popular discontent.

One day they visited the spacious apartment in Hradčany Square where the Korbels had lived when they returned from London after the war. The foursome knocked on the door and was invited in to look around. A whole

The Körbel men: Arnošt Körbel, center, with sons, Josef, left; Jan, right. *(Courtesy of Madeleine Albright)*

Mandula and Josef Körbel, Prague, 1930s.
(Courtesy of Madeleine Albright)

Madlenka in a stroller in Prague with Cousin Dagmar and Dagmar's sister Milena, who was killed in the Holocaust.
(Courtesy of Dagmar Šímová)

Madlenka and her doll,
London.
(Courtesy of Madeleine Albright.)

Madlenka, sister Kathy,
cousin Jara.
(Courtesy of Dagmar Šímová)

During the early war years, the Körbels spent some time
living in a house named The Old Cottage on Bank Mill Lane
in Berkhamsted. *(Courtesy of Inge Woolf, current owner)*

When they returned to
Prague after the war, the
Körbels lived in an apart-
ment on the second floor
of this building in
Hradčany Square. The
ground-floor restaurant,
U Labutí, is still there.
*(Courtesy of Hana Paříková,
restaurant owner)*

Madlenka in Belgrade wearing a typical Czech costume. With her governess, sister Kathy, and a friend, Nicholas Jankovic.
(Courtesy of Madeleine Albright)

Madeleine in Switzerland, 1948.
(Courtesy of Madeleine Albright)

Madeleine's graduation picture, Wellesley College, Class of '59.
(Courtesy of Wellesley College)

Madeleine with the twins: Alice (*left*)
and Anne, 1961.
(*Courtesy of Madeleine Albright*)

Madeleine and Joe Albright (*left*) with
a guide in Sofia during a trip to Eastern
Europe in 1967.
(*Courtesy of Marcia Burick*)

Madeleine, her mother, Mandula, and
the twins, age five, 1966.
(*Courtesy of Madeleine Albright*)

Madeleine with Alice. *(Courtesy of Madeleine Albright)*

Madeleine worked on the staff of the National Security Council. Seen here with Senators John Glenn and Edward M. Kennedy, May 9, 1979. *(Courtesy of Madeleine Albright)*

Madeleine with her mentor, Maine senator Edmund S. Muskie, at the White House, where Madeleine is wearing her National Security Council badge, January 1980. *(Courtesy of Madeleine Albright)*

Madeleine and her sister, Kathy Silva, 1983.
(Courtesy of Madeleine Albright)

The Golden Girls—Barbara Mikulski, Madeleine Albright, and Barbara Kennelly at Bill Clinton's second inauguration, January 1997.

Ambassador Albright with her daughters, *(from left)* Alice, Anne, and Katie.
(Courtesy of Madeleine Albright)

Secretary of State Madeleine K. Albright being congratulated by President Bill Clinton after her swearing-in ceremony, January 23, 1997. *(Official White House photograph)*

Albright threw out the first pitch at the Baltimore Orioles' opening day at Camden Yards. She is seen here with Cal Ripken, April 21, 1997. *(Official State Department photograph)*

Vladimír and Dagmar Šíma in their fifth-floor Prague apartment, December 1997. *(Photo by Ann Blackman)*

A real friend. Eduard Goldstücker in his Prague apartment in December 1997. Goldstücker was a close friend of the Körbel family. Even though he was an official with the Czechoslovak government and a Communist Party member, he invited the Körbels to stay with his family in his London apartment when they fled to the West in 1948. They arrived exhausted and slept for several days. *(Photo by Ann Blackman)*

Secretary Albright has coffee and pastry with Letohrad resident Věra Ruprechtová (standing) in the room where her father used to do business. Mrs. Ruprechtová is the granddaughter of Arnošt Körbel's business partner, Jan Reinelt, who owned a match factory that sold its wares as far away as Prague. *(Courtesy of Letohrad mayor Petr Šilar)*

Secretary Albright wearing her trademark black Stetson, arriving in Moscow with Deputy Secretary of State Strobe Talbott, February 1997. *(Official State Department photograph)*

family was living in what had been little Madeleine's bedroom. The sight brought back painful memories and left Madeleine sad.

They were visiting Prague at a tense time. Charles Jordan, executive vice chairman of the American Joint Distribution Committee, a relief agency for needy Jews overseas, had recently disappeared. He had walked out of his hotel to buy a newspaper and was never seen again. A few weeks later his body was found floating in the murky waters of Prague's Vltava River.

Throughout Eastern Europe there had been periodic harassment of Jews and Jewish organizations, and in the months following the Six-Day War in June 1967 between Israel and her Arab neighbors, the harassment erupted anew. The *New York Times* reported that tensions were so high that Czechoslovaks, including party members, who normally received Western visitors, had warned them "not to come, not to call and not even to write."[4] The Albrights and their friends arrived only a month later.

Marcia Burick remembers an afternoon that devastated Madeleine Before Madeleine left for Prague, her mother received a letter from Petr Novak, the sole surviving member of a prominent Jewish family that had hidden the Körbels after the Nazis invaded Czechoslovakia in 1938, prompting Madeleine to pay him a visit. Night after night, the family had sent the Körbels to hide in different manor houses they owned around Prague, enabling the Körbels to evade the Gestapo.

When the Körbels returned to Prague after the war, they found that all but one member of the family had been killed. The only survivor was a teenage boy, Petr, a prodigy cellist, who had played in concert halls throughout Europe. The Nazis had sent the boy and his family to the Theresienstadt concentration camp, where they slashed his wrist, cutting the nerves to ensure that he could never play the cello again and leaving him in a kind of living death.

On the afternoon of Madeleine's visit to Petr, members of the Albright party took off in different directions, hoping to thwart the secret police. Steve walked in the direction of one of the universities he was visiting, Joe in another. Marcia lingered behind Madeleine, far enough that they did not seem to be together, but close enough to keep an eye on her friend and make sure that she was safe. "It sounds very James Bondish, but she had reason to be frightened," Burick says.

Albright, who recalls only pieces of the story now, says she found Petr's apartment and was greeted by two elderly women who had been friends of her parents and had visited the Korbels in Belgrade. Albright thinks the women may have been caring for Petr Novák, who was by then dying of stomach cancer. One woman had a stiff finger, the result of nerve damage.

They told Albright a story that she had not heard before. Because her father had been a rising star in the Czechoslovak Ministry of Foreign Affairs, he had been placed on the Gestapo's Most-Wanted List, tried in absentia, and sentenced to death. Madeleine was shocked and deeply upset by the revelation.

When she returned to the hotel, Burick says, Albright collapsed sobbing, devastated at what she had learned. "There but for the grace of God, there but for the grace of God," she cried over and over. Marcia put her arms around her friend and held her. "She kept saying that [Petr] had nothing and nobody because his family had saved her family," says Burick. "I kept saying they would have been killed anyway or maybe they would have escaped." Madeleine could not be consoled.

Because they did not dare discuss anything important in their hotel rooms, which they assumed, probably correctly, were bugged, the friends sat in the lobby to talk about what Madeleine had learned on her visit. As she related the conversation, Joe kept clinking his car keys on a coffee table to make it difficult for listening devices to pick up what she said.

Madeleine told the group that for the years Petr was in the camps, a boy of fourteen, fifteen, and sixteen, he decided that the best way for him to survive would be to join the Communist Party. Later, he became disillusioned and became a Zionist. But by that time, the Iron Curtain had closed around Czechoslovakia, and he could not escape. In the summer of 1967, shortly before the Albrights' visit, the man had led a pro-Zionist rally in Wenceslas Square in support of Israel in the Six-Day War. He was jailed by the Czech Communist government and told the authorities, "I can either die in the putrid air of your prison, or I can die in the putrid air of Prague, because I am dying of stomach cancer." They let him go, and he died a short time later.

Josef Körbel may have been on the Nazis' hit list because he was a member of the Czechoslovak political elite. But he also could have been on it because he was born Jewish. Burick says she is sure that Madeleine and her Zionist friend did not discuss the Körbel heritage. "She would have told me," Burick says.[5]

Albright says today that she does not have a strong memory of the afternoon and does not remember if she even saw Novák, whom she has since learned was related to her. Their grandmothers, she says, were sisters. But she does remember being terribly upset at the news that her father had been tried in absentia. She says also that she never questioned her parents' explanation of how her grandparents died in the war.[6]

The Americans had another errand while they were in Prague. Frank Gotlieb, a fellow graduate student at Columbia and also a Czech, had asked them to take a present to his father, a second violinist with the Prague symphony orchestra. Steve and Marcia went to Symphony Hall to deliver the gift. When the musician was not there, they left it for him. That evening, he came by the hotel to thank them. He found the four friends sitting again in the lobby having a drink. The man was deferential and turned to Marcia, not Madeleine. He had brought her something very special, he said. Opening his bag, he pulled out a wooden drinking mug. "I've brought you a korbel," he said. Marcia lit up, delighted with the symbolism of the gift. "Oh my goodness," she said, "what a coinci—" Her sentence was halted in mid-word by Madeleine's sharp kick in the shin under the table. When the man had left, Marcia turned to Madeleine and asked quizzically, "Don't you think that's incredible? What a coincidence." Madeleine's reply was curt and quick. "It's not a coincidence," she snapped. The word *korbel* was old-fashioned Czech, not one that a person would use in everyday conversation. "It was like somebody saying 'Come to my house for a chalice of wine,'" Madeleine explained. It was the man's way of letting her know the authorities were aware she was Marie Jana Korbel, the daughter of a defector. She interpreted it as a warning to be cautious.[7]

13

The Demanding Professor

"Brzezinski was the single best professor I ever had."
—Madeleine Albright, February 6, 1997

GRADUATE SCHOOL IS DIFFICULT under most circumstances. For a mother with three children and a husband whose job forced the family to move every few years, it was a formidable challenge to mind and body alike. Madeleine Albright took three leaves of absence from her doctoral studies, but she finally won her Ph.D. in political science—almost thirteen years after she enrolled in 1963.

The two titans in her field at Columbia in those days were Marshall Shulman and Zbigniew Brzezinski. Shulman, a moderate Democrat and a soft-spoken, articulate man, had advised Secretary of State Dean Acheson on Soviet affairs during the Truman administration. Shulman predicted in the seventies that the Cold War would end through détente, and that the Soviet Union would evolve into a somewhat more benign world citizen. He argued that the East-West confrontation was essentially a political and economic competition, and that there was an overemphasis in the United States on military saber-rattling. Brzezinski considered such talk foolish, if not dangerous. Brzezinski, who had been born in Poland in 1929 and had grown up in France and Germany before fleeing to Canada in 1938, was a rabid anti-Communist, a hard-line Democrat with far more conservative views toward the Soviet Union and Eastern Europe than the Republican Party.

Albright found herself drawn to Brzezinski. Not only were they fellow Eastern Europeans, who shared a worldview passionately anti-Communist, but she also admired his stiletto intellect and blunt manner. He was a demanding professor who insisted that students come to class prepared. No matter how hard students worked, he always pushed them harder. His piercing eyes could wilt them in seconds. "What, where, why, how do you game this out?" he would snap, demanding clear, concise answers with absolutely no holes in the argument. "If they were proposing a policy, I wanted students to tell me how they would get it adopted, how they would get it implemented, and how they would override likely obstacles," he says. "Otherwise I would say, 'That's not a policy. It's just a wish, and I'm not interested in wishful thinking.' "[1]

He recalled his own graduate school days at Harvard when he took a seminar from Barrington Moore, a distinguished professor of social science. Most of his fellow students turned in eighty- to ninety page papers; Brzezinski's was nine pages long. "I thought, 'Oh boy, I'm going to be fried,'" Brzezinski says. "But I think I got the highest grade in the class. Moore wrote on the back, 'This is exactly the point.' That's when I learned length is no compensation for thought." It was a point Brzezinski made often in his own classes.[2]

If a student got an A in one of Brzezinski's courses, the professor wrote the student a personal note of congratulations because he gave out so few. It was considered high praise if he commented, "Hmm, that's interesting," or "Good job."[3] The whole point of the class, he says, was to teach students to stand up to him and respond: "I wasn't there to pat them on the back."[4] He rarely let a student or subordinate see him angry; rather, with biting sarcasm, he would make the person feel stupid and intellectually naked. Some hated him for his attitudes.

Albright, however, developed a thick hide and an uncanny knack for earning the respect of bosses who terrorized other subordinates. She became a favorite of Brzezinski. He respected her organizational talents and her easy manner in dealing with people. Privately, he recognized that he could be difficult and admired how skillfully she dealt with him.[5]

Their area of expertise, Eastern Europe and the Soviet Union, was clearly delineated in their minds: black and white, good and evil. America was fighting a corrupt system that they understood from direct experience.[6] The underlying assumption of the hard-liners was that accelerating the pace of military competition played to American advantages and Soviet disadvantages. They advocated forcing the pace. During the Cuban missile crisis in 1962, Brzezinski had sent a telegram to Kennedy adviser Arthur M. Schlesinger, Jr., urging dramatic action: "Any further delay in bombing missile sites fails to exploit Soviet uncertainty."[7]

It was at Columbia, as one of only a few female students in Brzezinski's class, that Albright learned that she had to be better prepared than the boys if she expected to be taken seriously.[8] "Brzezinski was the single best professor I ever had," Albright told *Time* magazine shortly after becoming secretary of state. "I took a course from him in 1965 in comparative communism. It was the best course I ever took. He just expected the most amazing things from his students. Half the assignments were in Russian. He had great respect for his students. He really drew you out. He's such a totally clear speaker. He speaks in perfect paragraphs. I learned analytical skills from him. When I was in college, I read every one of his books. He has an ability to conceptualize, but also to change his mind. I really do think that strategic thinkers who never adjust their strategy or their thinking are not useful."[9]

The period of the late 1960s was a confrontational time in American politics. Uprisings swept from one college campus to another as students protested against the country's military buildup in Vietnam; the materialism of a comfortable, status-conscious middle class; and growing problems with civil rights. College presidents found themselves pummeled both by antiwar radicals who grew their hair long and smoked pot as symbols of rebellion, and black-power advocates sporting "Afros," each group pushing its own agenda and program of studies.

Columbia University was no oasis. In May 1968, just as the deep lavender azaleas to the west of Low Library[10] were bursting into bloom, student rebels occupied five buildings for nearly six days. Led by the leftist Students for a Democratic Society and the all-black Student Afro-American Society, more than 130 people—including 12 police officers—were injured in tussles between demonstrators and police. There were 698 people, mostly students, arrested and charged with criminal trespass, resisting arrest, or both. "A majority of the university's 17,000 students and 2,500 faculty members undoubtedly shared the initial goals of the strike," reported *Time* magazine. "But many were also appalled at the hooligan tactics of the demonstrators, who had held university officials captive, broken into offices and overturned furniture."[11]

The demonstrations meant little to Albright. She was not so much antiwar as she was anti-Communist. She wrote a paper at this time comparing Marshal Tito to Ho Chi Minh, illustrating the differences in communism. She was nearing thirty, the mother of three, and married to a man who had fulfilled his military obligation. The demonstrations annoyed her. "I found

[them] a pain in the neck," Albright says today. "I don't know how else to describe it. The libraries would be closed. It was such a struggle for me to come in and leave the children. People were doing their oral exams while demonstrators were climbing in the windows. I was in a different period in my life."[12]

That spring Albright was awarded a master's degree in political science. She had spent most of the year writing her thesis on a subject of dubious interest to a campus of antiwar radicals: "The Soviet Diplomatic Service: Profile of an Elite." It was a dry, scholarly paper, some one hundred pages long, and not especially revealing, but little more could be expected. The Soviet Union was a closed society where not even first names of government leaders were printed in the newspapers. In one chapter she showed her interest in how women fared in the top ranks of Soviet diplomacy: "In spite of the fact that the Soviets were pioneers in appointing the first woman ambassador in the world, Madame Kollontai, the 111 diplomats are all men."[13]

Albright was, however, a fan of Senator Robert F. Kennedy, who entered the 1968 presidential race to challenge President Johnson's prosecution of the war in Vietnam. Albright had met Kennedy four years before when he was running for the Senate and went to *Newsday* to ask for the newspaper's endorsement. "I thought he was dedicated and smart," Albright says today. "I found him a compelling person."[14] Wini Freund says she and Albright attended a gathering on Long Island when Kennedy ran for president in 1968. "Bobby became our political hero," Freund says. "We liked his stand on civil rights and social justice."[15]

But tragedy intervened. On June 4, after winning the vital California Democratic primary, Kennedy was shot in the head after making his victory speech in the Ambassador Hotel in Los Angeles. Joe Albright, then a *Newsday* editor in New York, called Wini Freund's husband, Mike. It was after midnight. Albright asked Freund, a physician, for his professional judgment about whether he thought Kennedy could survive the head wound. Freund, a urologist, had no idea. The two families followed developments through the night and were crushed when Kennedy died. "It was a worse blow for us than when JFK was killed," says Wini Freund. "We felt very close to him."[16]

With her master's degree in hand, Albright began work on her Ph.D., a degree that would add the title "Dr." to her name, as it had to her father's more than thirty years before. For her dissertation, she chose to study the role of the press during Czechoslovakia's 1968 Prague Spring, the brief period of liberalization that was crushed by Soviet tanks on August 20, 1968, just months after it began. It pained her that on her visit to Prague the previous summer, she was too preoccupied to pay much attention to the growing dissident movement.

Yet during her research at Columbia, Albright made friends with several Czech dissidents visiting the United States. One was Jiří Dienstbier, a young, rakish journalist and ex-Communist who was working as a Radio Prague correspondent in New York. "I was asked if I could help a woman working on a doctorate on Prague Spring," Dienstbier says. "I was her unofficial consultant. It was a period of tremendous change in Czechoslovakia, and every day I expected that I would be recalled. The Communists considered me an enemy of the people. I was anti-Socialist."

Dienstbier was recalled in September 1969, but he cabled his Communist bosses to say he was taking a holiday. He sent his five-year-old son to stay with friends in North Carolina, and he and his wife took a two-month tour of America, traveling from one coast to the other. When he returned to Czechoslovakia on November 30, 1969, he was thirty-one years old. The Communist leaders took his passport, and he would not see it again until November 1989, when his old friend and colleague Vacláv Havel proclaimed the Velvet Revolution that overturned forty-one years of Communist rule.[17] Albright kept in touch with Dienstbier through the years, visiting him on her periodic trips to Prague. When Havel became president of the Czech Republic in 1989, he made Dienstbier his first foreign minister. It was Dienstbier who introduced Albright to Havel when she visited in 1990 while on a survey mission for the National Democratic Institute.

14

Crossroads

"She was the best chairman of any board I have been on before or since."
—Harry McPherson, distinguished
Washington lawyer and old-line Democrat, March 25, 1997

THE ALBRIGHTS MOVED TO WASHINGTON in late 1968, but they did not want to sell their Long Island house. Instead, they decided to rent it. One of those who came to look at it was Jean Kennedy Smith, who brought along her sister-in-law Ethel Kennedy. Madeleine was star-struck. "She was so excited that she called me up and asked me to witness the fact that the Kennedys were looking at her house," Winifred Freund says.[1]

In Washington, the Albrights purchased an elegant, three-story redbrick house, not far from the one they had before and even closer to Georgetown University. Circular stairs at the entrance set it apart from other houses on the block. With Joe's family contacts, they were soon part of the capital's glittery social circuit. They gave a counterinaugural party at their new home to mourn the ascendancy of Richard Nixon to the White House. Among the guests were Senator Edward M. Kennedy and Senator J. William Fulbright.

Like many women of her generation, Madeleine used her spare time to become involved in the local community. It was the end of the sixties, and the women's movement was grabbing headlines. The question of whether married women with children should work outside the home was a hot topic of discussion. The Albrights enrolled the twins in the Beauvoir Elementary School, one of the capital's elite private elementary schools on the grounds of Washington's National Cathedral, atop Mt. St. Albans, overlooking the city. Madeleine decided to devote her spare time to the school.

She joined Beauvoir's board of trustees in 1968 and later became its first female board chairman.[2] "She was the best chairman of any board I have been on before or since," says Harry McPherson, who worked as White House counsel in the Johnson administration. "She had intellectual grasp, financial acumen, and political savvy, even though we failed at what we were ultimately trying to do."[3]

What they were trying to do was not easy. With the backing of Beauvoir principal Frances Borders, who led the school from 1965 to 1979, Albright and McPherson waged an uphill campaign to change the structure of Beauvoir. "I was interested in using teaching approaches that would engage children more," Borders says. "There was a rigidity, and children did not fit in as individuals. Madeleine bought into this." They wanted to expand the school and shape the curriculum according to the theories of Jean Piaget.[4]

Borders had introduced Albright to the writings of the distinguished Swiss psychologist, who made enormous contributions to understanding the intellectual development of children. In the late 1950s and 1960s, when English translations of Piaget's works became available in the United States, educators concerned about a crisis in American education studied his theories for fresh ideas.[5]

Piaget believed that a child's way of structuring reality is different from that of an adult, and that a child goes through a fixed sequence of stages in the process of learning.[6] One of Piaget's conclusions was that until children finish the third stage of childhood, between the ages of ten and eleven, they live in a phase of innocence and fantasy that is utterly fresh. "Piaget believed that if you teach children as young innocents, you should keep them in the same environment until they make this change naturally," McPherson says, "and that if you take them out of a benign, sweet-spirited, and permissive environment and put them in a hard-nose, get-the-answer-and-get-it-now atmosphere before they make this natural change, you do them a disservice." In other words, an environment where a child could be free to experiment until the age of eleven would be more beneficial to children than a highly structured environment.

Beauvoir classes went from kindergarten through third grade. It was considered a preparatory school for the other two schools that share the Cathedral grounds—St. Albans for boys and the National Cathedral School for girls. Both have challenging standards and rigorous expectations that make the schools enormously competitive, an atmosphere that puts an exacting pressure on parents as well as children.

Borders and Albright were convinced that by expanding Beauvoir to kindergarten through fifth grade, the younger children would thrive in a more relaxed, nurturing atmosphere. "There is a change in kids at that time which marks the beginning of the phase beyond early childhood," Borders says. "It also gives children a chance to develop leadership skills in school, which is helpful to children below them. We thought that with an extra two years, they would be better supported to move to higher grades."[7]

McPherson says the plan failed, not for lack of academic merit but because St. Albans and the National Cathedral School did not want to give up the financial contributions they received from parents and grandparents of younger students.[8]

Albright was more successful on other school fronts. She worked to diversify the student population, which had been almost entirely white. "When I arrived here in 1965, you didn't try to have more than a token black in every nursery school class," Borders says.

As a board chairman, Albright demanded the participation of her all-volunteer trustees. When they did not attend meetings, she was not hesitant to approach them, even if they were well-known Washington personalities, to suggest that either they resign to make room for someone who could make a real contribution to the school or start attending meetings. Jack Valenti, a former Lyndon Johnson aide, who became the premier lobbyist for the motion picture industry, was among those who were given the choice.[9] Valenti acknowledges the reprimand. "I was traveling a lot at the time, and I was an absentee board member," he says.[10]

In another victory, Albright succeeded in convincing the board to form two classes at each grade level to allow room to accept siblings of children who were already enrolled. "I admired and appreciated her style of thinking on the board," says Borders. "She was a very honest woman and didn't avoid dealing with issues and dealing with them forthrightly."[11]

The years were restive ones for Joe. In the summer of 1968, Harry Guggenheim's health began to decline. He blamed his problems on a combination of hepatitis and arthritis, but he had also been diagnosed with prostate cancer.[12]

And he was irate over the publication of the book *Naked Came the Stranger,* the literary creation of a group of *Newsday* reporters, who wrote the novel as a spoof intending to lampoon best-selling authors Harold Robbins and Jacqueline Susann. The cabal of reporters and editors each wrote a steamy chapter and put them together under the pseudonym "Penelope Ashe." The cover featured the derrière of a well-proportioned, naked woman. The concoction shot up the best-seller list before an Associated

Press reporter, who knew the authors, unveiled the true identities of "Penelope Ashe."[13] One chapter featured a character with a not-so-subtle likeness to Captain Harry. It read: "Meet the Baron. Tired Old Tycoon . . . Hardhearted invalid . . . He found a new use for his wheelchair when . . . Naked Came the Stranger."[14] The results were instantaneous. "Harry went ballistic and wanted to know who wrote it," says Jim Toedtman. "Moyers didn't know, and it was the beginning of the end for him."

Within a year, the relationship between Harry Guggenheim and Bill Moyers was strained almost to the breaking point. While they had long differed politically, there was growing skepticism in the country about President Nixon's strategy to end the Vietnam war. Guggenheim was convinced his own paper, under Moyers' editorial control, was out to get Nixon, and he was particularly displeased by *Newsday*'s coverage of the Vietnam Moratorium, a nationwide demonstration against the war that was held on October 15, 1969. He wrote a memo to Moyers saying that *Newsday* had been "sucked into the deception perpetrated by the organizers of the Moratorium. . . . Our left-wing city room accepted the propaganda without question."[15]

That fall, Guggenheim had what Moyers thought was a small stroke. The following August, Captain Harry suffered a major one. As his health deteriorated, his personality became more difficult and his paranoia increased. He decided to sell *Newsday* to the Times Mirror Company, which owned the *Los Angeles Times*.[16] A condition for the sale was that Moyers would leave, Toedtman says. Employees hoped the Albright family, which held 49 percent of the stock in *Newsday,* would buy the paper. A note, tacked to a newsroom bulletin board, read: "Pray for Joe."[17]

Josephine Albright, Joe's mother, returned from a trip to Italy and called Harry, her brother-in-law, several times, but he could not be persuaded to change his mind. "Your children are all New Left," he said, "and I don't approve of that." When Guggenheim reached an agreement with Otis Chandler, publisher of the *Los Angeles Times,* Joe Albright appealed to Chandler to let him run the paper. Chandler turned him down. "He was not of my style," Chandler said.[18] With no chance of a family member in charge, the Albrights sold their stake in the newspaper to the Times Mirror Company. For their minority 49 percent, Times Mirror offered a combination of common stock and convertible preferred stock totaling $37.5 million— about $5 million more than Captain Harry got for his 51 percent. On October 27, 1970, the paper was turned over to the fast-growing West Coast chain.[19] In March 1971, a decade after he had come to the paper, Joe Albright announced his resignation. It became effective that April.[20]

*   *   *

In September 1971, Eduard Goldstücker visited Josef and Mandula Korbel in Colorado. Korbel had invited his old Czech colleague and friend to lecture at the University of Denver. But when Goldstücker arrived, Korbel was in the hospital, recuperating from an operation for stomach ulcers.[21] "I visited with him in the hospital," Goldstücker said. The two men never met again.

From the Wellesley Class of 1959 Record Book for 1974

Korbel, Madeleine
Mrs. Joseph Albright
Husband: Journalist (Williams 1958)
Children: Alice (12½), Anne (12½), Katie (6½)

Chairman, Governing Board, Beauvoir School, Washington, DC.; member Board of Trustees Negro Student Fund; Opera Society of Washington.

"My life has been a combination of working on my Ph.D. dissertation in Political Science at Columbia, raising our children, various Board work, and fund raising for Political candidates, not necessarily in that order. The combination is great, hectic, satisfying and it seems to work."

15

A Demanding Senator

"He was a wonderful example of an American public servant. He had his head screwed on right. But he was tough. There was no question about it."
—Madeleine Albright, February 6, 1997

HARRY MCPHERSON had known Madeleine Albright for several years and was impressed with her fund-raising ability at Beauvoir. Like Pamela and Averell Harriman, other wealthy Democrats whose social connections helped them raise money for the party, the Albrights had a wide circle of well-heeled friends. McPherson, a close Muskie adviser, asked her to help out with a fund-raising dinner for Maine senator Edmund S. Muskie, the front-runner for the Democratic presidential nomination in 1972.[1] Sheppie Abromowitz, who was working on issues research for Muskie, encouraged Albright to accept. "It's such an endless mess, those dinners," Abromowitz says. "Madeleine had a committee of Cleveland Park matrons. They sold tickets, made telephone calls, did the tables. Madeleine really knew how to do it."[2]

Four years before, Muskie had been on the ticket with Vice President Hubert H. Humphrey, who stepped in as Johnson's surrogate when the president decided not to seek reelection. Even after they were beaten by Richard Nixon, Muskie emerged on the national scene as a level-headed, reliable politician with a reputation as a strong campaigner.

Before the 1972 primary season, Muskie had been anointed by the press as a favorite to defeat Humphrey and Senator George McGovern of South Dakota in the race for the Democratic nomination. George Wallace, a

Southern Democrat, was running a populist campaign in hopes of gaining a broker's role at the convention. Four years after antiwar sentiment had pushed Johnson off the ballot, the Vietnam war continued to drain the nation's energy and patience, and antiwar protests were still gathering momentum. The race actually had been shaped in the first summer of Nixon's presidency, when a young Senator Edward M. Kennedy, the last surviving Kennedy brother, drove his car off a bridge at Chappaquiddick Island, drowning a young woman who had worked in Bobby's campaign. The ensuing questions about Kennedy's character—he admitted he panicked and left the scene of the accident with the woman trapped inside her submerged car—took him out of contention and sent Muskie's stock shooting up. The Maine senator's loyalist staff had a small button printed that said "FMBTB"—For Muskie Before the Bridge. Madeleine was FMBTB. She worked out of Muskie's campaign headquarters at 1972 K Street in downtown Washington with a bright, enthusiastic team. "Essentially, she was an intern, volunteering," says Leon Billings, an environmental expert and senior adviser to Muskie.[3]

For young women entering the job market today, internships represent the kind of summer jobs they get when they are twenty and twenty-one, offering a gofer's eye view of an organization that is often more important to building a résumé than it is interesting. In 1972, Albright was thirty-five years old, a mother, and entering the workplace for the first time.[4]

When Muskie lost his temper—and his political footing—in the New Hampshire primary and dropped out of the presidential race, Madeleine was asked to stay on to work for his Senate staff. But as her children were still small—the twins, eleven; Katie, five—and she was continuing to work on her doctoral dissertation, she signed up as a part-time volunteer. "I think of Madeleine in the context of my late wife, who was often passed over for jobs," says Billings. "These are women who stayed home with their families in the 1960s and had an enormously difficult time reentering [the job market] and reestablishing themselves. What is remarkable about Madeleine is that she was not only able to enter but that she has been so successful. This is a Cinderella story."[5]

In 1975, Muskie began laying the groundwork for reelection to a third term in the Senate. A young Maine congressman, William Cohen,[6] an up-and-coming first-term lawmaker who had impressed independent-minded Maine voters when he was one of the few brave Republicans in the House Judiciary Committee to vote to impeach Richard Nixon, was seen as a potential threat. Muskie had been preoccupied with his presidential campaign, and staffers worried that he had not spent as much energy as usual on state business. Fearing that voters might turn on him, Muskie's staff urged the senator to devote more attention to Maine. Muskie beefed up constituent services, such as responding to inquiries and answering the mail, and set out to increase his base of campaign donors.[7]

He turned to Albright, who had already proved her mettle at political fund-raising. He liked the way she worked through problems in an orderly way, and she seemed to have the capacity to present issues in a succinct fashion.[8] In May 1975, Alan Platt, who had served for two and a half years as Muskie's legislative assistant for foreign and defense policy, left the staff. When Albright came to work, she assumed much of his portfolio.[9]

Although her specialty was foreign affairs, Albright acted as a generalist, overseeing such domestic issues as the postal service, health, aging, welfare, social security, and political affairs.[10] In fact, during Albright's time with Muskie, the senator devoted less time to foreign policy issues than he had previously. He had secured a seat on the Senate Foreign Relations Committee in 1971, when he began to think seriously about making a run for the presidency and realized he needed greater experience in foreign policy. Arkansas senator William Fulbright, chairman of the Foreign Relations Committee, assigned Muskie to head the subcommittee on European Affairs. In 1973, Muskie moved to the subcommittee on Arms Control and International Law and Organization, where he served as chairman until January 1975, when he became head of the Senate Budget Committee. The result was that in the last half of the 1970s, Muskie devoted most of his energies to budget and environmental issues.[11]

Nonetheless, Albright remained busy. In addition to handling various domestic policy issues, she directed the legislative section of the senator's office and coordinated legislation with the various Senate committee staffs. She was responsible for approving all "Dear Colleague" letters from Muskie to other members of Congress, as well as overseeing all issues correspondence and general floor action.[12]

Muskie was a man with old-fashioned values who was not used to dealing with women as professionals. As a member of a Senate staff of more than fifty people, which included several subcommittees, Albright was one of only two women in a senior position. Most of the male staffers were in their thirties.[13] Albright, a mother of three daughters, was pushing forty.

If this bothered her, she did not let it show, and she never complained. While many of her friends were taking up the battle cry of the women's movement, demanding equal pay and access to jobs and careers they had long been denied, Albright was more inclined to blend in, to laugh at the jokes of her male colleagues, to put them at ease by not challenging them.

"Madeleine never had any trouble being one of the boys," says Leon Billings. "It was clearly a man's world, and the women who were effective in that world participated rather than protested."[14] Albright participated.

The American workplace was becoming a confusing battleground for the sexes in the mid-1970s. Most men and many women had little understanding of the women's movement. If anything, they were put off by the stridency of feminist leaders, who called on women to shed their bras, stop shaving their legs, and take to the streets to demand equality. More important and far more central to the issues they confronted was the fact that many men and women were threatened by the idea of women thinking of themselves as equals. "It was asking for trouble to be a feminist at this time," says Cokie Roberts, an ABC correspondent who graduated from Wellesley in 1964, five years after Albright. "You had to show you were one of the guys. To be a feminist was threatening. This was a very unsettled time."[15]

The sputtering economy unsettled it more. High inflation, high interest rates, and stagnant growth forced millions of couples who once planned to live on a single paycheck to recalculate and conclude that the only way to maintain their standard of living was for both spouses to go to work.

Emily MacFarquhar, a close friend of Albright's from their Wellesley days, says that she and Albright used to argue about feminism. Unlike Albright and many others in their college class who had married directly after graduation, MacFarquhar had gone to London to pursue a career as a journalist. She believed in the issues that the feminist movement represented. "I was a more committed feminist," says MacFarquhar. "In Madeleine's initial years, she didn't experience what she thought was any gender discrimination. She didn't feel it with Muskie or on the National Security Council. Gender didn't hit her in any real way until she got to the United Nations. Feminism wasn't an important cause for her until recently."[16]

When Muskie hired Albright, there were not only few women in senior positions in his office, but there were not many anywhere on Capitol Hill, especially in the field of foreign policy. The most prominent were Sally Shelton, who handled foreign affairs for Senator Lloyd Bentsen of Texas; Paula Stern for Senator Gaylord Nelson of Wisconsin; and Dorothy Fosdick for Senator Henry M. "Scoop" Jackson of Washington. "The rest were men, and when you looked at the State Department and the National Security Council, there were virtually no women," says Sally Shelton, who later married CIA chief William Colby. "It was a tough period."[17]

So tough, in fact, that when, in February 1975, *New York Times* columnist William Safire wrote a piece on the solidity of the "old boys' network," he came up with only three women who might measure up: Shelton; Jessica Einhorn, a junior officer in the monetary office at the Treasury Department (and now top financial officer at the World Bank); and Doris Kearns, who had worked in the Johnson White House and was then professor of government at Harvard. "Like the old boys, the new boys admire girls but not as professional associates," Safire wrote.[18]

Albright tested that standard as a member of Muskie's staff. Though Muskie might have been an "old boy" and may have harbored some old-boy chauvinism, he was a man of great integrity who treated his staff—men and women alike—with respect. "The good and the bad was he treated everyone equally," says Alan Platt. "There were some senators whom I would describe as politically incorrect or who might have made sexual advances on their staff. That was not an issue with Muskie. He was difficult because he was demanding of all staff."[19] Albright later acknowledged that Muskie's commitment to treating all aides—old, new, male, female—with parity provided her with a sense of standing and self-assurance that would be crucial to her subsequent success.[20]

As Albright discovered, however, equal treatment from Muskie was a mixed blessing. He had a well-earned reputation as one of the most difficult senators to work for on Capitol Hill, a man with a sharp mind, infused with a volcanic temper.[21] Muskie required his staff to organize material succinctly, to assemble enough background material to answer any question he might raise, and he tested people with a third degree. The challenge was to survive his brutal interrogation.[22] "Ed Muskie intimidated everyone, and he made almost everyone cry, including yours truly," says Leon Billings. "He would yell and scream and swear. He had the capacity to be so overbearing that you could leave a room questioning your own parentage, not just his." Billings says that Muskie had legislative assistants who were afraid to be in the same room with him and would communicate with him only by memo. But not Madeleine. She briefed Muskie regularly, patiently outlining the issues and explaining how the votes from other senators lined up. "I don't think I ever saw Madeleine blush," says Billings. "I don't think I ever saw Madeleine intimidated. I don't think I ever saw Madeleine cry."[23]

That is only because she kept her emotions under control in the office. Many men considered women too emotional to hold positions of responsibility. Tears would have merely confirmed their conviction. "She would have killed herself before she would cry in front of Leon Billings," says Anita Jensen, who worked for Muskie as a legislative aide and shared a back-room office with Albright. But Muskie could be relentless. He engaged in a charade with his staff that sometimes bordered on warfare, insisting that aides were forcing him to go to too many places and participate in unnecessary events. No one took him seriously, of course, but his diatribes could be exhausting. Muskie would yell: "What do you think I am—a tube of toothpaste that you can just squeeze and squeeze and squeeze?"[24]

Occasionally, when the assault of insults was too much for anyone to handle, Albright would retreat to the office bathroom in tears. It was not just Muskie's temper tantrums but the ambience of oversized male egos that would regularly collide as each staff member insisted that his or her issue take precedence. "The boys were always lifting their legs and saying 'This is my territory,'" says Jensen. "It was a pain-in-the-ass environment for a lot of us, trust me. But you weren't allowed to say anything because, one, it wasn't done, and two, you wanted to keep your job. Madeleine handled it very well. I never saw her become hysterical, and I can't say the same thing about myself."[25]

When they had had enough, Albright and Jensen would retire to the Senate cafeteria, which they dubbed the Pink Palace. Albright would have coffee; Jensen, a cigarette.[26]

What made Albright different? What emotional or intellectual armor did she possess that allowed her not only to stand her ground with Big Ed but thrive in the process? "For Madeleine to hold her own in that environment is reflective of a fairly secure personality and a fairly intelligent approach," Jensen says. "I won't say she was never upset by the guys. It was impossible not to be upset by them at least once in a while. But I don't think she ever allowed it to undermine her sense of who she was. She could make a clear distinction between what was work and what was game playing." Billings says Albright liked the challenge of engaging in political discussions with Muskie.[27] Though he might tear into people, he did it on intellectual, not personal, grounds.[28] "I honest to God believe she enjoyed it," Billings says. "Muskie was a towering intellect. To be able to hold your ground against him was very energizing."[29]

Albright also fared well with Muskie because her thought processes and style of thinking appealed to his independent mind. Albright was a practical thinker. "She's not inclined toward big abstract theories, and she's very operationally oriented and achievement-oriented," says Platt. For his part, Muskie was also a somewhat unpredictable thinker. He did not always follow the straight, liberal line. Instead, says Platt, "he listened to different arguments at different times and decided as he saw it how to go."[30]

Albright has her own view of why she was able to work well with such a demanding personality and how it shaped her. "The fact that I wasn't twenty-five years old when I worked for Muskie made it a little easier," she says. "He always yelled about things to me rather than yelling at me. We had a great relationship. He admitted to me that he used his temper as a device. His questioning followed such a line that it made you realize that you had to have all your facts before you ever went in there."[31]

Albright had no personal agenda to push, but it would not have mattered if she had. Muskie demanded that his staff members reflect his agenda, not their own. But he liked people who came up with new ideas or unusual ways of looking at issues. If an aide wanted Muskie to act on an issue, he or she would submit a one-page paper outlined in a way that the senator could absorb it quickly. If Muskie decided to act on the proposal, he invited the person into his office, which was dubbed the "lion's den." Muskie would sit at his desk and grill the individual with every question he could think of.[32] "No matter how well you were prepared on a subject, he always pushed you further and harder," says Platt.[33] "He had a great ability to get to the core of things and push his staff members beyond what they thought they knew or could do."[34]

Sometimes Albright burrowed into the complex issues herself in order to brief her boss; at other times, she relied on specialists on her staff. In October 1977, when the landmark *University of California* vs. *Bakke* affirmative action case was before the Supreme Court, Albright studied the intricacies of the issues in order to brief Muskie and endure the inevitable grilling. "She was ready and anxious to get up to speed on everything, including things like this that she had no reason to be familiar with," Jensen says.[35]

At another point, Albright was summoned to brief Muskie on Senate efforts to expand Medicaid to cover abortion in cases of rape, incest, or health risks to the mother. Albright, who had been raised Roman Catholic and converted to Episcopalianism, was pro-choice. Muskie, a Roman Catholic, was generally obdurate on the subject of abortion, and this discussion made him grumpier than usual. "What health risks to the mother?" he demanded. Albright buzzed Anita Jensen, who had handled the details of the case, and asked her to come into Muskie's office. "Senator Muskie wants further examples of the kind of health issues that can arise," Albright explained. Jensen began to list them, starting with kidney failure and high blood pressure. "High blood pressure?" Muskie bellowed. "I have high blood pressure. What about hangnails?" Albright looked at Jensen. Jensen looked back. They did not have to exchange words.[36]

It was in foreign affairs that Albright was most comfortable. In September 1977, she wrote a memorandum to Muskie recommending that he lead a congressional delegation to the Middle East, but she warned him that in "discreet conversations with those not directly involved with Capitol Hill, we have found what we might call 'pitfalls' of the trip." The delegation, she wrote, should make clear that it would not negotiate for President Carter, who sets U.S. foreign policy. Also, she told Muskie that if he decided to make the trip, there would be considerable press coverage. To keep himself out of trouble and avoid embarrassing headlines, he should be careful how he answered questions about the possibility of a Middle East settlement and a Palestinian homeland. "Too much talking during the trip might prove damaging," she wrote. Muskie must also realize that his answers would be scrutinized both in the United States and abroad. "The maintenance of impartiality will be difficult at best," she said. "There are so many more Arab countries to visit. Arab hospitality is legendary, and Israeli abrasiveness lives up to its advance billing. It is apparently difficult not to be overwhelmed by an Arab campaign of appearing reasonable."[37]

Despite the controversy that it generated, the women's movement was gaining in strength and numbers, as well as political clout. Jimmy Carter, who had defeated Gerald Ford for the presidency in 1976, was eager to appoint women to visible posts in his administration. The Foreign Service was no exception. In most cases, the State Department jobs traditionally open to women were in cultural affairs, public relations, or personnel. After Sally Shelton was offered a middle-level policy position in Latin American affairs, a male Foreign Service officer approached her and asked, "Why do you want to work as a deputy assistant secretary? You'll never be taken seriously. Wouldn't you be more interested in the Bureau of Cultural Affairs?" She shrugged and laughed. "That was indicative of the climate in which we worked at the time," she says. "My colleagues were almost all men, and nobody questioned their qualifications."[38]

Partially as a result of her own perseverance, partially because of the emerging clout of the women's movement, Albright was beginning to blossom in Washington. Unfortunately, her father, her hero and lifelong mentor, was not able to enjoy her success. After being ill for several years, Josef Korbel died of pancreatic cancer in Denver's Rose Memorial Hospital in July 1977. He was sixty-seven. "I was devastated," Albright says today. "I still am devastated. Every day I wish my father was alive to see what is going on."[39]

What struck Albright about her father was that once he started his life over in America, he did not retreat to the past. "I remember going to the Library of Congress to do research, and there were little old people there, older men, who were doing work in the Slavic section," Albright says. "They kept calling each other 'Your Excellency' and saying, 'As I have said to Beneš . . .' They were living in the politics of émigré groups. My father moved to Denver and started a new life and did not look back. I used to ask him, 'Are you sorry?' And he said, 'Never, I love teaching. I love this country. I never think I have done the wrong thing.'"[40]

Josef Korbel was occasionally more revealing about his fate with colleagues who shared some of his experiences. Several years before he died, Korbel visited the University of Wisconsin in Madison for a two-day conference. Over lunch at the faculty club with two fellow East European scholars, the group discussed their war experiences. One was Michael Petrovich, a University of Wisconsin professor. The other was Milan Radovich, the university's librarian, a Yugoslav, who was jailed from 1948 to 1953 for his opposition to communism. "He [Korbel] said that because he was known as a Jew, he would have been in the first group of the Nazi liquidation," says Radovich. "He said he would have been in the first phase because he was a political opponent of the Nazis and a good friend of the Czech democratic leaders. . . . I remember his firm statement that he would not have survived as a Jew. Those were his exact words."[41]

Friends, family, colleagues, and students remembered Korbel warmly at a memorial service held by the Graduate School of International Studies on July 20, 1977. Former students praised him as a scholar, teacher, and human being, a man of "unsurpassed integrity and genuine human compassion."[42] One student remarked that Korbel "is probably the finest human being I have met. He is surely the most worthy of emulation, yet truly impossible to emulate."[43] Recalling Korbel's experiences in Czechoslovakia and his decision to flee his homeland, colleague and editor Russ Porter observed: "Only men and women of infinite resources of spirit, of resiliency and spiritual strength beyond the understanding of those of us who have lived so easily and so safely for so long, could emerge from such losses of country and home and family relationships and fortunes and remain so apparently unscarred. That was the price that Josef Korbel and his family paid for our rich privilege."[44] Korbel, said Porter, "taught us to appreciate a little the dearness of great freedom. He taught us that a love for this country is neither a shibboleth nor chauvinism."[45]

Yet with all the effusive tributes, it was Mandula Korbel who summed up her husband's life most simply, and most poignantly. In the personal essay she wrote as a tribute to her husband of forty-two years, she did her best to capture the essence of Josef Korbel: "On [a] high mountain near Denver is a little cemetery and there on the wall of a mausoleum is a plaque with the name: Josef Korbel. 1909–1977. Maybe one day somebody will wonder who was this man with such [an] unusual spelling and why was he buried in the mountain in Colorado.

"Well, I would like to write something about him, because his life was rather unusual, even more unusual than the spelling. He is buried in the mountain, because he loved the nature, because he loved fishing, because it was in Colorado where he spent many happy years after an active life in many different countries and fields. He used to say often, I was in so many glorious jobs but to be a college teacher in a free country is what I am enjoying best."

16

The White House

"My chronological age and my professional age never matched, maybe until now. I was always older than I should have been for the job because it took me longer to do it."

—Madeleine Albright, February 7, 1998

MADELEINE ALBRIGHT ENJOYED her work with Ed Muskie, but the surprising political fortune of the Democratic Party would soon carry her to 1600 Pennsylvania Avenue. Jimmy Carter, a former naval officer, businessman, peanut farmer, and one-term governor of Georgia, narrowly defeated incumbent Gerald R. Ford in the 1976 presidential election. Carter capitalized on the anger and distrust that Americans felt toward the federal government in the years following Vietnam and Watergate and campaigned as an outsider, a man who would fix the vexing problems in Washington. He promised in his inaugural address to "adjust to changing times and still hold to unchanging principles." Following the ceremony, in a gesture intended to portray him as a man of the people, he led the parade in a dramatic walk down Pennsylvania from the Capitol to the White House.[1]

But if Carter's anti-Washington sentiments appealed to voters, they won him few allies in Congress once he got to the White House. Carter's failure to develop a friendly and productive working relationship with Democrats and Republicans on Capitol Hill threatened both his domestic and foreign policy agendas.[2]

Albright was a Democrat with Capitol Hill experience, exactly the kind of person Carter needed to help coordinate relations with Congress. The president had tapped Zbigniew Brzezinski, Albright's graduate school professor and mentor at Columbia, to serve as his national security adviser and direct the National Security Council staff, a group made up largely of promising young careerists from the State Department, Pentagon, and intelligence community.[3] The official job of the national security adviser is to present foreign policy options to the president, but recent advisers—McGeorge Bundy for John F. Kennedy, Walt Rostow for Lyndon Johnson, Henry Kissinger in the Nixon administration—had expanded the role and helped develop policy.[4] Over the years, the NSC has advised the president on some of the most serious threats facing the United States from abroad, such as the Cuban missile crisis in 1962, the war in Vietnam, and the Cambodian attack on the American ship *Mayaguez* in 1975. During Brzezinski's tenure, the council's toughest challenges would be Iran's seizure of fifty-two American diplomats in Tehran and the Soviet Union's invasion of Afghanistan.

Brzezinski had only a textbook understanding of Capitol Hill[5] and realized, after a year punctuated with missteps, that he needed the support of someone with knowledge of congressional operations. Who better than Albright, a former student who had worked on the Hill? It was a natural match. In March 1978, a year into the administration, Brzezinski invited Albright to serve as the NSC's congressional liaison. It was an opportunity, he says, "she grabbed with both hands."[6] Albright agrees. "Despite the fact that it was a man's world, I was so glad to be there," she says. "The truth about me is that I am always grateful to be doing what I am doing. I'm not a person who wishes I were someone I am not or who is dissatisfied with what I am doing. The idea of being in the White House was great."[7]

Albright had distinguished herself on Muskie's staff as a hard worker. She had developed a good understanding of domestic legislation under consideration on Capitol Hill and recognized that foreign policy issues were negotiable commodities for members of Congress, that frequently they would be willing to trade votes on foreign matters of little interest to their constituents for support on projects closer to home.[8]

Albright learned quickly that working at the White House was less glamorous than it sounded. She was given a cubbyhole of an office in the basement of the West Wing, a few steps from the Situation Room. She even had to share it with another aide. But White House office space is the most fought over real estate in the country, and the location pleased her. Like staffers in every administration, she would have preferred a desk in a White House washroom to a sunny suite in the spacious Old Executive Office Building next door. Echoing her father's view almost thirty years before at the Paris Peace Conference, when he tried to snag a hotel room closer to key negotiators, Albright told interviewers that a West Wing office "makes a tremendous difference. There's no way you can underestimate the importance of proximity"[9] to the president.

Albright was a shy, almost awkward woman when she arrived at the NSC. Christine Dodson, who worked as Brzezinski's administrative officer, found the new staffer hesitant to speak up or express her opinions. Policy meetings in Brzezinski's office often included not only his key staff but any number of individuals who ranked lower than Albright. Yet many of them had sharper elbows when it came to spending time with the boss. Albright hesitated to attend meetings without an explicit invitation, even if she was expected to be there. For that reason, she often arrived late. "There would be a knock at the door," says Dodson. "It would open, and there would be Madeleine, usually with a little sweater over her shoulders and holding a set of papers. She would literally ask, 'May I come in?'"[10]

Dodson took it upon herself to push Albright to be more assertive.[11] There was only one other woman on the NSC roster, and she was considerably younger. So partly because they were the same age, Albright and Dodson became fast friends. One morning Dodson was sitting in her office reading the *Washington Post* when she came across a story about a reception for the National Symphony. The co-chairs were listed as "Mr. and Mrs. Joseph Medill Patterson Albright." Dodson was amused. She had learned that Madeleine's husband was named Joe Albright, but that was all she knew about him. Taking the newspaper with her, she walked to Madeleine's basement office and showed her the page. "Isn't this a coincidence?" she asked. "He has the same first and last names as Joe." Madeleine got a funny look on her face. "It's not you, is it?" Dodson asked in surprise. "Yes, it is," Madeleine said softly, and she started to cry. Touched by her friend's reluctance to flaunt her Social Register status, Christine burst into tears as well. "How could you not tell me?" she asked. Madeleine's reply: "There was no reason to. I'm sorry."

Christine smiled. "Don't be sorry," she said. "It must mean, among other things, that you have a lot of money." Madeleine smiled back. "We do,"[12] she said. Dodson was impressed that Albright felt no need to brag about her social life at the office, an unusual trait in the world of Washington politics, where self-importance and name-dropping are acquired skills. Along the corridors of power it is not unusual for people to decorate their offices *and* their homes with photographs of themselves and recognizable personalities. (The more informal the pose and the more intimate the inscription, the better. Receiving-line pictures are déclassé, conveying the impression that one has no more status than a ten-second handshake.)

Carter had first met Brzezinski when he was governor of Georgia and

Brzezinski was director of the Trilateral Commission, an organization of prominent figures in government, business, and academia from the United States, Canada, Western Europe, and Japan. The group's goal was to foster economic stability by promoting cooperation among the world's capitalist powers. As director, Brzezinski was responsible for recruiting members. Among those selected was the promising young governor of Georgia.[13]

Brzezinski was a natural choice as national security adviser. The Columbia scholar thought in broad geopolitical terms and provided Carter with an overarching philosophical framework within which to organize his relatively narrow understanding of global politics.[14] Though Carter was determined to establish the direction of foreign policy and set priorities himself, he wanted Brzezinski to play the role of the idea man and the NSC to provide the strategic analysis.[15] For the top spot at the State Department, Carter selected Cyrus Vance, an Establishment lawyer who had served as a U.S. negotiator during the Vietnam peace talks. If Carter respected Brzezinski's intellect and academic credentials, he was drawn to Vance for his precision, attention to detail, and knack for problem solving.[16] Though Carter respected Vance's diplomatic skills, he selected him for the top post at State largely because he thought he would be a strong manager and team player who would loyally pursue the policies originating from the White House.[17] Brzezinski would be the strategist; Vance, the tactician.

Brzezinski was a demanding boss. He required each staffer to write a one- to two-page report for him every day before leaving work. Failure to do so was grounds for dismissal. He expected his staff to keep him informed of potential problems, as well as any press contacts they had had that day. "It put the burden on them to keep me informed, and it also controlled my understanding of leaks," Brzezinski says. Like a college professor, he would write in the margins: "OK," "well done," or "come see me."[18]

Jimmy Carter, who made no pretense of his discomfort with the capital's elite establishment, thought he had achieved a neat balance between intellectualism and professionalism when he selected Brzezinski and Vance to be his chief foreign policy advisers. The reality, however, was that the three men failed to map out a clear demarcation of their roles in the foreign policy apparatus. The muddling of the division of authority between the State Department and the NSC had disastrous consequences. Vance and Brzezinski, men of different temperaments and different skills, frequently offered Carter conflicting advice. With only limited background himself in foreign affairs, Carter often ended up vacillating.[19]

The turf war between Vance and Brzezinski reflected the broader tension that existed within the Democratic Party over the direction of the administration's foreign policy. Vance represented the liberal wing of the party, the chief spokesmen of which were Muskie and Carter's vice president, Walter Mondale. A gentleman of the old school, Vance believed that the United States and the Soviet Union possessed mutual interests that should be used as a starting point for building diplomatic relations.[20] Vance felt that trust could be built step by step and favored emphasizing those areas in which the two powers had overlapping interests, such as arms control.[21] He was more interested in negotiation than the projection of power and talked openly of the need to learn lessons from Vietnam.[22]

Brzezinski spoke for the more conservative and hawkish element of the Democratic Party. Born in Poland and raised in Canada from the age of ten, he attended McGill University and came to the United States to do graduate work at Harvard. His wife, Muska (Wellesley '53), was the grandniece of former Czechoslovak president Eduard Beneš. Brzezinski's personal and academic connections to East European history influenced his conception of world politics. He felt that Vance's stance toward the Soviet Union was naive,[23] and he argued that Moscow was a global troublemaker. Progress toward détente and strategic arms limitations should be the reward for better behavior, not the starting point of American foreign policy.[24]

The battle between Brzezinski and Vance played itself out in several foreign policy areas, but particularly during negotiations with the Soviet Union over the SALT II Treaty. Vance was a primary proponent of the treaty, which called for some limitations on the development of nuclear weapons, while Brzezinski had some reservations about Vance's approach.[25] Presented with conflicting advice, Carter waffled.

If Vance and Brzezinski were ideological foes, they were polar opposites in style as well. Vance was soft-spoken and polite. Brzezinski was adversarial, a brusque man with a penchant for self-promotion. Tension between the two was inevitable.

Albright's start at the White House was marked by a tension of its own. Brzezinski's decision to put her in charge of congressional relations did not go over well initially with some of Carter's senior domestic policy advisers, who shared a parochial view of U.S. foreign affairs. They wondered why it was necessary that the NSC have its own congressional liaison.[26] Albright herself sensed the hostility.[27] David Aaron, Brzezinski's deputy, however, wanted Albright to work in the White House because he felt that the staff of Frank Moore, who was in charge of legislative affairs, had no sense that foreign policy was important. At the president's insistence, Moore had spent so much political capital pushing the Panama Canal treaty that selling foreign aid was, as Albright put it afterward, "like trying to sell leprosy."[28] Aaron hoped Albright would be a strong spokeswoman for the NSC's interests within a White House dominated by domestic policy advisers.[29]

Despite the initial skepticism among her colleagues, Albright quickly established strong working relations with other members of the White House staff and demonstrated that she would play a useful role as congressional liaison.[30] She plunged immediately into the debate over U.S. arms sales to the Middle East, an issue that would prove pivotal to Carter's search for peace in the troubled region. The president had agreed to sell supersonic jet fighters to Israel, Egypt, and Saudi Arabia to maintain parity between the Arabs and Israel. The move incensed the American Jewish community, which had formidable political clout on Capitol Hill. To Carter, the arms sale was crucial to U.S. credibility in the Arab world. If Congress defeated the plan, it would almost certainly doom his hope of winning a peace treaty between Egypt and Israel. To placate the Jewish lobby, Carter offered an additional twenty F-15s to Israel.[31]

Albright knew that the success of the arms sale was critical to Carter's goal of achieving any peace agreement between Israel and her Arab neighbors. Talks between Israel, Egypt, and the United States eventually led to the signing in September 1978 of the Camp David Accord, one of the few shining moments of the Carter presidency. It provided for Egypt's official recognition of Israel and the return to Egypt of lands occupied by Israel during the Six-Day War in 1967.[32] Many hoped the agreement would serve as a framework of peace for the Middle East that would end three decades of hostilities between Israel and the Arab world.[33]

During the debate over the arms sale, Albright worked with Brian Atwood, the State Department's congressional liaison, as well as colleagues at Defense, to count votes, watch for shifts in the political wind, and find issues the administration could use as bargaining chips with particular members of Congress. They gathered material for administration fact books, organized briefings for congressional staff, and helped develop legislative strategy.[34] In April, only a month after she went to work at the White House, Albright informed Brzezinski that the administration strategy was working. "Feedback from the Hill indicates that we are well out in front of the power curve on the arms package proposal and that our briefings and information packets have had a positive effect," she reported.[35] With Bob Beckel, a Democratic political adviser with excellent relations on Capitol Hill, acting as White House point man for lobbying, Albright became the tactician at the other end of the telephone, suggesting members of Congress for him to contact. She acted as an information source within the Executive

Branch for members of Congress and people in other departments. "I can't stress enough the importance of the people part of my NSC job," she said at the time. ". . . I would know which people in the departments I could work with, what kind of information they were giving them, how close they were to the source. They would know about you, too, and you develop your own network."

On May 15, 1978, after hours of debate, the Senate voted 54–44 to defeat a resolution that would have killed the arms sale.[36] Albright later reasoned that if Congress had defeated the proposed sale of aircraft, Camp David would never have taken place.[37] She also felt that her role in the process was critical. "Although I clearly cannot take credit for our foreign policy legislative victories . . . I honestly believe that my coordinating role was useful in developing an Administrative message pulling together briefings and Presidential meetings in the White House, and telephone calls to Members."[38]

Networking was a skill Madeleine Albright knew something about. Her job as congressional liaison was to coordinate an interagency legislative effort, bringing together individuals from various departments responsible for national security legislation to plan legislative strategies. She ran an interagency group on the foreign aid bill and participated in a similar committee that developed the legislative strategy for the SALT II Treaty.

Albright believed that to present the administration's views on the SALT II to Congress, she needed to learn the arcane language of arms control. With NSC staffer Karl F. Inderfurth, she signed up for a biweekly tutorial given by Roger Molander, the council's arms control expert. After eight or ten hours of classes, she could discuss the throw weight of the MIRVed missile, the range of the Soviet's Backfire bombers, and the difference between GLCMs and SLCMs[39] as well as anyone else on the NSC. "We used to quiz each other on the acronyms in the halls," Inderfurth says.[40]

Albright was responsible for advising Brzezinski on how key issues would fare in Congress. Because the NSC frequently approached issues with little regard for their domestic political ramifications, Albright tried to sensitize members of the NSC staff to the importance of the Legislative Branch, doing her best to make her colleagues aware of legislative problems and the need to track legislation.[41] It was a difficult task to get Brzezinski and his staff to consider the political implications of foreign policy choices during the decision-making process rather than after it.[42] "One of the accusations made originally about Brzezinski was the feeling that he didn't have enough of a sense how foreign policy issues played out on the Hill," Albright said when she left the White House.[43] As a way of keeping the NSC staff up to date, Albright would invite staffers to informal meetings with members of Congress and their aides. In addition, every Saturday morning she wrote a report discussing relevant legislative activities over the previous week and then distributed it to the rest of the NSC staff. Albright hoped this would reinforce the fact that the NSC "couldn't just create policy in a vacuum."[44]

In her legislative reports, Albright briefed Brzezinski on how various issues and pieces of legislation were playing out in Congress, noting the support or opposition they faced, and suggesting possible strategies to win congressional approval of the administration's foreign policy initiatives.

Unlike most official White House memoranda written in a legalistic, bureaucratic style, Albright's comments were expressed in plain-spoken English. In an April 1978 memorandum to her old professor, written after he had met with Democratic senators Patrick Leahy of Vermont and John C. Culver of Iowa, Albright reported: "Senator Culver reacted by saying that our repeated statements about Soviet strength create a perception problem. We need to build up the confidence of our allies rather than always saying the Russians are so awesome."[45]

Albright's earthy, unassuming style was sometimes tinged with sarcasm. In a November 30, 1979, memo to Brzezinski outlining Congress' reaction to Carter's initial handling of the Iran hostage crisis, Albright ended with a playful jab at Congress: "The quote of the week by Congressman Hansen: 'I support military action in Iran provided that it doesn't result in violence.' "[46]

As the months went by, Albright became more and more comfortable giving the sometimes arrogant Brzezinski advice on dealing with others. Before he was to speak to a group of high-powered Colorado businesspeople who came to Washington for a few days of briefings in March 1979, she wrote: "They are generally well read and well informed. It is important not to talk down to them."[47] In September 1980, Brzezinski was summoned to Capitol Hill to testify before the Senate Foreign Relations Committee to explain his role in the Billy Carter case, in which the president's brother accepted $220,000 from Libya's renegade dictator Muammar al-Qaddafi. Albright accompanied Brzezinski to the hearings and coached him in his responses. "This was the first time a national security adviser had to testify before Congress, and [Madeleine] was very helpful in [showing] me how to micromanage senators and how to play them," Brzezinski says. "She was very effective in guiding and helping me."[48]

It was in this job that Albright became an important link between the Carter White House and Capitol Hill, cultivating the conservative Republicans frequently ignored by many liberal Democrats. "There's often a real divide there," says Brian Atwood, who coordinated with Albright every day.

"But she was able to bridge that divide by understanding how people on Capitol Hill think. She was a good envoy from Capitol Hill to the Executive Branch. She would challenge people and say: 'Do you know what Senator So-and-So will say about that?'"[49]

Alan Platt, whose responsibilities as congressional liaison at the Arms Control and Disarmament Agency put him in frequent touch with Albright, says one of her greatest assets was her ability to reach consensus on issues. "I think a distinguishing characteristic of her . . . is that she has a very good ability to try to find common ground among different people. In her work for Muskie and for Brzezinski, she was able to bring together people of widely differing ideas and find some consensus positions. And her job for Brzezinski was to do exactly that and to try to form bipartisan coalitions with people on Capitol Hill."[50]

Albright understood that Carter needed to do more than recognize Republicans; he needed to court them. Although the president had the luxury of Democratic majorities in both houses of Congress, his relations with Congress suffered from Brzezinski's failure to meet with congressional members as often as he should have. Albright did her best to make sure her boss paid more attention to Capitol Hill and cultivated better relationships with senators and congressmen. At the end of one memorandum reminding Brzezinski of a meeting with newly elected members of Congress, Albright coached: "You should try to stay for the wine and cheese—a good chance to mingle."[51]

In a memorandum to Brzezinski in April 1979, just before he was to meet with eight new Republican senators, Albright outlined the senators' foreign policy views. She listed Maine senator William M. Cohen in a group she called "Conservative, but some chance of working with them." Of Cohen, whom President Clinton appointed secretary of defense when he named Albright to the State Department, she wrote: "He is most unpredictable and when he was in the House, he had a bad record of supporting the administration on foreign policy issues."[52] Of the famously crusty Wyoming senator Alan K. Simpson, she wrote: "He has been much more open-minded than we originally expected—that is not saying much however."[53] In May 1979, Brzezinski was dispatched to pacify Senator Sam Nunn, chairman of the Senate Armed Services Committee, who had questioned President Carter's commitment to maintaining a strong defense against the Soviet Union. Albright suggested he use the occasion to signal Nunn that Brzezinski, his ideological partner inside the White House, was gaining influence with the president. "I believe that Nunn can be reassured and kept on the reservation by being told that his views are not fully, but increasingly, shared within the administration,"[54] Albright told Brzezinski in preparing him for the meeting.

African nationalism and the East-West struggle for control of the Third World presented Albright with her first opportunity to fence with Senator Jesse Helms. More than any previous White House administration, the Carter team pressed the case for black nationalism in Africa. The United Nations imposed economic sanctions on Rhodesia (now Zimbabwe) in 1965, when the colony's white-supremacist government declared independence from Britain. The United States participated in the sanctions regime until 1971, when it lifted the ban. But in 1977, Carter persuaded Congress to reimpose sanctions.[55] Carter's call for majority rule in the overwhelmingly black country was consistent with his policy of promoting human rights beyond U.S. borders. But Helms, then considered an extremist even in his own minority party, regarded civil rights for blacks as a Communist plot—whether in his own native North Carolina or in faraway southern Africa. He was fighting to lift the Carter administration's sanctions against the white-minority Rhodesia regime, and as a White House lobbyist, Albright tried to thwart his attempt. But rather than dismiss Helms as a kook, as her boss might have done, Albright gave her time, if not her support, to the southern Republican. In a July 1978 memo to Brzezinski, Albright wrote: "Spent a great deal of the day trying to get Senator Helms' assistant off our collective backs. He wants to make a deal on Helms' Rhodesia amendment."[56]

Events in Iran presented the most poignant and emotional foreign policy crisis of Carter's presidency. In early 1979, Islamic revolutionaries overthrew the shah of Iran, forcing the longtime American ally into exile. Muslim fundamentalists loyal to the Ayatollah Ruholla Khomeini took power. When the Carter administration permitted the shah to seek cancer treatment in the United States, Iranian students, bent on revenge, stormed the American embassy in Tehran on November 4, 1979, and seized fifty-two American hostages. The Khomeini government condoned the embassy takeover and refused to release the hostages unless Carter pledged not to interfere in Iranian affairs and agreed to return the shah's wealth to Iran.[57] Carter refused and dedicated his presidency to freeing the hostages, refusing for months to leave the White House while Americans remained captive. When a daring airborne rescue mission ended in fiery failure on a remote desert airstrip the following April, Secretary of State Vance resigned to demonstrate there were some measures that even the consummate diplomat could not abide.

The news media saw in Vance's resignation a telltale sign that Carter's foreign policy was in disarray, shredded by the constant tension between the secretary of state and Brzezinski.[58] Carter replaced Vance with Ed Muskie, who, though he possessed no particular expertise in foreign affairs, commanded tremendous respect on Capitol Hill. Most important, however, Muskie was plain-spoken. Carter chose him because he hoped the tall man from Maine would effectively explain foreign policy to the American people.

If Carter hoped that his new secretary of state would be a better fit with Brzezinski than Vance had been, he was sadly mistaken. Despite their common Polish heritage, Muskie and Brzezinski soon saw each other as rivals. The joke in the capital was that they were "Poles apart." Albright was torn between two mentors. She later remarked that had Carter been reelected, there would have been "a shoot-out in the next administration."[59] "Brzezinski was being really aggressive while Muskie was learning the job," says a longtime friend of Albright's. "I think her heart was with Muskie, even though she was working at the White House. He was more like her, more of a politician with a very subtle mind."[60] Albright resolved her dilemma without alienating either man: She refused to choose between them. Using the same diplomatic skills that she exercised on the Hill, she kept communication open between NSC and State, serving as a bridge of common sense between the two temperamental Poles.

Privately, Albright told friends that Brzezinski was tone-deaf when it came to Capitol Hill, that he would go up there and talk but not listen, then come back to the White House thinking he had set things right. Muskie, on the other hand, used the skills and credentials he had won with twenty-one years in Congress and had taught to Albright. He waded into battles personally and listened to both sides. He would talk to both Republican and Democratic caucuses, explaining complicated issues in terms members of Congress could use to sell the issue to voters at home.[61]

When she left the NSC after Carter's defeat in 1980, Albright said that her experience taught her the importance of picking issues that the White House could win to give the president a list of victories and let him distance himself from issues "if you thought that you were going to go down the tubes."[62] Another lesson she learned, and one that would become important to her as secretary of state, was the need to prioritize foreign policy issues. Her rationale was simple: A president should not ask members of Congress to vote on six or seven tough issues at the same time.

Albright also learned about the importance of stroking the egos of members of Congress, that there is no better coin of the realm in the nation's capital than proximity to power. She made sure politicians could open a conversation with folks back home with those golden words: "When

I was at the White House . . ." During her time there, she organized elaborate White House dinners for members of Congress and brought in cabinet secretaries with maps and charts to lay out the issues.[63]

Finally, Albright's stint at the NSC reinforced her father's emphasis on the necessity for a leader to speak and act forcefully. Josef Korbel criticized Czechoslovak president Eduard Beneš for appearing weak, and his daughter saw the same flaw in Carter. "A lot of it is style," Albright explained later. "Consider a Cabinet room with twenty people in it, and those of us who knew him knew that the quieter he got, the madder he was, and that didn't exactly help him to be forceful." Also, she said, Carter had an "unfortunate speaking style in strange rhythms where he'd go up at the ends of sentences and smile in the wrong places."[64]

Carter was bright and studied issues until he learned the finest details, but he often failed to communicate his desires to Congress. "We all finally learned the trick that when the President said, 'I understand,' that really meant he disagreed with a person, and so he had a way of not really coming to terms with members of Congress," Albright said. "They themselves would turn around and say, 'I'm not quite sure what it is he wants.' "[65]

Month by month, year by year, Albright was absorbing the lessons and culture of political Washington, just as she had absorbed the politics of Eastern Europe at her family's dinner table in Denver. Yet even though women were flocking into the workforce and breaking through barriers in almost every sphere of American life, the world of American foreign policy was still very much the domain of the white male establishment. "Madeleine was Brzezinski's liaison to the Hill, and I think she performed very ably there," says Richard Moe, who was Mondale's chief of staff both when Mondale was a senator and vice president. "Yet there is no question that the foreign policy crowd is an old-boy network. This was an obstacle for her every step of the way. She kept hitting glass ceilings. The rest of the world was changing, but the foreign policy world was not changing at all. She was cast into this role as congressional liaison and wasn't taken as seriously on substantive matters as she should have been. She was very sharp and very intelligent and very well-read and studied hard, but she was put into a process role instead of substantive policy role."[66]

The sense that she was kept out of the loop affected Albright's ability to do her job. One year into her tenure, she wrote Brzezinski a memo reviewing her performance over the previous twelve months. She told him that she could do a better job of updating him on congressional problems if he kept her better informed: "I am not a secret information junkie, but I think it would be helpful if I could see some additional cable traffic," she wrote.

"Most of what I get is about room reservations for [congressional delegations traveling abroad]. I often find out substantive material with Congressional impact, i.e., Iran, Afghanistan, Vietnam from the people I deal with at State or Defense. Other than just feeling stupid and put-down which I can deal with, I cannot be useful if I have to scrounge information."[67]

Moe believes that the discrimination must have bothered Albright, but he says that she did not show it: "She never complained about it. But it had to frustrate her. Some of the guys in this crowd can be insufferable. They can be insufferable to white males. They tend to be full of themselves and see foreign policy as a prerogative that ordinary mortals can't grasp. It was the culture of the times that she was fighting."[68]

Privately, some of Madeleine's friends worried that she was working too hard at the White House and not spending enough time with Joe; that she was spending too many long days, too many evenings, too many Saturdays, caught up in the all-consuming workload of the White House. One old friend spotted Joe at the 1980 Democratic convention in New York with a woman "who was clearly not his sister." They were riding an escalator together in Madison Square Garden, and while it was not clear that they were romantically involved, the friend thought to herself, "What is Joe doing with her? Uh-oh."[69] She said nothing about it to Madeleine.

When Carter lost the election to Ronald Reagan, Albright's White House days drew to a close. It had been a rich and rewarding period, but the last days were as emotionally draining as they were dramatic. The hostage crisis, which had gone on for fourteen months, was in its most delicate stage since the aborted rescue mission. Intense negotiations through third parties in Europe continued right up to Inauguration Day, January 20. Carter insisted he would not pay ransom, but the deal eventually produced $8 billion to Iran from frozen Iranian assets.

That morning, Albright drove her old red station wagon to the White House, and she and Christine Dodson loaded their belongings inside. Then they drove to Andrews Air Force Base, where much of the outgoing White House staff gathered to watch Carter board the presidential aircraft for his return flight to Georgia. At the airport gate, Brzezinski spotted the two women and had security officers bring them through the crowd to watch their vanquished leader's departure. Just as Carter started up the staircase to the plane, he reached over and whispered something to the wife of one of the hostages, who was standing in the receiving line. She burst into tears and began hugging and kissing the former president. Albright and Dodson looked at each other and realized the hostages must have been released. Carter had learned by telephone only moments before that, as Ronald Reagan was sworn in, Iranian authorities gave permission for a plane waiting on the runway at Tehran airport with the hostages aboard to take off for the West. The crisis that had crippled the Carter presidency was Reagan's first triumph.

With mixed emotions—happy for the hostages and their families, sad that Carter's presidency was but a memory—Albright and Dodson climbed back in the car and drove to Crisfield's, a plain but popular fish restaurant in Silver Spring, Maryland, just outside the capital. Over a late lunch at one of the yellowing Formica tables, Albright and Dodson discussed their own lives. When they finished, Albright looked at her friend and said, "The only thing I am sorry about in our relationship is that you don't have the same Cinderella marriage I do."

From the Wellesley Class of 1959 Record Book for 1979

Korbel, Madeleine (Mrs. Joseph Albright)
Husband: Joe
Children: Alice (17)
Anne (17)
Katie (11)

I have been unbelievably lucky in the last 20 years—without sounding too much like Pollyanna—I am married to the same man I met while at Wellesley, I have three daughters—all of them relatively well put together. The twins are seniors in high school . . . and Katie is . . . excited about all her pursuits from science to ballet. Joe is an investigative reporter—working for a chain of newspapers which owns the Atlanta Constitution—now well-read in Washington. We have lived in Washington for the last 10 years and believe that for us it is the best of all possible worlds.

In terms of my career—all I can say is that all my interests have finally come together. Most of my friends know it took me an embarrassingly long time to get my Ph.D. from Columbia, but I finally did. The reason it took me so long was that I got over-involved in community activities and politics. I was Chairman of a local school board, worked on Ed Muskie's presidential campaign in '72 . . . was prepared to stay forever—or at least six years—when Zbigniew Brzezinski, "my professor" at Columbia, called to ask if I wanted to come to the White House to do Congressional Relations for the National Security Council. . . .

On the negative side, my new job leaves little time for anything else but family—so have not seen my friends as much as I would like. Also am not getting as much exercise as I should—therefore the perennial weight problem. My excuse is that I eat up all my discipline working 12 hours a day.

In re-reading this, I'm afraid I sound a little too self-satisfied. Believe me—I don't think everything I do every day is perfect—but I really am having a wonderful time. Knock on wood!

17

Divorce

"Heaven has no rage like love to hatred turned,
Nor Hell a fury like a woman scorned."
    —William Congreve, *The Mourning Bride,* Act III, Scene viii

ONE WEEKEND in late November, Madeleine invited Christine Dodson to join her at the Albrights' Virginia farm. It was time to clean the swimming pool before closing it for the winter. Most women of Albright's social class hired people for this task. Not Madeleine. She insisted on doing it herself. "It was just the two of us, nobody else," Dodson says. "When we reached our hands into the pool filters, they were full of frogs. I kept thinking, 'You have enough money. Get somebody to do this.'"

That same morning, Toby, the Albrights' golden retriever, had a run-in of his own. He was skunked. The two women rushed to the nearest store to buy tomato juice, which is supposed to help eliminate the smell. When they returned to the house, they gave Toby a bath, a messy proposition under any circumstances, a revolting one when a big mop of a dog shakes himself, spraying everyone in his vicinity with a pungent shower of soapy, red skunk scent. "So there we were, frogs in one hand, washing Toby with a hose with the other," laughs Dodson.

Madeleine arranged the weekend in order to pick up Joe at Dulles Airport when he returned from a business trip. Christine was not particularly fond of dogs under ordinary circumstances, and this had not been an ordinary day. When they met Joe at the airport, he offered to sit in the back with Toby and took the place directly behind Madeleine, who was driving. Dodson thought Joe seemed delighted to see his wife. Even though he was seated in back, Joe hugged Madeleine and kissed her and kept saying how happy he was to be home. "He couldn't keep his hands off her," Dodson says. "It got to the point where I said, 'Careful, we're going to have a wreck.'"

Not long afterward, Madeleine and Joe were having lunch at the Four Seasons Hotel in Georgetown with Marcia Burick, the friend who had accompanied them to Eastern Europe in 1967. Madeleine was recounting her recent trip to Poland, where she met Polish Solidarity leader Lech Walesa. When Madeleine excused herself from the table to visit the ladies' room, Joe turned to Burick and said, "Isn't she fabulous?"

But it was only the very next month, on January 13, 1982, that Joe Albright told Madeleine he wanted out of the marriage. It was eight o'clock in the morning when Joe said to his wife, "This marriage is dead, and I'm in love with somebody else."[1]

Madeleine Albright associates the date with the day of the Air Florida crash, when an ice-heavy jetliner lifted off from Washington National Airport, clipped the 14th Street Bridge, and crashed into the frozen waters of the Potomac River.[2] It was the day her own personal world crashed, the day the woman who had tried so hard for so long to be an accepted member of the team again found herself rejected, not just by the person whose world of money and social status had given her young life new direction, but the man she loved, the father of her children. Madeleine was stunned.

She also needed to talk, and that night she called Christine Dodson. "Is there anyone in the room with you?" Albright asked. When Dodson replied that her mother was nearby, Albright asked if she would move to a different location. Then Albright broke the news: Joe wanted a divorce. Dodson was incredulous. "This must be a joke," she said. Madeleine's reply: "This is not a joke at all."[3] Joe Albright, who had joined Cox Newspapers, had met the other woman at the 1980 Republican convention in Detroit.[4] Her name was Marcia Kunstel, a woman ten years his junior who was also a reporter for Cox.

Romance was fairly common on the campaign trail in the 1970s and 1980s. News reporters and political staffers were away from home for long periods of time, traveling in the same bizarre, airborne campaign bubble, living on expense accounts, staying in different hotels every night, eating in the best local restaurants. It was like a luxury camping trip, interrupted only occasionally by a weekend at home.

It was also a time when the status of women was a topic of constant debate. Many young women were postponing marriage to pursue their careers, and many companies, including news organizations, were under pressure to promote women. It was not unusual for female reporters on the campaign trail to be a decade younger than the men, many of whom had wives at home. Nor was it unusual for men to find themselves attracted to their independent female colleagues. The trend was not restricted to the campaign trail. As the roles that men and women play in marriage went through all kinds of contortions, the divorce rate soared. It became so common that schools added a new line on their forms asking with which parent the children live.

There are those who say Joe had a wandering eye, that as early as Madeleine's graduate school days he was frequently seen gazing at one of her fellow students.[5] Others who knew the young couple well disagree, insisting that Joe became disenchanted with the marriage only after Madeleine turned her energy and attention to her own career at a time when his was floundering, that she had too many early-morning breakfasts at the White House for most husbands to accept.[6]

If Madeleine Albright had any idea that her marriage was in trouble, she did not confide it to many friends. Two or three months before she learned that Joe wanted a divorce, Madeleine told one friend on a walk that something was wrong with her husband, but she did not know what. The friend figured that Joe was depressed over his career. "We were shocked at their divorce," the friend says. "Joe seemed so very proud of her."[7] Marcia Burick, who had been divorced two years before, thought that it was wonderful that her friend had such a supportive husband. When she learned the Albrights' marriage was dissolving, she was incredulous. "I couldn't believe it," Burick says.[8]

Telling the children they were planning to divorce would be traumatic for both Joe and Madeleine. Friends say Joe Albright wanted to give the kids a cover story, but that Madeleine insisted they sit the children down and tell them the truth—their father had fallen out of love with their mother. "The children were aware of the facts and that there was another woman," says one confidant.[9]

Madeleine was distraught and overwhelmingly sad. Her friends worried about her. When a man leaves a woman—or, for that matter, when a woman leaves a man—it is a huge blow to the self-esteem of the one who is abandoned. Yet Madeleine seemed to take it harder than most. Christine Dodson was talking to her on the phone one day in July from her family home on the Greek island of Mytilini and could not bear to find her friend so unhappy. "Get yourself over here," she said. Albright agreed to a visit. When she arrived, Dodson sent a friend to the Athens airport to pick her up, but there was no one there who resembled the woman Dodson described. "She was in one of her thin phases, gaunt actually," Dodson says. "She was wearing a white dress, with this white face and blond hair."[10]

Mytilini, or Lesvos, as it is often called, is a large Greek island in a gulf formed by the Turkish coast in the northern corner of the Aegean Sea. Local residents refer to themselves as "Lesvians." Dodson's huge, two-story stone house, built in 1864 and located on the eastern side of the island, has a large balcony that overlooks a narrow stretch of sparkling water that separates it from Turkey. In fact, Turkey is so close that when she is standing on the balcony, Dodson can see trees and traffic along the Turkish coast.

Albright arrived exhausted, both physically and emotionally. The two women dragged a long, narrow pillow out onto the balcony floor. Albright stretched out on her stomach and slept there for the better part of a week. When she was not sleeping, the two friends swam, sunned themselves, and talked endlessly about their lives. "Madeleine considers this her turning point," Dodson says.[11]

When she returned to Washington, Albright began to think about her future. She had spent most of that last year as a fellow at Washington's Woodrow Wilson International Center for Scholars, writing a paper on the role of the Polish press during the Solidarity Movement. A year before, she had begun learning Polish. Walter Mondale was putting a campaign staff together for a 1984 presidential bid and asked Albright to be deputy campaign manager. She was also thinking about teaching. "I thought if Joe was actually leaving, it made more sense to be a professor than to be a political person because it was steadier work," Albright says. "It was totally scholarship mentality. I needed to be serious and earn a living."[12]

On January 31, 1983, Madeleine and Joe Albright were officially divorced. Madeleine's hurt and anger were evident to anyone who talked to her. And to her friends' distress, she talked relentlessly about it. "She remained bitter over Joe for reasons we can understand, personal hurt," says a man who knew her well at the time. "Some of it could be the rejection of her whole social construct. She has harnessed her insanity for the most part, but sometimes it comes out."[13]

For years, Madeleine Albright poured out this bitterness to friends, telling them that Joe was jealous of her success, that he could not deal with a strong woman, and that she never would have made much of her professional life had she stayed married to him.[14] People were sympathetic, but after a while, even her friends had had enough. Several told her to shut up about Joe, to get on with her life, that her demeanor was unbecoming.[15]

Privately, some of Albright's friends wondered how she could have been married for twenty-three years and still be surprised when her husband announced that he wanted a divorce. Was she wearing blinders? Could she possibly have been in touch with her husband's feelings and their own relationship if she did not recognize that Joe was souring on the marriage? "He walked out and she didn't have a clue why?" asks an old friend. "Come on. Give me a break."[16]

Whatever the case, one aspect of the divorce is not in dispute. The settlement left Madeleine, the onetime refugee child, a wealthy woman, many times a millionaire. Along with a sizable chunk of Albright family money, she got the couple's elegant, three-story redbrick home in a comfortable section of the capital's historic Georgetown, as well as their weekend farm in Virginia.[17] It also left her a middle-aged, single mother of three, aching to chart a new path. "It shook her up and made her reevaluate her life," says her Wellesley friend Wini Freund. "But it contributed to her strength. Our generation of women never expected this to happen to them."[18]

No one knows what goes on in someone else's marriage. Yet to most friends, the Albrights' had seemed like a strong one, which is what made it so hard for Madeleine's friends to accept the idea that Joe asked for a divorce.

Many of the couple's mutual friends tried to stay friendly with both Madeleine and Joe, but as in many cases of divorce, neutrality was impossible. "Madeleine felt anyone who had anything to do with Joe was disloyal to her," says a longtime male friend. "But until the time when she became United Nations ambassador, I think she would have dropped everything if he came back. I don't know when the psychological and emotional switch happened, but it finally did."[19]

Just after becoming secretary of state, Albright went to Helsinki as part of her two-week, round-the-world trip to meet leaders. At the time, Joe was a newspaperman in Moscow, and it was very likely that he would cover the event. When Albright worried aloud to friends that she would probably run into him, they pointed out gently that she had nothing to worry about. She was the one, after all, who had become secretary of state.[20]

Albright once told friends that Joe would not set foot in the United States while his "ex-" was secretary of state.[21] But Joe and his wife, Marcia Kunstel, did move back to Washington in the summer of 1997, in time to promote a book they wrote while on assignment in Russia. They are coauthors of *Bombshell: The Secret Story of America's Unknown Atomic Spy Conspiracy,* the story of Ted Hall, an eighteen-year-old physics prodigy who had worked on the Manhattan Project, which made America's first nuclear devices, and gave information to the Russians. In April 1998, they left for a foreign assignment in Beijing.

In the last five years, Joe and Madeleine Albright have become friendlier with each other than they have been in years. Much of the bitterness they once felt has dissipated. The weddings of their daughters helped, as did the growing political success that Madeleine enjoys.[22] Today, fifteen years after they parted, Madeleine Albright says that while her own childhood had not prepared her for divorce, she has finally put her own behind her. "[My parents] adored each other," she says. "They met when they were young and went through nine zillion things together. For me, people stayed married. I adored Joe. I'm sorry. But I am over it."[23]

PART THREE

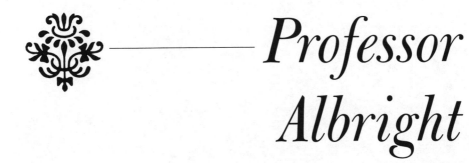

Professor Albright

18

On Her Own

"I watched her confidence grow."
—Peter Krogh, September 9, 1997

MADELEINE ALBRIGHT IS DIVORCED. The dissolution of a marriage is never easy, whenever and however it hits, but some years in a woman's life are more difficult than others. In Albright's case, the twins were twenty-one. Anne was a junior at Dartmouth; Alice, a junior at Williams. Katie was fifteen, a freshman at the National Cathedral School in Washington. But it was Albright who was at the most vulnerable age of all. She was forty-five.

She was also a single mother. "I was saved a lot of the things that single mothers worry about," Madeleine Albright says today. "I had a very good job teaching at Georgetown, and I had enough money and an ex-husband who had been very generous and very generous about the kids. So I did not have the horrible problems single mothers had."[1]

Still, she worried incessantly about her youngest daughter. "Katie and I are good friends now, but when she was a teenager," Albright says today, "I used to wander around the house paralyzed with fear that she was out too late. My kids are the greatest source of everything that goes on. But I worried if [Katie] would come home, if she was doing her homework, if she would get into college."[2]

Ronald Reagan was in the White House. The Democrats were in exile. Republicans had been happily replacing them in government jobs all over town. Albright, who had spent a year poring through thousands of pages of

Brzezinski's White House papers in preparation for a book he was writing, had accepted a teaching job at Georgetown University's School of Foreign Service. The school had been looking for a professor with a background in Eastern European studies to fill a position in the field of comparative politics. It was a perfect match for Albright. The school was even conveniently located, only three blocks from her house, close enough to walk home for lunch.

The job was described as an interdisciplinary teaching post, which meant that practical experience was considered important. But most of the courses that the new professor taught fell under the auspices of the Government Department, which was oriented toward scholarship and pure academics.

The university was at a crossroads, trying to establish a reputation for academic excellence. School officials were eager to make an aggressive move for more prominence and prestige. Visibility was critical. The school had just completed construction of the $32 million Salaam Intercultural Center (Madeleine Albright is one of thirty names listed on the donor plaque), and the Donner Foundation had recently provided money to launch a new program specifically aimed at women interested in the foreign service. Its purpose was to bolster their professional self-confidence, introduce them to female role models, and begin the process of networking.

Two finalists competed for the open faculty position. One was a man, respected in the field and possessing an impeccable résumé and a long list of published articles. The other was Albright. In spite of her impressive government credentials, she had no teaching experience. And except for her Ph.D. dissertation, she had written almost nothing of an academic nature—no books and few articles.

As part of the selection process, each candidate had to give a lecture on comparative politics to a class of Georgetown students. The established professor, obviously overconfident, felt it unnecessary to prepare. His lecture bombed. Albright did her homework. She put together a vibrant presentation and stole the show. "No contest," says Peter Krogh, who was dean of the School of Foreign Service at the time.[3]

Privately, Krogh was more pleased than he let on. In the early 1980s, all big organizations—universities included—were under pressure to promote women within their ranks. The problem was finding those who were qualified. Students' reactions to Albright gave Krogh ammunition to make what could have been a controversial decision. "There was no affirmative action here," he says. "If the Government Department had been all alone in making the appointment, they probably would have gone with the other fellow because scholarship was more important to them. But for us, a really effective teacher with real-world experience and the credentials of having worked for Brzezinski was a natural."

Like her parents some thirty-five years before, Albright was starting over. The circumstances were vastly different, but her life was taking a new, unrehearsed turn. "I knew all that work on getting a Ph.D. was worth it," she says. "I could not kind of sit around."[4]

From the beginning, Albright was comfortable in the classroom, just as her father had been at the University of Denver. In September 1982, she began teaching Modern Foreign Government, a required course for sopho-mores, which meant that not all who registered were enthusiastic about tak-ing it. But for most of the one hundred students in her section, Albright made the class come alive. The students loved her. "She taught the course in her classroom," says Krogh. "She taught it as she walked across the campus. She taught it in her lovely Georgetown home. She taught it at her farm in Virginia. The students were always with her. She was like a Pied Piper."[5]

Albright branched out from undergraduate classes to teach graduate courses in Foreign Policy Decision Making, United States–Soviet Relations, and Contemporary International Relations. "Women students have a ten-dency not to talk, and she made a point of drawing them out," says Nancy Soderberg, a Georgetown graduate student who followed Albright's tracks into government and Democratic politics. "She would ask them questions and force them to get involved in a conversation."[6] Jan Kalicki, who taught at Georgetown with Albright and now works at the Commerce Depart-ment, was stunned one day in 1983 when Albright, the guest lecturer in his American foreign policy class, walked in carrying a stack of internal NSC documents from the Carter White House that she had declassified. She began passing the once-sensitive documents around to enthralled students to give them a sense of how politics affects policy decisions.[7]

Albright became one of Georgetown's most popular teachers. Students voted her their outstanding teacher in 1988, 1990, and 1991. She was also asked to direct the school's Women in Foreign Service Program. She brought in the few females who had risen through the ranks of the foreign service to give lectures. She organized workshops to show students how to prepare résumés and dress for job interviews. She invited them to informal seminars over dinner at her house and shepherded them around Washing-ton, introducing them to individuals who could be helpful to their careers. Always generous with friends, Albright was expansive with students as well, opening her Rolodex, literally and figuratively. "The record of women and their placement in careers has been stunning in the last five years," says

Krogh. "The program owes a lot of its success to Madeleine's early efforts to raise the visibility and consciousness of women."[8]

Privately, Albright was starting to date again, an awkward situation for divorcées, even in the best of times. In July 1982, six months after Joe told her he wanted a divorce, she attended a cocktail party at the DuPont Circle home of Barry Carter, a smart, handsome Georgetown Law School professor. It was not the first time they had met. He had attended a $1,000-a-plate dinner Albright had given for Walter Mondale in her home shortly before she and Joe split. Joe was not home that night. He believed that as a news reporter, it would be a conflict of interest for him to attend a fund-raising dinner for a politician, so he took his daughters to the movies instead.[9]

Carter, four years younger than Albright, had worked on the National Security Council staff under Henry Kissinger in the Nixon administration. Since then, he had held various high-level jobs in government that gave him extensive background in foreign policy, national security, and trade. Divorced from Margie McNamara, the daughter of Robert S. McNamara, who was secretary of defense in the Kennedy and Johnson administrations, Carter dated a select group of bright and beautiful women on the Washington social scene. Not long after his cocktail party, he invited Madeleine to dinner at Nora's, a popular restaurant not far from his house.[10]

Madeleine enjoyed Carter's companionship. To get herself in better physical shape, she began swimming regularly at Georgetown University's Yates Field House, wearing earphones to listen to her favorite music.

She and Carter shared a special interest in Democratic politics.[11] Walter Mondale was preparing another presidential bid and began a series of breakfast meetings at his law firm to discuss foreign policy. He used the meetings both to keep current on the issues and to keep his ties to people who might serve in his campaign if he decided to run. Usually twelve to fifteen people attended. Albright and Carter were regulars.

Bt the spring of 1983, a few months after Albrights' divorce was final, Carter and Albright were spending most of their time together, usually at her house in Georgetown. He had no children from his previous marriage and enjoyed the company of Albright's girls. He even chaperoned a party Katie had one evening.[12]

Carter was an avid canoeist. That July, he led a whitewater canoe trip in northern Maine. The group, which included Albright, her three girls, and one boyfriend, took a private plane with canoes strapped to the pontoons. After flying to Umaskis Lake, the plane landed softly on the water, letting the canoes slide in. They spent three days camping and canoeing the rapids of the Allagash River.[13]

For the most part, Albright's and Carter's lives revolved around the university, where Albright helped launch another program: the Georgetown Leadership Seminar. It was the brainchild of Alan Goodman, then the university's associate dean, whose idea was to fill the gap created when Henry Kissinger stopped conducting his summer leadership seminars at Harvard.[14] For almost twenty years, the Harvard International Seminar brought together mid-level foreign officials, diplomats, and journalists from all over the world. It was an imaginative and creative way to expose promising individuals who were likely to become prominent world leaders to American political and intellectual life. And for Kissinger, it created a network of international contacts that served him well in diplomacy and later as a consultant. The Harvard program ended when Kissinger joined the Nixon administration in 1969.[15]

In 1981, Georgetown University had resurrected the concept in the form of an annual weeklong seminar in October, bringing together twenty-five to thirty young government specialists, politicians, business leaders, military officers, and journalists from across the globe. Speakers included the cream of the Georgetown faculty and as many Washington newsmakers as school officials could lure to the campus. In three years, the program grew in popularity and prestige. It was so successful that graduates began holding reunions in their home countries. Albright attended one in Tel Aviv. Graduates include the prime minister of Taiwan, Vincent Siew, and former French prime minister Alain Juppe. From the start, Albright was a prominent participant. She became a member of the program committee in 1982, her first year at Georgetown, and was on the speaker's list most of the years between 1984 and 1993. "It has been our flagship program, and Madeleine has been in the midst of it," Krogh says.[16] It was also a flagship enterprise for Albright that combined her joy of teaching with an opportunity to build an international network that would be important to her in the years ahead.

Albright also participated in a Georgetown program that exposed her to a medium of growing importance in American politics. Beginning in 1981, Krogh moderated a PBS series called "American Interests," a weekly, thirty-minute foreign affairs talk show that brought in policy experts to debate various foreign policy issues. In 1985, "American Interests" was replaced by "Great Decisions," which Krogh also moderated. Between 1989 and 1991, Albright was a regular participant; the others were Karen Elliott House, a *Wall Street Journal* reporter and editor, who was considered the moderate, and Richard Allen, chairman of the Asian Studies Center of the Heritage Foundation. Allen, who had served as Reagan's first NSC adviser, was the conservative. Albright was cast as the liberal. Every week the panelists discussed a different topic.

The most salient foreign policy issue of the late 1980s was Mikhail Gorbachev's efforts to reform the Soviet Union. Peeling back the layers of communism proved a monumental task that eventually turned his countrymen against him, but it was one that Albright and other Russia experts watched with growing fascination. While Albright knew her subject well, she was not an accomplished commentator. Yet, gradually, she began to perfect the plainspoken style that would become one of her greatest assets as a diplomat. When Krogh asked a question about the causes of the democratic revolutions sweeping across Eastern Europe, Albright answered succinctly. "Well," she said, "it was really the infection of the thought that people could have their government the way they wanted it."[17]

One "Great Decisions" show in 1990 concentrated on the relevance of the United Nations in a post–Cold War world. Albright argued that though the role of the U.N. had been effectively mooted by the power struggle between the United States and Soviet Union, the organization would become a crucial player across the globe as new problems and issues emerged in the new post–Cold War climate.[18]

Over the three years and twenty-four shows that she taped for "Great Decisions," Albright's performances improved. She covered a gamut of issues: the drug war, Central America, the Middle East, Central Europe, Japan.[19] "I watched her confidence grow," Krogh says. "She always managed to come out of discussions well, but she gained in strength and effectiveness."[20] Albright credits the alphabetic priority with helping her learn how to do TV. "Georgetown put out a book of experts," she says. "Because my expertise was the Soviet Union and because my name began with *A*, I would get called a lot, primarily to do foreign television. I would get Finnish TV or something. They would come to my office. I figured nobody will see this, so I got comfortable with the camera."

Albright was right. While the PBS series had wide viewership, it was not the kind of prime-time news show that the Washington press corps scrutinizes for changes in policy and nuance. In short, it was a good place to practice the fine art of delivering the sound bites that would become her trademark. It also gave her an appreciation of the conservative point of view. "You know, I don't think you're the right-wing monster I expected," she once told Allen after a show. His reply: "You snatched the words right out of my mouth. You're not the leftie you purport to be."[21] At the same time, Albright started doing weekly commentaries for Voice of America, another media outlet that offered her an opportunity to develop her skills as a commentator, as well as an audience for her views and opinions.[22]

Albright eventually faced being denied tenure in a classic publish-or-perish decision by the faculty. Because she was on the tenure track, she essentially had seven years to be granted a lifetime position or leave. Although her government experience was valued in the School of Foreign Service, it was clear she would not receive tenure unless she published some substantial scholarly work. For a while, Albright agonized over the issue. "I thought, if you are a professor, you ought to have tenure," Albright says. Then she reconsidered. "I thought, why do I need tenure? Money is not an issue. And there is always something [else] interesting to do."[23]

Friends say that, privately, Albright felt that Georgetown officials did not treat her as well as they could have, that they were more demanding of her time than of men in the same position.[24] Nonetheless, it was not a fight that she was likely to win. She chose to leave rather than press her case. "There was no point in Madeleine taking on the battle unless she was prepared at her age to take a two-year sabbatical to write a book, and no one in their right mind would have advised her to do that," Krogh says.[25]

Another snub that Albright endured at the university was that she was never invited to be a full voting member of the Government Department. In essence, her colleagues never accepted her as a full-fledged member.[26] Friends say it rankled her, but Albright never let her feelings show.[27] She had trained herself well.

From an early age, she had learned to adapt, whether in language, culture, academic mores, or national politics. At every juncture, Albright rarely let adversity drain her deep well of energy and enthusiasm. Instead, she set her sights on new challenges, from mastering an arcane subject to breaking through a known barrier to making an unexpected friend.

During this period, Albright's widowed mother moved to Washington to be closer to her children. One weekend, Albright invited her mother and Christine Dodson to accompany her to the family farm in Virginia. Happy to be away from the city and able to relax, Albright plunged into needlepoint while she and Dodson chatted about their children. Afterward, Mandula Korbel told the younger women that one aspect of the visit had disappointed her. Knowing that they were politically sophisticated and enjoyed discussing international events, she had spent the previous week reading newspapers, determined to learn everything she could about places like Africa so she could follow the conversation and ask intelligent questions. But their conversation never even touched on current events.

Dodson says that she and Albright had mothers who were quite similar, women with no professional ambition of their own, eager to support their husbands, and sometimes overbearing in the concern they showed their children. "We were difficult daughters," Dodson says. "We both had powerful fathers, and our mothers were the classic second fiddles, focusing enormously on their children, insisting they tell them everything they do and don't do."[28] Long after she was married, Christine Dodson's mother would visit and insist on doing the cooking, sure that her daughter was not capable in the kitchen. Mandula Korbel would ask Madeleine, who was used to traveling and had been almost everywhere, "Did you pack an extra set of underpants?" Dodson explains the dynamic: "These women want to participate as much as possible in the lives of their children, but they don't understand the lives of their children. So they interfere, and it is very annoying, but it is not [their] fault. It is our fault because we do not stop. These women needed sweet children, and we [were] impatient."[29]

If the early eighties were a time of adjustment for Albright personally, she did not leave a lot of time for brooding. To her friends, it seemed that she poured her various energies, which have always been prodigious, into her budding career. As she honed her skills as a teacher and a television personality, it was a time of professional development. With the girls almost grown, a time of reflection and refocusing for any parent, Albright was entering a new phase of life. For twenty-three years, Joe had been Number One. Now Number One was Madeleine.

From the fall 1983 Wellesley Alumnae Magazine

I was appt. director of new women in Foreign Service Program and William H. Donner professor of international affairs at Georgetown University School of Foreign Service. The new program addresses the distinct challenges that women face when pursuing careers in international affairs, particularly in societies abroad where traditionally women have not been treated as equals. . . .

19

The Golden Girls

"Our values and concerns are the same. We've gone through the same things in life. We've seen what it's like to grow up in a situation where girls are treated differently from boys."[1]

—Geraldine Ferraro, March 25, 1997

WOMEN OF ALL SIZES AND AGES were dancing in the aisles. Red, white, and blue balloons billowed from the rooftop. It was July 19, 1984, the Democratic convention in San Francisco. Amid the joy and pandemonium breaking out on the convention floor, Geraldine Ferraro accepted her party's nomination to become the first woman vice presidential candidate.

The moment was electric. Democratic women whose lives would soon become indelibly entwined—Barbara Mikulski, Barbara Kennelly, Wendy Sherman, Anne Wexler—crowded onstage, clapping, cheering, shedding tears of joy. Donna Shalala, then president of Hunter College in New York, was in her apartment, watching the proceedings on television. Madeleine Albright, soon to be named Ferraro's campaign foreign policy adviser, was not senior enough in the campaign hierarchy to have earned a spot onstage. Instead, she watched with Barry Carter from the convention floor.[2]

Thirteen years later, January 24, 1997, these same women came together for a more subdued but equally magical moment. The setting this time was the Benjamin Franklin State Dining Room on the seventh floor of the State Department, an eighteenth-century-style, neoclassical chamber with twenty-one-foot-high ceilings, set off by fluted Corinthian columns of French red marble and eight cut-glass chandeliers. A portrait of Benjamin Franklin by the Scottish artist David Martin hangs over a carved marble fireplace on the east wall. An equestrian portrait of George Washington by Thomas Sully hangs over an American Hepplewhite sideboard,[3] looking over the room where some of the greatest minds in twentieth-century diplomacy have shared their ideas. Standing at the end of a long receiving line, Madeleine Korbel Albright, fifty-nine years old, accepted the congratulations and hugs of scores of old friends who were there to celebrate the fact that one of their own had finally broken through.

Albright had been sworn in as America's first female secretary of state the day before. The excitement in the room was palpable. Wearing a striking purple dress with matching long jacket, Albright beamed as these old friends cheered, clapped, and, once again, shed tears of joy.

Although Ferraro's campaign had ended in failure, it had been a watershed, an event that triggered a slow, steady climb of political women toward the top of the ladder. In their own ranks, Mikulski had risen from Maryland congresswoman to become the senior woman senator in the U.S. Senate and planned to run for a third term. Kennelly, a Connecticut congresswoman, had become a member of the House Democratic leadership and was flirting with a run for governor. Sherman, who had been Mikulski's top aide in the mid-eighties, would eventually move back to the State Department to become Albright's trusted counselor. Shalala, called "Boom Boom" by her friends for her propensity for attacking problems from all directions, was secretary of health and human services, one of the only members of the Clinton cabinet around for a second term. And Wexler, who had worked in the Carter White House before heading Ferraro's vice presidential campaign, was chairman of the Wexler Group, among the capital's most prestigious lobbying firms.

Yet it was Albright, propelled into public life when she became foreign policy adviser to Ferraro, who shattered the glass ceiling to reach the top echelon of the U.S. government. Albright, a woman betrayed by a husband who left her for a younger woman, had triumphed over bitterness and adversity. She had become a star. "As I watched her take the podium at the reception, I became very emotional, which is unusual for me," Ferraro said afterward. "I had this picture in my mind of Madeleine in 1984, leaving my plane and standing alone on a tarmac and having to find her way back to Washington because she had to teach a class. This was such a low time in her life. She had been so bruised by the divorce, and she had worked so hard to get where she is, harder than anyone I know. At that moment, when she looked out at us all, I realized that she was representing all women who have had a tough life and haven't achieved their goal. For all of us, Madeleine had broken through."[4]

*   *   *

If it was Madeleine who had broken through, it was Ferraro who gave her the first, intoxicating taste of the national limelight. When Democratic presidential candidate Walter Mondale plucked the sassy Queens congresswoman out of a handful of contenders to become his running mate in 1984, she had admitted to author Gail Sheehy that she was not as strong as she would like to be in foreign affairs.[5] Recognizing a potential problem, the Mondale campaign team looked to two foreign policy experts: Barry Carter and Albright.

Foreign policy is a tricky field for presidential candidates. Unless the country is at war, politicians do not win elections by demonstrating their grasp of national security issues. But they can lose elections on foreign policy if they appear incompetent. Voters do not want a leader who seems naive, untested, or who cannot lead them through a world crisis. An inarticulate answer in a presidential debate can impair the chance of success in an election, as President Gerald R. Ford discovered in 1976, when he insisted Poland was outside the Soviets' sphere of influence in Eastern Europe. Voters want the assurance that their candidate can hold his own in a dangerous and complicated world.[6]

As a three-term congresswoman, Ferraro was more familiar with foreign affairs issues than most House members, but she needed to be able to respond to questions quickly and confidently. And like every woman who sticks her head through the door once labeled "men only," she had to be better prepared than her opponent. "We knew that the media would test her," says John Sasso, who was Ferraro's chief of staff. "The question 'Could you press the button?' came up in every interview. We needed to demonstrate her surefootedness and knowledge." Ferraro was determined not to embarrass either Mondale or the millions of women who looked to her for leadership. She would need a savvy coach. Albright appealed to her because she had a reputation of being cool under fire.[7]

From the start, Ferraro and Albright liked each other. They were both mothers, both ambitious, and unlike so many campaign staffers who are one, two, and sometimes three decades younger than the candidate, Albright and Ferraro were about the same age. While there is little free time on a presidential campaign, Ferraro always sat next to Albright when she had a few minutes to spare.

Working together, Carter and Albright coached the candidate. "They started from the beginning and briefed me on one topic at a time," Ferraro said. "I would tape their briefings and then get into the bathtub and listen to them until I could respond to whatever was the issue of the day." Ferraro's husband, John Zaccaro, sometimes called into the bathroom, "Who's in there with you?" Ferraro would shout back, "Oh, just Barry Carter again."[8]

By listening to the tapes two and sometimes three times, Ferraro familiarized herself with the issues. "If I didn't understand something, they would practically draw pictures for me," she says.[9] Albright was putting into practice a lesson her father taught her: Engage the local citizenry to get them on your side. It was not enough for Ferraro to understand foreign policy issues. She had to be able to discuss them in terms voters—not just diplomats—could grasp. "She knew that I had to speak on a level that folks could understand," Ferraro says. "So that's how she explained things to me."[10]

Ferraro's team figured that her toughest foreign policy test would come during her nationally televised debate with Vice President George Bush, her Republican opponent. With Bush's background as CIA director and U.N. ambassador, and his daily national security briefings, he could be expected to field almost any international affairs question with ease. The Democratic hopeful's advisers expected a cheap-shot question meant to make Ferraro appear ignorant and were determined that she be prepared. Albright drilled her on capitals of the world and put two scenarios in the briefing books. If Ferraro knew the answer, she would give it. If she did not, Albright coached her to say: "First, I have a question for you. What is the capital of Burkino Faso?" If, as they expected, Bush was unable to identify the African country above Togo and the Ivory Coast, Ferraro would reply triumphantly: "Ouagadougou." Albright made Ferraro repeat the name of the capital until she could pronounce it without stumbling.[11]

Just as Sasso predicted, the press corps bore down upon Ferraro. Three days after the debate, Marvin Kalb asked her on *Meet the Press,* "Are you strong enough to push the button?" Ferraro's reply: "I could do whatever is necessary to protect this country."[12] In October, just three weeks before the election, ABC's Ted Koppel used his *Nightline* show to give Ferraro a foreign policy exam, grilling her about her position on the Reagan administration's "Star Wars" for developing a defense against Soviet missiles. And he demanded to know her position on "first use" of nuclear weapons. When she replied, Koppel challenged her answers with follow-up questions.[13]

Albright was furious and did not forget. When Koppel showed up at Georgetown University after the election to address the School of Foreign Service, Albright was seated in the first row. A student asked why the candidates had not focused more on the issues, and Koppel replied that he had invited all four candidates to discuss them on *Nightline,* but Ferraro was the only one to accept. "That's right, and you did a number on her," Albright shouted at him. Koppel looked perplexed. He did not recognize her.[14]

In the end, Ferraro made a fatal campaign mistake by not dealing quickly or completely with questions that arose about her husbands real-estate investments and tax returns. She received kudos from many quarters for her poised conduct in a withering ninety-minute press conference at Kennedy Internation Airport, where she fielded questions from some 200 reporters about the couple's personal finances, but she emerged from the controversy as damaged goods, largely because she never put it to rest. The issue provided Ferraro's opponents in both parties with enough ammunition to keep her on the defensive throughout the campaign, thereby undermining the Democratic ticket. This was the excuse the old-boy Democrats used, mostly in private, to sustain their long-standing argument that Ferraro was not the right choice for vice president. Yes, Republicans had a field day, but they had an effective echo on the Democratic side.

Over the years, Ferraro, Mikulski, Kennelly, and Albright formed what could be called the Old Girls' Network, a closely knit group of women who share all aspects of their lives, from politics to Premarin. In the process, they have become inseparable friends, a passage perhaps best illustrated by the morning they rode bikes together at Ferraro's place on Fire Island, pedaling along the boardwalk that runs beside the beach, belting out the theme song from *The Golden Girls* at the top of their lungs. Ferraro and Kennelly whizzed ahead while Mikulski, not the most athletic of the group, struggled to keep her bicycle upright.[15]

Born in the midst of the Depression, Ferraro, Mikulski, Kennelly, and Albright all came from immigrant families—Italian, Polish, Irish, and Czech— and all were raised in the Roman Catholic Church. "Our values and concerns are the same," Ferraro says. "We've gone through the same things in life. We've seen what it's like to grow up in a situation where girls are treated differently from boys. We laugh at the same things. We view problems from the same direction."[16]

Though they are also approximately the same age—Ferraro, Mikulski, and Kennelly have summer birthdays within a few weeks of each other— they are quick to point out that Ferraro is the oldest. It fell to her to throw a joint sixtieth birthday party for the group, which they had at Washington's popular Galileo restaurant. But Ferraro failed to realize that Albright, whose birthday is in May, had another year to go. "Waa-iit a minnn-ute," piped up Albright, when she realized she was being lumped into the newly sixty crowd. "I'm still fifty-nine." Ferraro shook her head. "Jezuz," she said in mock disgust, "now I'm going to have to throw another one of these next year."[17]

Actually, the group has been meeting together over dinner for years. "We have a foxhole friendship," says Mikulski. "It started on Gerry's campaign, which was very intense. We'd sit together on planes, trains, buses. You really get to know each other that way. When it was all over, we were very sad, but we had to move on."[18]

It was over because President Ronald Reagan soundly trounced Mondale and held on to the White House. Ferraro knew that if she tried to stay in politics by running for the Senate, she would be scrutinized more closely than Reagan had been when he ran for the presidency. Once again, as had happened in '84, she would be subjected to a more rigorous examination because she was a woman. And although she had been a member of Congress and had traveled fairly widely, she needed more hands-on experience abroad. In September 1985, she visited the Soviet Union. Albright accompanied her as a staff aide and acted as interpreter for Ferraro's official meetings.[19]

Ferraro says that at the request of a New York rabbi, they took with them videotapes of the Bible for a group of Jewish dissidents. To avoid detection of the religious materials, which were banned by the Communist authorities, they hid the tapes in a suitcase to get through Customs. Once in the city, they telephoned dissidents from pay phones on the street, knowing that their hotel phone was probably monitored by the KGB.

After a quick sightseeing trip to Leningrad, where they spent an hour or so browsing through the Hermitage, Ferraro and Albright arrived back in Moscow by train. It was 10:00 P.M., and they had not had dinner. In those days, Moscow restaurants closed immediately after the dinner hour. Albright announced that she would go out and find something that they could eat in their hotel room. In a few minutes, she returned grinning. She was carrying a can of caviar, a bottle of vodka, and a bag of Fritos. Soon they were having a fine old time eating, drinking, and making jokes for the benefit of the listening devices in the hotel walls. "We acted like teenagers," Ferraro says. "And God, was I sick. It was a long time before we ate caviar again."[20]

The friendship deepened. Albright was visiting Ferraro at her Fire Island home in August 1985 when Gerry got a 2:00 A.M. call that her elderly mother was being taken to the hospital. Albright got dressed, hopped into a boat with Gerry, and accompanied her to the hospital. After Ferraro's son was arrested on a drug charge in February 1986, Albright flew to New York to be with her. When Ferraro did run for the Senate in 1992, Albright flew to New York on primary night to have dinner with the candidate and watch the returns. Ferraro was devastated when she lost the Democratic primary by less than 1 percent. Albright stayed overnight to be with her friend. "She's laughed with me and cried with me," Ferraro says. "I don't have to explain anything to her. We talk about all the girl stuff, but we talk about the other stuff as well."[21]

Barbara Mikulski was first elected to Congress in 1976. The daughter of Polish immigrants who ran a grocery in East Baltimore, she had been a social worker who led the fight to save East Baltimore's ethnic neighborhoods from a sixteen-lane highway. That exposure helped boost her onto the Baltimore city council. After an unsuccessful run for the Senate against popular Republican incumbent Charles "Mac" Mathias, she ran for the House in 1976 and won.

When Walter Mondale chose Ferraro as his running mate in 1984, he appointed Mikulski as one of the co-chairs of his campaign. When the Democrats lost, Mikulski had to reassess her own future. A five-term congresswoman who could count on reelection, she had her eye on running for the Senate in 1986. But Mathias, a liberal Republican known for his strong stand on civil rights, would give her a hard race. "I had to decide three things," says Mikulski: "Was there a 'there' there for me politically? Was there a 'there' there for me to raise the money? And was there a 'there' there for me to face losing and not be in politics at all?"[22]

Mikulski had just watched Ferraro, one of her closest friends, accept a historic opportunity—and end up losing not only the election but her House seat as well. Mikulski did not relish the same risk. She turned to Madeleine Albright, who had been a frequent seatmate on Ferraro's campaign plane, for a sounding board. "She helped me formulate and ask myself these questions," Mikulski says. "Especially the magic question: Are you ready to roll the dice and go up—or out? That's a lot about what our friendship is about—very concrete advice."

Before she had to challenge the veteran Republican, Mathias decided not to run. Mikulski seized the opportunity and won. Her introduction to the Senate, however, was not easy. At four feet eleven inches, Barbara Mikulski hardly looked like the tall, pin-striped, steel-gray stereotype of a U.S. senator. "Okay," she says, "Madeleine and I are both on the chunky side. We have, shall we say, the East Central European body type." Mikulski does have presence, however. She marches into a room like a blocking back. And she has humor, often referring to herself as "The Little Engine that Could."

Mikulski can intimidate male senators twice her size, but like many people who purposely create a tough persona, she can be unusually thoughtful and sensitive, especially to other women. As one of the first women elected to the Senate, she knew how difficult it was to succeed in an overwhelmingly male microcosm. And when other women joined the club, she strengthened the female minority by organizing her own power workshops. In these seminars, she holds forth on such arcane but necessary skills as how to draft a bill, how to get appointed to the best congressional committees, how to build a reputation as an effective senator. "This is an empowerment model," Mikulski says. "Capitol Hill can be a lonely place, even though people are in constant motion. But activity is not a synonym for relationships. The media can be punishing, so you need to find little havens of hospitality."

Mikulski has taken it on herself to build those havens. Seeing how valuable her monthly dinners with Albright, Ferraro, and Kennelly were, she began organizing monthly dinners for the growing club of women senators. The rules are simple: no staff, no memos, and everything, including the crab cakes and chardonnay, is off-the-record. "The boys always build in fun and friendship," says Mikulski. "They don't just sit around and share their feelings. They use sports as a way to bring themselves together whether it's in a sky box or a bowling alley or a duck blind. There is the joy of shared mission."[23] For Mikulski and Albright, the missions vary. "Madeleine and I talk about everything from weight management to arms control," Mikulski says. "And in some ways we both feel arms control is easier. It's about telling other people what to do."[24]

One of the Golden Girls' shared interests is the dissident movements in Eastern Europe. Madeleine was friendly with the late Rita Klímová, who became the first non-Communist Czechoslovak ambassador to the United States in 1990. Albright and Mikulski thought it would be helpful to Klímová to meet some American women who were political activists. They arranged a dinner at Mikulski's home in Baltimore's historic Fells Point, which overlooks the city harbor. Mikulski invited two friends of Czech origin: Antonia Klima Keane, an associate professor of sociology at Maryland's Loyola College who had been Mikulski's first campaign manager and part of the original group to save the neighborhood, and Dr. Mildred Otenasek, professor emeritus of economics at Notre Dame of Maryland College and a National Democratic committeewoman who had been one of the prime movers in Maryland of John Kennedy's presidential campaign. After a walk around the waterfront, the women began trading war stories, sharing the problems they faced as they had organized protest movements on different sides of the Atlantic at approximately the same time. "What struck us was that in a free society, I went on to be elected to the Baltimore city council," Mikulski said, "but in Czechoslovakia, Rita went to prison."[25] It was a story

Mikulski used to illustrate how women's lives have intertwined and how female politicians like herself have been shaped by the feminist movement, just as they have contributed to its success.

Barbara Bailey Kennelly was first elected to Congress in a special election in January 1982. The daughter of the legendary Democratic Party boss John Bailey, who dominated Connecticut politics for almost thirty years, she was elected to the House to succeed William R. Cotter, who died of cancer. It was a spirited campaign, and Kennelly won with 54 percent of the vote.

Although born into a family with a long tradition of holding public office—her paternal grandfather served on Hartford's city council and her paternal grandmother, a suffragette, was the first woman to hold municipal office in Hartford—Kennelly followed a path similar to most women of her generation. She married shortly after graduating from Washington's Trinity College, raised four children (three daughters and a son), and supported the political ambitions of her husband, Jim Kennelly, a brilliant, charming, and sometimes moody lawyer who was a rising star in Connecticut politics, often mentioned as a potential gubernatorial candidate.

In 1967, Jim Kennelly was elected state representative from Hartford and later served two terms as speaker of the Connecticut House. In 1970, he ran for Congress and lost. It was the seat he sought that Barbara Kennelly went on to win.

Like Albright, Barbara Kennelly spent her early married years as a housewife, carpooling the kids and doing volunteer work. In 1975, when her youngest child, John, was ready for first grade, she thought about teaching. But when a vacancy opened on the Hartford city council, party pols arranged for her to get the job. Three years later, she was elected secretary of the state—the same year her husband lost a bid to become Connecticut's lieutenant governor.[26]

When Barbara Kennelly was elected to Congress in 1982, thanks in good measure to the political network built by her father, she was forty-six years old. Jim Kennelly had joined a prominent Hartford law firm; two of her children were teenagers; and she spent most weekends commuting between Hartford and Washington. There were only a handful of women in Congress, and she became friends with Ferraro, another politician with teenage children and a commuter marriage who shared similar political views. The women played racquetball together. Although both were long-time tennis players, they took lessons to learn the new sport and played in the early morning on courts not far from their congressional offices.

Two years later, when Ferraro's name surfaced as one of those Mondale was considering as his vice presidential running mate, Kennelly went to the Woman's National Democratic Club in Washington and gave a speech supporting her friend. Patricia Schroeder, a six-term congresswoman with her own White House ambitions, was distressed. "Pat cried and was mad at all of us," Kennelly says.[27]

Kennelly traveled with Ferraro during the first and last weeks of the vice presidential campaign, as did Albright. And that is where their friendship began. "Madeleine and I hit it off right away," Kennelly says. When the campaign ended in defeat, Ferraro invited them all to her house in St. Croix for New Year's Eve. It was the first of many such holidays they would spend there together. Ferraro, an accomplished cook, brings everything frozen to make sure no one spends much time in the kitchen. "We swim and boat and snorkel," Kennelly says. "We go totally natural."

By 1992, when Bill Clinton was elected president, the Golden Girls had become inseparable friends, as well as each other's close political advisers. Over dinner one night, they joked about whom they might invite to Clinton's inaugural celebration as their dates. Mikulski mentioned a Maryland football player. Albright, whose relationship with Barry Carter was long over, settled on Tom Dodd, brother of Connecticut senator Chris Dodd and later named ambassador to Uruguay. Kennelly had had a crush on him when she was in college.[28]

When Clinton appointed Albright to be U.N. ambassador, Kennelly and Mikulski traveled to New York to watch her chair the Security Council. "We wanted to be right there on the U.N. floor when it happened," Mikulski says, grinning. They spent the night with Albright in her elegant ambassadorial suite at the Waldorf Towers, curling up in the den after dinner to talk.

While the 1992 election had brought a welcome change of jobs for Albright, it was bad news for Ferraro, who lost her bid for the Senate. She was not sure what she would do next. Albright, who had once attached herself to Ferraro's star, was now in a position to help. When news reports surfaced a few months later that large numbers of Bosnian women had been raped during the ethnic cleansing, Ferraro raised the issue with Albright. "Madeleine," Ferraro asked, "what the hell are you going to do about this?" Albright replied that she planned to appoint Ferraro as a delegate to the United Nations Human Rights Commission, which would be meeting for six weeks in Geneva. "So now," Albright said, "what in hell are *you* going to do about it?"[29]

Ferraro spent two years with the commission, which she later headed, before quitting to join *Crossfire,* a verbal slugfest on CNN that pits conservative against liberal commentators. She sparred with former White House chief of staff John Sununu and Republican Pat Buchanan. The biggest plus for Ferraro: It offered her increased visibility for another Senate bid.

Privately, the Golden Girls were worried. Barbara Kennelly's husband, Jim, had serious health problems. Barbara was under enormous stress as she tried to juggle her House responsibilities with her wish to spend as much time with Jim as possible. But she could not just quit her job to take care of her husband: She was the one who carried the health insurance.[30] During a particularly difficult period, Ferraro flew to Washington to be with her. Mikulski checked in almost daily. Albright called regularly. On October 11, 1995, after lying in a coma for ten days, Jim Kennelly had a heart attack and died. Barbara was devastated. Mikulski, Ferraro, and Albright cleared their schedules to go to Connecticut for the funeral. "The pain of losing a husband is like childbirth," Kennelly says. "No one ever tells you how much it hurts."[31]

That New Year's Eve, Ferraro insisted Kennelly join her family in St. Croix for the holiday, as she had done with Jim for years. As midnight approached, Kennelly told Ferraro that she was leaving the neighborhood party they were attending and would walk back to Ferraro's place alone. Ferraro would not hear of it. Together, the two friends walked down the hill to Ferraro's condominium. "She had a good cry and felt better," Ferraro says.

When Clinton was elected for a second term in 1996 and selected Albright to be his top diplomat, Kennelly started rethinking her own career. In the fourteen years since she had first been elected to the House, Mikulski had moved on to the Senate. Between bids for the Senate, Ferraro had launched a television career. And Albright, who was an unsung staffer on the National Security Council when Kennelly was first elected, had outdistanced them all.

Kennelly, the fourth-ranking Democrat in the House, had become a senior member of its powerful Ways and Means Committee. She was also vice chairwoman of the House Democratic Caucus, an honor, but one that carried little power. She was restless and thought about running for governor of Connecticut. Twice before she had passed up opportunities to run. This time she agonized. She was not a wealthy woman, and her husband's death had been a major loss.

Her friends worried how she would hold up if she ran and lost and gave up her comfortable House seat in the process. Kennelly listened, knowing that these women not only understood the risks, but that they had her best interests at heart. "It's hard to do things that are risky for a lot of reasons," Kennelly says. "I look at Madeleine and think that she has always excelled, but that she was willing to take a risk. I say to myself, 'It took courage for Barbara [Mikulski] to move from the House to the Senate. Geraldine has refused to ride on the laurels of being the first woman to run for vice president. And who would have thought a sixty-year-old woman could start a television career?' It made me feel like, 'Hey, what have I done?' These are my friends and maybe I could do better. I'm thinking maybe I should do more, make a move."[32]

The congresswoman spent the month of August at her family beach house in Madison, Connecticut, mulling over her choices. On Monday, September 23, a radiant Barbara Kennelly announced her decision in Hartford's Old State House, one of the oldest legislative chambers in the country. After fifteen years in Congress, she was a candidate for governor of Connecticut.[33] It would be a difficult uphill race.

Ferraro took a similar path. After spending New Year's with her husband at their vacation house in St. Croix, she announced that she would seek the Democratic nomination to challenge Alfonse M. D'Amato, known by his city detractors as Senator Pothole. No one had been able to wrestle the seat from him in seventeen years.[34]

Mikulski planned to seek a third Senate term. By the spring of 1998, she had become such a formidable presence—and collected $1.4 million in campaign contributions—that she faced little serious Republican opposition. "The fact is, probably the strongest Republican couldn't beat Mikulski," one GOP operative told the *Washington Post*.[35]

Wendy Sherman met Albright during the Mondale-Ferraro campaign. As chief of staff to Barbara Mikulski, she traveled on Ferraro's campaign plane whenever her boss went along. Sherman had encouraged Mikulski to take the job of co-chair of the campaign because the four-term congresswoman was thinking of running for the Senate in 1986 and needed to increase her visibility. In a strategy memo to Mikulski, Sherman explained that a leadership position in Mondale's presidential campaign would give Mikulski the opportunity to meet big Democratic givers from all over the country. She was proved right when Mikulski raised more money in 1986 than she ever had before.

It was during Michael Dukakis' presidential campaign in 1988, when Sherman ran his Washington operation, that she and Albright became close friends. Four years later, after Clinton was elected, Sherman took a job at the State Department handling legislative affairs, which put her in daily contact with the powers-that-be on Capitol Hill. In 1996, she was named president of the Fannie Mae Foundation, an organization that provides affordable housing opportunities to communities throughout the United

States. She was there only a year when Albright became secretary of state and persuaded Sherman to return to Foggy Bottom to join her inner circle.

Sherman's link to the Golden Girls explains a lot about them all. Twelve years younger than Albright, she is one of a cadre of professional women who act as a support group for their older bosses, providing shrewd political advice as well as reassurance. They are a sounding board for a generation of women who did not start their careers as feminists and still have a tendency to doubt their abilities, no matter what they have achieved. Like Sherman, who is married and has a teenage daughter, these younger women struggle to balance family life with careers and look to the older women as role models, mentors, and friends. "We give them confidence that they will have staff and political people who are totally loyal to them and who can also work with the guys," Sherman says. "We are the ones who can walk into the ladies' room with them and have the conversation you sometimes have to have. We can say 'Do this' or 'Stop worrying,' all the things guys say to each other in the men's room."

The bond these women share is not only critical to their political success but crucial to their understanding of themselves as well. Albright, Ferraro, Mikulski, and Kennelly are peers, women who grew up in the 1950s and saw the rules of society change a decade later. Each has had her own struggles, personally and politically. Each has succeeded in what is still very much a man's world. When one has trouble, health problems, children with growing pains, or personal self-doubts, the others have rallied, no questions asked. It is the essence of their friendship.

The generational link with Sherman and some of their younger aides is equally interesting. There is a mutual sharing of trust and respect; loyalty is more important than professional advancement; the physical, emotional, and professional experiences of those a decade older become the road map for friends who follow in their path. It is a gift that Albright has both given and received.

20

Moving Up

"People were envious and started seeing that Madeleine would play a key role in a
Dukakis administration. She had to hold her ground."

—James Steinberg, October 3, 1997

IT WAS IN THE 1988 presidential campaign of Massachusetts governor
Michael Dukakis that Madeleine Albright came into her own. In the '84
campaign, she had been a member of the candidate's foreign policy team,
but she actually spent more time advising the *vice presidential* candidate on
foreign policy, traveling on Ferraro's campaign plane, carrying her black
briefing books. This time Albright became principal foreign policy adviser to
the *presidential* candidate, Dukakis himself. Madeleine was moving up.

During the eight years of the Reagan presidency, Albright had positioned
herself to become a player in Democratic politics. She hosted a series of
working dinners at her Georgetown house where Democrats-in-exile
debated the issues of the day. To ensure that the evenings were not boring,
she limited the guest list to sixteen, served cocktails in her cozy living
room, and insisted that all conversation be off-the-record, which allowed
people to speak frankly. A buffet dinner would be served. Nothing fancy.
Maybe just a chicken casserole and salad. "No one ever went for the food,"
one regular says.[1]

Christine Dodson, who had prodded Albright to become more
assertive, could not get over the change in her old friend. One day when
Dodson was staying with Albright at her Georgetown home, Albright mentioned that she was the luncheon speaker at the Woman's National Demo-

cratic Club on New Hampshire Avenue and invited Dodson to come along. "I remember her standing at the podium and this roaring lion quality came out of her," Dodson says. "She had this poise and this articulateness and this complete confidence in her ability to speak. It was stunning."[2]

Equally stunning to Dodson was how disorganized Albright could be at home. "She must be the most untidy person in the world," says Dodson. "She undresses and drops everything wherever it falls." Albright's housekeeper usually came to the rescue, but she was afraid to touch anything in Albright's office, which was just off the living room. On several occasions, Dodson told her friend that the mess was unacceptable, embarrassingly so. When Albright paid no heed, Dodson took a photograph of the office and gave it to Albright as a present. "This is what the room looks like," Dodson said. Albright called in an architect, who moved her office to the third floor.[3]

Christine Dodson tells the story not to embarrass Albright but to show that when Albright thinks someone is well-intentioned, she listens. "She knows she has five or ten friends who will tell her the truth," Dodson says. "I suspect this is how she deals with world leaders. She figures out their intent. If she needs to correct something that is not well done, she can change [direction]."[4]

As is often the case with senior campaign advisers, Albright had the luxury, if there is such a thing as luxury in a presidential campaign, of spending most of her time in Washington while junior Dukakis staffers (read: younger) baby-sat the candidate. In fact, the situation often works well for both the home team and the one on the road.

Young politicians are easily addicted to the circus atmosphere of a presidential campaign, thirteen to fourteen months of escalating tension and travel in what amounts to a sealed cocoon, a bubble that crisscrosses the country with its own rules, its own nutty culture, its own frenetic pace. In this hermetically sealed world of expense-account meals, mindlessly repetitive campaign events, ever-changing schedules, and minicrises that take on momentous importance, an easy camaraderie develops between an adrenaline-driven campaign staff and an irreverent press corps, a silent handshake based largely on a tacit understanding that the fortunes of those who make the news and those who report it are not unrelated, that they can be and often are intertwined. And then there are the campaign junkies, those in the press corps and the campaign world whose professional lives revolve around the peripatetic cycle of election campaigns. Emotionally and physically, this is not a grown-up's world, and not a world the fifty-one-year-old Albright chose to jump into again. Instead, as a senior campaign official expected to lure opinion makers into the center ring of the Dukakis circus tent, she remained largely in the nation's capital during the primaries, close to Capitol Hill, close to international thinkers, close to home.

Her staff consisted of James Steinberg, a former national security adviser to Senator Edward M. Kennedy, and Nancy E. Soderberg, a former budget analyst for a Boston bank and Georgetown graduate student to whom Albright had become a mentor. Steinberg was designated as the person to do much of the plane travel with Dukakis during the primaries. Wendy Sherman, whom Albright had met during the Ferraro campaign, was running the Washington operation for Dukakis, coordinating issues and developing relations with Capitol Hill.

As a governor, Dukakis had little more than a passing familiarity with foreign policy. He had lived in Peru while a college student at Swarthmore, was fluent in Spanish, and, as a descendant of Greek immigrants, had a particular interest in Greek-Turkish relations. Yet although he was a good student of history, he lacked a comprehensive worldview. Most of what he knew about foreign affairs came from reading the *New York Times*. While he understood, say, the basic economic problems facing developing nations, he had developed no grand strategy for U.S. foreign policy. In both depth and breadth in international affairs, Dukakis could not touch his rival, George Bush, who had been U.N. ambassador, U.S. envoy to China, and director of the Central Intelligence Agency before becoming Ronald Reagan's vice president. Bush had been training for the presidency since Yale. Dukakis' goal in life was to be governor, but he rode the economic recovery called the "Massachusetts Miracle" into the Democratic presidential race. Patricia O'Brien, who was Dukakis' campaign press secretary, remembers driving with the candidate when he returned from a presidential campaign swing to Boston. As his car sped under a bridge, the governor looked up and shook his head. "We've got to get these painted," he said. It was the State House, not the White House, that was Dukakis' passion. The White House was an afterthought.[5] Foreign policy could be Dukakis' Achilles' heel. His staff realized that its job was to assure voters that he was qualified to negotiate with Mikhail Gorbachev.[6] Albright had her work cut out for her.

Susan Estrich, a Harvard law professor and veteran of Democratic politics, who had met Albright during the Mondale/Ferraro campaign and now was number two on the Dukakis team, pulled her friend aside.[7] "The problem this time is that he doesn't know much more than Gerry [Ferraro] did, but he's a helluva lot more arrogant," Estrich said. "He doesn't know that he doesn't know as much as he doesn't know."[8]

Then there was the public perception of Dukakis himself, fostered by his opponent. In a national political climate that had grown increasingly conservative under Reagan's stewardship, the Bush campaign operation portrayed Dukakis as the ultraliberal governor from the dangerously liberal state of Massachusetts, a mercurial politician whose view of the U.S. role in the world was shaped more by Vietnam than by Munich. The appointment of Albright helped counter that image. Dukakis' campaign staff viewed her selection as a plus, because she was more conservative than the candidate in her international outlook. She was not one of those liberal advisers from the Kennedy School priesthood that Dukakis had known for years. Albright, with her Eastern European background, independent views, and strong belief in a powerful America, brought Dukakis credibility.

She brought another strength to the job. After her years dealing with the tempestuous egos of Ed Muskie and Zbig Brzezinski, Albright was, in the long run, not intimidated by Dukakis, who could be stubborn and bone-headed on issues, aloof, and arrogant with his staff. He was a strong debater, and when staffers challenged him on issues, he would often lunge back at them. "You had to be prepared to hold your ground and not rise to the bait," Steinberg says. "If you got past that, it was okay." Steinberg had an instinct to debate Dukakis; Albright knew it was more effective to talk him through issues, although she was not always confident in her own ability to get him to listen.[9]

While Albright was clearly the senior partner in the foreign policy cluster, she never pulled rank on Steinberg, whose daily exposure to the candidate offered both of them important insight into his temperament. By working carefully together, they were able to get Dukakis to adopt a more subtle approach to the country's nuclear force posture, to back off his plan to withdraw American troops from South Korea, and to reverse his opposition to many new strategic weapons systems. "Madeleine played an absolutely crucial role in the campaign," says Steinberg, now deputy national security adviser and still a close friend of the secretary. "She had a lot of impact on his recalibrating the way he saw and talked about the United States." Albright's sense that it was a good thing that the country was strong and active internationally was a real counterweight to some of Dukakis' instincts.

To her female friends on the campaign, Albright confided that she did not think that she was getting through to Dukakis. "She was frustrated because he wouldn't listen to her," says a staffer, who often sat in the back of the campaign van with Albright when she traveled. "There was a timidity about Madeleine. She was trying to get him to pay attention, and he would cut her off. It threw her off and made her more tentative, and she asked her friends how to get through to him."[10]

Albright was also still smarting from her divorce six years before. "She was still deeply wounded," says this campaign colleague. "She was dieting and drank this awful liquid goo. Her daughter Anne was getting married, and she said that she was damned if she would show up at the wedding not looking good."[11] Albright had dieted off and on for years, once by eating kelp, which is a form of seaweed. She lost so much weight before Anne's wedding that she got her dress size down to 10. But she was so busy on the campaign that she did not have time to shop. "I went to Saks Fifth Avenue and found a Mary McFadden on sale that was perfect for her," says Winifred Freund. "Madeleine is not a clotheshorse." There was another aspect to the purchase that pleased Albright: The dress was on sale.

In the fall of 1988, the amount of money the United States should spend on defense was again an issue of contention between Democrats and Republicans, and Dukakis' staff was concerned that the candidate's opposition to excessive spending not make him look weak. Determined that he meet the minimum standard in national politics for being pro-defense, Estrich and Albright went to brief him. Looking Dukakis in the eye, Estrich began, "You say that you'll spend what it takes to make America secure." Dukakis erupted, insisting that he could not say those words, that the country was already spending too much on defense. Albright looked horror-stricken and gave Estrich a "How can he say that?" glance. Then she patiently turned to Dukakis and said, "Michael, you have to spend what it takes to make America secure." Estrich nodded. "Michael, you have to believe that," she said.

Hoping their student had absorbed the weight of their argument, the two professors walked out of the room. Estrich told Albright she should never reveal the conversation they had just had with Dukakis. Albright did not. Ten years later, Estrich was still impressed at her friend's discretion. "I've been with Madeleine in rooms where candidates have made absolute fools of themselves," Estrich says. "Anyone else at that level of foreign policy would walk out of the room and leak it. Madeleine not only doesn't burn you, but figures out how to teach the clod."[12]

Albright coached Dukakis and broadened his perspective by bringing other foreign policy experts to meet with him, including Congressman Lee Hamilton of Indiana, a senior Democrat on the House Foreign Affairs Committee, and Senator Sam Nunn of Georgia, a key figure on the Senate Armed Services Committee. From her growing network of friends who jumped back and forth between politics and academia, Albright developed a team of individuals who were not household names but on whom the campaign could draw at a moment's notice to craft a position paper or draft a speech: Martin Indyk, executive director of the Washington Institute for

Near East Policy; Robert Lieber, a Middle East specialist at Georgetown University; Pete Hakim, a Latin America expert in the Carter administration. All regulars at Albright's Georgetown salon, they were the kind of dinner party guests who were more likely to be discussing the role of Circassians in the Jordanian army than the "legs" on a good merlot.

Campaigns are cutthroat operations. There is often less competition between the Democratic and Republican candidates than among campaign staffers who sense that they have picked a winner. People whose idea of heaven had once centered on spending two consecutive nights in the same bed start thumbing through the "Plum Book," mulling over its list of government jobs subject to presidential appointment. The extent of an aide's ambition can usually be measured in reverse proportion to his degree of insistence that he would never move to Washington and cannot wait to return to Dubuque.

A campaign aide's status is measured in "face time," the amount of time he or she spends with the candidate. Even the most generous individuals find their access and proximity difficult to share. One of Albright's longtime friends in the news business was deeply hurt when Albright would not intervene to secure a television interview with Dukakis. "When she got on to an important person, that was it," says this friend. "You couldn't approach him. She felt a proprietary sense."

Although Dukakis lagged behind Bush for much of the campaign, he enjoyed a brief surge in the polls in July, emerging from the Democratic convention seventeen points ahead. Democrats, banished from the White House for twelve years, could almost smell the Rose Garden and began jockeying for position. Unhappy with having to deal with a woman in charge of foreign policy and unwilling to take her seriously, some of Dukakis' outside advisers tried to get around Albright and send position papers to him directly through the governor's office. They were not clever enough to realize that staffers in his state office would send the papers on to Albright, who then knew exactly who was trying to circumvent her. "People were envious and started seeing that Madeleine would play a key role in a Dukakis administration," Steinberg says. "She had to hold her ground."[13]

The advantage in the polls was short-lived. By August, Bush was nine points ahead of Dukakis. Democrats hoped that two upcoming presidential debates would reinstate their candidate. Debates are high-stake, high-pressure events, and Dukakis' team was convinced that the quick-thinking governor would prevail over Bush, who had a goofy tendency to transpose events and garble his syntax.

Ever since 1960, when Richard Nixon lost the first televised debate to

John Kennedy, largely because of his sweaty brow and five o'clock shadow, style has mattered as much as substance. Dukakis spent more time than his staff thought necessary trying to decide whether adding shoulder pads to his suit jackets would make him look bigger. Media consultant Robert Squier spent half a day adjusting the angle of the podium to make Dukakis look taller. When the candidate participated in a debate, aides would try to enhance his presence by placing a stool behind the lectern for him to stand on. Sneaking it discreetly onto the stage without his opponent seeing it became a game of skill. At one point, Squier built a ramp with a rise too subtle for a camera to catch. "We're going to make this slope so gradual that construction will start in your hotel room," Squier told the candidate.[14]

The Dukakis staff, frustrated by the candidate's refusal to accept policy suggestions from inside the campaign, turned to an outsider to advise Dukakis on the debate. Bill Clinton, the smart, likable governor of Arkansas, was reluctant, but he eventually agreed to help prepare the Massachusetts governor for his face-to-face meetings with Bush. It would be the first time Albright met Clinton.

Clinton arrived in Boston on Saturday morning, September 24, and joined the staff preparing Dukakis for the Sunday debate the next night in Winston-Salem, North Carolina. Crime was a major issue, and Bush intended to show that Dukakis was soft on crime by highlighting the case of Willie Horton, Jr., a convicted murderer who, while on furlough from the Massachusetts prison system, stabbed a man and raped a woman. Dukakis had inherited the penal system from his Republican predecessor, and it had not been an issue until Al Gore raised it in the New York primary.[15] Estrich wanted Dukakis to offer a mea culpa, admitting his original decision to support a furlough program for murderers had been a mistake. Patricia O'Brien, the campaign press secretary, wanted her candidate to visit the rape victim—with television cameras rolling—and apologize. But Dukakis, always cool to the personal touch, refused. They appealed to Clinton to intercede. In a folksy manner, the Arkansas governor told Dukakis that he had a similar problem in his state, that he felt terrible for letting the guy out of jail, and that he felt real remorse. Dukakis, Clinton implied, could express the same feeling. The problem was that Dukakis did not believe he had made a mistake. Watching Clinton, Estrich thought to herself, "Why aren't we working for this guy?"[16]

At another point, Dukakis looked at his briefing books and said, "I don't ever want to see another reference to country club Republicans." Clinton, a more astute politician, who understood that Republicans took care of core constituents, looked puzzled. "Why not?" he asked. Discouraged at how poorly the preparations were going, the group broke for lunch. Estrich, Clinton, Albright, and Squier went out for Chinese food and returned to grill Dukakis for five or six hours more. By evening, everyone was exhausted and disheartened. The prep team adjourned to Boston's South End for dinner, then went on to a popular bar. It was a dark night for political junkies on a sinking campaign ship.

Estrich drove her campaign-leased blue Chevrolet. Clinton sat in front. Albright, Squier, and Clinton aide Bruce Lindsey sat in back. Their destination was the Four Seasons Hotel, where the campaign press corps was lodged. When they arrived, a hotel bell captain informed them that the bar was overcrowded. He would not let them in. Furious, Squier marched into the bar and announced, "I have the governor of Arkansas, the director of the Dukakis presidential campaign, and the brightest star in American foreign policy in my party. This hotel will not let us in, so we are taking our business elsewhere."[17]

With that, the group drove off to the less prestigious Lafayette Park Hotel, across from the Dukakis campaign headquarters on Chauncey Street, where campaign advisers were staying. There the bar was closed, whereupon Clinton invited the group to his hotel room and opened the mini-bar. Sitting on Clinton's hotel room floor, they laughed uproariously at what presidential campaigns actually come down to: the vanities, the games, Dukakis and his shoulder pads, the angle of the lectern. At 3:30 A.M., someone looked at a watch. They had to be on the campaign plane in less than four hours. Clinton walked the women to their car, and Estrich drove Albright to her apartment, where they agreed that Clinton's ear was politically tuned to the issues on which Dukakis was deafest.

The next night, Clinton, Albright, Estrich, and Squier watched the debate from the staff holding room and were delighted that their candidate did better than they had expected. Afterward, they stood around a piano and sang Beatles songs while the Duke's new press secretary, Mark Gearan, played.

21

Training Ground

"Certain parts of my life contained what I called my Scholarship Personality. I thought I had to earn everything and that I couldn't afford to do anything. I used to worry about it and not buy clothes. The other [part] is that if there is something that needs to be achieved, I should try to achieve it."

—Madeleine Albright, February 7, 1998

THE 1980S WERE dreary times for the Democrats. Ronald Reagan had enjoyed two terms as a popular leader, and George Bush roundly defeated Michael Dukakis for the presidency in 1988, leaving Democrats to wander in the political wilderness for four more years.

The '80s were hard on Albright as well. In January 1985, Barry Carter had shocked Albright by announcing that he was moving out of her life.[1] "Madeleine had three lovely daughters and raised them," Carter says. "She was a caring mother. I wanted to have children. It was clear we were at different stages of our lives."[2]

That July, Albright joined the board of a small think tank called the Center for National Policy. The liberal center had been started in 1981 by a group of people organized by political consultant Ted Van Dyk, a former speechwriter and strategist for Hubert Humphrey. In response to a growing feeling that Republicans had usurped the Democrats as the party of ideas and that more creativity was needed to address public problems, Van Dyk put together a board of directors drawn from the cabinets of the Kennedy, Johnson, and Carter administrations. Edmund Muskie was chairman of the board in 1989 when the center started a search for a new president to replace Kirk O'Donnell, a former aide to House Speaker Thomas P. "Tip" O'Neill, who was leaving to return to practicing law. Finding a new leader to run the small, underfunded organization was a tough sell, and Albright was a member of the search committee. With a budget of barely $1 million and a staff of only eight or nine full-time professionals, the center was hidden in the shadows of bigger, better-known, and better-financed think tanks, such as the liberal Brookings Institution or the conservative Heritage Foundation. Frustrated at the committee's inability to find a suitable candidate, Richard Moe, a longtime Democratic operative and chair of the search committee, called Harry McPherson, another board member, to say he had a radical idea but one that might work. "What about Madeleine?" Moe asked McPherson. The seasoned elder Democrat, who had been a key party adviser since the Johnson days, suggested that they take Albright to lunch. Albright's reaction to the proposition was noncommittal, but Moe remembers that "she didn't immediately turn it down."[3]

In fact, Albright was hesitant to accept the position. "She went through an agonizing process," says Wendy Sherman, who was a consultant to the center at the time. "I pushed her really hard to take it, as did others. I thought it was a very good platform and that it was time for her to be head of something. It was one of those moments in which she had to catapult herself into seeing herself differently."

Albright knew the center was still in the process of trying to define itself and that a major fund-raising effort was necessary. Privately, she told friends that she was not sure she had a vision for the organization. "It was one of those moments when she had to take a risk and a chance because it was time for her to emerge as more of a leader, someone in her own right," Sherman says.[4]

Muskie, the board chairman, did not share his search committee's enthusiasm for the idea. He had high regard for his former staff member, but that was part of the problem. He thought of her as a staffer. As chairman of the board, he wanted the job to go to someone who was better established, a sure rainmaker. And there was something else: She was a woman. Muskie thought the job should go to a man, and he told her so directly. Albright heard him out. Once the search committee convinced Muskie that she was the right person for the job and offered it to Albright, Muskie was very supportive.[5]

It was the right decision. Under Albright's stewardship, the center became the stage that Albright's friends thought she deserved. She made it a place where her combined interests in foreign policy and politics found a voice. Her job was no longer that of the supportive woman providing answers for political candidates to recite, but to offer them herself. "For all of us, there comes a moment in our career path when we confront whether we will remain as a staffer or become a principal," says Maureen "Mo" Steinbruner, who was Albright's vice president at the center and succeeded her as president. "Becoming a principal is not a choice everyone can make. If you make that choice, there are certain things you do to change your sense of yourself—the sense of relationships, the way you present yourself. It probably comes intuitively to some people and not to others."[6]

The process did not come naturally to Albright. Like everything she had done her entire life, she had to work at it, work at articulating views that made it clear she was in charge, work at sounding decisive, work at offering judgments instead of simply providing facts. "It doesn't happen overnight," says Steinbruner. "You feel it. This was a place of passage for her."

As she had been during her days associated with the Beauvoir Elementary School, Albright was determined to make a difference. To put the center in better financial health, she recruited new board members who brought dollars with them. They included Maurice Templesman, the diamond importer and longtime companion to Jacqueline Kennedy Onassis; John Cooke, head of the Disney Channel; and David Maxwell, head of Fannie Mae. She teamed up with the Times Mirror Company's Center for the People and the Press, which conducted surveys about Americans' opinions about foreign and domestic policy issues. The two groups released their results together, and the center planned "Square Table" panel discussions, drawing upon both Democrats and Republicans to discuss the issues raised in the surveys. "It was a place for her to have a range of activities that would allow her to interact with the policy development process in a way you don't get if you are teaching one course at Georgetown," Steinbruner says. "This put her in the process in a legitimate, useful way. It was important to her."

Albright had enjoyed the television panels at Georgetown University, and the center offered a broader arena. "This was the place where she began to understand her talent at communicating," says Wendy Sherman. "The center became a place where she could go on 'The Today Show' and comment on foreign and domestic policy. It was a phenomenal training ground for her now very sophisticated skills in public diplomacy." It was also an opportunity to practice her new role, to comment on events for which she had no direct responsibility. "The stakes aren't so high," Sherman says. "You can experiment a little bit and use your own style and get comfortable with what that style is."[7]

Her timing was lucky, too. On the international scene, communism was falling apart in what was then the Soviet Union, and the small countries of Eastern Europe that Albright had spent a lifetime studying were struggling to cast off the Soviet yoke and establish open markets and democratic rule.

Albright did not need to stretch to offer an analysis. She had been honing her lines on this subject for more than three decades.

When the 1992 campaign season rolled around, Albright decided not to commit herself to one candidate because that would have conflicted with the leadership of the nonpartisan center. In the end, that did not matter. The relationship with Bill Clinton that began in prepping Dukakis for the presidential debates four years before had remained intact. When Clinton was seeking to expand his own meager foreign policy credentials and sought admission to the Council on Foreign Relations in 1989, Albright recommended him.[8] The council would give Clinton entrée to the elite chamber of America's foreign policy establishment. He did not forget who helped put him there.

As the months went by, Mandula Korbel's health deteriorated. She suffered from scleroderma, a painful disease causing thickening of the skin that also affected her lungs. "There is more to life than breathing," she joked to friends. But soon her breathing became difficult. On October 8, 1989, Mandula Korbel died. She was a fun-loving woman who understood people and considered her family to be her life's work. In her later years, she took great joy from her grandchildren, bragging to relatives about the musical ability of one grandson and the athletic prowess of another. Because she was never fluent in English, her children were astounded to find among her personal papers her essay about her husband and her life, all written in hesitant English. "The more I talk and think about [my parents], the more remarkable I think they are," Albright says. "They made us feel normal. If you tell the story, it seems heroic or textured, but what they were was great parents."[9]

PART FOUR

 *Madame Secretary*

22

Madame Ambassador

"This experience has been invaluable for her work as secretary of state. There are people who go through this organization for five years and don't have the networks and contacts and relationships to fall back on as she does."
—Kofi Annan, Secretary-General of
the United Nations, January 15, 1998

WHEN BILL CLINTON was elected president in November 1992, Madeleine Albright was not confident that she would get a plum appointment. She had not played a crucial role in his campaign. Samuel R. "Sandy" Berger, a close Clinton friend since their days together on George McGovern's losing presidential campaign, had served as Clinton's senior foreign policy adviser prior to the election. But because he did not feel that he had enough heft in foreign policy issues, Berger brought in Anthony Lake, a former NSC staffer, as his boss. Nancy Soderberg became a foreign policy adviser based in the campaign's Little Rock headquarters, a good position for a relatively young staffer who was willing and able to move. Albright had recommended her former graduate student for the job. Strobe Talbott, a recognized expert on Russia and a Clinton pal since they were Rhodes Scholars at Oxford, was still employed at *Time* magazine in Washington, but he was in regular touch with the candidate. His wife, Brooke Shearer, was a top aide to Hillary Clinton, traveling with her on the campaign trail.

There are only so many key foreign policy jobs in a campaign, and Clinton's inner circle was in place. Albright, who had not worked full time in the campaign, became part of the outer circle, a group tapped on occasion to write position papers for the candidate and advise him on special issues. "It was out-ski time," says a political campaign veteran. "As of the [time of the] convention, she was feeling very much that her role was limited. It was clear to me that some of the men were doing everything in their power to keep Madeleine out, and she felt it, as she had all along." Why would they try to keep Albright, a rising star in the foreign policy world, at a distance? "Because if they let her in, she'd end up the fuckin' secretary of state," explained the campaign aide.[1]

After almost twenty years as a Democratic campaign operative, starting as a volunteer for Ed Muskie in 1972 and culminating as the top foreign policy adviser to Michael Dukakis in 1988, Albright had developed an intricate network of friends and advisers. She did not need a ringside seat inside Clinton's campaign tent to know what was going on. She could call Soderberg. Because she had trained her, Albright trusted her friend's perceptions and instincts. "It's the women who don't have those relationships who fall on their faces," Soderberg says. "What happens is that they say, 'Okay, I will get tough to be taken seriously.' Then nobody wants to deal with them. Madeleine has this network of women, and men, whom she can call to ask, 'What's the real story?'"

The real story was that Clinton liked Albright. His approval of her was her secret weapon. Soderberg recalls that after she handed Clinton a paper with a list of people planning to attend a meeting, he underlined Albright's name and wrote "good" in the margin.[2] Like many men in top management positions, Clinton mouthed the right words about being comfortable working with strong women. He certainly had married one. And while few people pretend to understand the dynamics of the Clintons' marriage, everyone agrees that they are a strong political team. Yet many women insist that the Clinton White House remains largely the domain of white men, in spite of the president, who prided himself on hiring large numbers of minorities and women. Women, some at high levels, expressed dismay that they were treated in a patronizing manner and not accorded the same stature as their male colleagues.[3] Dee Dee Myers, Clinton's press secretary for the first two years of his administration, noted despairingly: "You get the title, but you don't get the job."[4]

Soderberg compares a political campaign to freshman year in college, during which savvy students develop a network of friends whom they can call to ask what's going on. "The policy [world] is more straightforward," Soderberg says. "You need to know the dynamics, the personal fights, the personal ambitions, the egos, someone who will say 'Here's the inside scoop.' You need to know the behind-the-scenes policy, the give-and-take of what's going on."[5]

One of the benefits of presidential politics is that campaign veterans train the next generation of political operatives. Soderberg was grateful to Albright for fine-tuning her former student's political antennae. "What happens to many women is that they don't have role models when they are young," Soderberg says. "They don't have an inner circle of people to tell them what's really going on. As a result, the advice they get is always a little off—and it gets worse as they become more senior. By the time they're forty, they can have a series of not the most brilliant recommendations." Albright made sure that did not happen to Soderberg.

After his election, Clinton asked Albright to run his National Security Council transition team. Though this was a clear indication that he held her in high esteem, Albright did not head any of Clinton's lists for top positions in the new administration. When Donna Shalala arrived in Little Rock to be interviewed by the president-elect for a cabinet job, she found Albright sitting alone on the porch of the governor's mansion, surrounded by packing boxes. "Gee, whatcha gonna get?" Shalala asked her old friend. "I don't think anything," Albright replied. "I don't think it's going to work out." Shalala tried to cheer her up. "Oh, come on," Shalala said. "He's going to appoint you to something. I know it."[6]

The president-elect first offered the position of U.S. ambassador to the United Nations to Ronald Brown, who, as chairman of the Democratic National Committee, had played a crucial role in rebuilding the party and Clinton's winning the election. Brown, who had often been the "first black" to fill any number of important positions, did not want to be seen as following in the path of civil rights leader and former Atlanta mayor Andrew Young, Carter's U.N. ambassador. Brown made it clear he wanted a different post.[7] Clinton also considered Condoleezza Rice, who had served on the National Security Council staff in the Bush administration and was teaching at Stanford. Clinton decided to appoint a Democrat and dropped Rice from his list.[8] Another possible choice was Richard Gardner, a longtime student of the United Nations and Albright's former Georgetown neighbor. But the president-elect was being pressured by a range of people, including his wife, to add more women and minorities to his cabinet, and the U.N. post had been elevated to cabinet rank by several of Clinton's predecessors. He eventually named Gardner to be the U.S. ambassador to Spain and chose Albright—by now a part of his foreign policy team—for the U.N. post in New York.

When Clinton introduced his cabinet selections to the press in Little Rock in December 1992, Albright referred to herself as a Czech immigrant, spoke of her father, and said how proud she would be to sit at the United

Nations behind the nameplate that reads "United States of America." She had written her brief acceptance in longhand on a yellow legal pad. Her words brought tears to the eyes of many in the room, including her daughters and the president-elect.

A few days later, a Christmas party Albright gave at her home in Georgetown turned into a celebration of her selection. A young Senate aide came up to her and told her how difficult her confirmation hearings would be, perhaps trying to promote himself as the best person to guide her through the Byzantine confirmation process. He went on at length, outlining the problems she would face, the outlandish questions, and the irascibility of the senators on the Senate Foreign Relations Committee. Albright stood there, not sure how to respond. Then, not content to have inserted only one foot in his mouth, the Senate aide added that Clinton had not really cried at her introduction in Little Rock; it was his allergies that brought tears to his eyes. Albright was stunned, as amazed at the man's insensitivity as she was concerned that he might be right.

James P. Rubin, an arms control specialist who had become a personal and professional friend of Albright, overheard the conversation and rolled his eyes at the man's insensitivity. Rubin, who was then on the staff of the Senate Foreign Relations Committee, which would consider her nomination, took Albright aside to reassure her, predicting that she would be confirmed unanimously by the Senate. He offered to help prepare her for the hearings.[9]

Rubin and Albright had met in 1988, when she was advising Dukakis on foreign policy, and Rubin was directing research for the Arms Control Association, a nonprofit special-interest group in Washington. The next year, he joined the staff of the Senate Foreign Relations Committee as Delaware senator Joseph Biden, Jr.'s senior policy aide on the panel.

Ever since 1990, when they had had their first lunch of bratwurst and beer at a small restaurant on Massachusetts Avenue called the Cafe Berlin, Albright and Rubin had relied on each other as sounding boards for policy advice and job counseling. Rubin had arranged for Albright to brief Biden after she returned from a trip through Eastern Europe following the collapse of Communist rule. Albright reciprocated by arranging for Rubin to participate in seminars held by her Center for National Policy.

Rubin is a tall, intense man with curly black hair and gray eyes. A bright, street-smart New Yorker, he can be cheeky one minute, charming the next. Everyone calls him Jamie. Although he's young enough to be Albright's child, the two share an intellectual bond, cemented by an insatiable interest in foreign policy and international politics. Albright and Rubin were further bound by their accord on one of the most vexing foreign policy issues of the 1990s: Bosnia. The Balkan war was the defining issue of Rubin's adult life. In March 1992, fighting broke out between Muslims and Serbs in the former Yugoslavian republic of Bosnia and Herzegovina, where the population is made up of a volatile mix of Serbs, Croatians, and Slavic Muslims.[10] Bosnian Serbs, with the support of neighboring Serbia, undertook to "cleanse" the country of Muslims, forcing them from their homes and, in some cases, executing people en masse or imprisoning them in concentration camps reminiscent of those run by the Nazis. Serbian troops frequently raped Muslim women. The Bush administration, unable to win agreement on a course of action among its European allies, declined to intervene directly, but supported economic sanctions against Serbia and a "no-fly" zone over Bosnia. Secretary of State James A. Baker III summed up the administration's position with an apt southern aphorism: "We don't have a dog in that fight."[11]

Rubin, who had been too young to be actively involved in the debate over U.S. involvement in Vietnam, was captivated by the complex issues raised by Bosnia. As a Senate staff member in the winter of 1991, he had visited all six Balkan Republics and came home convinced that the only way to stop the fighting was through direct American military intervention. "All the other issues—whether it was the Contras, China, the Soviet Union, Eastern Europe, the Berlin Wall, Vietnam—had been debated for years in the Democratic policy world," Rubin says. Bosnia was different, an issue that created new bedfellows and new alliances. "I have a friend with whom I had agreed on every other thing all my life—on nuclear weapons and arms control and the Russians and why Reagan was dangerous—who fundamentally disagreed with me on Bosnia," Rubin says. "It was complicated. You could be a liberal, an extreme liberal, and be against the nuclear arms race or against the dangers of nuclear weapons and for the war in Bosnia."[12]

In Albright, he found an ally. "Here was a fellow Democrat who didn't think I was crazy for wanting to use force in Bosnia," Rubin says. "Most of my other Democratic friends would mouth the right words as a criticism of Bush, but when push came to shove, they weren't really ready to see the United States go to war because they were fundamentally antiwar."[13]

Albright sailed through her confirmation hearings. And Rubin's prediction had been correct: The Senate vote on her nomination was unanimous. Albright invited Rubin to join her staff as a senior adviser and press spokesman. He had never worked with the press before and says he told his new boss: "I'm happy to work in sales, as long as I can work in production."[14] It's the kind of clever one-liner—a bit too cute to be spontaneous—they would soon be polishing together in New York.

*   *   *

Madeleine Albright was sworn in as the United States Permanent Representative to the United Nations on February 3, 1993. On her way to the ceremony in the ornate Old Executive Office Building, Albright's limousine pulled up at the gate to West Executive Avenue, the block-long private street between the old EOB and the White House. Her driver told the uniformed security guards at the gate that his passenger was about to become the American ambassador to the United Nations. The guard was not impressed. "Show me her I.D.," he said.[15] A few minutes later, Vice President Al Gore swore Albright into her new job. Her daughter Katie held the family Bible.

Accompanied by Karl Inderfurth, a colleague from her Carter NSC days, Albright caught the shuttle to New York for her first meeting with her counterparts from the other permanent members of the U.N. Security Council: France, Britain, Russia, and China. Not until they reached LaGuardia Airport did Albright realize how much her life would change, that she had, in fact, crossed a major divide. The longtime Washington staffer, who had spent years coaching others for the big time, was now, at last, a Washington insider in her own right, a member of the president's cabinet. She also had an impressive title, ambassador: Ambassador Albright. Her Excellency. A long, shiny, and heavily armored black limousine was waiting for her at LaGuardia. As the driver, George Ford, held open the door, a big grin spread across Albright's face, and she climbed into the backseat.

After a brief stop at the U.S. mission at the corner of First Avenue and Forty-fifth Street, she and Inderfurth drove around the corner to the French mission at One Dag Hammarskjold Plaza, where former secretary of state Cyrus Vance and Lord David Owen of Great Britain were waiting to present the outlines of their new peace plan for Bosnia. As Albright and Inderfurth entered the conference room on the forty-fourth floor of the modern office building, they spotted Vance and Owen, along with Yuli Vorontsov, the tall, courtly Russian envoy. Vorontsov wondered to himself what this "lady professor" would be like. What did she know about diplomacy?[16]

Inderfurth, a tall man with chiseled good looks, known to friends as "Rick," had been a special assistant to National Security Adviser Zbigniew Brzezinski in the late 1970s and had had an office on the first floor of the White House West Wing, not far from the Oval Office. Albright's office had been in the basement. Inderfurth later joined ABC News as a television correspondent and covered arms control and, after that, Moscow before leaving the network to join the Clinton campaign. Albright brought him aboard as U.S. representative for special political affairs with responsibility for

U.N. peacekeeping, disarmament, and security issues. Taking a deep breath, he surveyed the scene with a newsman's eye. A magnificent sunset was settling over Manhattan. "What an entrance to this job," he thought. "This is unbelievable."[17]

Albright's headquarters was now New York, but she wanted to keep a base in Washington as well, and planned to spend as much time there as possible. In addition to giving her cabinet rank, Clinton named her as a member of the handful of advisers who make final recommendations to the president on vital national security issues.

Previous U.N. ambassadors, including Adlai Stevenson, George Bush, Daniel Patrick Moynihan, and Jeane J. Kirkpatrick, represented their government at the United Nations but had little input in the making of foreign policy. Thomas Pickering, the career diplomat who later became ambassador to Russia—and, still later, one of Albright's top deputies—was widely admired at the United Nations for his ability to come up with creative formulas to resolve sticky dilemmas. He dominated the Security Council as no other American ambassador had, impressing easily ruffled diplomats with his ability to substitute one resolution for another with both ease and grace.[18] But he spent little time in Washington, largely because Bush's secretary of state, James Baker, resented having to share the limelight with the popular Pickering.

Several earlier ambassadors were accorded cabinet rank, but none had the kind of power that Clinton gave Albright when he picked her for the job.[19] To be sure, she was subordinate to the secretary of state, Warren Christopher, and received instructions as her predecessors had. But Albright, as one of the Principals, had a voice in drafting these instructions.

Meetings of the Principals' Committee convened in the Situation Room, a soundproof, top-security communications center in the White House basement. At the start of Clinton's term, members included the secretaries of state and defense, the national security adviser, the chairman of the Joint Chiefs of Staff, the director of central intelligence, and the U.N. ambassador. Because it blurs the lines of authority, most modern secretaries of state have opposed having a subordinate, such as the U.N. envoy, sit at the table, but Christopher was secure in his relationship with Clinton and comfortable having Albright at the meetings.

As president-elect, Clinton had promised an administration that "looks like America" in all its diversity. One of the other Principals put it more bluntly: "Frankly, he wanted another woman in the cabinet."[20]

Clinton's foreign policy team gathered informally on Wednesday mornings in Tony Lake's bright West Wing corner office for breakfast, brought up from the White House mess. CIA director John Deutch usually had what the others called "industrial-strength, virtual-reality sausages." Albright always ordered the same thing: a poached egg and rye toast.[21]

Albright was assertive and never hesitated to make her point during the breakfast sessions, although less so when the group gathered for more formal meetings in the Situation Room. She frequently arrived with a clear point of view and stated it firmly, although she was reluctant to engage her colleagues in sustained debate. This was particularly apparent in her exchanges with General Colin Powell, chairman of the Joint Chiefs of Staff. Her reticence occasionally frustrated Lake, an impatient man who showed his annoyance by looking at the clock and drumming his fingers on the table. After the group had been meeting for about a year, Lake learned that Albright felt he was cutting her off, and he made a special point to call on her, even if she had not made it clear that she wanted to speak. If Albright was in New York and participating by video conference, Lake trained himself to look up at the television monitor over his head, to be sure to include Albright in the discussion.[22]

A reluctance to jump into a debate is not uncommon for professional women. Georgetown professor Deborah Tannen, author of *You Just Don't Understand,* says women are often hesitant to speak up in groups, in part because their socialization as children does not prepare them for it. Boys are expected to call attention to themselves. "Research on boys at play shows they learn to use language to negotiate their place in a group by vying for center stage," Tannen says. "They learn to challenge each other and deflect challengers. Girls' social life tends to focus on a best friend, and they use language to negotiate their closeness. Girls are critical of other girls who stand out, or try to attract attention to themselves. Another part of many women's reluctance to speak out is fear of saying something that will offend or anger someone."[23]

To maintain her presence in Washington while she was away, Albright needed a good staff in the capital. She chose Frances Zwenig, a former aide to Massachusetts senator John Kerry, as her top policy adviser, and David Scheffer, an international lawyer, who had helped her prepare for her confirmation hearings. Their offices were on the sixth floor of the State Department. When Zwenig left in November 1994, Albright appointed political pro Elaine Shocas to take her place.

Shocas, a native of Worcester, Massachusetts, had been an attorney on the Senate Judiciary Committee. She also had served as a prosecutor in the Civil Rights Division of the Justice Department and the U.S. attorney's office and handled legislation for the American Federation of Teachers. In the mid-1980s, she was counsel to the treasurer of the Democratic National Committee. She also worked as counsel for Senator Edward Kennedy and was responsible for the confirmation of all federal judges. She handled congressional issues and convention matters for his 1980 presidential campaign.

Shocas is shrewd and hardworking, a dedicated staffer with a solid reputation and a taste for politics.[24] Behind a tough, no-nonsense facade is a woman with a good sense of humor who sizes up people quickly and steers clear of the press. Her job for Albright, whose daily schedule read like an airport flight plan, was that of a strategist, to think past the day's meeting with the president and to decide what Albright should be doing next week, next month, next year.

Albright met Shocas in 1986, just after Shocas returned from the Philippines, where she had been monitoring elections as a member of the National Democratic Institute for International Affairs. Albright remembers their first encounter because she noticed Shocas had fang marks on her wrist. She had been bitten by a poisonous snake during an overnight ferry ride from the island of Mindanao to Manila. Shocas joked that it was the snake that died. The women were professional friends and did not socialize often. They got to know each other better during the transition period preceding Clinton's inauguration in January 1993, when Shocas handled arrangements for Congress, the Supreme Court, the cabinet, and the Joint Chiefs of Staff.

Albright added another staffer to her inner circle, Suzy George, a 1990 Mount Holyoke graduate who grew up in Chappaqua, New York, and had recently earned a law degree from George Washington University. She had been an intern in the White House office of legislative affairs and first met Albright in 1990, when George was working as an outside adviser to the National Democratic Institute for International Affairs. When Shocas began putting together a U.S. mission staff, she wanted someone, preferably a lawyer, who was smart enough to understand policy and write cables but young and flexible enough to do advance work for upcoming trips. The United Nations was filled with people who thought of themselves as policy experts; Shocas was looking for someone with common sense, someone who would be as loyal to her as she was to Albright. Suzy George fit the description. Shocas called George to offer her the job the Tuesday night before the law school graduate took her New York State bar exam. She would work in Albright's Washington office. Albright calls her "Elaine-in-training."[25]

Rubin, Shocas, and George became Albright's eyes and ears, watching out for her interests, keeping track of her schedule, and making sure she was kept in the White House loop, politically and socially. They were fiercely protective of her reputation: Shocas, the lioness; Rubin, the pit bull; George, the aide-de-camp. Like Albright, they were all single, type-A workaholics. Soon they would think of themselves as family, an unlikely foursome bound together not by blood but loyalty, energy, and ambition, driven by democratic ideals and a determination to keep Albright's star sparkling.

The new ambassador loved her job from the start. She moved into the ambassador's $27,000-a-month suite atop the Waldorf Towers[26] and had the rooms painted a soft cream. She borrowed contemporary art—huge paintings by American painters Jackson Pollock and Louise Nevelson—from the Metropolitan Museum to hang in the living room. "Enjoy this because it's an incredible moment in time," she would tell harried aides. "We don't know when it will end." Albright could operate on four or five hours' sleep, sometimes rising at 4:30 A.M., just as she had done as a graduate student, but now to read the *New York Times,* the *Washington Post,* and the *Wall Street Journal.* Often she did not retire until after 11:00 P.M. When she arrived home at night, she frequently flipped on *Larry King Live* or *Nightline,* never hesitating to phone staffers if an interesting point was raised during either program. Privately, she joked to friends: "I sleep in George Bush's bed."[27] It was also the same bed former U.N. ambassador Adlai Stevenson shared for a time with Joe Albright's aunt Alicia Patterson.

During the Cold War, the United Nations was virtually paralyzed by the fierce competition between its two most powerful members, the Soviet Union and the United States, each of which wielded a veto in the Security Council. After the collapse of communism, the international organization slowly transformed itself into a more influential force as it monitored ethnic conflicts and other tensions around the world. President Bush and President Clinton pushed it to take on a more active role, to move from peacekeeping to peacemaking. Albright called it "assertive multilateralism,"[28] a term that made her the butt of jokes after unfocused and passive behavior by the international community led to failures in Somalia and Bosnia. She says that she abandoned it because it took too long to explain.

Although hobbled by its own entrenched bureaucracy, the international organization began to accumulate at least some of the power and authority that its founders envisioned for it at the end of World War II. Albright dubbed it "the global 911 number," the switchboard for distress calls from around the world.[29] Because it was operating as an international emergency squadron, its docket was always full. Between 1990 and 1993, the Security Council authorized the Persian Gulf war, tried though unsuccessfully to stop the wars in Croatia and Bosnia, supervised elections in Cambodia and peace in El Salvador, and sent troops into Somalia to feed the starving and try, unsuccessfully, to disarm the warlords who supplanted the government there.[30]

The U.N. Charter gives the fifteen-member Security Council "primary responsibility for the maintaining of international peace and security." Each of the council's five permanent members holds veto power over council actions. Albright, the only woman ambassador on the Security Council during her tenure, often joked that she would write a book about her experiences entitled "Fourteen Suits and a Skirt."

Albright's Security Council colleagues were tough professionals, curious about the new U.S. representative and not sure how she would fit in. Albright understood this. She proceeded slowly, often sitting quietly through their meetings, listening instead of talking. "She wasn't intimidated," says U.N. secretary-general Kofi Annan, who came to know her well. "When she was ready to make a move, she said what she thought." But not right away. "Being the only woman brought its own dynamics to the situation," Annan says. "I don't think it bothered her much. It may have bothered some of the others more than it bothered her."[31]

Gradually, Albright's style began to emerge. Her colleagues enjoyed her winning personality and her self-deprecating sense of humor. They appreciated her willingness to have a one-on-one dinner when there was a thorny issue to work out. They were also struck by what one called "her hot temper and fairly short fuse."[32] Her views on some issues, such as Bosnia, were black and white. "She was not prepared to see the chiaroscuro," says a colleague. "She was always going for the jugular." Albright, says one, was not above using "a form of emotional blackmail, like, 'Oh my God, I can't rely on my friends? What am I going to do?'" This colleague added, however, that the American ambassador never held a grudge: "If she went off the deep end, I always found the next day was kiss and make up. There was no lasting resentment there."[33]

Kofi Annan says that Albright imparted "a certain freshness, a certain direct approach." She spoke in a language that did not allow ambiguity or misinterpretation. "Working and operating with diplomats who, like lawyers, are trained to obfuscate rather than clarify, it was good to see [her forthright approach]," he says.[34] One day in the summer of 1994, Albright approached Annan, who was then in charge of the U.N. peacekeeping operation in Bosnia. "The U.N. is chicken," she said. "You're afraid of getting into action there." Annan, a soft-spoken Ghanaian, said of Albright: "I admired her for her bluntness. She doesn't mind standing alone, but she also has a capacity to work for a consensus. She stakes out her position very clearly."

Sir John Weston, the experienced British ambassador to the United Nations who worked closely with Albright, says that even if it meant getting into an occasional tangle, he preferred her direct approach to those who deal in winks, nods, and fencing. "I'm not saying she didn't have subtleties of maneuver and diplomacy," he says, "but her manner was straight out."[35]

Americans have always been ambivalent about the United Nations, content to use the world forum to promote democracy but reluctant to surrender any of its own sacred sovereignty. For years, the U.S. government has been in arrears in its dues payments. By the end of 1997, it owed more than $1 billion, mostly in unpaid assessments for peacekeeping operations.[36] The country's delinquent financial status has been a source of deep resentment among other member countries, despite U.S. claims that it has financed the bulk of U.N. operations by virtue of the body's proportional funding formula. In November 1996, the General Assembly was so displeased that it ratified a decision to oust the United States from the committee that manages the organization's financial affairs. Furious at the affront, Albright called one of her fellow permanent representatives in a rage. "This is going to cause an explosion on Capitol Hill," she said. "What are you going to do about it?" The other ambassador replied, "Madeleine, what do you mean, 'do something'? We just had an election, and you lost. That's called democracy." Albright was not appeased. "You don't realize that this is going to cause absolute mayhem on the Hill," she continued. "You have to stop it. Do it. Have a recount. Vote again." Her ambassadorial colleague explained that the vote reflected U.N. unhappiness with U.S. failure to pay its dues. Albright was unmoved, insisting something had to be done to reverse the action. "Madeleine," the ambassador said finally, "stop being petulant."[37]

For all the posturing and grandstanding that went on in open Security Council meetings, it was the informal, shirtsleeve sessions that were most conducive to honest talk. Yuli Vorontsov, Russia's representative, remembers one beautiful, clear day in late August 1993 when he and Albright were sitting under a Chinese apple tree at the Russian mission's dacha, or getaway estate, in Glen Cove, Long Island. By summer's end, the small apples had turned a deep crimson, and Vorontsov was admiring their ruddy color. He had organized the daylong retreat for his colleagues to discuss long-term projects. They were all sitting on the lawn on easy chairs, sipping peaty, Russian tea, and enjoying a respite from the recent humidity. The subject of sanctions came up. Vorontsov argued that punishing a foreign government by restricting trade or travel is not usually very effective, that it punishes powerless citizens—"the little people," he called them—more than it does a country's leaders. Albright disagreed, insisting that sanctions are effective and that if the local populace is not happy with the status quo, they should learn to get rid of the leader. "In a democratic society, that may work, yes," Vorontsov told Albright. "In the next elections, they might vote against him. But if he is a dictator, who will push him out?" Albright listened, which impressed her Russian counterpart. "That is a wonderful quality she has," Vorontsov says. "Very often diplomats see in front of them their own instructions and don't listen to what the other guy is saying. It is possible to have a give-and-take with Madeleine."[38]

Albright loved a good debate, but she was less at ease with her U.N. colleagues than was her predecessor, Thomas Pickering. He enjoyed chatting in the hallways and schmoozing before official meetings. She was less likely to join in the active debate at Security Council meetings and did not attend as many sessions as Pickering.[39] Even after she'd been on the job for a few months, many of the other permanent representatives still knew little about her. Vorontsov was surprised one day when he was giving what he considered to be an important address and saw Albright remove the earphones that provide simultaneous translation. Annoyed, he confronted her when he had finished. "You're not interested in what I am saying?" he asked. Albright's reply startled him. "I was listening to it," she responded in unaccented Russian. Vorontsov took note.[40]

Within the confines of the U.S. mission in New York, Albright was an exacting boss. David Scheffer, the lawyer whom Albright had hired to be her senior counselor in Washington, found out just how exacting she could be when, to prepare her for an appearance before a congressional committee, he gave her a brief explaining the budget crisis facing the United Nations. Looking at a sheet of numbers that showed the various amounts that the United States had paid the organization and how much the country remained in arrears, Albright took out a pencil and added the tables by hand. "David," she said, "these figures don't add up. I have to testify in front of the committee in twenty minutes." Sure enough, in his haste to get the information for Albright, Scheffer had added incorrectly. "Those were some of my tensest moments with her," Scheffer says. "It was an idiotic mistake. She knew the process well enough to know that she had to have everything precisely correct in order to make her case as strong as possible with the Hill."

Scheffer, a specialist in international law, learned quickly that Albright had no patience for obfuscatory language and insisted that he get right to the point. She wanted to be told about complicated issues such as the U.N. budget crisis in terms that she could use to explain the issue to Congress. "She knew that she had to understand it the way a member of Congress would understand it," Scheffer says. She had, after all, learned at Muskie's feet and, like him, demanded that her staff have the facts.

Albright was a stickler for detail on small matters as well. She insisted that her aides double-check the name of every guest to make sure each place card was spelled properly. And if an aide made a typographical error in a letter, Albright would catch it.

The ambassador often asked staffers to come to her apartment on Saturdays and Sundays for strategy sessions. Wearing blue jeans and sweaters, they would spend hours at her dining room table discussing upcoming events. Albright was obsessed with planning ahead. Practically every meal during the week was booked for diplomatic functions. She did not particularly like conducting business while eating, but she had little choice. There was a monthly breakfast with the Russian delegation, another with the Japanese—usually rice, fish, and a raw egg, which her staff called "weird."[41]

Albright instituted regular lunches with representatives from different countries. When she realized that only 7 of the 185 delegates to the U.N. General Assembly were women, she organized a monthly get-together that the women took turns hosting at their residences. In a spoof of the G-7 group of industrialized democracies, Albright's "girls" also called themselves the G-7. "It was a privileged forum," says Louise Frechette, the Canadian ambassador to the United Nations, who was named deputy secretary-general in December 1997. "It made the American ambassador very accessible to a very small group, some of whom came from very small countries."[42] Before the women's first luncheon, Frechette was startled to get a call from Albright's office asking if she planned to bring a photographer. "It made me laugh," Frechette says. "I'm a public servant, not a politician like Madeleine. It had never occurred to me." The regular meetings irritated some of the male ambassadors, who resented the special access that Albright gave her female colleagues. "The men felt left out and resented it," says Kofi Annan. "They would have liked to sit and have a meal with her. Many asked, 'When will we get our turn?' The men, who usually call the shots, were on the outside."[43]

Although virtually every meal was a ceremonial event, Albright tried to stick to her diet, but it was not easy. She has a weakness for sweets, finding it difficult to resist when pastries, ice cream, and cookies are passed. Her weight ballooned. Although she had struggled for years to control it, the problem was one her staff knew better than to discuss. It is hard to imagine Henry Kissinger's staff ever fretting about his weight, but a woman's dress size is often a key not just to how she sees herself but to how others perceive her. Albright was no exception. In hopes of reducing, she began seeing a Washington nutritionist, who explained the chemistry of food and how to achieve a better balance in what she ate. In New York, Albright's resident chef at the U.S. mission, John Wiecks, started making low-fat soups, using chicken soup instead of cream as a base. Her favorites were leek, fennel, broccoli, cauliflower, and pumpkin.[44]

From the beginning, Albright set herself apart from most of Clinton's other top foreign policy advisers. She was more articulate in explaining American positions than Warren Christopher, who was too lawyerly to excite a crowd. And she was comfortable projecting American force. The question of whether the American military should intervene to help resolve the brutal ethnic war raging in Bosnia had become a front-page issue. It was the most difficult foreign issue facing the administration, and for years, the Clinton administration failed to come up with a coherent and consistent policy. The president's top foreign policy advisers offered differing advice from the start.[45]

Tony Lake, the national security adviser, had written a confidential memo to Clinton early in the administration, arguing that Bosnia was becoming a cancer on Clinton's foreign policy, sapping it of strength and credibility. Lake, a cerebral college professor who had resigned to protest the invasion of Cambodia when he worked for Henry Kissinger in the Nixon administration, was a proponent of some kind of strong action in the Balkans. He believed that sound foreign policy required a moral compo-nent[46] and sought a policy that would halt the systematic genocidal "ethnic cleansing" and the random destruction of cities.[47]

In the other corner, Colin Powell, who had served in Vietnam and over-seen the U.S. victory in the Persian Gulf war, was set on convincing Clinton to refrain from using force in Bosnia. He argued that bombing would be ineffective and that at least a hundred thousand American ground troops would be needed to guarantee the peace. He was unequivocally opposed to the use of ground forces without a clearly stated, achievable objective.

Albright, along with several others in the Principals meetings, advocated using stronger military pressure on Bosnia. Albright's view had been formed by the dissolution of her native Czechoslovakia at Munich in 1938, which had become a metaphor for political betrayal. During one NSC meeting,

Albright confronted Powell: "What's the point of having this superb military you're always talking about if we can't use it?" she demanded. Powell was dumbfounded. His own view, which had become known as the Powell Doctrine, was that the United States should intervene militarily only when there was a clear goal that was achievable through military action. "I thought I would have an aneurysm," he wrote in his memoir. "American G.I.s were not toy soldiers to be moved around on some sort of global game board."[48]

On August 3, 1993, Albright wrote a toughly worded memo to Clinton that crystallized the country's stakes in Bosnia, arguing that military pressure was the only way to succeed and urging that the issue be put in a larger political perspective. In the memo, titled "Why America Must Take the Lead," Albright contended that the administration should reexamine its fundamental assumptions that the Europeans had a greater stake in resolving Bosnia than the Americans. Muddling through was no longer an option. If the president failed to deal with Bosnia, it would eventually overshadow his entire first term. Albright argued that the United States had to stop thinking of Bosnia as a tar baby and that Clinton had to realize that, whether or not it was fair, America's stewardship of foreign policy would be measured by its success in the Balkans. "The essence of any new strategy for Bosnia must recognize the one truth of this sad story," she wrote. "Our only successes have come when the Bosnian Serbs have faced a credible threat of military force. Hence, we must base our plan on using military pressure to convince the Bosnian Serbs to negotiate a suitable peace settlement."[49]

Clinton read the memo over the weekend and was impressed. When he convened his foreign policy team in the White House the following Monday, he told the group that he liked Albright's memo: "I don't agree with every one of her prescriptions, but I agree with her paper," Clinton said.[50]

While surefooted in domestic policy, Clinton was always more tentative in laying out foreign policy. It would be another two years before Albright's views sunk in and the president took her advice. In September 1995, a United States–led NATO air campaign called Operation Deliberate Force produced three weeks of precision bombing on Bosnian Serb military targets. When the bombing worked, and Bosnian Serbs showed up at the bargaining table in Dayton, Ohio, Albright took a verbal shot at Powell. "I felt some vindication," she said. "It wasn't easy being a civilian woman having a disagreement with the hero of the Western world. But maybe he'd want to rewrite that page now."[51]

President Clinton took the long view. "While she was not alone in urging a forceful course, she was out there early," he said in March 1998. "She was doggedly persistent on this Bosnia thing from the get-go. She pushed, and she pushed, and she pushed in an entirely appropriate way. . . . She was always out there, and that made a big difference to me."[52]

Lake says that he did not agree with Albright's proposal that the United States "should just go in and blast them. I was looking for a more focused way to use force."[53] He was also looking for the right timing. Unlike others at the table, Albright was in the enviable position of being able to voice her opinion forcefully and unequivocally without being responsible for the decision's consequences. She was the advocate. The others at the table were the action officers. The difference was crucial.

Albright and Lake had a long history together. Lake met Albright in 1972, when he was foreign policy adviser to Ed Muskie, but he had little contact then with Albright, who was merely one of many volunteers. He got to know her somewhat better during the Carter administration, when she was at the NSC and he was director of policy planning at the State Department. Lake did some consulting for Dukakis when Albright was the Democratic presidential nominee's principal foreign policy adviser. When Clinton ran for president, Lake and Sandy Berger filled the role Albright had played for Dukakis.

Lake could be exasperating, and Albright put up with him for a while. But as her self-confidence improved, she was less reticent in letting Lake know what she thought. The national security adviser made a trip to New York one day and neglected to inform Albright that he was meeting with foreign dignitaries. When she learned that he was there and had not checked in with her, she was furious and chewed him out in front of some of her aides. The incident angered Lake, and he asked to see her in her office. They settled their differences and made a point of showing the staff that they were back on good terms by emerging with their arms around each other.[54]

Albright's penchant for spending much of her time in Washington frustrated some colleagues at the United Nations. They resented it when she arrived at a meeting late, explaining that she had just taken the shuttle from Washington, and launched into a discussion they had already finished. "We would either have to stop and reexplain it or say, 'Madeleine, why couldn't you be here?'" reports one ambassador. Such reprimands angered Albright. "There is nothing she hated more than being told she had missed out on this because she hadn't been there," the diplomat says. "It enraged her." Albright would tell them it was to their advantage to have an American ambassador who was part of the president's cabinet. Her colleagues understood, but begrudgingly. "I saw the strength of that argument," said one, "but there was a downside."[55]

Many of Albright's colleagues hoped she would be more like Tom Pickering, a master at personal diplomacy, who was known as "The Magician." But instead, for some, Albright became known as "The Queen of Mean." When the Chinese representative could not vote on an anti-Cuba statement until he received instructions from his government, Albright kept the Security Council in session until 4:00 A.M., when they finally arrived.[56] She once called a speech by the Iraqi deputy prime minister "one of the most ridiculous" she had heard at the United Nations. And she told French defense minister François Leotard to mind his own business. After the Iraqi press dubbed her a snake, she appeared in the Security Council sporting a serpent-shaped brooch. When the Iraqis called her a witch and a Georgia woman opposed to sanctions sent her a broom, Albright displayed it like a trophy in her office.[57]

One highlight of Albright's years of public service came in January 1994, when she accompanied President Clinton to Prague. As they exited Air Force One, Secretary of State Warren Christopher broke with protocol and asked Albright to present Clinton to her friend Czech president Václav Havel. "It doesn't get much better than this," Albright said.

Albright spent a lot of time traveling. In her first two years in the job, she visited peacekeeping operations in Ethiopia, Somalia, the Sudan, Mozambique, Croatia, Slovenia, Moldavia, Georgia, Armenia, and Azerbaijan.[58] Because peacekeeping became such an important part of the U.N. operations, Albright cultivated a strong relationship with General John M. Shalikashvili, who replaced Powell in October 1993 as chairman of the Joint Chiefs of Staff. She visited Fort Polk, Louisiana, to see how American troops were trained for the role. She spent one Thanksgiving in Haiti, sharing the holiday dinner with members of the 22nd Infantry, and she gave a pep talk on peacekeeping to officers at the Naval War College in Newport, Rhode Island.

"Shali," as he is universally known, often invited Albright to visit U.S. troops overseas on peacekeeping duties, and she accepted whenever possible. The U.N. ambassador realized that the administration needed the military's support for the interventions that she often advocated at the White House. Albright flew into Mogadishu when U.S. troops were deployed. Wearing a flak jacket, she drove through town in an armored personnel carrier. She arrived in Cambodia aboard a rickety Russian helicopter that was flying Japanese peacekeepers along the Vietnam border. She toured Sarajevo in helmet and body armor.[59]

In March 1996, she traveled to the ruined Croatian city of Vukovar in Eastern Slovenia, an area under Serb control. Her mission was to pressure local Serb authorities to cooperate in a range of refugee and war crimes issues. While she was walking through a marketplace afterward, she was jeered and cursed by Serbian demonstrators, who screamed, "Kucko, kucko." The only member of her party who understood what the demonstrators were yelling—"Bitch, bitch"—Albright turned and murmured grimly to an aide, "I think it's time to go."[60] They walked quickly into town, the angry crowd in pursuit. As Albright got into her car, the motorcade was pelted with heavy rocks and stones. One large stone broke a window in the staff van behind her, shattering glass all over two aides, James O'Brien and David Scheffer. "My first reaction," says Scheffer, "was 'Get us the hell out of here. Drive this car fast.' "[61]

Albright enjoyed putting on a blue-and-white U.N. helmet and chatting with the soldiers. She also liked the publicity that surrounded these trips. A master of the photo-op, she knew that a female U.N. ambassador bumping around in a personnel carrier or jumping off a Black Hawk helicopter was likely to make the newspapers back home. Albright's colleagues, however, often bridled at her penchant for publicity. During the March trip to the Balkans, Albright went to a mass gravesite near Janje in northeast Bosnia with a cluster of reporters. Her mission was to pressure Serbian strongman Slobodan Milosevic to cooperate with the war crimes tribunal. But fearing that too much publicity would also result in more pressure on the Defense Department to become active in war crimes investigations, which the Pentagon was avoiding, Pentagon officials got Albright to scale back the press conference that she had planned.[62]

A few days after Albright returned from Eastern Slovenia, her old friend and mentor, Ed Muskie, died. The U.N. ambassador, who had started her career as a volunteer in his office almost twenty-five years before, was asked to deliver the eulogy. "The truth is, this man was my role model," she told mourners at the Church of the Little Flower in Bethesda, Maryland. When she finished, Albright folded her notes and walked back down the steps from the altar. As she passed Muskie's coffin, she stopped for a brief moment and touched the top of the casket in a silent farewell.[63]

It was at the United Nations that Albright developed her reputation for clever one-liners. When an official of the repressive Burmese government insisted that there were no human rights violations in Burma—"You can see that the people are smiling here," he said—Albright snapped: "I had a lot of friends in Czechoslovakia who used to smile, but only because they were scared."[64]

After Cuban jet pilots shot down two civilian planes from a Miami Cuban exile group over the Florida straits in February 1996, Albright read the transcript of the Cuban pilots bragging about taking out the Americans' *cojónes,* Cuban slang for testicles. "God, it's disgusting," Albright said. The pilots used the word *cojónes* numerous times. Albright suggested to the White House that the best place to release the transcript to the court of world opinion was at a press conference in New York. Nibbling a sandwich at her desk, she turned to Rubin and remarked quietly: "It's not *cojónes.* They're cowards." They looked at each other. "I wonder if I should say that?" Albright wondered aloud. "I'm going to call Elaine. She'll tell me if a woman can use this word and whether or not it's appropriate." Albright, Shocas, and Rubin got on the phone together. Elaine Shocas gave the okay: "It works." But the line needed more pizzazz.[65] With a little tinkering, they crafted Albright's most famous sound bite: "Frankly, this is not *cojónes,* this is cowardice." It was vintage Albright, a clever quip not only guaranteed to make instant headlines, but one that had a subliminal, macho message calculated to suggest that she was one of the boys. President Clinton loved it and kept a bumper sticker with the quote in his office.[66] "You can't teach somebody that," he says. "You can't send [someone] to school to learn that."[67]

The remark went over better with the American public than it did in the diplomatic community. Nor did it impress Albright's old friend from her NSC days, Christine Dodson. Not long after the incident, Albright was in Greece on business and Dodson, who lives there six months of the year, invited Albright to a popular Athens restaurant for dinner. "I took her head off about the comment," Dodson says. "I told her it was inappropriate for a woman to say this. I really chewed her out." At the next table, a group of businessmen were conversing in both Greek and English over dinner. When they finished, they rose and faced Albright. "Mrs. Ambassador," said one, raising his glass of wine. "A toast to you for your forthright behavior and ability to call *'cojónes' cojónes.*" Dodson was furious. Before the men could sit down, she told them angrily in Greek, "You shouldn't say that. I've been telling her it's inappropriate for a woman of her level to feel that she is one of the guys and say something like this." The men were dumbstruck. No one at either table said a word.[68]

Albright's colleagues at the NSC were impressed by her ability to accomplish difficult tasks. In the summer of 1994, the refugee crisis in Haiti came to a head. In 1991, military thugs had ousted the elected president, Jean-Bertrand Aristide, and in the intervening years, neither the efforts of President Bush nor President Clinton to return Aristide to power had been effective. A trade embargo of the impoverished nation did little to weaken the military's grip.[69]

When, in July 1994, thousands of Haitians fleeing political repression and poverty crowded onto overloaded boats headed for Florida, the Clinton administration came under pressure to stanch the flow.[70] Few people, however, thought the United Nations would take action to oust Haiti's military junta and return Aristide to power. But Albright told Clinton, "If I have the authority, I think I can do it."[71]

At the Security Council in New York, Albright told her counterparts that six thousand U.N. troops would be needed and that the United States would supply the bulk of the force. "Who decided on six thousand?" Vorontsov asked her during one meeting. "Why not three thousand or twelve thousand?" Albright conceded that she was following guidance from the Pentagon and was not sure how the number was reached. Not possible, too expensive, said Vorontsov. When Albright returned to press her argument, she was armed with statistics as to precisely why six thousand troops were needed, how they would be split into groups, and where each group would be deployed. Vorontsov was convinced. "It was her logic, not her charm, that changed my mind," he says. "She is very effective."[72]

For Albright and the United Nations, it was a historic moment, the first time that the United Nations agreed to use force to restore democracy in a sovereign state. "People don't appreciate the importance of her four years at the U.N.," says Strobe Talbott, Albright's deputy secretary of state. "It taught her the best and worst of multilateralism. It also taught her how important it is to bring along not just individual governments but collections of governments."[73]

Vorontsov agrees with Czech president Václav Havel that Albright's effectiveness, like that of Henry Kissinger, is a product of her European background. She has a broader understanding of the history, tradition, culture, and thinking of foreign governments than most American leaders because she has lived under different regimes and can identify with different points of view. "She understands that one of the characteristics of Yugoslavs is stubbornness," Vorontsov says. "She knows this because she lived in Belgrade as a child, when her father was stationed there. They are tremendously stubborn, like mules really, not because they don't want to understand something but because they don't want to change their views. Madeleine understood how hard it would be to deal with [Serbian leader Slobodan] Milosevic because she lived there. It is very important."[74]

Vorontsov said it was not so much Albright's gender that differentiated her from the State Department's Russia specialists—Strobe Talbott and Tom Pickering—but her perspective. "Madeleine has a broad and theoretical knowledge," he says. "She never served in Russia, but she understands the

Slavic mind. Strobe Talbott was there as a journalist and understands public opinion and what makes Russia tick. Pickering served there as a top diplomat and knows how things move and how they don't." Who speaks the best Russian? "Strobe," says Vorontsov. "Pickering musters some phrases but doesn't speak it. Madeleine understands everything but only speaks when it is very much needed. But when she speaks, it is without an accent, just as she speaks English without a foreign accent."[75]

Vorontsov was so impressed with Albright's background and grasp of foreign policy issues that he leaned over to her during a Security Council meeting in 1994 and told her that she would be the next American secretary of state. "Oh no, the country isn't ready for a woman," she replied. When Albright was selected for the job more than two years later, Vorontsov asked her if she remembered his comment. "I do remember," she said, "but I didn't believe you."[76]

Albright may have impressed Vorontsov, but she disappointed some colleagues at the United Nations with her lack of attention to detail. Professional diplomats who prided themselves on understanding the fine points of an issue were aggravated by her penchant for stating a broad position and then defining it in a sound bite. "It's very frustrating if you can't have a conversation with a senior counterpart with a certain level of detail on the drafting of something," says one ambassador. "She wasn't used to it. She didn't regard it as her job, and she would hand it off to others."

She did not, however, shy away from controversy, even when U.N. colleagues were directly involved. More than a year before U.N. secretary-general Boutros Boutros-Ghali's five-year term was up, she decided that the fiercely independent Egyptian should be blocked from a second term. Although she knew that such a move would be controversial within the United Nations, she brought her idea to the attention of the Principals. The Clinton administration blamed Boutros-Ghali for the failure of the 1993 peacekeeping mission in Somalia. The inability of the U.N. force to reestablish civil authority came to rest on President Clinton's shoulders when eighteen U.S. Army Rangers were ambushed and killed during an unsuccessful attempt to capture a Somali warlord. Although the Rangers were being commanded by U.S. officers, they were in Somalia under a U.N. mandate.

Albright and Boutros-Ghali disagreed about the role of the United Nations in international diplomacy, as well as internal management of the international body. Boutros-Ghali insisted that the United Nations control the international force operating in Bosnia and refused to cede to British and French officers the right to authorize air strikes against the Serbs. Operational commanders complained that delays in the U.N. chain of command destroyed the effectiveness of the air strikes. Furthermore, Congress, which controls U.S. payments to the United Nations, saw Boutros-Ghali as the embodiment of U.N. mismanagement and an obstacle to reform. With the American government more than $1 billion behind in payments for dues and assessments, Albright feared that the United States would see its influence wane. In October 1995, she instigated a campaign to keep him from seeking a second term.[77] Although the United States had no replacement in mind, she persuaded Christopher and Lake that the Egyptian had to go. The strategy was to tell Boutros-Ghali to withdraw and quietly support Kofi Annan, the under secretary-general and a Ghanaian who could garner substantial Third World support.[78] "It was a difficult and intense period," says Annan. "For a long time, one didn't know what would happen or when the issue would be resolved or for how long it would drag on. She was seen as playing hardball."[79]

At the United Nations, many diplomats were aghast at Albright's treatment of the secretary-general, and suggested she had a personal vendetta against him. When other Principals expressed concern that the United States was isolated on the issue, Albright refused to back down.[80] On November 19, in a 14–1 vote, she was the only member of the Security Council to vote against Boutros-Ghali for a second term. Because each of the five permanent members has veto power, Albright's vote put Boutros-Ghali out of the running. The Clinton administration pushed Annan for the position.

The diplomatic grumbling over Albright came to an abrupt halt two weeks later when Clinton nominated her to be secretary of state. Suddenly those who had criticized her tactics wanted to be on her good side. On December 13, eight days after Albright's nomination, Annan was unanimously elected the new secretary-general. "Foreign diplomats who only recently had predicted that Albright was leading the United States into a major fiasco suddenly reappraised her role as architect of a strategy that achieved the twin goals of derailing Boutros-Ghali and hand-picking his successor," reported the *Washington Post*.

Many of those who have watched Albright's evolution over the years say that she changed at the United Nations, that the friendly, easygoing woman they had known showed a new tendency to be imperious and somewhat dismissive of those who got in her way. Another view is that she became two people, sometimes the big-shot personality, sometimes the easygoing pal her friends had known for years. "The person I knew in Washington is quite different from the public person she became in New York," said one official who worked closely with her.[81]

Clearly, the once-retiring aide had become an assertive principal. She not only carried out administration policy but initiated it. Never one to suffer fools, Albright also began letting her impatience show. In June 1995, during celebrations in San Francisco for the fiftieth anniversary of the United Nations, which Clinton had agreed to attend, she was waiting on the tenth floor of the Fairmont Hotel for an elevator that would take her to the hotel basement to meet the presidential motorcade. Albright became irritable when the elevator did not arrive. A security man assured her that it would be there in thirty seconds. But the ambassador looked him in the eye and announced that she was not waiting. With that, she picked up the hem of her long red dress and started down ten flights, her pumps clicking all the way. Near the bottom, she spotted an elevator and jumped on, but it turned out to be a freight elevator that deposited her in the hotel kitchen. A hotel staffer showed her a door that led to the basement, but the Secret Service had locked it as a security precaution. When Albright finally found her way to the basement, a big San Francisco cop approached her and asked where exactly she thought she was going. Albright pulled herself up to her full five feet three inches and said that she was the United States ambassador to the United Nations and was there to meet the president. You're going nowhere, the policeman told her. Just then Albright's aide spotted a State Department security man who recognized her and let her join Clinton's party.[82]

Albright understood that if she were to have any chance at higher office, she would need to spend time with people who could influence the decision. In September 1995, the United Nations was sponsoring the fourth International Conference on Women, this time in China. Albright was appointed to lead the U.S. delegation. She asked Hillary Clinton to be honorary chair. Each was to give a major address at the conference. As the leader of the delegation, Albright was responsible for overall planning and scheduling, a gargantuan task made particularly tricky by Beijing's role as the conference host. There was no U.S. ambassador on the ground in Beijing to cement relations with wary Chinese officials, who were just beginning to realize that the gathering could become a forum for attacks on the Communist regime's treatment of women and families. What's more, before the conference convened, Chinese authorities intercepted Chinese dissident Harry Wu as he reentered the country, focusing world attention on Beijing's unenviable human rights record. There was speculation that the U.S. delegation, including Mrs. Clinton, would boycott the conference. "Wu is us" became the slogan of the day in the First Lady's office quarters. China, which had signed up for the conference thinking it would be a glorified fashion show, now realized that it was about to be invaded by thousands of prominent—

and uppity—women who intended to address such controversial issues as human rights, abortion, and family planning.

To the disappointment of some officials, Albright did not take a hands-on role in organizing U.S. participation in the conference. Delegates learned that when they had a problem, they could get more done by calling Melanne Verveer, Hillary Clinton's top assistant, than by calling Albright. "Madeleine was a figurehead," said one participant.[83] She did, however, make a key political decision. Instead of arriving in China a few days before the conference to resolve a host of last-minute problems, as organizers had expected, Albright accepted an invitation to accompany the First Lady, who planned to arrive, make her speech, and depart in twenty-four hours.

Several women who attended the conference were surprised by what they interpreted as Albright's play to share the limelight with Hillary Clinton. "She flew in and made a cameo appearance, the visible piece, and then left," said one top official. "It was the first time I was consciously aware of what a public persona she was. It's also the first time I was sure she was campaigning to be secretary of state."[84] On the other hand, few individuals turn down a chance to travel in such exclusive company. Not only are such trips considerably more relaxed than commercial flights—presidential aircrafts are outfitted with rooms that resemble lounges with soft easy chairs and comfortable sofas—it *is* an opportunity to exchange views, get to know each other better, and talk discreetly without the possibility of misinterpretation by third and fourth parties.

Logistics for the China trip were complicated by the wedding of Albright's daughter Katie, who was to be married the weekend the conference started. Albright attended the festivities, then flew directly to Hawaii to meet the Clintons, who were vacationing there. When Albright's plane touched down in Honolulu, President and Mrs. Clinton were waiting for her at the airport. Albright literally walked across the tarmac from her plane to board the presidential plane.[85] Once in Beijing, Hillary Clinton made headlines around the world with a bold address that indirectly criticized China's coercive family-planning tactics. It was time to "break the silence" on human rights abuses against women, she said to repeated cheers from an enthusiastic audience. "It is a violation of human rights, as when women are denied the right to plan their own families, and that includes being forced to have abortions or being sterilized against their will."[86] When her speech was over, Mrs. Clinton flew on to Mongolia. To the annoyance of others in the U.S. delegation, Albright flew to Burma to meet Daw Aung San Suu Kyi, the human rights activist and Nobel Peace Prize winner.

It was not the only time Albright made sure she was in the right place at the right time. In 1995, when the United Nations sponsored a social policy summit in Copenhagen, Albright showed little interest in its substance or issues. "She wasn't engaged at all," says a U.N. official who worked with her. But when Albright learned that Vice President Al Gore would make an appearance, she flew to Copenhagen to attend his speech. "If she spent a day there, I would be surprised," said one observer. "She took a plane, went to a meeting, and took a plane right back."[87]

The next year, Albright had another opportunity to spend some airplane time with Hillary Clinton. Both women were scheduled to speak at the American Bar Association's annual meeting in Orlando, Florida. The First Lady asked Albright to join her for the flight. David Scheffer, who accompanied the women, was impressed by their chemistry. "It was fascinating," he says. "They were clearly close. They joked, talked frankly, and slipped back and forth between policy issues and family talk." The First Lady discussed visiting colleges with her daughter, Chelsea. Albright, who had recently returned from a trip to Cyprus, explained the political problems between the Greeks and the Turks. "They each had a sense of what was important and zeroed in on it, sometimes in a humorous way, sometimes seriously," says Scheffer.

Some U.N. staffers—career bureaucrats, as opposed to the nearly all-male cadre of ambassadors—were disappointed by what they saw as Albright's lack of interest in the status of women who were employed by the organization. They say that despite Albright's appearances at international women's conferences and similar functions, she mainly went through the motions and did little to advance their cause. The ambassador did convene a series of meetings to discuss the problems of women employees at the United Nations, and followed them up with an outline of initiatives. Yet according to one observer, her commitment "was less than intense. She really had no interest in it."[88]

As the presidential campaign season rolled around again and Clinton prepared to run for a second term against Republican presidential candidate Bob Dole, Albright began to talk privately with friends about her future. Anne Wexler, a high-powered Washington lobbyist who knew her from the Ferraro campaign days, spent the night at Albright's Waldorf suite every few months. They would stay up late, gossiping about who was up and who was down in Washington and speculating about what lay ahead. "We would sit in her library with our feet up, occasionally talking about the far-fetched notion that she would be secretary of state," Wexler recalls. "Madeleine would always say, 'Oh, the boys will never let it happen.' "[89]

Shortly after Clinton's reelection in November 1996, Albright, whose name was said to be on the "short list" of candidates to succeed Christopher, was invited to be a special guest at a nine-woman lunch group organized by CBS *60 Minutes* star Lesley Stahl and ABC's Lynn Sherr (Wellesley '63) of 20-20. The high-octane crew, which meets once a month, also includes literary agent Esther Newberg; federal judge Kimba Wood; journalist Jurate Kazickas; Manhattan assistant district attorney Linda Fairstein; Faye Wattleton, president of the Center for Gender Equality; novelist Anna Quindlen; and Ellen Futter, president of the American Museum of Natural History. The luncheon, held at Sherr's newly refurbished apartment near the United Nations, included much laughter and joking. The subject of face-lifts was raised. Albright said nothing. Several of her friends had discussed the possibility of her having one—maybe just a little tuck or two under the chin— but they had not summoned the nerve to mention it to her.

Inevitably, the conversation turned to men. Albright asked their advice. "What do you think?" she said. "Should I bring a date to the Inaugural?" The group launched into a debate on the pros and cons. Do you want to dance? someone asked. A collective groan. No one ever dances at Inaugural balls. Okay, if she does take a date, it has to be someone of equal stature. She does not want to worry about introducing him or whether he is having a good time. Maybe someone like diamond importer Maurice Templesman, Jackie Onassis' companion before she died and an occasional guest at Albright's New York dinner parties. No, no, someone else said. The press would have a heyday. How about Tony Lake, whom Clinton had nominated to be director of the CIA? Nope. Better to stay out of the gossip columns. The name of a wealthy widower was mentioned. Forget it, said one of the attendees, somewhat huffily. He's taken. Albright shook her head and gestured to her security detail waiting outside the apartment. Maybe, she said, she would just bring her daughters.

Although Albright had a busy social life in New York, it was largely a formal one. The lunch group was different. She loved the laughter, the girl talk, the easy, informal camaraderie with a group of smart, high-profile, professional women. "She enjoyed it on two levels," said a friend, who did not attend. "First, it was fun. But she also enjoyed being the pooh-bah addition. Lesley [Stahl] had had a lunch group for years in Washington and New York, and Madeleine had never been included before. She was finally playing with the big girls."[90]

Albright had been playing with the big boys for years, but this was an even more exclusive circle. If it were high school, they would be the popular clique—team captains and student leaders—the ones invited to the best parties. With these women as her friends, Albright could afford to be a little sassy. She had loved the lunch and asked when the next one would be. For a few hours, she had become one of the gang.

When Clinton nominated Albright to be his secretary of state, members of the lunch group were delighted. They sent her a Hermès scarf decorated with colorful international flags. At Esther Newberg's suggestion, they included a note that read: "We didn't think he had the *cojónes.*"[91]

**From the Wellesley Class of 1959 Record Book for
Its 35th Reunion in 1994**

Madeleine Korbel
Madeleine Korbel Albright

United States Representative to the United Nations

Alice, Williams '83, and her husband, Gregory Bowes, recently moved to London with their son, David, born in May '93. Greg manages the London office of Greenwich Capital and Alice has resumed work as Vice President at J.P. Morgan.

Anne, Dartmouth '83, is a public defender in Seattle where she lives with her husband, Geoff Watson, a professor of law at the University of Puget Sound.

Katherine (Katie), Williams '89, is graduating from law school at Georgetown. She will be clerking for a judge in Baltimore.

23

The Brass Ring

"Her career evolved. It wasn't planned. Reporters ask me if she always wanted to be secretary of state. That's like saying, 'Did she want to go to the moon?' It was way out of the realm of possibility. She never thought of that. Even when she worked for Dukakis, it wasn't discussed seriously."

—Winifred Freund, March 22, 1997

JULY 1996. Madeleine Albright and Hillary Clinton were traveling together in Eastern Europe, a trip designed to show support for the fledgling democracies. The highlight was a few days touring Prague. They dined with Czech president Václav Havel and walked across the historic Charles Bridge at night, passing the statues of fourteenth- and fifteenth-century Baroque saints whose charcoal shadows cast eerie, ghostlike silhouettes against the Gothic stone walls. Pausing for a moment, they looked back at the breathtaking panorama of Hradčany Castle, shimmering in a golden hue of spotlights. It is one of the most spectacular views in all of Europe.

With Secret Service agents in tow, they spent an afternoon wandering through the narrow, cobblestone streets of Old Town Square, chatting about their children and the professors they had at Wellesley, stopping in a café. They looked at the astronomical clock on the fifteenth-century Town Hall Tower, where, on the hour, a skeleton begins by tolling the death knell and turns an hourglass upside down. The twelve apostles parade around, and a rooster crows. The women even visited the Jewish Cemetery together, though they did not go into the nearby Pinkas Synagogue, where the names of thousands of Holocaust victims are painted on the walls. Albright did not know at the time that the names included three of her grandparents.

One afternoon, just after dusk, Albright took Hillary Clinton to see her childhood home, a large, second-floor apartment located over a small restaurant called U Labutí on Hradčany Square, right outside the castle gates. Madeleine and her family had lived there when they returned to Prague after the war. Roman Bohuněk, the headwaiter, was standing outside on the sidewalk when Havel's presidential motorcade approached, apparently headed toward the castle. He joked that they were probably coming to the restaurant but was actually shocked when the stretch of black limousines pulled up and stopped in front of him. Within seconds, security agents jumped out, swarmed into the restaurant, cleared the bathrooms, flushed the toilets, and jabbered into the tiny microphones protruding from their sleeves. As it turned out, the official party never did go inside. Hillary walked with Havel the short distance to the castle. The next morning when he came to work, Bohuněk saw Albright giving Hillary Clinton a tour of the house.[1]

Another afternoon, Havel, Albright, and Clinton piled into a Chevrolet Suburban and were driven to Wenceslas Square, where a protest rally in November 1989 sparked the country's Velvet Revolution, which brought down four decades of communism. Inspired by the scene, the threesome broke out singing "Good King Wenceslas."[2]

One morning, Havel walked the women through the castle, showing off a theatrical mural in his private office that includes a hand-painted comic portrait of the KGB agent who trailed him in his dissident years. During their tour, Hillary and Madeleine slipped into the powder room for a private chat. A photographer snapped a shot of them talking earnestly to one another just inside the entrance. Albright keeps the photo behind her desk. At the bottom, Hillary inscribed: "To Madeleine, who leads fearlessly where others may fear to tread—with great affection from your friend in 'the girls' room.'"

No one doubts that Albright's friendship with the First Lady was helpful when Albright's name surfaced as a possible secretary of state, but helpful in a much more subtle way than conventional wisdom would have it. The First Lady does not make things happen by working the West Wing overtly. Does she have influence? Everybody thinks so. But after the highly publicized health care fiasco, she has figured out how to let the president know her views without going to the West Wing and attending meetings.[3] "She doesn't need to leave notes on his pillow," says Melanne Verveer, the First Lady's chief of staff.

Not surprisingly, Albright is closer to Hillary than she is to Bill Clinton. "With the president, she is almost flirtatious," says one top official. "But she touches base with Hillary all the time, advises her on international stuff, sends her memos and materials. And they both schmooze about Wellesley. Madeleine's great champion for this job was Mrs. Clinton. Knowing that, there was never any doubt in my mind she would get it."[4]

Hillary and Madeleine had become good friends, soul mates a decade apart with a common interest in American politics and women's issues. While they share a Wellesley connection, the bond is stronger than just college ties. Each is an ambitious, hard-driving woman with an earthy sense of humor and a disarming ability to poke fun at herself. In another setting, they could exchange jobs. For in an ironic way, each was originally trained for the position the other holds. Hillary Clinton, the lawyer, would make a fine cabinet secretary. Madeleine Albright, the fifties gal, might have been a politician's wife.

But there is much more to Albright's appointment than friendship with the First Lady. Women have not risen to the top of their organizations in greater numbers because men are often uneasy with them. Albright is a woman with whom the president and vice president were comfortable. They trusted her judgment and liked the way she expressed her opinions. Those advising Clinton against Albright had never worked with her as closely as Clinton and Gore had.[5] Moreover, Bill Clinton always had an instinct for grand symbolic gestures, and gender issues were no exception. "You tell him, Jesus, boss, that's never been done before, and it's a good way to get him to do it," says a senior Clinton administration official. "You show him a glass ceiling, and he'll pick up a rock."[6]

Clinton did not pick Albright for the job simply because she is a woman, but her sex did not hurt. He realized that the women's vote had been a big factor in his election—women had favored him over Republican candidate Bob Dole by seventeen points[7]—and women's groups were lobbying the White House to pick a woman for one of the top cabinet jobs. "He liked the idea that she was female but could be tough in the role," said Michael McCurry, Clinton's press secretary.[8]

In fact, Clinton had been thinking of appointing Albright to be secretary of state for some time. In May 1993, Albright's first year at the United Nations, Clinton sent her a fifty-sixth birthday present that suggested he had a bigger job in mind for her. It was a photograph of them together, shot when Albright had presented Clinton with a first edition of Thomas Jefferson's writings on Virginia. Referring to Jefferson's role as the country's first secretary of state, Clinton wrote on the photo: "You are a worthy successor to Jefferson in diplomacy and ever so much younger, even on your birthday."

McCurry did not realize how committed Clinton was to the idea until one day in August when he received a call from *New York Times* reporter

Elaine Sciolino. She was preparing a piece about Albright for the *Times Sunday Magazine* and told him she had it on good authority that Clinton was seriously considering her for secretary of state. "I'd be cautious about that," McCurry replied. "A lot of people are saying that, but I don't know if it's true." McCurry is respected by reporters because he gives them careful guidance on their stories. If he cannot tell them something, he does his best to explain why. If he does not know the answer to a question, he says so—and he does his best to get one. So McCurry walked into the Oval Office and told the boss about Sciolino's call. "You don't have to participate in the story, but how would you like it to turn out?" McCurry said. The president did not hesitate. "Make sure Albright is in it," he said.[9] McCurry was surprised. "What kind of reaction do you think she'd get in the Arab world?" he asked. Clinton replied that he thought she would do fine, that, actually, he has found Arab leaders to be more progressive than conventional wisdom would allow.[10] "Syria has a lot more women in parliament and influential positions in government than a lot of non-Arab countries," Clinton says today. "So I just figured it wouldn't be a problem with a lot of them, and the others would have to find a way to work through it [because that] is important to what our country is about. What are they going to do when we elect a woman president? Sooner or later, that's going to happen."[11]

When Sciolino's long, complimentary piece about Albright appeared in the *New York Times Magazine* in September 1996, Albright's staff was privately thrilled that the cover featured not just Albright, but pictures of former Maine senator George Mitchell and Richard Holbrooke, also contenders. "It was really important for her not to be campaigning for this job, and there were people who were going to be unhappy that she had this magazine story," says an Albright confidante. "For her to be on the cover with all the guys made her less of a target. At least they could say they got their picture on the cover of the *New York Times Magazine*."[12]

Most of those who lined up against Albright were described in the press as "members of the administration with the strongest ties to the American global establishment."[13] They included Treasury Secretary Robert Rubin and presidential confidant Vernon Jordan, who served on the transition team. When Thomas Pickering, the ambassador to Russia, was dropped from the list, four names remained: George Mitchell, a former federal judge and Senate Democratic leader, who had helped prepare Clinton for the campaign debates with Bob Dole; retiring senator Sam Nunn, who had been chairman of the Senate Armed Services Committee until the Republicans gained control of Congress in 1995; Holbrooke; and Albright.

Clinton admired Holbrooke, the chief negotiator of the Dayton peace agreement on Bosnia. Like Albright, he was an astute diplomat, good at closing a deal, and comfortable in front of cameras. Clinton also appreciated Holbrooke's ability to "rattle the china," as one White House aide put it, a trait that enabled him to crack heads in a tough negotiation.[14] These were all attributes that impressed Clinton. George Mitchell's star, however, was fading: congressional Republicans thought him too partisan. Neither Tony Lake nor Colin Powell was ever a serious contender. Lake, dubbed "Mr. Peepers" by the press for his scholarly, horn-rimmed spectacles, was Clinton's choice to become CIA director, and the Democrats had little incentive to polish the already stellar résumé of Powell, who was considered a potential rival of Vice President Al Gore in the next presidential race. Talbott, a Clinton confidant from their Oxford days, took himself out of the running. Conservatives in Congress considered him soft on Russia and were sure to contest a Talbott nomination. While Clinton thought he could win a confirmation fight, he knew that the hearings would be used to excoriate U.S. policy toward Russia. Talbott, unwilling to let his nomination be used as a political battering ram, pushed both Albright and Holbrooke as worthy candidates.

In discussions with Clinton, which often lasted about forty-five minutes each, several members of the administration argued that to name Albright would be a major mistake, that she was not intellectually up to the job; "that it would be viewed by the foreign policy community as a 'lite' appointment, not a serious one," one official said.[15] Albright's critics argued that her penchant for toughness would be mistaken for simpleness and rashness, traits a woman might emphasize to persuade people she could not be pushed around. "They saw her as quick of wit but questioned her ability to manage the immensity of American foreign policy and the superstructure of the State Department," said one former cabinet member.[16] "They saw her as a competent debater who could carry out instructions, but not a visionary."

Clinton listened, but he disagreed. He thought of Albright as a team player, known for expressing her differences with others privately. He was impressed that after he added cabinet rank to her position as U.N. ambassador and made her a part of the Principals Group, she did not try to go around Secretary of State Warren Christopher, her superior in the bureaucracy, by using National Security Adviser Tony Lake as her point of contact with the White House. Albright was more articulate than Christopher, and certainly more telegenic, but she was careful not to set herself up as his rival. "She worked very much in tandem with Christopher," says McCurry, who was Christopher's press spokesman at the State Department before going to the White House. "She stayed completely within the boundaries that were established at the State Department before going to the White

House. She would never do a Sunday talk show without checking with Christopher's staff first."[17]

Also important to Clinton, he found the U.N. ambassador to be good company, someone who shared his outgoing, friendly, and optimistic personality, a woman who did not put on airs and was quick to laugh at a man's joke. At the Denver economic summit that took place in late June 1997, Madeleine had a private dinner with Russian foreign minister Yevgeny Primakov and Deputy Secretary of State Strobe Talbott. They ate at one of those restaurants that feature such Wild West exotica as rattlesnake and buffalo buns. When Talbott ordered Rocky Mountain oysters, Primakov turned to Albright, whose spoken Russian is not as fluent as her comprehension, but good enough that interpreters are unnecessary when she and Primakov are together. Addressing Albright with the personal Russian pronoun reserved for family and close friends, as he always does, Primakov said he had a slightly off-color story about such dishes. Would Madeleine be offended if he told it?

Albright not only did not object, but reminded the Russian foreign minister that her most famous quote was about Cuban pilots and *cojónes*. Primakov smiled. He told her of an American couple who ended a wonderful day by going into a popular restaurant in Spain. When they could not decide what to order, the owner arrived at their table and said that bull fighting was popular in the area, and he had a local specialty that he was sure they would enjoy. The couple agreed. When a big plate of fried rounds appeared on their plates, they dug in. The dinner was delicious, so good in fact that they decided to go back the next night and order the same meal. But this time when their food arrived, there were only two tiny fried morsels on the plate. The couple called over the owner and complained that this was not the dish they enjoyed the night before. Sure it is, said the owner, but the matador does not always win.[18]

Albright roared.

Clinton also appreciated Albright for her ability to explain why he should make a certain decision on foreign policy grounds and lay out the political impact of the decision. "She has the ability to think out of the box, to think two, three steps down the road," says Erskine Bowles, Clinton's chief of staff, who sees his role as making sure Clinton hears all sides of an issue before he decides it. "She also has an extraordinary ability to communicate a very complex situation in an understandable manner."[19] Few foreign policy advisers have such a visceral feel for policy and politics. Clinton recognized that talent and valued it.[20]

Also, Albright had instigated the U.S. move to block Secretary-General

Boutros Boutros-Ghali from a second five-year term, which had won her and the White House points with Congress. She knew that her fellow permanent representatives at the United Nations would resist, but she did not waiver.[21] Clinton was criticized by foreign leaders for the decision and the awkward way in which the Americans carried it out. But he appreciated Albright's steadfast position in the face of powerful opposition from her U.N. colleagues.

He also noted that she had been ahead of most others in the administration in pushing for American military intervention in Bosnia. She argued, correctly as it turned out, that Bosnian Serbs were slow on their feet and would not challenge American soldiers. Clinton would say later that the memo Albright sent him favoring stronger action in Bosnia was the clearest, most persuasive one that he had read. She also won U.N. authorization for U.S. intervention in Haiti when State Department officials said it would be impossible.

Albright and Holbrooke were, without question, the most serious contenders. In terms of substance, they were not far apart. Neither would have to spend much time mastering the issues. Yet Holbrooke, for all his negotiating prowess, had one big disadvantage: He not only accepted the limelight, he thrived on it and sought it out. "Holbrooke never got to the front of the parade because there was too much risk associated with the reward," said one official close to the decision making.[22] Albright lapped up publicity as much as Holbrooke, but she was more adept at interoffice politics, careful to publicize events in a way that never upstaged or offended the president, Lake, or Christopher. She was also less outspoken in senior policy meetings. With Albright, Clinton was told, "we get Holbrooke without the neurosis."[23]

One member of Congress lobbying strongly against Holbrooke was Delaware senator Joseph Biden, Jr., who had become a Clinton confidant on foreign policy matters. Biden not only did not like Holbrooke, he favored almost any alternative. Several of Biden's former staffers, including Jamie Rubin, had gone to work for Albright; others had jobs at the White House. The senator, once chairman of the Judiciary Committee, planned to give up his ranking position there to be a ranking Democrat on the Foreign Relations Committee. He let the White House know of his opposition to a Holbrooke nomination. Clinton, with a number of important treaties and initiatives before the Foreign Relations Committee, had no interest in crossing words with Biden. The president needed a strong, ranking Democrat on the Foreign Relations Committee to help him take on the chairman, Jesse Helms.[24]

Albright knew she had a good shot at the nomination but that it was not a done deal. Over dinner one night with Gerry Ferraro, Albright mentioned that presidential confidant Vernon Jordan, who was interviewing cabinet candidates, had told her not to lobby Clinton for the job, that lobbying would be offensive to the White House and would backfire. "Did he tell you that he would take your case to the president himself?" Ferraro asked her friend. "No," Madeleine replied hesitantly. "Then it's bullshit," said Ferraro.[25]

The weekend before Thanksgiving, Marcia Hale, an Albright friend from the Ferraro campaign who had gone on to work in the Clinton White House as director of intergovernmental affairs, came to New York for a weekend visit and stayed with Albright. That Saturday afternoon they sat talking in the privacy of Albright's living room. Hale, wearing jeans and relaxing on a couch, sipped a glass of wine. Albright, who had a dinner engagement and was dressed in a tailored suit, sat in an armchair, balancing a cup of tea. Albright discussed what her chances were of getting the job and asked Hale for advice. Hale cautioned her friend not to launch a public campaign, saying that would put unnecessary pressure on the president, which he would not appreciate. It was familiar advice, but coming from a friend of hers this time, not the president's camp. Albright confided that she had to be careful not to let her own expectations get out of line. Although the two are good friends, Albright was discreet. She told Hale that she felt comfortable with Hillary Clinton, that she and the First Lady had a good trip to Prague and that Hillary was aware of her interest. Yet Albright was careful not to relate to Hale exactly what she and the First Lady had discussed. "She knew that, basically, it would come down to what the president wanted and what he thought," Hale says.[26]

As often happens when he faces personnel decisions, Clinton was torn. He was determined to avoid the rancor that had ripped previous foreign policy "teams." The notorious rivalries that pitted Henry Kissinger against William Rogers in the Nixon administration and Zbigniew Brzezinski against Cyrus Vance in the Carter years may have provided the presidents with an array of policy recommendations, but Clinton wanted no such contests on his watch. For years, the national security adviser has vied with the secretary of state for the president's ear, a tug-of-war between institutions and personalities that author Leslie G. Gelb once called "the historical struggle between the palace guard and the king's ministers."[27] Clinton wanted a team with good chemistry. In his first term, the president had picked a senior statesman to be his top diplomat. For his second term, he planned to be more active in foreign policy matters and wanted an atmosphere in which he would be the chief policy designer, and others would carry out his vision. With Albright at State and former Republican senator William Cohen of Maine at Defense, he might get the chemistry he wanted. "He encourages people to approach situations from a different viewpoint, so Bill [Cohen] is one side of the coin and Madeleine the other," says Bowles. "He likes that because he gets two very fresh perspectives."[28] Unlike during the Nixon and Reagan years, there was seldom much head banging among Clinton's top foreign policy aides. Policy disagreements were more often matters of nuance than ideology.

But as usual, the president took his time, and as he did, Albright became increasingly distressed. She knew that she had tremendous opposition from inside the White House and the foreign policy establishment. Many foreign policy regulars simply did not trust a woman to handle the job, particularly this woman, who prided herself on toughness. They never expressed this thought directly—that would have been politically incorrect—but it was in the air. Former White House chief of staff Leon Panetta indicated to Ferraro that he supported Albright, but said he was getting a lot of questions from people who wanted to know how she would be received by countries that did not hold women in high regard. "Have you ever heard of Golda Meir and Margaret Thatcher?" Ferraro barked back.[29]

Others suggested that Albright's low profile at cabinet meetings was proof that she was not ready for the big time. One former high-ranking administration official insists that during Clinton's first term, Albright was simply not a major force in the cabinet, that when there was a discussion of foreign policy, it was led by Christopher. Unintentionally, this critic underscored an essential element in Albright's mode of operation: Christopher's job was to lead the foreign policy discussion in a cabinet meeting. To have usurped him, as others tried to do, was not Albright's style. Her forbearance was a trait Clinton appreciated.

Even Albright's seat in cabinet meetings made it difficult to jump into conversations. The Cabinet Room is located on the first floor of the West Wing of the White House. Lit by six brass wall sconces and two large brass chandeliers, the room radiates formality. Three French doors open to the Rose Garden. Cabinet members sit along the eighteenth-century mahogany table in descending rank, each assigned to a chair—a $1,500 reproduction of an eighteenth-century Queen Anne armchair—with his or her title engraved on a brass plaque in the back. Albright, who was a member by presidential choice but had no department in the government, sat near the end of the twenty-two-foot oval table,[30] well "below the salt" and "totally at the edges and physically not proximate enough to be a powerful force," according to one participant. In four years, few heard her say anything in this setting that they remembered."[31]

However, the real business of state is rarely conducted in cabinet meetings. They are held because they are expected or because there is a need for broad interdepartmental discussion. Most policy work is done in smaller groups. It was in these settings that Albright could be a force.

Shortly after the election, White House aides leaked to the *Washington Post* that Albright was in a "second tier" of candidates,[32] a remark that infuriated her high-powered female friends and, in their view, probably paved the way to her getting the job. "That was like, *kazam!*" says Mikulski. "It was an insult to all of us who have worked so hard and played by the rules. And it gave us the opportunity to launch a full-court press."[33]

That they did. The Golden Girls kicked into action. With Wendy Sherman orchestrating the battle plan, the White House was deluged with calls from congresswomen and women's groups. Mikulski called Clinton and Vice President Gore and lobbied Hillary Clinton over a veggie-burger lunch at the White House mess.[34] Kennelly wrote personal letters to the Clintons and placed a telephone call to Gore. "I'm getting lots of calls from women," Gore told Kennelly. "Wait a minute, Mr. Vice President," Kennelly replied, "I'm calling not because she's a woman; I'm calling as a member of the House leadership, and I'm not calling because she is a woman but because she is the most qualified candidate." To Albright, Kennelly said: "If your friends don't do this for you, who will?"[35] When Albright ran into Health and Human Services Secretary Donna Shalala outside the White House mess, she asked in a whisper, "Whadayahear? Whadayahear?" "Keep your head down and stay cool," Shalala whispered back. Albright nodded.[36]

Even Clinton's closest aides have trouble reading his mind when he is making personnel decisions. Few realized that Albright had been his top choice from the beginning, that Holbrooke was never as close to getting the job as rumor had it. Clinton became more and more convinced that he had been right all along, that Albright brought experience from the field, that he liked working with her, that he trusted her judgment. "She never lets the perfect be the enemy of the good," says one White House aide privy to Clinton's thinking. "But she's not going to do something she thinks is wrong in order to be practical."[37]

The day before he made his announcement, Clinton went to the Army-Navy Country Club in Arlington, Virginia, across the Potomac River from the Capitol, to mull over his choices while he practiced hitting golf balls. It was just before sunset, and he liked to use that time to think. He wanted to be sure that he had the right chemistry, and he reviewed the field again. If he picked Mitchell for State, he would not put Cohen, another senator from tiny Maine, at Defense. The pieces in the puzzle had to fit together. Clinton resented the intense lobbying of the women's organizations, and contrary to the feminists' view, if anything had come close to derailing Albright as his top choice, that was it. But he had listened to all the arguments. When everyone had finished, when Albright's critics finally rested their case, the president shook his head. "I'm going to go with my instincts on this," Clinton said to himself.[38]

When he returned to the White House, Clinton called Leon Panetta out of the Christmas Congressional Ball on the State Floor of the White House. The president asked his outgoing chief of staff to come up to the family kitchen.[39] He had made his decision. Madeleine Albright would be his secretary of state. "A lot of big decisions in life you have to get all the information you can," Clinton says. "Then you make it on instinct."[40]

Panetta, however, was not the only one who knew. The president had already let at least one other person in on his secret. He told Hillary first.[41]

24

Madame Secretary

"I realized that some people would consider it a little bit of a reach."
—President Clinton, March 4, 1998

MADELEINE ALBRIGHT WAS NERVOUS. She knew there was a good chance Clinton would select her to be his secretary of state, but it was not a sure thing. On Wednesday, December 3, 1996, late in the afternoon, Erskine Bowles, Clinton's tall, owlish incoming chief of staff, called the U.S. mission in New York, where Albright was waiting for the decision. Bowles, a nononsense businessman who brought a new degree of organization to the chaotic Clinton White House, had two questions: "If the president calls and extends you the offer to be secretary of state, will you accept?" Albright said she would. Then: "Will you be home to receive a call from the president at nine o'clock tomorrow morning?" In what had to be the biggest understatement of her life, Albright said yes, she would be there. "That's when you could feel the sheer joy and excitement of it all," Bowles says. "I had offered other cabinet jobs to people, but there was never the same sense of 'God, this is wonderful.' "[1] Bowles says making the call to Albright was the highlight of his time at the White House. He was so delighted by her excitement that he told his wife of the choice. Crandall Close Bowles (Wellesley '69) was ecstatic.

Albright, Shocas, and Rubin took a 9:00 P.M. shuttle flight to Washington to be in the capital when the call came. Wanting company, Albright asked Shocas to spend the night at her Georgetown house, and the two sat up late talking. For six months, Shocas had felt intuitively that Clinton would choose Albright for the job when Christopher left, as he was expected to at the end of the first term. A longtime political operative, she had figured the odds every way she could, and each time, it came out with Albright as number one. But at Albright's insistence—and with her own sense of superstition—Shocas instructed Albright's staff to make no move, however small, that would give anyone the impression the job was expected to go to Albright. But if—*if*—Albright was tapped, Shocas, the consummate planner, had a strategy outlined in her head.

The two friends were up early the next morning. They sat in Albright's living room drinking coffee, again talking, talking. At 9:45 A.M., the phone rang. When Albright answered, a White House operator told her the president was on the line. He wanted Albright to be his next secretary of state. When she hung up the phone, Albright gave Shocas a big hug. "You were right," Albright told her friend. They decided she should wear a red dress for the swearing-in ceremony.[2]

Albright's staff wanted Albright to be able to acknowledge the obvious—that she would be the first woman to hold the position—without actually having to say so. But how to craft the right line, set the right tone, find the right sound bite. With only a few hours before the decision would be announced at the White House, a speechwriter went to work.

Early that afternoon, in the formal elegance of the Oval Office, an ebullient Clinton announced he had chosen Albright to be secretary of state. Surrounded by her family, Albright alluded to the historical significance of her nomination with a hokey line that she thought of herself just before leaving her house. Turning to Christopher, she said, "I can only hope my high heels can fill your shoes."

The following morning, Albright made a triumphant trip back to New York to accept congratulations from her aides at the U.S. mission. She took a 9:00 A.M. Amtrak train. As she boarded one of the cars and walked down the aisle, virtually every passenger was reading a morning newspaper featuring her picture on page one. After Albright took a seat, the conductor approached to say congratulations. A few minutes later, a twelve-year-old girl came up and asked her to autograph her photograph in the *Washington Post*. Albright penned a quick note: "You can be anything you want to be." A few more people came up. Moments later, the conductor said that people in the next car knew she was there and wanted to come see her. He asked if she would mind walking to the next car to say hello, rather than have passengers filling the aisles. Albright checked with her new bodyguards. They agreed. When the secretary-designate opened the doors separating the cars, cheers erupted. Passengers jumped on their seats. Teenagers whistled. Albright made her way down the aisle, shaking every hand. When people from the next car heard the commotion and tried to join in, Albright agreed to greet them as well. Eventually, she walked the entire length of the train, posing for pictures, signing autographs, accepting congratulations.[3]

The rest of the world greeted Clinton's choice just as he had hoped it would. Newspaper editorials gushed over the decision. Women's groups rejoiced. And Albright herself, who had taken to the treadmill to lose thirty pounds in the months before her nomination,[4] looked happier and more fit than she had in years.

The reaction of the diplomatic corps was welcoming but tempered. Albright had worked with hundreds of foreign officials at the United Nations, met scores more on her international travels, and was on a first-name basis with virtually every ranking ambassador in Washington. But when her selection to be secretary of state was announced, world leaders who had watched her on CNN wanted to know more. Sir John Weston, the respected British ambassador to the United Nations, sat down at his desk and drafted a character sketch, which he sent in a cable to his home office:

> Albright is both a politician and a woman to her fingertips, warm, friendly, approachable and emotional, with a quick, intuitive grasp of people and situations, from which she can usually distill a clear and often pithy view. She likes jokes and needs attention. Among her many attractive traits are a certain spontaneity, an ability to laugh at her own expense, a sense of fun and up to a point, a readiness to listen to advice which may not be what she wants to hear. She can be quite quick-tempered when crossed. She is sensitive to any hint of being patronized, but she is not one to let the occasional spat lead to a lasting grudge.
>
> At the same time, one cannot assume that in a given case, the intellectual logic of the political scientist and her instinctive or emotional reaction to a situation will be mutually consistent or that this matters to her if they are not. She is modest and unpompous, and knows she has got on in life by sheer application rather than innate brilliance. Not having a spouse to turn to, she values private chats with and advice from friends. . . .
>
> In her job here at the U.N., American observers say she has grown considerably since her arrival. Her public presence is self-confident, she is at her best on the big issues in front of a microphone laying down a line which has U.S. interests at its centerpiece, or reducing a

complex and arcane subject to a few simple propositions for the mass audience.

Inside the Security Council, she conveys a mixture of authority and insecurity. She is not good at devising a detailed game plan for pursuing broad objectives. This can make her look flat-footed, even gauche, in detailed handling. As someone with an academic background, she knows intellectually that the world does not dance solely to an American tune and that compromises are necessary, but her behavior can belie this. And she is not always good at accepting the need to apply to the United States the same standards and expectations she requires of others.

She depends heavily on advice and reassurance from her team. There is a mildly irritating tendency to create a fixed position and then to look around for others to save her from the detailed consequences of it. She has not shown much gift for influencing her instructions from Washington in tight, time-urgent situations, with somewhat wooden results in situations requiring quick, tactical play. This has often surprised me, considering her cabinet-rank status. Her reactions to being exposed or brought under pressure from sudden turns of events are sometimes tetchy, verging on the panicky.

She has not given her attention to second-order issues, rarely attending informal consultations of the Security Council except on subjects like Iraq, Haiti, or Israel or other matters of direct interest to the White House. While taking strong positions on U.N. reform, including finances, she has never made any real effort to study or understand the dossiers. Rather than the professional diplomatic technique of negotiations, drafting and detail, her style is to set up energetic briefing meetings or foreign tours at which she lays out the U.S. position and assesses political responses. From there she instructs her subordinates to find compromises on whatever she judges the necessary point of compromise to be. It's very difficult to see her taking a lawyer's interest in the fine print of complex negotiations, such as on the Middle East or Cyprus. Although generally liked in the U.S. Mission here, I doubt whether she is an effective internal manager.

To make the transition from being a forceful spokesman of the administration's policy at the United Nations to being the effective source of that policy will be a big challenge for Albright. She has certain givens. She makes no apologies for projecting the U.S. interests vigorously. She has drive and energy. She will presumably be a warmer and more colorful high level interlocutor than her predecessor. Being the first woman secretary of state may carry its own bonus.

The question is whether she will be able to extend both the range and depth at which she can operate effectively. Her strength lies toward a style of diplomacy favored during the classic East-West relations period, e.g., her intellectual fascination with Russia; relatively narrow-gauge political preoccupations; and human rights–related issues with a strong public resonance, where she has also extended her reach in recent years into Africa.

Towards China and the Far East, generally her attitude appears more one of perplexity. Towards the European Union, a somewhat mistrustful acceptance because of the usual American difficulty in reconciling the aspiration for a united Europe with the fact that the Europeans will sometimes want to stand up firmly for their own interests. I do not see her taking naturally to some of the more complex international economic and technical agendas that Ministers increasingly have to face. But here, presumably, the quality of her tenure will depend greatly on the strength of those she appoints as senior advisers. A further blossoming and expansion of her range may yet occur and thus surprise her critics again.[5]

Madeleine Korbel Albright breezed through the confirmation process. The Senate vote was 99–0. She was sworn in as secretary of state on Thursday, January 23, 1997, by Vice President Al Gore. Wearing a glittering American eagle pin in her lapel and with her daughters at her side, she repeated the oath of office and made a short, emotional statement. "My life reflects both the turbulence of Europe in the middle of this century and the tolerance and generosity of America throughout its existence," she said. "As I stand here today in this office, which symbolizes the power and purpose of the United States, I think especially of five people: my mother and father, who taught me to love freedom; President Václav Havel, who helped me to understand the responsibilities of freedom; and Edmund Muskie, who gave me the confidence to know that no barrier or ceiling should stop me from serving freedom in my own life; and someone I did not know, Thomas Jefferson, who, as our first secretary of state, set the right diplomatic course for this nation."

The next day, at her first press briefing in her new role, Albright outlined her priorities: controlling the spread of weapons of mass destruction; keeping the Middle East peace process on track and consolidating the peace in Bosnia; paying increased attention to Latin America, South Asia, and Africa;

fighting international terrorism, drug trafficking, and international crime; and working for human rights, democracy development, and a healthy environment.

She also gave the press corps a geography lesson in how she classifies different countries: the World According to Albright. The largest group understands the rules of international diplomacy and the rule of law. The second group consists of evolving democracies that would like to be a part of the international system. The third group consists of rogue states, those countries that feel important when they disrupt the international system. And fourth, the failed states.[6]

It was an impressive show. There were so many friends and acquaintances who wanted to offer congratulations that the State Department held two afternoon receptions. Albright greeted each guest personally, beaming as she stood on a seemingly endless receiving line, embracing such old friends as New York financier Felix Rohatyn, Lesley Stahl, and the grande dame of Democratic politics, Pamela Harriman, America's ambassador to France, who was jetting back to Paris that evening.

That night she appeared on CNN's *Larry King Live* and talked about the importance of Americans understanding such foreign policy issues as terrorism, international crime, and global warming. "People always think of foreign policy issues as only guns," she said. "Foreign policy issues are those issues that average Americans care about."[7]

Only a handful of the people closest to her—and one reporter—knew that another issue brewing, personal rather than policy, was about to dispel the euphoria.

25

Bombshell

"As so often is true in life, great moments of happiness are accompanied by great moments of sadness. And so clearly this is a very bittersweet time for me."
—Madeleine Albright, February, 2, 1997

MADELEINE ALBRIGHT was at the top of her game, the first woman to reach the highest ranks of the U.S. government, the toast of the capital. She had achieved a dream that only months before few thought possible. Her father would have been delighted.

The good times, however, were short-lived. Before Albright's confirmation, she had received a call from Michael Dobbs, a Belfast-born *Washington Post* reporter, who had spent years as a foreign correspondent in Moscow and Eastern Europe and was now covering the State Department. He wanted to write a magazine story about her origins and asked if she had any relatives in the Czech Republic. Albright was pleased. She knew Dobbs to be a good reporter with a sense of history and thought he would put her story in context.[1] The tale Dobbs eventually told was enormously distressing to the new secretary, a personal shock made all the more difficult to absorb because it unfolded so publicly. Dobbs' account of how he pieced the story together differs somewhat from the one told by Albright and her team. Cousin Dagmar provided this author with additional detail.

When President Clinton tapped Albright, she became an instant media magnet. But following the custom that nominees awaiting Senate confirmation do not upstage the senators, she refused requests for interviews. She did agree, however, to take a call from Dobbs, because his story would not be published for another month, well after she was sworn into office. Albright says that during the twenty-minute conversation, she encouraged Dobbs to go to Prague and gave him the names of her father's friends, as well as that of her sixty-nine-year-old Czech cousin, Dagmar Šímová, whose maiden name was Deimlová. "I thought we had a good working relationship," Albright says.[2]

As Dobbs recalled it, Albright told him that she had a cousin, but they had lost contact. "She was very vague about her and didn't seem to know her name," Dobbs said. "At least she wasn't going to give it to me."[3] Dobbs went to the small village of Letohrad, where Albright's father was born, and soon located Cousin Dagmar, who lives in Prague.[4] When he went to see her, Dagmar told Dobbs that she had met with Albright several times over the past few years. But it was apparent that the two were not close.

Dagmar says that she was annoyed with Albright because during visits to the Czech Republic, the American cousin never went out of her way to see Dagmar. "I always learned from the newspapers or television that she was in Prague, and I didn't know why she didn't give me a ring," Dagmar says.[5]

When Albright visited Prague with President Clinton in January 1994 on a consolation trip, after NATO put off the Czechs' request for entry into the Atlantic Alliance, Dagmar called the American embassy to ask which hotel the U.N. ambassador was staying in. "I thought I would try to contact her, and I knew she wouldn't find me, even if she wanted to, because we had moved," Dagmar says. "So I said I must do my best to contact her because I was very upset by her not calling me when she came to Prague." An official at the American embassy suggested that Dagmar attend a press conference that Albright would be giving and arranged for her to be admitted. Dagmar says she knew that a press conference was not a convenient place to contact someone, but she wrote a letter with her new address and phone number and planned to give it to Albright. "When the press conference ended, she got up and almost ran out of the room," Dagmar says. "I rushed after her, but a bodyguard came between us." Dagmar says that she gave the letter to the security agent and asked that he deliver it, but Albright told her later it never arrived.[6]

By sifting through public records in Prague, Dobbs had learned that Albright's parents, who had raised her in the Roman Catholic Church, had been born Jewish. He also discovered that three of Albright's grandparents had died in the Holocaust, as had more than a dozen other relatives.[7] Cousin Dagmar confirmed the family secret that Albright insists had been kept from her.

Dobbs' profile of the new secretary was scheduled to run in the *Washington Post*'s Sunday magazine sometime after Albright took office, but what began as a soft historical piece tracing her roots in Eastern Europe was quickly exploding into hard news. Discerning the truth from reluctant newsmakers is often a reporter's hardest task, requiring a delicate balance of hardball tactics, diplomacy, and spadework. Instead of confronting the new secretary directly, Dobbs worked the edges first. He called Albright's daughter Anne. It was Friday, January 24, the day after the confirmation and swearing-in and the day of her mother's State Department receptions.[8] Anne, a thirty-six-year-old Maryland lawyer who had recently started her own firm, had talked to reporters about her mother before. But this situation was different from any she had encountered. Dobbs peppered Anne with difficult questions, reducing her to tears.[9]

The next day, a Saturday, Dobbs called Winifred Shore Freund and Emily Cohen MacFarquhar, who are among Albright's oldest and dearest friends. "He started out with the Bermuda shorts and knee socks questions, but soon it was clear that wasn't why he called," MacFarquhar recalls. Dobbs asked if she knew that Albright's grandparents had died in the Holocaust. MacFarquhar said no. After their respective interviews, Freund and MacFarquhar compared notes and placed a conference call to Albright.[10]

Dobbs insists that before calling Anne or Albright's friends, he first told Jamie Rubin, the secretary's spokesman. He says that he did that even before Albright's swearing-in. Rubin believes it was shortly after the ceremony that Dobbs first telephoned him to say he had learned that Albright's grandparents were Jewish and had died in the Holocaust. Rubin says that he was shocked by the news and is certain he would not have forgotten had Dobbs told him earlier. He remembers that Albright and her staff had just moved into their seventh-floor offices and that the call came through while the new State Department press secretary was admiring his sweeping view of the Lincoln Memorial. After he and Dobbs finished talking, Rubin raced down Mahogany Row—the private inner corridor that links the offices—to consult Elaine Shocas, the secretary's new chief of staff. Shocas was just settling into her new quarters, a few steps from Albright's. On her desk was a souvenir she had picked up in Angola, a defused land mine. It was a tacit reminder to proceed carefully because one never knows what lies ahead. When Rubin burst into her office, Shocas saw immediately by the look on his face that something was seriously wrong. Closing the door, he turned to her and said: "Where's Madeleine? We have to talk to her."

Albright had just heard the news from Anne, who was extremely upset when she talked to her mother. Anne told her mother that she had just had a call from Dobbs. "He told me that all Grandma's family died in the concentration camps," Anne cried. She told her mother that she was sorry she had not been nicer to her grandmother Mandula. "Now I understand why she was so protective of us," Anne said. The secretary was furious. "Anne had been adorable to her grandmother," she says. "She was totally devastated."[11] Albright considered Dobbs' treatment of her daughter unconscionable. "Madeleine was upset that Dobbs called Anne first," says MacFarquhar. "He was very abrupt, throwing it in her face. Madeleine saw it as an underhanded assault on her daughter. She was so angry at him. She was angry about what she considered a sneak attack."[12] Dobbs says he later wrote Albright a note and, referring to his call to Anne, said he understood such matters of personal identity are difficult.[13]

An entire week went by. Dobbs presented his findings to Albright during an hour-long meeting in her cherry-paneled private study at the State Department on Thursday, January 30. Steve Coll, editor of the *Washington Post Magazine*, was also present. Document by document, Dobbs showed Albright what he had uncovered. He held up a small black-and-white photograph of little children and demanded: "Can you identify the people in this picture?" Albright said she could. "That is my cousin," she began. "The person in the stroller is my sister, and the little girl standing there is me." "No," said Dobbs, "that is your cousin. It's you in the stroller, and that is her sister, who died in a concentration camp." Then Dobbs handed Albright a copy of a page from a book that lists people who were sent to the Theresienstadt concentration camp and the dates of their deaths. "Have you seen this document?" he asked. "No," Albright replied, "I have not."[14]

Albright handed Dobbs a document. It was the personal essay her mother had written describing the family's dramatic escape from Czechoslovakia in 1939. She had written it after her husband, Josef Korbel, died in 1977 but had never shown it to her children; her children found it among her personal papers when she died. Albright used the letter to show Dobbs that her family fled Prague because of political persecution, not because they were Jewish. What could be better proof that they did not know about their background, Albright asked, than an eleven-page, single-spaced history written by her mother in longhand that never mentioned the word *Jewish?*[15] Mandula Korbel had gone to her grave with the family secret intact.

Originally, Dobbs had sketched his story to Rubin as a piece about what it was like to be born in Czechoslovakia and how the debacle at Munich affected her thinking as a diplomat. When the reporter did not touch on these questions, Albright was surprised. "Aren't you going to ask me about anything else?" she said. He was not. Dobbs later called the meeting "contentious." Albright's view was stronger. "You would think we were in court," she says.[16]

The interview was awful for Albright. She was deeply hurt and felt that she had been treated as if she had done something wrong. "Who are these people?" she asked Rubin afterward. "Who do they think they are?" She says she was surprised by Dobbs' findings, but she was infuriated by the confrontational style in which they were presented to her and to her daughter. Nonetheless, she thanked him for his work, saying that the information was important to have.

Dobbs was under enormous pressure as well. He was a veteran reporter with a world exclusive. He could not afford to be wrong. He needed to satisfy himself, and his editors, that Albright was as ignorant of her family history as she insisted. As dogged as reporters often appear to be, dropping a bombshell on an unsuspecting official is a gut-wrenching experience, and such interviews are not always conducted in as polite or diplomatic a manner as they should be. Dobbs concedes he wishes he had handled it differently. In his stories, there is not a hint that he thought Albright was being untruthful.

But Albright had no way of knowing what the newspaper would say. That weekend, she called Katharine Graham, chairman of the executive committee of the Washington Post Company, whose own extraordinary rise came when she inherited a mediocre newspaper and built it into the nation's premier political daily. Graham, whom Albright considered a friend, had recently published a memoir (for which she would later be awarded a Pulitzer Prize) in which she discussed her own Jewish heritage. The secretary of state told Graham that the issue was a very personal matter and asked to see Dobbs' story before it ran. She said she did not expect the *Post* to make changes, but she wanted her family to have time to digest the information before it became public.[17] Graham, an experienced news executive who had handled many newsroom crises, told Albright that the *Post* never shows news subjects a story before it is in print. But she referred the secretary to her paper's top editors and placed a call herself to *Post* executive editor Leonard Downie, Jr. Downie assured Graham that Dobbs was a tough reporter but fair. When Graham later talked to Dobbs, the writer explained that in order to be sure there were no holes in his story, he had felt it necessary to be aggressive, and that in the end, he was convinced that Albright had not known her family's history.[18]

At a meeting that week at the White House, Albright took Clinton aside and told him what she had learned. The president was sympathetic. He told her that when the media focused on his family background, he learned of a half-brother he did not know he had.[19] To make sure that the chairman of the Senate Foreign Relations Committee did not hear the story first from the newspapers, Elaine Shocas called Jesse Helms. "Oh, the poor darling," Helms said sympathetically.[20]

Albright's team of advisers met to figure out how she could control the story and not be thrown on the defensive. In the end, she disclosed the news herself—in effect, scooping Dobbs on his own exclusive.

CBS's *60 Minutes* reporter Ed Bradley had a piece on Albright in the works and an interview scheduled at her Georgetown house for Sunday afternoon, February 2. During the taping, in response to a question from Bradley that had been suggested by a source, Albright said that she had just learned that her parents were Jewish and her grandparents had died in the Holocaust. Jamie Rubin saw producer Michael Rosenbaum's eyes light up like flashbulbs. "Boy, has this ever been out before?" Rosenbaum asked. Rubin knew then the story would not hold. He had to work quickly. The next morning, Monday, February 3, he called the *Washington Post* to say CBS would probably break the story that night on the evening news.

Rubin also called Barry Schweid, a veteran Associated Press State Department correspondent respected for his broad knowledge of foreign policy issues. Schweid had already put in a pro forma request for an interview with the new secretary. "How about today?" Rubin asked. Schweid was taken aback. Normally such interviews are scheduled well in advance. But like any crack reporter, he loves the sound of the fire bell and thrives on beating his colleagues on important interviews. He accepted immediately. Rubin suggested that they meet for a quick lunch to discuss the terms.

Over a tuna fish sandwich in the State Department cafeteria, Rubin told Schweid that the secretary would not mind talking about her family history. Schweid, who is more comfortable asking about world issues than personal matters, shrugged. "I thought I'd ask a question or two about that and get on with asking about what are we going to do about China," he says.[21]

The interview took place in Albright's office. Both Schweid and Albright were ill at ease. Schweid opened by saying he hated to get into personal questions, but would she mind if he asked about her background? Albright was ready. "Sure," she said. She told him about letters she had been receiving recently that contained information about her family history, "some of which was completely off the wall."

But apparently not all of it. "In the midst of this," Albright continued, with uncharacteristic awkwardness, "there would be an occasional something that would say—not specifically saying you're of Jewish origin but saying—I can't remember the way it was framed, but basically, something like that. But with the time that I was named to be the secretary, the news kind of got . . . a trickle turned into a flood, and there was more and more information. It began to make more sense to me."

Suddenly she was speaking so softly that Schweid says he had to strain to hear her: "[Dobbs] found that my grandparents had actually died in Auschwitz. So this was obviously a major surprise to me because I had never been told this." Schweid, who calls himself a traditional Jew who lost numerous family members in the Holocaust, asked if she felt satisfied that her grandparents died at Auschwitz. "No," she replied. "No. I have to say that the information seems fairly compelling to me, but I want to check it out, obviously." Schweid apologized again for delving into personal questions and then asked if both sets of grandparents had been Jews.[22] "Both," Albright replied.

SCHWEID: You didn't know?
ALBRIGHT: . . . I had some papers under which—where it says "religion," they had something which I don't exactly know how to translate.[23]

Although Schweid did not press her, Albright was referring to her birth certificate. More than a year later, Albright produced the document for this author, effectively making it public for the first time. In the space marked "religion," her parents wrote "*bez vyznání,*" which means, roughly, "without denomination" or "without confession."

Schweid decided to move on. "More comfortably . . ." he began, and he launched into a convoluted question about Peru and the U.S. policy on terrorism. Within no time, both Albright and Rubin started to shift in their chairs. "I realized she was giving me a boilerplate answer," Schweid says. "I knew I had either used up my time on the family stuff, or this is why I was permitted to see her."

Schweid went back to the AP office in the State Department news room and filed his story:

WASHINGTON (AP)—A church-going Roman Catholic as a young girl and a practicing Episcopalian as an adult, Secretary of State Madeleine Albright said today she has concluded she was born Jewish. She also has learned two of her grandparents perished in the Auschwitz concentration camp.

Calmly discussing her background in an interview with the Associated Press, Albright said, "This obviously was a major surprise to me. I had never been told this."[24]

When Schweid finished writing, it was dinnertime. The story would appear in the morning papers. He knew he had to write a new version for the afternoon papers and file it by midnight, but he was hungry. He drove to the Tel Aviv Cafe in the northern suburb of Bethesda, Maryland, for a bite to eat.

CBS news producers saw Schweid's story on the wire and knew that they would have to go with the segment on Albright's Jewish background before the weekend. They decided to run it on the *CBS Evening News* that night. With the AP story and the CBS segment flashing around the world, the *Washington Post* was forced to preempt its Sunday magazine piece with a weekday news story. In effect, the State Department public relations machine had forced the *Post* to play catch-up on its own exclusive. On Tuesday, February 4, the newspaper ran a page-one piece under Dobbs' byline. The headline: "Albright's Family Tragedy Comes to Light."

The story was riveting. The avalanche of news stories that followed raised embarrassing questions for Albright about how an avid scholar of Eastern Europe could possibly have been ignorant of her own family history for so long. The damning charge was that she was either lying or pitifully naive. In either case, she had been in office barely two weeks, and her credibility already was at stake.

Cousin Dagmar says that she discussed the situation with Dobbs not to embarrass her newly famous relative but because Dobbs called her to ask if it was possible that Albright and her family did not know. Dagmar insists that she did not mean to spill a family secret, that it never occurred to her that her American cousins were ignorant of their Jewish heritage. "I didn't know what to say," she says. "I had no idea."[25]

Did Madeleine Albright know? The question inevitably pops up whenever her name is mentioned, even in casual conversation. How could she *not* have known? Her cousin Dagmar is not the only one who says she does not understand. So do many of her family friends, who lived through the wartime years with the Korbels. They do not want to challenge the secretary of state. They do not want to get into a sparring match. Some do not even think it matters. But they wonder. And more often than not, they bring it up without being prompted. "Look," says Eduard Goldstücker, who was Korbel's close friend for many years, "I very much doubt Madeleine's statement that she had no knowledge of it until recently. It seems improbable that a woman her age, having lived through all these decades, never came face-to-face with this realism." Goldstücker says he is not sure what to make of it: "Maybe she suppressed the memory, which is very understandable, so she can deny it with a good conscience."[26]

Comments Albright and her staff made at the time of the revelations confirm that she had been receiving information for several years about her Jewish heritage. For whatever reason, she never pursued it. While her remarks did not contradict each other, they were not spoken in the plain English for which the secretary is famous.

To everyone who asked, and even at times to those who did not, Albright insisted that her parents never talked to her about the family's Jewish heritage, that she had no idea members of her family were killed by Nazis. *Newsweek* quoted Jamie Rubin saying Albright received "some communications" in November that "for the first time made her wonder whether she really might have Jewish origins."[27] Albright told Ed Bradley that "with the opening up of Czechoslovakia and with my naming as secretary of state, there has been some very compelling evidence that the *Washington Post* found, that my family was indeed of Jewish origin and that my grandparents may, in fact, have died in a concentration camp."[28] Albright told *Newsweek* that her brother, John Korbel, had visited their father's hometown in the early nineties, and nobody had said one word to him about the family background.[29]

At a bilateral meeting between the United States and Mexico on February 8—four days after the *Post* story—Albright said that since the opening up of Czechoslovakia in 1989, she had been getting many letters and that "as a result of some of these letters, I began to see that there was, indeed, the possibility that my family was of Jewish origin."[30] To ABC's Sam Donaldson on February 23, she said that what had shocked her about Dobbs' revelations was that it was "the first time I had heard about the fact that my grandparents had died in a concentration camp; not the fact that my family was originally Jewish. That I had learned earlier."[31] This was not the first time Rubin, who is Jewish, had raised the question with Albright. Ever since he began working with her at the United Nations, Rubin would occasionally say to her: "Hey, my friends say you gotta be Jewish." Albright found it amusing and always responded by saying that it was not true; she had been raised Catholic. The November 1996 "communications" Rubin had mentioned to *Newsweek* were actually only one letter that made her rethink the situation.

Unlike other letters to Albright that had basic facts about her family history wrong, this one, sent to the American embassy in Prague, seemed to have correct names and dates. "You should be less categorical about this," she told Rubin. "It seems possible." During the White House security checks performed before Clinton nominated her for the job, Albright told investigators that she might have Jewish ancestors. They said, in effect, so what? Over a Christmas skiing holiday in Aspen, she discussed it with her family.[32]

For Albright, whose selection as secretary of state represented not only a moment of professional triumph but a personal one as well, the news of her family history, and the curiosity it provoked, was a devastating blow. It was not that she had a Jewish background; there was, obviously, nothing "wrong" with having Jewish forebears. But the harsh way in which she learned the news, and the second-guessing of her parents' motives, infuriated her. "I went from being sad to sick to mad," she says.[33]

What startled those around the new secretary was that her parents, whom she adored, had allowed their children to remain ignorant of a poignant aspect of their heritage—the deeply tragic deaths of their grandparents in the Holocaust. American Jews were particularly incensed, insisting that she had to know she had Jewish blood, that it was insulting that she was denying a heritage that they celebrate, that if they could shoulder a lifetime burden of anti-Semitism, so could she. To many, Jews in particular, there was the question of a cover-up.

Whatever their religion, many people in Albright's social and academic circles lead lives that have been blessed. While many Jews came forward to say that they, too, had not known their family heritage, others were unwilling to believe that there are families with pasts too painful to talk about, that there are individuals for whom a private trauma in an earlier period has left them outwardly normal yet emotionally fragile in ways they choose not to discuss. For war veterans, this behavior is deemed acceptable by such observers. For Albright's parents, who were war veterans of a different sort, it was not.

In her book *Children of the Holocaust,* Helen Epstein writes that many of the children of survivors absorbed their families' attitudes toward the Holocaust with a kind of "wordless osmosis." "Those children of survivors whose parents had sealed off their past responded by sealing off their own," she writes. "Those whose parents talked openly about their experience were most at ease with the subject while others, whose parents tried to forget it, had little to say themselves."[34] This description seems to fit the Korbel family.

At what should have been her moment of triumph, Albright was beleaguered. She was angry and hurt that many people did not believe her. This was, after all, the woman who had told America on her first day as secretary of state that she would "tell it like it is" about issues such as human rights. Yet in less time than it would take to recycle yesterday's newspapers, Madeleine Albright appeared reluctant to tell it "like it was" about herself.

Even Albright's admirers were perplexed. She was a Czechoslovak-born teacher and politician who prided herself on her knowledge and study of Eastern Europe, the daughter of a Czechoslovak diplomat who fled his country twice, first to escape the Nazis, then its Communist rulers. It stretched the imagination to believe that she was truly ignorant of her family history. How could a precocious child who had grown up in a close family that had lost loved ones to the Holocaust have missed, ignored, buried all the clues all her life? When her parents explained that their own parents had "died in the war," did she never ask *how* they died? Albright answered the question herself. "If you are told your grandparents died during the war of old age, would you not believe your parents?" she says.[35]

Many of Albright's friends see her lack of curiosity about her family heritage as an act of denial, an unspoken agreement not to delve into painful matters of the past that her father and mother chose, for whatever reason, not to discuss with their children. If Henry Kissinger minimized the persecution and anti-Semitism he felt as a child growing up in Nazi Germany,[36] Albright appeared to have ignored her background altogether.

Perhaps this was the box in the family closet Madeleine Albright chose not to open, one that had been there so long it had become part of the woodwork, uncomfortable evidence of an earlier life that at some visceral level, however deep, she understood was off-limits, a subject too sensitive to be probed.

Some friends even believe that she ignored the clues on purpose. After all, they told each other, it was hard enough being a woman trying to make it to the top echelon of American government; it would be harder still for a Jewish woman. Kissinger, who lost thirteen members of his family to the Nazis,[37] had become secretary of state almost twenty-five years before and dealt successfully with Middle Eastern nations. But he was, after all, a "he." How would the Arabs react to a Jewish woman as the American secretary of state? In Prague, stories circulated that it was the Syrians, deeply distrustful of the alliance between the United States and Israel, who first dug into her Jewish past and leaked it.

It is apparent that the Israelis knew. Gad Yaacobi, Israel's ambassador to the United Nations when Albright was there,[38] told reporters that he had known about her Jewish history for several years. He had mentioned it to then—Prime Minister Yitzhak Rabin and Foreign Minister Shimon Peres, but he had never mentioned it to Albright.[39] It would not have been in Israel's interest to embarrass the new secretary of state with information she did not know or did not want disclosed.[40]

For Albright, who wanted to savor the electric moment in history that her father could only have dreamed of for his daughter, the past suddenly came crashing in on her. There was hardly time to react, to think about her answers, and no time to do her own research.

Political Washington dines on stories of personal intrigue, and within hours, Albright's Secret Past had become a staple of the capital dinner party circuit. How could she not have known? Isn't Korbel a Jewish name? What does she think she's hiding?

ABC's Cokie Roberts (Wellesley, '64), who was raised Catholic, and her husband, Steven V. Roberts, whose grandparents were Jewish, defended Albright against charges that she was opting for an easier life by denying her heritage. "Easier life?" they wrote in a column that appeared in the *New York Daily News*.[41] "Look at it: In wartime London she was a refugee, in totalitarian Czechoslovakia she was a democrat, in small-town Denver she was a foreigner and at Wellesley in the 1950s she was a Catholic. In some ways that was a lot tougher than being Jewish. Old-line Protestants discriminated equally against both groups, but Jews had more of an intellectual cachet while Catholicism was equated with simplemindedness."

Other pundits, however, were in high dudgeon. At the *New York Times,* Philip Taubman, deputy editor of the editorial page, wrote a piece that began: "Madeleine Albright must have known."[42] Frank Rich, a *Times* columnist, devoted several pieces to the story. "The question of what Madeleine Albright knew about her past and when she knew it is hardly of Watergate significance," he wrote.[43] "Her religion, whatever it is, is irrelevant to her job, for which she is abundantly qualified. But her story isn't going away just yet, in part because it upsets more than a few American Jews, and in part because she seems to be shading the truth."[44]

Albright was so upset and hurt by Rich's column that she arranged a telephone interview with him that took place an hour after she arrived home from her first, eleven-day trip around the world as secretary. "Was I totally surprised about my Jewish background?" she asked rhetorically. "No. I had hints along the way. . . . I feel pretty stupid. It's like seeing a bunch of dots and when a person puts it all together, it makes sense. . . . I had not been sensitive enough to signs that my background was different [from what] I thought it was."[45]

Piecing the story together herself would prove as painful as it was difficult. As she often does when she's nervous, Albright picked up the phone to discuss the situation with her friends. One evening near midnight, she called Kati Marton, a New York writer, whose diplomat husband, Richard Holbrooke, had been Albright's chief rival for secretary of state. The three had known each other a long time.

Fifteen years before, Marton made a discovery similar to the one Albright was confronting. On her first trip back to her native Hungary since her family fled after the abortive 1956 anti-Communist revolution, Marton interviewed a Holocaust survivor who told her that Marton's grandparents had been in one of the first Hungarian transports to Auschwitz. Like Albright, Marton had never been told of her Jewish heritage. When Albright's story spilled onto the front pages of the nation's newspapers, Marton felt enormous empathy for the emotional upheaval she knew her friend must be experiencing. Despite the late hour, she was eager to reach out and offer the kind of reassurance and solace that she had needed. "Madeleine was very rattled, and she was emotional," Marton says. "She asked how I told my children, how I dealt with it, and how it affected my relationship with my parents."[46]

In their conversation, Marton explained to Albright that she, too, had been raised a Roman Catholic. She had been told her grandparents died during the siege of Budapest in 1945. Her parents, André and Ilona Marton, both distinguished Hungarian journalists, had been arrested by the Communist regime in early 1955 on trumped-up charges of spying for the United States and imprisoned. When they were released, they came as political refugees to the United States, where Endre Marton resumed his career covering diplomatic affairs for the Associated Press. That was 1957, when Kati Marton was nine years old. Her job, which Marton says her parents conveyed to her in every way they knew how, was to become the all-American girl: "Learn the language. Adapt to the culture. Be successful. And above all, be grateful."

It was not until almost twenty years later that Marton learned that there was more to her parents' story. "Refugees like Albright and me do not have normal relationships with our parents," she wrote in an article in *Newsweek,* comparing her experience to Albright's. "We don't simply love them; we revere them. We know that they have been through great and terrible things, that they risked everything to bring us to this strange and wonderful country with its strange and wonderful ways. I had seen my parents' courage in the face of the communists. Now I learned that there were things about these heroic people—and about me—that I knew nothing about."[47]

Marton's parents never looked back. "Our family's history would begin here," she wrote. "As my parents saw it, there was danger in looking back. There were problems enough in being a refugee; why compound them by adding 'Jewish' to the list of things we had to overcome? They had too much history. I did not have enough. They felt that to be American meant not having a past, or at least having the freedom to choose what to remember. I felt the opposite. To me, America means the freedom to unabashedly embrace your heritage, whatever it might be."[48]

As her late-night conversation with Marton continued, Albright defended her parents' decision not to tell their children about the family history. "Essentially, my feeling was that her affinity was more with my parents than with me," Marton says. "I felt that even though she and I are closer in age—I'm twelve years younger than she is—she felt more comfortable with their thinking than mine. I represent the postwar generation that wants the truth, the whole truth, and thinks that truth has its own merit without embellishment, and my parents' generation represents fear of the truth. The truth can hurt, and they have been hurt by it. In fact, she was kind of explaining that to me, basically using some of the same language that my parents had—that we will never understand what they went through and their need to protect us."[49]

Albright had already disclosed the news that her family was Jewish. Now what she desperately needed was time to adjust to the knowledge, to discuss it with her family and digest the undeniable fact that her father and mother had not leveled with her. In her view, it was a private matter. She decided to consider her public discussion closed. "I've explained this as well as it can be explained," she told Rubin. "If people don't want to believe me, there's nothing I can do."[50]

She wanted to stop others from talking about it as well. In hopes of refocusing news about Albright, which was becoming increasingly critical, her staff tried to silence as many people as possible, including friends, other family members, and officials in both the U.S. government and local Czech municipalities. Over several working dinners on State Department trips, Jamie Rubin told journalists that Albright would not cooperate with the handful of people who were writing books about her phenomenal rise.[51] Shocas, her chief of staff, wrote a letter to biographers stating Albright's position. "Her decision is based on the time demands and inevitable distractions that would result from her involvement in these projects," Shocas wrote. "The members of Secretary Albright's family have also decided not to participate in these book projects, and we would appreciate your respecting their decision. The Secretary has advised her friends and colleagues of her decision on this matter." In short, no family members would be permitted to "tell it like it is" about Albright—*or their own family history*—and friends would be discouraged from doing so.

Albright decided to investigate her family background privately. But with such a visible new job, not to mention the crush of foreign policy issues that demanded her attention, she knew it would be impossible to do the work herself. She enlisted her brother, John Korbel, a partner with the Price Waterhouse accounting firm, and her sister, Kathy Silva, a middle-level official at the Department of Education, to make a family fact-finding trip. Each had visited Prague in the early 1990s. Kathy had accompanied Albright several years before when Albright was invited to speak at the Palace of Culture. Dagmar remembers spending three days showing Kathy around the city, that they attended the lecture together, and that Kathy had trouble walking because she had had an operation on her foot. They also went on a shopping trip for garnets, a local semiprecious stone.[52]

In February 1997, John Korbel, his wife, Pamela, and Kathy Silva left for Prague again. Carrying a notebook and a video camera, they visited the Old Jewish Cemetery and the Pinkas Synagogue, where the names of their grandfather and grandmother are listed among those who died in the Holocaust. One afternoon they visited with Cousin Dagmar.[53]

Today, Dagmar Deimlová Šímová is a cultured, well-spoken woman whose short stature, wide cheekbones, high brow, and narrow chin bare a strong family resemblance to Albright and her sister. Her English is flawless, the accent slightly British, her voice gravelly, her manner proper and polite. Nine years older than Madeleine, Cousin Dagmar has distinct memories of the war years, which she lived through as a teenager when Madeleine was but a little girl. In fact, both in Prague and in London, Dagmar often acted as her baby-sitter.

Dagmar Šímová and her husband, Vladimír, a retired electrical engineer, live on the fifth floor of an aged apartment building, located just outside the center of Prague in a section of the city called Nusle. A drab cement staircase winds from floor to floor. Their apartment is tiny. One enters through a narrow kitchen of 1930s vintage. The living room is clean, comfortable, and worn; the wallpaper faded; the sofa and easy chairs covered with thin batik dustcovers. Despite the fact that they have met Albright numerous times over the past few years, there are no visible pictures of their famous cousin on display. Cousin Dagmar's life is clearly Spartan, a far cry from the world of Georgetown and the hunting and ski lodges that Madeleine Albright and her family have known.

Dagmar says John Korbel and Kathy Silva arrived at her apartment about

3:00 P.M. and stayed until 11:00. First they had tea, and then, over dinner, they drank red wine and had a long talk about family history. "They were nonplussed because it was all new to them," Dagmar says. "Actually, they found the situation difficult to handle. It wasn't pleasant at all for them."[54]

Albright's cousin says that she showed them family pictures, as well as two Theresienstadt Memorial books that list the names and fates of victims of the Holocaust: "We looked up all the relatives, and they took notes." Asked if she believes their claim that they knew nothing about their Jewish background before, Dagmar replied, "Yes, I do believe them. They were surprised. They couldn't imagine why they hadn't been told."

Cousin Dagmar, who had been besieged by news reporters when the first stories broke about the family history, says the Korbels asked her not to speak to the press again. "But it was too late," she says. "They should have warned me earlier. If I had known they didn't want me to talk to the press, I could do the simplest thing in the world. I could write to the people who live in the house where my grandfather used to live and ask them not to give my address to anybody." That was the way she was most easily found in the former Communist country, where public telephone directories were still rare.

On February 14, the Korbel family took the three-hour drive over rolling countryside to Letohrad, the picturesque town where their father had been born. They had refreshments in the town's chateau, a fourteenth-century fortress that serves as the town community and social center. So many international news reporters surrounded the building and camped out on the town square to report on their visit that the Korbels were forced to flee out a back door into an unmarked car they hoped would go unrecognized by the press.[55]

They visited with Letohrad mayor Petr Šilar, who showed them the Korbel family tree that officials in the community had assembled. They also visited the house where their grandfather Arnošt Körbel had lived. What they learned was that the inherited property had been divided into three parts and that Josef Korbel's share was seized by the state when he defected. In 1949, Cousin Dagmar sold the two thirds of the property that the family still owned to the Otava family.[56] Upon Josef Korbel's death, the Otava family purchased the remaining third from the state. Jarmila Otavová now runs the town museum in Žamberk, which oversees the only Jewish cemetery in the area.[57]

Věra Ruprechtová, who had known Arnošt Körbel as a child because she was the granddaughter of his business partner, entertained the Korbels in her home. She says they were very emotional during their visit to her apartment, that they were moved to tears as they realized they were sitting in chairs once used by their grandfather. She added that they asked her not to discuss the Korbel family with the press.[58]

Shortly after they returned to the United States, Kathy Silva wrote a letter thanking the family's new friends in Letohrad for their hospitality. The letter said that the Korbel family was surprised to learn that their grandparents were born Jewish and died in the gas chambers. Silva mentioned that Dagmar Šímová had sold her father's house and concluded by saying that the family had learned how the Nazis and Communists appropriated property from private individuals.[59]

In June 1997, four months after the Korbel visit, Mayor Šilar, a big bear of a man with a salt-and-pepper beard, showed this author a big scrapbook of letters, pictures, and historical detail about the Körbel family. He began the scrapbook when international news stories about Albright put Letohrad on the map.[60] The scrapbook contains copies of four letters he sent to Albright.

Written in Czech, the letters detail her family's fate in the Holocaust. One, dated February 25, 1994, and mailed to the United Nations in New York, where Albright was serving as the American ambassador, said that birth records of Josef Körbel had been found in the "birth register of the Jewish community" and that her paternal grandparents "died in the gas chambers." Two others were dated August 26 and August 29, 1994, and mailed to the American embassy in Prague at the time Albright was visiting. The fourth was dated December 6, 1996. Šilar says that he does not know if Albright read any of the letters. He never received a reply.[61]

American ambassadors to the United Nations receive thousands of letters each year from around the world. Few reach the ambassador, but all are read by aides. If Albright never saw these letters, as she claims, it could have been the result of poor staff work. Or perhaps she neglected to read them.

Šilar says the Korbels were insistent that town officials not discuss their visit or the Korbel family history with the press. He says that Tomáš Kraus, executive director of the Federation of Jewish Communities in Prague, who accompanied the Korbels on the visit, also warned him not to "stir the waters" by speaking with reporters. Picking up the scrapbook and pointing to a picture of Kathy Silva, Šilar said she was the most insistent, that she explained to him that discussing personal matters in public was disagreeable. He said John Korbel agreed. Šilar says he would have gone along with their wishes, but officials in another town nearby had started discussing details with reporters. He wanted his community to get credit for being the hometown of the now-famous Korbel family.[62]

Kraus, one of the leaders of the Jewish community in Prague, concedes that he asked local Letohrad leaders not to talk to reporters, and he thinks it was a necessary precaution. "It was [the Korbels'] wish that they not talk to the press," Kraus says. "There was nothing to hide but they wanted to digest it first for themselves. There was damage done by the first [*Washington Post*] story."[63]

Kraus, whose parents are both Holocaust survivors, says it is quite common for children like the Korbels not to have been aware of their Jewish origins, that some survivors can talk of nothing else and others find themselves unable to bring it up at all. "After the war, my father published several books in which he described his every step in Terezín, Auschwitz, the Death March, labor camps," Kraus says. "My mother had the exact same experiences, but she never told me a word about the Holocaust. She was trying to erase it from her memory as if it never existed."

In June 1997, three months after the Korbels' trip to the Czech Republic, Cousin Dagmar agreed to a series of interviews with this author in hopes of putting the family history in perspective. She says that she was aghast at the distress and headlines that her revelation caused Albright and her family. Dagmar showed no bitterness and, in fact, seems genuinely fond of her American cousins, whom she has seen from time to time over the years.

Dagmar conceded, however, that she remains mystified at how Albright and her siblings could have remained ignorant of their family history for so long, that Madeleine never discovered her parents were Jewish or that six of her closest relatives—two grandmothers, a grandfather, Aunt Markéta, Uncle Rudolf, and Cousin Milena—had died in the Holocaust. She said that when she and the Körbels returned to Prague after the war, there was certainly discussion of the tragedy in the apartment—"Of course there was"[64]—and that she does not know how Madeleine, then eight years old, could have avoided overhearing any of the conversations: "I can't imagine how she could have been kept aside."[65]

In a subsequent interview a month later, her mood softened after a private breakfast with Albright. Dagmar qualified her comments, saying that the conversation in her apartment had been between her and her uncle Josef, Madeleine's father: "But with the others, there was not much conversation. I'm surprised how little. But Kathy was three, and Madeleine was eight. It was not a topic for small children."[66]

In Washington, Albright remained fixated on the subject of her Jewish heritage, much as she had on her divorce some fifteen years before. In each case, delicate layers of family lore had been peeled back, leaving her feeling raw and vulnerable. During dinner party discussions and in informal conversations with friends, she talked about it endlessly. She asked one old friend who had known and respected her father if he felt differently about him. When the friend said, "No, of course not," Albright seemed relieved.[67] To many, Albright appeared to be struggling to understand the motives of her father, whom she loved deeply and emulated all her life. The careful cocoon he had woven to protect his own life and that of his family had split open.

As is often the case in Washington, Albright had to endure countless jokes about the controversy wherever she went. At the annual white-tie Gridiron dinner in March, where the capital's hoariest print journalists spoof government VIPs, Copley News Service economics writer Finlay Lewis played the State Department spokesman: "Ladies and Gentlemen of the Press," he began. "We've had Catholic secretaries of state. We've had Episcopalian secretaries of state. We've had Jewish secretaries of state. Now we have all three—and he's a woman."[68] All eyes turned to Madeleine, who made no move to feign a chuckle. One person who could see her face watched her grimace.[69]

The jokes did not let up. At a joint Washington birthday party later in the spring for Kati Marton and producer-director George Stevens at the Stevens' elegant nineteenth-century home in Georgetown, President Clinton was a surprise guest. Recuperating from knee surgery, he was on crutches and did not plan to stay for dinner. But once he arrived, he enjoyed himself so much that he showed no signs of leaving. Dinner was delayed, then delayed again. When the president finally departed and the guests sat down to grilled bass, Stevens announced that he had one more surprise. "Oh no," shouted *Washington Post* columnist Richard Cohen. "Don't tell me you're Jewish, too?" The room erupted in laughter, except for Albright, who gripped the stem of her wineglass so hard that her knuckles turned white. Nearby guests were afraid it would snap.[70]

Spring rolled into summer. Czech president Václav Havel sent word that he planned to award Albright his country's highest honor, the Order of the White Lion, and she decided to tack a one-day trip to Prague onto the end of the NATO summit in Madrid in early July. Albright invited Dagmar to the ceremony, where the cousin sat in a front row. Albright introduced Dagmar to President Havel.

The visit also gave Albright an opportunity to see her family names listed among the Holocaust victims on the walls of the Pinkas Synagogue. Albright would have preferred that this portion of the trip be private. She knew it would be emotional. But secretaries of state are not permitted such luxury. By making no advance announcement of her schedule, she hoped to limit the news coverage.

Albright arrived in Prague on Sunday, July 13. After a long day that had started in St. Petersburg in the morning and gone on to Vilnius, Lithuania, in the afternoon, her official air force jet with "United States of America" emblazoned on the side in bold blue letters landed at Prague's airport. American ambassador Jenonne Walker headed a group of Czech and American dignitaries who lined up to greet her. After shaking hands all around, Albright climbed into her limousine, and the nineteen-car motorcade sped off for the short drive into the city. As her entourage wound down the narrow, cobblestone hillside that buttresses Hradčany Castle and crossed over the Vltava River that divides the Malá Strana (Lesser Quarter) from the Staré Město (Old Town), dusk was just beginning to fall.

After a quick stop at the Hotel Inter-Continental, where she just missed American comedian Billy Crystal checking in, Albright walked two blocks through the dark, winding streets of the Old Jewish Quarter. With Leo Pavlát and Tomáš Kraus, leaders of Prague's Jewish community, at her side, she visited the historic section once again. This night, one year since her last visit, had special significance.

The press corps was kept cordoned off in an alley where reporters could not see Albright or hear her discussion with the Jewish leaders. She was accompanied by only one newspaper reporter, the *Washington Post*'s Michael Dobbs, who was chosen by Albright's traveling press corps to be its "pool" print reporter and take notes for them. The irony of Dobbs being the one to record Albright's reaction to proof of his story was lost on no one. Albright's staff was clearly annoyed, but knew it would cause a ruckus with the reporters if Dobbs was refused access or if the event was canceled altogether, as had been done on a previous trip to Belgrade when the traveling press selected Dobbs for the "pool." This time Albright's staff made sure Dobbs was kept as far from the secretary as possible.[71]

Walking through the Old Jewish Cemetery, the final resting place for Prague Jews since the fourteenth century to 1787, Kraus pointed out tombs of renowned rabbis and scholars and explained symbols that denoted the professions of people buried there.[72] They passed the marker thought to be that of Jehuda ben Bezalel and that of the famous Rabbi Löw, who is credited with having created the mythical Golem in the sixteenth century. Small scraps of paper are stuffed into cracks in the rabbi's tomb in hopes that he will grant their authors' wishes. With some twelve thousand graves buried twelve layers deep, the history is impressive. But it was history Albright had heard many times before. This time she was concentrating on her own heritage.

When she entered the Gothic doorway of the sixteenth-century Pinkas Synagogue, she knew she would see what she had missed on previous visits. Stopping a moment to adjust her eyes to the dimming light, Albright took a breath and gazed inside. Before her stretched the Memorial to the Victims of Nazism, the largest epitaph in the world, tragic testament to one of the most horrific chapters in history. Neatly hand-painted—last names in red, first names in black, with letters no more than a half a thumbnail high—the names of approximately eighty thousand Bohemian and Moravian Holocaust victims fill every wall in all four rooms, floor to ceiling. In the sanctuary of the synagogue, down in the corner to the left of the holy ark that holds the Torah, she found the names of her grandparents:

KÖRBEL, ARNOŠT 7. VI 1878 - 18.
IX 1942. OLGA 4. XI 1878 - 23. X
1944.

For anyone visiting the synagogue, sight of the names is powerful. For Albright, it appeared overwhelming. "You could see the emotion in her face," Kraus said later. "She just stood there." Afterward, Albright went into the Jewish Town Hall, a pink neo-Baroque building that was designed by an influential Jewish leader named Mordechai Maisel at the end of the sixteenth century. On the facade, a clock with Hebrew numbers keeps time counterclockwise. On the first floor, Kraus escorted her into a small, rather dingy room lined with Nazi card catalogues, each holding stacks of neatly typed cards that document the transport numbers and incarceration dates of many of the ninety thousand people sent to Terezín. It was compiled by the Council of Jewish Elders on orders from the captive leaders' Nazi camp guards. Albright looked at two cards that show both paternal grandparents were deported on July 30, 1942: Arnošt Körbel to Theresienstadt, where he died; Olga Körbel to Auschwitz.[73]

Twenty minutes later, Albright emerged from the Town Hall, the muscles in her jaw tense, the lines around her mouth drawn tight. Holding a statement that she had written early that morning, she spoke in an uncharacteristically small, quavering voice. On previous visits to the synagogue, it had never occurred to her to look for her family's name, she said. "Tonight I knew to look for those names—and their image will be forever seared into my heart."

The story of her Jewish heritage was no longer in doubt. It was fact, painful and public. Several times Albright paused to gather her composure. "As I stood looking at that melancholy wall, all the walls, I not only grieved for those members of my family whose names are inscribed there, but I also thought about my parents," she said. "I thought about the choices they made. They clearly confronted the most excruciating decision a human being can face when they left members of their family behind, even as they saved me from certain death."[74]

When she finished, she took off her glasses, folded them, and breathed a deep sigh. Albright turned quickly, head bowed, and walked off into the darkness. There were tears in her eyes.

26

Celebrity

"We have a responsibility in our time, as others have had in theirs, not to be prisoners of history, but to shape history. A responsibility to use and defend our own freedom, and to help others who share our aspirations for liberty, peace and the quiet miracle of a normal life."

—Madeleine Albright, April 10, 1997

AUGUST 1997. Mark Gearan, the director of the Peace Corps, was having lunch in a little country in the South Pacific called Tonga with its prime minister, Baron Vaea. "How do you get your news?" Gearan asked the official. "Through CNN," Vaea replied. He talked about the O.J. Simpson trial, confessed that he loves Larry King's interviews, then startled Gearan with a simple request: "By the way, tell me about Madeleine Albright."

What could Gearan tell this Tongan official about Madeleine Albright? She was old enough to be Gearan's mother. He got to know her when they sat together on the Dukakis campaign plane. Gearan had been sure to seat Albright next to Bill Clinton at a Democratic Governors' Association dinner in February 1992, to enable her and the Arkansan to become better acquainted. And now, only five years later, Albright was a celebrity. The sixty-year-old professorial diplomat was being mentioned by the prime minister of Tonga in the same breath with O.J. and Larry King. Gearan loved it. He also thought that Albright's newfound celebrity status would be an important component in American foreign policy.[1]

In a world where grassroots diplomacy has replaced grand summitry, celebrity enables a leader to command attention at every juncture, with voters, with world statesmen, and with the press. When he was secretary of state in the Nixon administration, Henry Kissinger, another professor-turned-diplomat, had used his special brand of statesmanship to become as much of a fixture on the Hollywood scene as he was in shuttle diplomacy. Dubbed "Super K" by *Newsweek,* Kissinger was a pop figure, a man with power, flair, and what Walter Isaacson, his biographer, described as "a fingertip feel for publicity," a man "whose heightened energy and presence helped [him] seem larger than life, both as statesman and celebrity."[2] When Kissinger spoke, people listened. The trick would be more complicated for a woman.

But it was an important trick to master. Albright was coming to power at a time when Americans were more concerned with domestic problems at home than bitter ethnic wars in newly developed countries they could not locate on a map, and politicians were spending more time stressing the need for immigrants to learn English than for Americans to master foreign languages. It was not just appropriate but critical to have a secretary of state who captured the attention of voters, as well as foreign leaders, a voice that helped people sort out the essence of an issue from the background noise. "A strong reputation can be an enormous help because people think they are dealing with someone who can make things happen," says Erskine Bowles. "It gives you power. But you'd better be able to follow up on it and do your homework and have the depth of knowledge to compete, because once you go in there, the expectations are also higher."[3]

Albright's sense of pride and excitement in her new job was contagious. Even cabinet members who had favored other candidates jumped quickly on board. Shortly after Clinton selected Albright for the job, a *Time* magazine reporter attending one of Hillary Rodham Clinton's White House round tables told Secretary of the Treasury Robert Rubin that she wanted to talk to him privately after the meeting. She had heard Rubin had pushed Holbrooke for the job and wanted to confirm it. "What's the topic?" Rubin asked. "Madeleine Albright," was the reply. Rubin grinned. "Isn't she wonderful?" he said. "I just had lunch with her." After the meeting, he scooted out of the room before he could be questioned further.[4]

Albright's first job was to choose her staff. She felt that the State Department had lost traction, that morale in the foreign service was low, and that the whole place cried out for strong leadership.[5] Albright asked Strobe Talbott, a Russia expert who had been deputy secretary of state under Warren Christopher, to remain in the job. A friend of Clinton, Talbott is both smart and loyal, and he provided a valuable link to the White House. Next, she recruited Stuart Eizenstat and Tom Pickering, two veteran public servants. Neither sought the job. Eizenstat, a former domestic policy adviser to President Carter and ambassador to the European Union in Brussels, loved his position at the Commerce Department as undersecretary for international trade. He supervised 2,500 people and considered the new post at State a lateral move. Pickering, one of the most popular foreign service officers in the diplomatic corps, had just retired after returning from Moscow, where he served as Clinton's ambassador. Albright respected his professionalism, directness, and clarity of thought. When the men hesitated, she called each three or four times to persuade him. Before accepting, the two men, old friends, talked several times a day. "I'll go if you go," Eizenstat told Pickering. "I'll go if you go," Pickering replied.[6] "I thought she was going to have the most exciting department in the government," Eizenstat said later, "that wherever she was, the action would be."[7]

Albright organized her staff like a Senate office, installing Jamie Rubin as her press strategist, eventually asking him to take on the dicey job of daily press briefings, akin to swimming with sharks. The job makes Rubin the public face of the State Department. With an audience that includes foreign governments, an international press corps, Congress, and the American people, it requires a mastery of the issues. Although he can be arrogant, Rubin is respected for his knowledge of the issues, as well as his understanding of Albright. Wendy Sherman left her lucrative job as president of the Fannie Mae Foundation, which she had held for only a year, to return to the State Department as Albright's counselor, a position in which she handles sensitive, substantive issues of special concern to the secretary. Albright elevated Elaine Shocas, who had become one of her closest confidantes, to chief of staff.

Of all those in the network—friends, mentors, advisers, colleagues, climbers—it is Shocas who knows the secretary best, who reads her moods, understands the body language, guards the gate. "I had no idea how close we were going to get and how important she has been in my life in terms of someone who is my confidante," Albright says. "Elaine is the only person who truly knows what I think. She has perfect pitch. She knows what the right thing to do or say is. She is not someone who sucks up to me. She is the person who makes the difference."[8]

Within a few months, Albright had assembled one of the strongest departmental leadership teams in modern history. It was a credit to her own forceful personality that these individuals, each tough in his or her own way, not only agreed to work with her but wanted to work with her. It also marked a newfound sense of professional security that Albright recruited strong subordinates.

As popular a choice as she was, her status as a household name was confirmed when National Public Radio's *Car Talk* anointed "Made A Lane All

Brite" as "secretary of halogen headlights." By spring, she had thrown out the first ball at the Baltimore Orioles' first home game of the season at Camden Yards. As always, she had done her homework. Before climbing aboard her plane for a quick weekend trip to New York, she had rehearsed her throw with her security agents at Andrews Air Force Base. Wearing high heels and with her pilots and other military personnel looking on,[9] she threw the ball against the brisk winds sweeping the airport tarmac, hoping to improve her distance. But when she got to the field and threw out the first pitch, her ball traveled about forty of the sixty feet from the pitcher's mound to home plate before hitting the dirt.[10]

Not that it mattered. The pitch was one of her few efforts that fell short. She was now more than just a team player, she was Clinton's brightest star, bringing more foreign policy expertise to the job than any modern secretary of state, with the exception of Kissinger. Most others, even those with some foreign policy background, were trained first as lawyers. "Madeleine has been living and breathing foreign policy for a very long time," says Talbott. "As a result, she has long since programmed into her software a lot of the basic stuff, much of which is still relevant to our issues. Her philosophy is that mastery of the brief is essential to a successful diplomatic encounter."[11]

For Albright, work is play. She is a quick learner, operating in two modes. As an academic, she reads a lot and absorbs encyclopedicly from briefing memos, but she is also a schmoozer, like Clinton, who likes to talk through issues. "Her method is Socratic," Talbott says. After she has read all the papers her staff has prepared for her, she often gathers aides around for discussion. They have learned to listen carefully when she says, "Now I want to ask a really stupid question." People narrow their eyes, sit forward in their chairs, and hold their breath. "It is never a stupid question," Talbott says. "It is always elemental and goes to the core."

Unlike most Democrats, Albright goes out of her way to woo Republicans, recultivating the bipartisanship that vanished with the Cold War. The concept that partisan politics ends "at the water's edge" is crucial to Clinton's foreign policy with both houses of Congress dominated by the Grand Old Party.[12] Her first trip as secretary was not to Europe or Asia, but a domestic excursion to Texas to visit former President Bush and former Secretary of State James Baker, whom she praised for their progress in Middle East peace negotiations. In April, she traveled to Michigan to honor former President Gerald Ford at the rededication of his presidential museum.

Albright puts considerable time and effort into courting Senator Jesse Helms, chairman of the Senate Foreign Relations Committee and one of the most outspoken critics of Clinton's diplomatic initiatives. In her capacity as American ambassador to the United Nations, she appeared with him in his home state before the Women's Fund of North Carolina. During a visit in March 1997, she spoke at Wingate University, a small, private college affiliated with the Baptist Church that is Helms' alma mater. She attended a private birthday party for Helms' wife and presented the senator with a blue T-shirt that read: "Somebody at the State Department Loves Me." The two arrived at the school smiling and holding hands, a flirtatious gesture that only a female secretary of state could pull off. When Albright boarded her Air Force jet for the trip back to Washington, she found a present from Helms: containers of North Carolina's famous pit-cooked pork barbecue, spicy sauce, and cole slaw.[13]

It is Albright's red-blooded American patriotism that appeals to Helms, an understanding that while they frequently do not agree on issues, they have deep respect for the underlying values of democracy that allow them to debate and disagree. "We both believe that the concept of individual liberty set out in the American Constitution remains, after more than 200 years, the world's most powerful and positive force for change," Albright told Wingate students. "And we both agree that if our freedoms are to survive through the next American century, we cannot turn our backs on the world."[14]

There is another reason for the unusual chemistry between the two. Unlike previous administration officials, Albright took Helms seriously. She did not refer to him, publicly or privately, as "Senator No." And instead of trying to deny him victories, she sought to compromise.

Before her confirmation hearings, she told Helms that she would consider his plan to reorganize the government foreign policy apparatus by eliminating the U.S. Information Agency (USIA), the Agency for International Development (AID), and the Arms Control and Disarmament Agency (ACDA). When she did review it, she proposed eliminating two of the agencies and folding AID into the State Department. As a result, for the first time in four years, the State Department got a budget increase, a 5.3 percent raise to $2.58 billion.[15] "It was not all Helms wanted," says Marc Thiessen, a Helms staffer on the Senate Foreign Relations Committee. "But he respected the fact that she met him partway up the road."

As all celebrities know, the limelight has its price. Privacy evaporates and puny controversies suddenly become page-one news. Albright wanted to learn more about her family heritage, but she knew an official trip to her father's hometown in Eastern Bohemia would turn into a media circus. Instead, she took a short vacation and made an unpublicized pilgrimage to the Czech Republic with two of her daughters and their husbands. They visited Letohrad, where her father grew up. Even that unofficial visit entailed a ten-car motorcade with security guards and a staff.[16]

Wearing a summery blue dress with a strand of white pearls, Albright toasted town officials at a reception in her honor, visited the homestead at 305 Tyršová Street, where her father lived, and stopped to have Turkish coffee and poppyseed pastry with Věra Ruprechtová. While a female security guard kept watch at the front door, Albright sat at the same mahogany dining room table where her grandfather had spent evenings going over his business records. Ruprechtová used the white china cups she keeps in a sideboard for special occasions. She told Albright that Communist officials sentenced her husband, a local judge, to hard labor for seven years in a uranium mine when he refused to jail local farmers for some minor infraction. "Madeleine asked me how I survived," Ruprechtová says, proudly displaying an autographed picture of Albright that the secretary gave her. Ruprechtová presented Albright with a picture of the Virgin Mary.[17]

Such private interludes are rare. As secretary of state, Albright travels in force. It sounds glamorous. The shiny limousine, its flags flying, is followed by a parade of cars and vans, attracting lots of attention. But it makes spontaneous private visits with family and friends almost impossible. Albright's social life is so programmed that an aide keeps a log of what she wears to each event.[18]

Albright keeps in occasional contact with Cousin Dagmar, whom she would likely not know much about if it had not been for the secretary's newfound fame. Albright does not like to talk to Dagmar about how wonderful her own life is in the United States and how lucky she thinks she has been. As a result, these conversations are not easy. "I try to talk to her, but when we are together, there is not a lot to talk about," Albright says. "I don't blame her for saying what she says. I just know what I know." Her own life, Albright believes, has been blessed, while Dagmar's has been difficult. "I think she would have to be a saint not to say some things that didn't have an edge to them," the secretary says.[19]

It angers Albright when people question the decision to leave Dagmar behind. She says Dagmar chose to stay in Czechoslovakia. "I can only believe certain things on the basis of my own experience," Albright says. "And my experience is that my parents were generous and warm and family-oriented. All they had was a small family. Why would they ever leave a piece of the family behind? I think [Dagmar] has said she had plenty of opportunities to leave at another stage. She told my sister, 'Why would I leave Czechoslovakia when I have a good job, and Vláda is an engineer, in order to start over in England?'

"My own belief is that she decided she did not want to leave. She may have not known we were going to the United States, but she certainly knew we were leaving. I think she was close to being an adult and made a decision to stay there because she was in love with somebody. She had lost her immediate family. She was, after all, not a daughter; she was a niece. She had been displaced during the war. She had found somebody she loved. Nobody knew what was going to happen, that this was going to be fifty years of horror. And she made a decision. I am desperately sorry about it. And if she says something . . . then she has a reason for saying it. I'm not going to put her down. But I cannot make up to her her life. I cannot."

As hard as the experience of delving into her Jewish heritage has been for Albright, the secretary believes that the new information has enriched her life. "I'm very glad I know this now," she says. "I really am. It makes me understand a lot about my parents. I don't want to overstate the humanity of my family, but there is a streak there that I am very proud of—people helping others."[20]

For the most part, Albright finds her superstar status a plus and puts it to good use. Unlike so many pompous bureaucrats who like to be addressed by their official title, she enjoys being called by her first name. When people stumble over the awkward but officially correct address, Madame Secretary, she says: "Call me Madeleine." She thinks it makes foreign policy more personal.[21]

Strobe Talbott says that she uses her celebrity to push the agenda and generate support for American foreign policy positions: "It means that someone who is very popular is associated with an endeavor that is not always popular, sometimes controversial, sometimes opposed, and sometimes the subject of great gnawing indifference on the part of the American people."[22] One reason Albright has garnered as much support as she has from the Senate Foreign Relations Committee, particularly on budgetary issues, is that the senators enjoy sharing the limelight with her. Even when they do not agree with her politics, they appreciate her firm convictions.

Albright spent her first year in office jetting from one foreign capital to the next, introducing herself to world leaders, taking their measure and letting them take hers. In February 1997, only a few weeks after taking office, she made a highly publicized world trip, visiting nine countries in eleven days. Sporting a black Stetson cowboy hat as a trademark, she did her best to assuage Russian concerns about the eastward expansion of the North Atlantic Treaty Organization and talked candidly with the Chinese about their dismal record on human rights. "The buzz of Washington is that

Madeleine Albright did a good job on her first trip as Secretary of State," the *Washington Post* gushed in an editorial. "She displayed a foreign policy fluency, and things came off well."[23]

In May, Albright read the riot act to leaders of the former Yugoslavia about their responsibilities in Bosnia. She gave Croatian president Franjo Tudjman a finger-wagging lecture in Zagreb for failing to live up to the peace accord that had been negotiated eighteen months before in Dayton, Ohio. Using language rarely heard in diplomatic circles, she told one of his cabinet members that she was "disgusted" by Croatia's failure to prevent attacks against Serbian refugees trying to return to their homes. Before she met with Serbian president Slobodan Milosevic in Belgrade, Albright's aides warned her that he would try to throw her off stride early in their session. Sure enough, while she was reciting a list of Serbian violations of the peace accord, Milosevic interrupted her with a patronizing smile: "Madame Secretary," he said, "you're not well informed." "Don't tell me I'm uninformed," she snapped back. "I lived here." Milosevic's smile faded, and Albright continued with her list of complaints.[24]

From the beginning, Albright went out of her way to cultivate a relationship with Russian foreign minister Yevgeny Primakov, a sometimes difficult personality who once headed the intelligence unit that succeeded the KGB. The two have developed a first-name friendship. Primakov respects Albright's toughness. He calls her *"Gospazha Stal"*—the Lady of Steel.[25]

Albright also has a close relationship with British foreign secretary Robin Cook. It's so close, in fact, that Cook felt comfortable confiding in her when he separated from his wife. It was the summer of 1997, the week that Cook's separation hit the British papers. Albright, who knew nothing of the situation, took a routine call from her British counterpart to discuss policy matters. When Cook came on the line, Albright opened the conversation with a normal greeting. "How are you?" she asked innocently. "Awful," Cook replied. "This divorce thing, all the publicity, the breakup with my wife . . ." Albright was sympathetic. She consoled Cook and tried to be reassuring. When she hung up, aides briefed her on Cook's messy love life. He had been having a torrid affair with his House of Commons secretary and planned to divorce his wife of twenty-eight years, who disclosed that he had had affairs with other women. "Goddamnit," Albright said. "Here I was sympathetic when he did the same thing to his wife that Joe did to me."[26]

At home, Albright made good on her promise to make foreign policy relevant to the American people, making nineteen domestic trips during her first year in office—more than any other secretary of state—trying to convince voters that foreign policy is as much about their jobs at home as it is about crises in distant lands. "Not only can foreign policy be cool," she told high school students in Houston. "It can be awesome."[27] During a trip to the United Nations for the opening of the General Assembly in October 1997, Albright took a side trip to the Theodore Roosevelt High School, located in a tough neighborhood of the Bronx. The students were so impressed that when she left the building, they crowded around the windows and yelled, "Go get 'em, lady."[28]

She did not fare as well four months later when she went to the country's heartland with Secretary of Defense Bill Cohen and national security adviser Sandy Berger to explain why the administration was threatening to use force against Iraq in a stand-off with Saddam Hussein over access to possible chemical and biological weapons sites.

At a gimmicky, campaign-style "town meeting" at Ohio State University, televised around the world by CNN, the officials were greeted with tough questions, skepticism about America's goals, and catcalls. When a young man complained that innocent Iraqi citizens would be killed by the bombing and asked how the speakers could sleep at night, Albright's reply was dagger quick: "What we are doing is so that all of you can sleep tonight."[29] But Iraq was quick to rebroadcast the heckles and catcalls that threw Clinton's team on the defensive.

In an era of instant communications, it is almost a prerequisite that a national leader be media savvy, able to pick up a news reporter's tricks and learn not only what to say but when, where, and how to say it. Mastering the technology, particularly television, allows a leader to command attention in ways that were not possible before satellite dishes became part of the neighborhood landscape. The trick is to communicate effectively in language voters understand.

Before the Senate was set to vote on the chemical weapons treaty in April 1997, Albright gave individual interviews to almost a dozen local television stations around the country. Purposefully discarding the gobbledygook acronyms that Washington officials substitute for English, she chose broad, easily understood phrases that might prompt voters to call their local congressmen. "This is a treaty that has 'Made in America' written all over it," she said over and over.[30] Her simplicity worked. In a show of remarkable bipartisanship, the Senate ratified the treaty, 74–26. The victory had not been guaranteed. While the accord had been negotiated by the Reagan and Bush administrations, it was strongly opposed by Republican conservatives, including the irascible Senator Jesse Helms. To appease Helms, who could have blocked the vote, Clinton chose the day the treaty came to a vote to approve a compromise version of Helms' plan to reorganize the State Department.

Abroad, Albright uses television equally effectively, sometimes offering to share the limelight with lesser-known diplomats as a way of locking them into a deal. During a visit to Bailundo, Angola, in January 1996, Albright wanted to pressure longtime rebel leader Jonas Savimbi into starting the demobilization process, a key commitment in the agreement to end nineteen years of civil war. After an hour-and-a-half meeting in a dingy, pink-walled guerrilla hideaway, the ambassador told Savimbi that the U.N. Security Council was prepared to take strong action if Savimbi's forces failed to disarm. When Savimbi agreed in principle, saying that he could demobilize about 650 soldiers a day, Albright pulled out a pad, figured they had twenty-five days before the deadline, and did some quick multiplication. Then she invited Savimbi to join her for the press conference that followed. With cameras rolling, Albright announced that the UNITA president had promised that 16,500 troops would turn in their weapons at U.N. assembly areas by February 8, 1996. Then turning to him, she said sweetly, "Right, Dr. Savimbi?" He nodded.[31]

In her first year as secretary, Albright was largely lucky. Long-term problems in the Middle East and Bosnia, the most volatile areas of conflict, continued to fester, but no new turmoil erupted. With the peace effort between Israel and the Palestinians all but collapsed following the election of a conservative Israeli government, Albright put the warring leaders on notice that she would work with them if they would negotiate seriously, but she was not going to waste her time. She lectured Palestinian leader Yasser Arafat on the need to show a "comprehensive, relentless and sustained" effort to stop terrorists and warned new Israeli prime minister Benjamin Netanyahu to avoid provocative actions like new construction projects on the West Bank and in Arab neighborhoods in Jerusalem. Using unusually blunt language for a diplomat, Albright said that "it is beyond my understanding" how Israel's decision to withhold millions of dollars in taxes it owes to the Palestinian Authority could be a security measure, as Netanyahu insisted.[32]

The greatest test of Albright's diplomatic skills, as well as her stamina, came in November 1997, when Iraqi president Saddam Hussein provoked a dramatic confrontation with the United States by expelling the American members of the U.N. team charged with inspecting and destroying Iraq's chemical, biological, and nuclear weapons and their production facilities. Albright was on a weeklong trip to South Asia meant to build a new relationship between the United States and the region. Visiting eight countries in seven days, she canceled appearances, dropped Bangladesh from her itinerary, and flew to the Middle East to shore up support on the U.N. Security Council and in the Arab world for the Clinton administration's demand that Saddam Hussein back down.[33] "Here she was, zooming between Doha, New Delhi, and Islamabad, thinking about one set of issues and having to deal with a very fast-breaking and extremely serious crisis in Iraq," says Talbott, who was overseeing negotiations from Washington. "She was thousands of miles away from the home office, keeping a grueling schedule and dealing with the worst miscreant in the world today, whose principal goal in the short term was to embarrass the United States. She also had to deal with some partners in the international community who were not, to put it mildly, completely on our program. It was tough."[34]

President Clinton has watched Albright's self-confidence grow. "Whenever you put a talented person in a position that has more responsibility than he or she has had before, if they have any sense, they will be cautious in the beginning and make sure they have the ground under them," he says. "I've watched her as U.N. ambassador and as secretary of state grow consistently more comfortable in her job. [She is] more assured in her judgments and more willing to provoke debate within our circle in a constructive way. She was always very outspoken about the things she knew about."[35]

In June 1998, Clinton appointed Richard Holbrooke to be ambassador to the United Nations, a position in which he would report directly to Albright. Holbrooke, a masterful strategist and negotiator who loves publicity and is on close terms with Al Gore and NSC adviser Sandy Berger, could easily make an end run around Albright if he chose to do so. In fact, when Holbrooke's name first surfaced for the job, some of Albright's associates were not sure they wanted him in a position to upstage the secretary. But then they thought again. Albright, by far the most popular cabinet member in the Clinton administration, had become a force in her own right. With her own constituency—which included the President—she could afford to have a high-profile player on her team. Nevertheless, before Holbrooke took the job, Albright sat down with him to outline the rules of the road for being on her team: Tread carefully.

One reason for Albright's effectiveness is that she combines that toughness and seriousness of purpose with a sense of fun. Having spent much of her life thinking about the issues and watching others in the job, she is obviously delighted to find herself in charge. "One of the reasons she is as good as she is and has such a high energy level and doesn't seem to get discouraged or exhausted is that it is a big kick," says Talbott. "She doesn't have the attitude others have brought to the job of 'Finally they had the good sense to select me.' Instead, she generates this feeling of 'Oh my God, do you believe I am here?'"[36]

Albright's popularity comes at a time when Americans are sick of national politics, disgusted with hypocritical politicians who refuse to reform campaign financing, and convinced that what happens in Washington has little impact on their daily lives. Vice President Gore jokes that he looks like a cardboard caricature of himself. And Bill Clinton waffles and weaves so much that well into his second term, people still wondered what he stands for. Charges that the president had sexual relations with a White House intern exploded in his second term, sending the news media into a frenzy and provoking Americans to question the moral and ethical standards of both politicians and the press. The public is fed up with evasive officials who do not answer questions and with news reporters who abandon any attempt at fairness and accuracy in a race to play "Gotcha."

Unlike so many politicians, Madeleine Albright does not feel she has to go out of her way to show that she is real. She is smart and sassy. She can explain the importance of mutual balanced force reduction in Europe and pinpoint the number of cruise missiles on a Tomahawk launcher—four.[37] But just as important, perhaps more so, she radiates an understanding of the real world. On a trip to Africa in December 1997, she was criticized for glossing over the undemocratic practices of leaders she met.[38] But what most Americans will remember from the trip is a picture of Albright cradling a dying baby. Not only is it unusual to see a secretary of state in such a public pose, there was another detail as well: She was holding the baby correctly. Women noticed.

Albright's greatest appeal is that she is just like us, only wealthier. She has had bad hair days and skirts with spots, runs in her stockings, a dog that was skunked. At some point, she probably even embarrassed her children. Americans see her as vulnerable, a wife rejected, a single mother who went back to work, prevailed, and raised good kids. She radiates a sense that if she can succeed at whatever happens to be the challenge of the moment, even in times of adversity, so can we. "I suck out of every day what there is to do," Albright says. "I really like my life, and I actually like myself. But I have not had a planned life."[39]

Unlike previous occupants of her office, Albright has elevated women's issues in America's international agenda, instructing American diplomats around the world that women's rights are a central priority of U.S. foreign policy. "Advancing the status of women is not only a moral imperative, it is being actively integrated into the foreign policy of the United States," she said at an International Women's Day ceremony at the State Department. "It is our mission. It is the right thing to do, and frankly, it is the smart thing to do."[40]

Ironically, many women professionals at the State Department were disappointed that in her first year in the job, Albright did not put her own words into practice and appoint more women to senior foreign service positions. It struck them as odd, perhaps even hypocritical, that the secretary was such an outspoken champion of women's rights on the international scene, but put few women in assistant secretary positions in her own department. "I think she's been captured by the old-boy network," says one veteran female foreign service officer. "Madeleine is doing a fabulous job talking about her commitment to women, but it is not reflected in her staffing pattern. And it is not a question of there not being competent women for the job. Nobody can make that argument anymore."[41] In truth, the three State Department officials closest to Albright—Elaine Shocas, Wendy Sherman, and Suzy George—are women. But Albright has filled five of the six top policy-making slots with men, as well as all the regional bureaus.

Eventually, and perhaps inevitably, some members of the foreign policy establishment began quietly questioning whether Albright was using her team effectively, whether she was delegating properly, and whether she relied too heavily on Shocas and Sherman, whom rivals referred to privately as "the ladies." One male colleague put it this way, "The kitchen cabinet team, which completely controls her, is all nonsubstantive." More damning was the charge that Clinton's foreign policy team substituted handwringing for policy. "While U.S. officials adopt dismay as a posture and mistake it for policy, other nations are making clear choices and hoping to gain national advantage in the rapidly developing power vacuum in world politics," wrote columnist Jim Hoagland in the *Washington Post*.[42] Another increasingly heard comment is that Sandy Berger has become the strategist behind the administration's foreign policy; that Albright is the mouthpiece. The view is too simplistic, but it cannot be dismissed entirely. The bottom line: Most of the men who dominate American foreign policy never fully accepted her as one of their own.

But, in any case, the months rolled on, many of Albright's old friends were amazed at how self-confident she had become, how forceful she was as a public speaker, and how she could command attention from the international press. They were also surprised that she was sometimes imperious. At a televised press conference in Prague with Czech president Václav Havel in

July 1997, that took place amid the ornate splendor of the presidential palace, Albright went out of her way to humiliate a nervous State Department interpreter who stumbled several times as he translated her statements for the Czech media. The secretary challenged the man's translations so often that he froze, forcing Havel's female interpreter to take over. Instead of politely correcting the aide's mistakes, Albright appeared intent on publicly showing she spoke Czech better than her official translator. Veteran news reporters witnessing the scene were slack-jawed at the display.

Old friends were struck by another change in Albright's public persona. Like so many politicians who go out of their way to stress their impoverished log cabin backgrounds, the woman who had always tried so hard to blend into American society is now using every opportunity to emphasize her European upbringing. "During all the years I knew her on the Hill, I don't recall her ever mentioning that as a formative part of her thinking, her life, or her career," says one old friend. "When we were having those let-our-hair down, soul-bearing conversations, that never entered into it. There was much more stress placed on her divorce and her breakup with Barry [Carter]. That was much more a factor in her conversations than her background."[43]

From most quarters, however, Albright got high marks for her first year in the job. Even conservatives thought she handled herself and the issues with aplomb. "I think the Clinton administration is doing much better this term than last," says Jeane Kirkpatrick, former ambassador to the United Nations and now a fellow at the American Enterprise Institute, a conservative think tank. "It is commonplace to hear people say today that President Clinton is a quick learner, that he is not making the same mistakes he made last term in foreign affairs. I think that is a fair conclusion, and it's reasonable to suppose that some of the credit goes to Madeleine. It's not all a consequence of the president being a fast learner. Madeleine Albright herself is probably more knowledgeable [on foreign affairs]. She was a fast learner on any number of global problems."[44]

The question is where she will go from here. The power and prestige that she clearly enjoys make it highly unlikely that she will retire quietly to the Virginia countryside to go antiquing and play with her grandchildren. And why should she? Albright could be a fine president or vice president. Although she has never run for elective office—and the job of secretary of state has not been a launching pad for the presidency since the nineteenth century—Albright is a natural leader who has worked on Capitol Hill and in the White House, has wide experience in foreign affairs, and a keen political sense. However, the U.S. Constitution permits only "natural-born" citizens to hold the two top elective offices, eliminating the 3 percent who are naturalized Americans from running.[45]

There have been proposals in the past to change the amendment, including several in the 1970s inspired by admirers of Henry Kissinger. When former Connecticut governor Lowell P. Weicker considered a bid for the Republican presidential nomination in 1976, the question was raised whether Weicker, who was born in Paris to American parents, was eligible to be president.[46] In 1983, former senator Thomas F. Eagleton, a Missouri Democrat, proposed an amendment that would make anyone who has been a naturalized citizen for eleven years eligible to be president. His move was prompted by his regard for Felix G. Rohatyn, the New York investment banker who engineered the rescue of New York City from its financial problems.[47]

One of Albright's closest friends shakes her head at the idea that this secretary of state would even consider a run for the presidency. "That she is not eligible to run is the beauty of it all," the friend explains. "It makes what would be scary in this town less scary because she is *not* the competition. Given how this place works—who's up, who's down, who's ahead, who's left behind, who's running for president, who isn't—it takes the issue off the table. The boys can deal with her because she won't be their competition. She would be more threatening if she could run for president."[48]

Even if there were a great groundswell of support for making Albright eligible, it is unlikely that Congress and the states would go through the necessary steps to amend the Constitution in time for her to benefit. A more likely possibility is that she might run for the Senate, which requires that a candidate be an American citizen for nine years. One friend tried to talk her into registering to vote at her Virginia farm to position herself for a Senate bid, an idea she considered once before, when she lived in New York. Albright herself says she has made only one decision about her future. When she leaves her current job, she plans to get a dog—another golden retriever.[49]

Albright takes advantage of any opportunities she has to relax with old friends. On May 15, 1997, her sixtieth birthday, the secretary flew to New York to spend the afternoon with Christine Dodson. Their birthdays are not far apart, and they like to celebrate together. Albright was running an hour behind schedule, and her security detail called Dodson repeatedly from the plane to keep her informed of when they would touch down at LaGuardia Airport.

They had an appointment with Georgette Klinger, owner of a chic New

York beauty salon. As a gift, Albright treated Dodson to a facial and makeup application; Albright had "the works": massage, facial, hairdo, makeup. It was the perfect respite from her usually chaotic schedule. At one point, a security man realized that she had disappeared into one of the facility's cubicles and started to look for her. "Opening one door after another, he startled any number of women in various stages of *déshabillé,*" Dodson says. Klinger offered the head of Albright's security detail a facial. He refused.

When Dodson was finished and waiting for Albright, Klinger inspected her makeup. "What are these two lines?" she said, pointing to Dodson's cheeks. "Bring me the number two cream." At last, Albright and Dodson emerged looking radiant. As they were walking down the winding staircase to the first floor, one security man said to another in a voice loud enough for them to overhear: "Are you sure we're taking out the same two women we brought in? Are you sure we haven't left the secretary in some cubicle?"[50]

It had been a wonderful afternoon. For lunch, Dodson had chosen a small French restaurant called La Mirabelle on the Upper West Side, where they were given a quiet table and a chance to have the kind of private talk that Albright rarely has time for in her new job. As they dug into their salads and began discussing personal matters, Albright looked at her old friend and said, "Suppose I had a date, somebody I'm semi-interested in. How would you do it?" She gestured to the security detail posted in various corners of the restaurant and said, "You always have these guys who have to sit at an angle so they can see you. Suppose a man reached over and took my hand. What would happen? It's impossible."[51]

Albright's romantic life has been the subject of great speculation since she became secretary. With all the hoopla and historic significance that surrounded President Clinton's first state dinner for newly installed Chinese leader Jiang Zemin, nothing caused such a stir as Albright sweeping in with her date, the television star and Shakespearean actor Patrick Stewart. Traditionally, the secretary of state makes an entrance alone, but Vice President Gore himself intervened to engineer a breach of protocol that put Albright on display with a man on her arm—the captain from *Star Trek,* no less.

And how she enjoyed the buzz! For all the fun she is having—the power, intellectual debate, stature, celebrity, trappings, insider status, travel— Albright appears to be a woman who likes a man in her life. Friends say that she likes everything a man can offer—personal security, intimacy, love, someone to share the mundane details of a day that no one else cares about, a person to laugh and cry with, who shares victories and cushions defeat. "I think she's aware that there is a price she is paying," says a confidante. "Because Madeleine, having been successfully in love and having had the experience of a woman who was loved and loved [back], misses that. She would like very much, if there is a chance before she dies or before she becomes too uninterested in the whole subject, to have had one more such experience. . . . She is such an affectionate person. She likes to hold people. She likes to hug [them]."[52]

There is no question that star status enhances a man's sex appeal, trumpets his eligibility, ignores his age. During a brief 1997 New Year's vacation, Jamie Rubin became engaged to CNN war correspondent Christiane Amanpour, a dark-haired beauty two years his senior and one of the best-known television reporters in the world. The couple got to know each other in Bosnia the previous summer and conducted a continent-to-continent romance.

As the months went on and it became increasingly apparent that Rubin was smitten, the other women in his life—Albright, Elaine Shocas, and Suzy George—decided that it was time to talk to him about his future. One night in Paris, the peripatetic team finished a meeting about the Middle East peace talks and went out for a last-minute dinner at Tante Louise, a small bistro, just off the Place de la Concorde. It was December 5, the first anniversary of the day Clinton asked Albright to be secretary of state, and they were in the mood to celebrate. The restaurant was crowded. They had a table on the second-floor balcony, overlooking other diners. Rubin, who has a taste for expensive wine, ordered a bottle of red Bordeaux.[53] Like a mischievous big sister, Shocas instigated a discussion of marriage, knowing that it would make him squirm. Albright chimed in. She told Rubin how she got married, that matrimony is the greatest thing in life, that if it feels right, he should do it or be sorry. Shocas agreed. Two weeks later, on a sandy white beach on the Caribbean island of Tobago, Rubin dropped to his knees and asked Amanpour to marry him.[54]

Power has historically attracted women to men. But it is not commonly thought of as an aphrodisiac that draws men to women. Many successful, once-married women of a certain age have little interest in tying another knot. They find work provides structure and control to their lives, a haven of activity that fills an emptiness that otherwise can eat away at them when a partner is no longer there.

But it would be too facile to infer that women like Albright, who reach a position of stature and attain a certain celebrity status, must choose between power and a man. A quarter of a century after the women's movement opened new horizons to both sexes, that stereotype can finally be retired. It would be "retrograde," Albright says, to assume that the trappings of power that enhance the appeal of a man do not work the same way for women. "You'd be surprised," she says. "You'd be surprised."[55]

Looking back over her life, she amplifies her thoughts and draws some distinctions: "I think it is a question of choice at this point, and time. I think guilt is kind of a middle name for women who have a career and children and a husband. Somehow it always was [for me]. Was I in the car-pool line, or did I leave the office when someone was sick? The classic example for me was before some huge [graduate school] exam, both kids had high fevers, and I spent all night up with them, and I thought I would never do well in school. That constant thing of never being able to devote myself full time to what I was doing—my schoolwork or the kids or my husband or whatever. So this is the first time in my life I can actually devote myself to what I love doing.

". . . There are [men] that I see, but it is on my terms, more than not. There is a sense of genuine liberation, where I can do what I want at the time I want and not have to go home and fix dinner or worry that somebody is waiting on a street corner to go to a movie. Do powerful women attract men? My own experience happens to be: yes, in a way that was not true before."

This does not surprise her, not too much anyway. "There are clearly men who do not like women who have more going for them than they do," she says. "But men who are strong and interesting and sure of themselves kind of think it's fun. . . . Not only is it not so bad, it's great."[56]

It has not always been that way. "I'm not saying there are not times in my life, especially after I was divorced, that I wanted to have more serious male relationships," Albright says. "But [now] I feel, in a way that I never have, totally fulfilled." She knocks on wood. "I really do. I love what I do. I can devote all my attention to it. I have the choice of seeing people when I want to, and I have a choice of seeing a whole different world of people. Washington is a closed group. I have lived here for thirty years. Now the world is open, and there are a lot of interesting people out there." Does she want to marry again? Albright's answer came quickly and without elaboration: "No."[57]

As much star power as she has today, Albright knows also that cachet is ephemeral, that, in Washington, no one becomes a sought-after guest by personality alone but because, for that particular moment, he or she is "hot." At the Sally Quinn–Ben Bradlee New Year's Eve party at the close of 1997, Albright was whisked around the dance floor by any number of eager partners, including her date, Australian ambassador Andrew Peacock. As men elbowed each other to cut in, she commented wryly to other guests around her: "The only reason they are all eager to dance with me is because I am secretary of state."[58] At the White House state dinner for British prime minister Tony Blair in February, she arrived with diamond importer Maurice Templesman as her escort. After an item had appeared in a local newspaper column that the two were dating, she picked up the phone, called Templesman, and said that as long as people were gossiping about them, would he like to be her date?[59] Templesman accepted.

Today, the decision of how she wants to spend her time, and with whom, is a matter of choice. It is a richness that Josef Korbel could not have envisioned for his daughter when he made his own brutal choices to ensure his family a better life in a free society, but it is one for which she has her father to thank. And does.

Albright *is* blessed. She has loving daughters, grandchildren to nurture, enormous stamina, money in the bank, men on her arm. Her friendships are intellectually and emotionally rich, her laugh contagious, her place in history secure. And in all likelihood, she will remain a star, a personality with values and convictions who has become a role model for men and women alike.

The refugee child who came to America's shores half a century ago has found a world of limitless promise and bountiful opportunity. Hers has not always been an easy road, yet after maneuvering around various obstacles and taking some detours, she has risen to a higher rank than any woman in American history. By law, the secretary of state stands fourth in line to the presidency of the United States.[60]

Finally, Madeleine Korbel Albright has arrived. What awaits her now, depending on the path she chooses, is what the secretary once so eloquently called "the quiet miracle of a normal life"—a garden with violets, new seasons to celebrate, a dog at her feet.

Acknowledgments

A BOOK, LIKE A fine meal, depends on the quality of its ingredients, timing, patience, and the inevitable dash of good luck. I have benefited from them all. Madeleine Albright's life story is more textured than that of anyone in public life today. She has a wide network of friends and colleagues, many of whom graciously shared their insights. And with both my children in college, it was a good opportunity to take on a new challenge.

At *Time,* Walter Isaacson and James Kelly encouraged and supported this project from the beginning. Isaacson's superb biography of Henry Kissinger served as an unsurpassable model. Washington Bureau chiefs Dan Goodgame and Michael Duffy let me pursue my work with as few extra assignments as possible. Joelle Attinger, always a friend, helped me jump each mental hurdle. Douglas Waller's broad knowledge of foreign policy and the State Department, as well as his moral support, was invaluable. Karen Tumulty and Viveca Novak patiently put up with my moods, read chapters, and generally kept me sane. Jef McAllister walked me through policy issues, Bruce Nelan through the arcana of arms control. Mark Thompson marched me through military matters. Christopher Ogden, himself an accomplished biographer, guided me through the process of actually producing a manuscript. Lissa August was tireless in her research and turned up such historical nuggets as the passenger manifests of the SS *Amer-*

ica and the RMS *Queen Mary*. Anne Moffet could put her finger on the most obscure references. Diana Walker was generous with her photographic talent. Garry Clifford of *People* was wonderful explaining Albright's era. Judith Stoler, as always, anticipated every need.

Also at *Time,* I am indebted to Sharon Roberts, Don Collins, Jr., Brian Doyle, Neang Seng, Wendy King, and Lona Harris for making every day easier.

Two individuals whose help could not be duplicated, and whose tireless work made Albright's story come alive, are Jan M. Stránský, a Czech-born American who lives in London, and David Rohrbach, a talented 1996 Yale graduate with an insatiable appetite for history. Jan Stransky is the grandnephew of Jaroslav Stránský, minister of justice and education in the postwar Czechoslovak government and a close friend of the Korbel family. Jan introduced me to numerous relatives in Great Britain and the Czech Republic who were friends and colleagues of Albright's parents, Mandula and Josef Korbel. Jan not only accompanied me on interviews, translating when necessary, but provided unique insight into the period surrounding World War II. He also painstakingly edited numerous drafts of the book, line by line. David Rohrbach served as my alter ego in Washington, concentrating much of his time on delving into the history through which Albright has lived. Dave was involved in all aspects of the last four months of the book. His imprint is deep. I am extremely grateful to both men for their dedication, energy, and friendship.

In the Czech Republic, Joe Monik was a superb historian, guide, and translator. His knowledge of Czech history and his written description of the Jewish history of Czechoslovakia were an inspired addition.

Thanks also for their research to Wilma R. Slaight, archivist, Wellesley College Archives, the Margaret Clapp Library; Lynn-Watson Powers at the Jimmy Carter Presidential Library; Daniel Lee at the Edmund S. Muskie Archives, Bates College; Ben Primer, archivist, Seeley G. Mudd Manuscript Library, Department of Rare Books and Special Collections, Princeton University; Steven Fisher, curator of archives and special collections, Penrose Library, the University of Denver; Richard Gelbke, archivist, the National Archives and Records Administration of New York; and Maryann Alt at the U.S. Mission to the United Nations.

Also, the Columbia University Rare Book and Manuscript Library, Bakhmeteff Archive; the University of Denver Library; the National Archives; the Library of Congress; the White House Historical Society; the Fine Arts Committee, the U.S. Department of State; the Berkhamsted

School for Girls, Berkhamsted, England; and the Czech Republic Ministry of Foreign Affairs, Prague.

At Scribner, I am deeply indebted to Lisa Drew, a superb editor, whose daily e-mails with advice, humor, patience, and general common sense kept me centered and on target. Blythe Grossberg, always eager to help, subjected herself to reading the initial draft, a thankless task. Jane Herman did a superb job as copy editor.

Special thanks to Cherie Burns, my agent at the Zachary Shuster Agency, who first came to me with the idea of writing an Albright biography, and found the publisher.

I am especially indebted to Henry Putzel, Jr., for his meticulous eye.

My own girls' network did its best to save me from embarrassment. Ellen Goodman, Patricia O'Brien, Lynn Sherr, Jurate Kazickas, and Melanie Nussdorf talked me through various chapters, read innumerable drafts, and held my hand, as they have for decades. Shelley Brody accompanied me on my first trip to the Czech Republic, starting off as a Holocaust adviser and coming home a dear friend. My daughter, Leila Putzel, joined me for a second visit to Prague and made the Baroque art world come alive while she kept me laughing. My sister, Carolyn Jacoby, who has a keen eye for people detail, was delightful company on my third fact-checking mission to Europe. Margaret Dalton literally walked me through the manuscript as we took our dogs out each morning. Marian Burros, as always, fed body and soul. Brooke Shearer helped me negotiate the complications of personal and professional friendships.

CNN's Richard Blystone and my Tenafly High School pal Nancy Turck, both in London, deserve a bow. Also in Washington, Cokie Roberts and George M. Ingram IV offered initial direction, as did Dr. Roy Coleman. Alan Platt guided me through the Muskie years. In Boston, Bob Levey offered personal analysis. In New York, Louis Putzel helped with research at Columbia University. In Hawaii, Max Putzel, my father-in-law, provided news articles he wrote as a young newspaperman in Prague.

What the book was missing until the very end—and what made an enormous difference—was the voice of the subject, Madeleine K. Albright. I deeply appreciate the hours she spent with me, her insights, the personal essay by her mother, which Albright provided, as well as family photographs from her personal collection.

My biggest thanks go to the almost two hundred individuals—friends and colleagues of Albright and her family—who spent countless hours offering ideas, impressions, and anecdotes. Most are named in the book.

Several people, who provided tremendous guidance, asked to be anonymous.

I am sorry I could not share the experience of writing an Albright biography with my parents, Jeannette and Samuel Blackman. Mom would have assessed every anecdote. Dad would have edited every draft, offering historic perspective. Their love lives on; it is their true legacy.

I am grateful to Estrella Damaso, whose care and attention to our family allow me to take on new challenges.

Endless days of writing were more bearable with Chief, our big golden retriever, sleeping at my feet under the computer table. He alone agreed with every word.

Most important: my husband and children—Mike, Leila, and Christof—to whom this book is dedicated. They are my life. Leila, kind and thoughtful like my mom, brings joy and sparkle to each day. Christof, tall and gentle like my dad, fills our hearts and home with music and song. Mike, soul mate, editor, and technical adviser, is my compass and keel. Together, we share every season, every dream.

Ann Blackman
Washington, D.C.
February 14, 1998

Notes

INTRODUCTION

1. *Caterer*, interview with Bill Homan, November 18, 1997.
2. Two confidential sources.
3. Douglas Waller, *Time* interview, February 1997.
4. Kirstin Downey Grimsley, "Avon Calling . . . on a Man," *Washington Post*, December 12, 1997, p. G1.
5. James Reston, *Deadline: A Memoir* (New York: Random House, 1991), p. 152.
6. Blackman interview with Václav Havel, Prague, July 14, 1997. The interview took place at 11:00 A.M. Havel was sitting in his spacious office in Hradčany Castle, site of the office of the Czech president. Taking deep pulls on a tall Pilsner beer, he talks at length about his friend.
7. Blackman interview with President Bill Clinton, March 4, 1998.
8. Ibid.
9. Interview with Lev Braun, July 22, 1997. He died in November 1997.
10. Remarks at swearing-in ceremony, the White House, January 23, 1997.
11. Korbel's curriculum vitae from the University of Denver states that he spoke English, Czech, Serbo-Croat, and French fluently, that he spoke Russian and German well, and that he had a good reading knowledge in Polish and Bulgarian.
12. Josef Korbel, *Twentieth-Century Czechoslovakia, The Meaning of Its History* (New York: Columbia University Press, 1977), p. 157.
13. Ibid., p. 129.

14. James P. Rubin, Prague, July 13, 1997.
15. Madeleine Albright, comments in Prague, July 13, 1997.

Chapter 1: Bohemian Spring

1. The feminine suffix "ová" is added to the family names of married Czech women if they end in a consonant or if it ends in the letter *a*. Female names ending in *y* become *a*. In most cases, this book identifies people by the male ending, as in Mandula Korbel. But if the women have been introduced to the author with the "ová" ending, as in Dagmar Šímová, or a name appears in writing, as in Marie Jana Körbelová, those are the names used.
2. Michael Dobbs, "Out of the Past," *Washington Post Magazine*, February 9, 1997, p. 11.
3. Josef Korbel, *Tito's Communism* (Denver, Colo.: University of Denver Press, 1951), p. 72.
4. Dobbs, "Out of the Past," p. 11.
5. Interview with Věra Ruprechtová, Letohrad, June 10, 1997.
6. Ibid.
7. There are also two large, autographed portraits of Madeleine Albright, who dropped in for coffee during a visit to her father's hometown in early September 1997.
8. Ruprechtová, June 10, 1997.
9. Ruprechtová says he provided 120 jobs.
10. Ruprechtová, June 10, 1997. Ruprechtová says she learned about it only recently when stories about the Korbels' heritage ran in local newspapers. She, too, was surprised, just as Madeleine Albright claims to have been.
11. Letohrad mayor Petr Šilar says that the document was located in late November 1997. Interview with Petr Šilar, Letohrad, December 4, 1997.
12. Mandula Korbel, personal essay. Because it is written from memory, the essay's dates do not always correspond with official documents.
13. Ružena Spiegelová was born in 1887, according to Šímová.
14. Interview with Eduard Goldstücker, Prague, December 5, 1997.
15. Blackman interview with Madeleine Albright, Georgetown, February 7, 1998.
16. The history of Les Hirondelles is from Frank Kraus of Mahwah, New Jersey, whose sister attended the school.
17. Dobbs, "Out of the Past," p. 12; Ruprechtová, June 10, 1997.
18. Madeleine Albright, response to written questions, January 13, 1998.
19. Mandula Korbel, personal essay.
20. Josef Korbel's official file at the Czech Ministry of Foreign Affairs.
21. Ibid.
22. Körbels' marriage certificate.
23. Interview with Jan Stránský, Prague, December 6, 1997. While he lived in Connecticut, the interview took place in Prague, where he was visiting. Stránský, author of *East Wind Over Prague*, died February 21, 1998, in Connecticut.
24. Mandula Korbel, personal essay.
25. Madeleine Albright, February 7, 1998.

26. Ibid.
27. Hugh Seton-Watson, *The East European Revolution* (London: Methuen & Co. Ltd., 1950), pp. 50–54.
28. Joe Monik research, Prague.
29. Madeleine Albright, response to written questions, January 13, 1998.
30. Interview with Dagmar Šímová, August 8, 1997.
31. Dáša is pronounced "Dasha." In an interview in her apartment in December 1997, Dagmar Šímová said that for the sake of clarity she would not object to being referred to throughout the book as Dagmar, or Cousin Dagmar. Her name changed from Deimlová to Šímová when she married.
32. Šímová, August 26, 1997.
33. Ibid.
34. Šímová, June 11, 1997.
35. Monik research on Jewish history.
36. Interview with Hana Hanšlová, Náchod, December 4, 1997.
37. Interview with Oldřich Šafář, Náchod, December 4, 1997. Šafář says that in the 1940s, the percentage fell to 3 percent, that of the 248 people from Náchod who went to concentration camps, only 16 survived.
38. Interview with Irena Ravel, Prague, June 14, 1997.
39. Although today the cemetery is run-down by Western standards, efforts are being made to repair tombstones and improve the grounds.
40. Walter Laqueur, "Madeleine Albright and Jewish Identity," *New Republic,* March 10, 1997, p. 28.
41. Interview with Michael Kraus, November 5, 1997.
42. Mandula Korbel, personal essay.

CHAPTER 2: THE ESCAPE

1. Josef Korbel, *Tito's Communism,* p. 3.
2. Interview with Jara Ribnikar, July 24, 1997.
3. Ibid.
4. H. P. Willmott, *The Great Crusade: A New Complete History of the Second World War* (New York: The Free Press, 1989), pp. 12, 13.
5. Hugh Seton-Watson, *The East European Revolution,* pp. 36, 53.
6. Robert Kee, *Munich: The Eleventh Hour* (London: Hamish Hamilton Ltd., 1988), p. 34.
7. Ihor Gawdiak, ed., *Czechoslovakia, A Country Study,* 3rd ed. (Washington, D.C.: Library of Congress, Federal Research Division, 1989), p. 31.
8. Ibid., p. 39.
9. Ibid.
10. Ibid.
11. Kee, *Munich,* p. 36.
12. Ibid., p. 132.
13. Willmott, *The Great Crusade,* p. 33.
14. Kee, *Munich,* p. 125.

15. J. F. N. Bradley, *Czecho-Slovakia: A Short History* (Edinburgh: Edinburgh University Press, 1971), p. 156.

16. Willmott, *The Great Crusade*, p. 33.

17. Ibid., pp. 3, 4, 33. Czechoslovakia had signed a mutual assistance pact with the Soviet Union in 1935, but Soviet intervention on Czechoslovakia's behalf was contingent upon France's fulfillment of her treaty obligations.

18. Kee, *Munich*, p. 209.

19. Ibid., p. 193.

20. Ibid., p. 155.

21. Willmott, *The Great Crusade*, p. 33.

22. Kee, *Munich*, p. 133.

23. Ibid., p. 130.

24. Gawdiak, *Czechoslovakia, A Country Study*, p. 41.

25. Kee, *Munich*, p. 129.

26. Ibid., p. 215.

27. Josef Korbel, *Twentieth-Century Czechoslovakia, The Meaning of Its History*, p. 121.

28. Kee, *Munich*, pp. 203–4.

29. Ibid., p. 204.

30. Bradley, *Czecho-Slovakia: A Short History*, p. 157.

31. Korbel, *Twentieth-Century Czechoslovakia*, p. 127.

32. Kee, *Munich*, pp. 170–71.

33. Ibid., p. 177.

34. Mandula Korbel, personal essay.

35. Interview with Jan M. Stránský, Prague, December 4, 1997. Stránský lives in London. He is also the nephew of the late Jan Stránský of Connecticut.

36. Ibid.

37. Ibid.

38. Kee, *Munich*, p. 204.

39. Paul E. Zinner, *Communist Strategy and Tactics in Czechoslovakia, 1918–1948* (New York: Frederick A. Praeger, 1963), p. 101.

40. Korbel, *Twentieth-Century Czechoslovakia*, p. 141.

41. Ibid., p. 126.

42. Ibid., p. 127.

43. Kee, *Munich*, p. 216.

44. Gawdiak, *Czechoslovakia, A Country Study*, p. 46.

45. Bradley, *Czecho-Slovakia: A Short History*, p. 159.

46. Korbel, *Twentieth-Century Czechoslovakia*, p. 156.

47. Willmott, *The Great Crusade*, p. 35; Gawdiak, *Czechoslovakia, A Country Study*, p. 44.

48. Korbel, *Twentieth-Century Czechoslovakia*, p. 156.

49. Kee, *Munich*, pp. 212–13.

50. Josef Korbel's official résumé at the Czech Ministry of Foreign Affairs.

51. Mandula Korbel, personal essay.

52. "Documents from the History of Czechoslovak Politics, 1939–1943: Relations of International Diplomacy to Czechoslovak Exiles in the West" (Prague: Czechoslovak National Academy Publishers, 1966).

53. Mandula Korbel, personal essay.
54. Ibid.
55. Korbel, *Tito's Communism,* p. 2.
56. Blackman interview with Madeleine Albright, February 7, 1998.
57. Mandula Korbel, personal essay.
58. Blackman interview with John Korbel, *Time,* January 27, 1997.
59. Mandula Korbel, personal essay.
60. Korbel, January 27, 1997.
61. Ibid.; Josef Korbel's official file at the Czech Ministry of Foreign Affairs; Mandula Korbel, personal essay.
62. Ribnikar, July 24, 1997.
63. Mandula Korbel, personal essay.
64. Interview with Dagmar Šímová, Prague, December 3, 1997.
65. Albright, February 7, 1998.

CHAPTER 3: BATTLEFRONTS

1. Mandula Korbel, personal essay.
2. Ibid.
3. Prokop Drtina, *Memoirs* (Nakladatelstvi Sixty-Eight Publishers, Corp., 1982). Translation by Joe Monik.
4. Interview with Dagmar Šímová, Prague, December 3, 1997.
5. Interview with Anna Sonnek, Canvey Island, England, May 26, 1997.
6. Blackman interview with Madeleine Albright, February 7, 1998.
7. Interview with Pavel Tigrid, Prague, June 11, 1997.
8. Albright, February 7, 1998.
9. Mandula Korbel, personal essay.
10. J. F. N. Bradley, *Czecho-Slovakia: A Short History,* pp. 162–63.
11. Ihor Gawdiak, *Czechoslovakia, A Country Study,* p. 48.
12. Bradley, *Czecho-Slovakia: A Short History,* pp. 163–64.
13. Josef Korbel, University of Denver and Czech Ministry of Foreign Affairs vitae.
14. Drtina, *Memoirs,* p. 510.
15. Albright, February 7, 1998.
16. Drtina calls it "propaganda."
17. Karel Brusak, *Notes on the Czechoslovak Section,* BBC Written Archives Centre.
18. Tigrid, June 13, 1997. Instinctively, Tigrid refers to his old boss as "KUR-bel," which was how his name was pronounced before he changed it after the war by dropping the umlaut to make it sound less German.
19. Interview with Jan Stránský, Prague, December 6, 1997.
20. Barry Paris, "Profiles: Unconquerable," *New Yorker,* April 22, 1991, p. 72.
21. Tigrid, June 13, 1997.
22. Interview with Eduard Goldstücker, Prague, June 9, 1997.
23. Josef Korbel, "Memorandum on J. Korbel's conversation with Mr. V. Clementis," Columbia University Rare Book and Manuscript Library, Bakhmeteff Archives, April 5, 1949. In the essay, Korbel says Clementis alienated his fellow Communists when

he deviated from the official Communist Party line at the time of the signing of the Soviet-German treaty in August 1939 and opposed it.

24. Ibid.
25. Interview with Avigdon Dagan, July 30, 1997.
26. Ibid.
27. Hubert Ripka, *We Think of You* (Library of Congress, Manuscript Division, Published by the Czechoslovak Maccabi, London, 1941).
28. Interview with Ctibor Rybár, Prague, June 13, 1997.
29. Walter Laqueur, "Madeleine Albright and Jewish Identity," p. 28.
30. Šímová, July 14, 1997.
31. Ibid., June 11 and July 14, 1997.
32. *Sunday Mirror,* February 28, 1988, p. 21.
33. Šímová, December 3, 1997.
34. Ibid., June 11, 1997.
35. *Sunday Mirror,* February 28, 1988, pp. 19, 21.
36. Šímová, June 11, 1997.
37. Ibid.
38. *The Lincoln Library of Essential Information,* 34th ed. (Columbus, Ohio: The Frontier Press Company, 1971), vol. 1, pp. 539–41.
39. Ibid., p. 541.
40. Albright, February 13, 1998.
41. Šímová, June 11, 1997. Similar stories were told throughout Europe during the war, and many people doubted they were true.
42. Drtina, *Memoirs,* p. 552.
43. Albright, February 13, 1998.
44. Drtina, *Memoirs,* p. 552.
45. Albright, February 7, 1998.
46. Ibid.
47. Leonard Mosley, *Battle of Britain* (New York: Time-Life Books Inc., 1977), p. 145.
48. Ibid., pp. 145, 154.
49. Ibid., p. 145.
50. Ibid.
51. Ibid., pp. 146, 152.
52. Ibid., p. 147.
53. Ibid., p. 146.
54. Ibid., p. 154.
55. Sonnek, May 26, 1997.
56. Ibid.
57. Drtina, *Memoirs,* p. 573.
58. Ibid., p. 566.
59. Ibid.
60. Interview with Jiřina Tondr, Henley-on-Thames, England, May 25, 1997.
61. Mosley, *Battle of Britain,* pp. 182–83.
62. Ibid., p. 183.
63. Ibid.

64. Ibid., p. 186.
65. Ibid., p. 187.
66. Ibid., p. 188.
67. Ibid., p. 190.
68. Albright, February 7, 1998.
69. The deed to the house shows that Jan Korbel, known in England as John Korbel, purchased the house on February 6, 1942, and sold it on April 15, 1954. Courtesy of Inge Woolf, the current owner.
70. Albright, February 7, 1998.
71. In old country houses, it was common to build fireplaces big enough to hold two chairs. The surrounding brick walls would keep people warm.
72. Interview with Inge Woolf, Berkhamsted, England, December 1, 1997. She and her husband, Michael Woolf, have owned the house since 1982.
73. Tondr, May 25, 1997; Sonnek, May 26, 1997.
74. Sonnek, December 6, 1997.
75. Interview with John Seymour, Berkhamsted, England, December 4, 1997. Seymour has been a resident of Berkhamsted since 1939.
76. Sonnek, May 26, 1997.
77. The church has moved, and the building is now occupied by the British Red Cross.
78. Sacred Heart Church records, Berkhamsted.
79. Ibid. The name "Císařová" includes the Czech feminine ending "ová." In references to the Císařs as a couple, the masculine ending is used.
80. Albright, February 7, 1998.
81. Sonnek, May 26, 1997.
82. Interview with Tomáš Kraus, Prague, December 3, 1997.
83. Stephen D. Kertesz, *The Fate of East Central Europe: Hopes and Failures of American Foreign Policy* (Notre Dame, Ind.: University of Notre Dame Press, 1956), p. 195.
84. Interview with Lev Braun, July 22, 1997. With Masaryk long dead, it is impossible to verify whether Braun's recollection of the episode would be the same as his. I called Braun on November 3, 1997, in hopes of interviewing him again and learned that he had died the day before. However, Ctibor Rybár, a good friend of Masaryk, says that while he did not hear Masaryk say this, it certainly was in character. "That was typical of Masaryk," he said in an interview in December 1997 in Prague.
85. Interview with Eduard Goldstücker, Prague, June 9, 1997.
86. Albright, February 7, 1998.
87. Ibid.
88. Ibid.
89. Ibid., February 13, 1998; interview with Joe Monik, February 17, 1998.
90. Imperial War Museum, February 12, 1998.
91. Albright, February 7, 1998.
92. Madeleine Albright, response to written questions, January 13, 1998.
93. Šímová, December 3, 1997.
94. Mandula Korbel, personal essay.
95. Interview with Diana Ely, December 12, 1997.
96. Albright, February 7, 1998.

97. Ibid.

98. Goldstücker, December 5, 1997.

99. Ibid.

100. Karel Brusak, *Notes on the Czechoslovak Section,* BBC Written Archives Center.

101. Imperial War Museum data.

102. Imperial War Museum brochure on the Morrison "Table" Shelter.

103. Mandula Korbel, personal essay.

CHAPTER 4: A LIVING HELL

1. George Kennan, *From Prague After Munich, Diplomatic Papers 1938–1940* (Princeton, N.J.: Princeton University Press, 1968).

2. Ihor Gawdiak, *Czechoslovakia, A Country Study,* p. 47; J. F. N. Bradley, *Czecho-Slovakia: A Short History,* p. 160.

3. Ibid., p. 47.

4. Josef Korbel, *Twentieth-Century Czechoslovakia, The Meaning of Its History,* p. 159.

5. Gawdiak, *Czechoslovakia, A Country Study,* p. 47.

6. Korbel, *Twentieth-Century Czechoslovakia,* p. 157.

7. Gawdiak, *Czechoslovakia, A Country Study,* p. 48.

8. Korbel, *Twentieth-Century Czechoslovakia,* p. 158; Gawdiak, *Czechoslovakia, A Country Study,* p. 47.

9. Interview with Irena Ravel, Prague, June 14, 1997; Michael Berenbaum, *The World Must Know* (Boston: Little, Brown and Company, 1993), p. 69. Ravel was seventy-five. During the interview, she was sitting in her stark, one-room apartment on the fifth floor of an ailing building in Prague. Her tiny sink held a bottle of washing soap, one of cooking oil, and another of rum. Her face, with its deep wrinkles, was a human frieze of suffering, a virtual map of Theresienstadt. As she talked, her words flowed in perfect cadence, a march of horrific memories long ago etched into her soul. With each recollection, her foot tapped nervously on the floor, slowly at first, then faster until she was punctuating each word with another tap. Ravel arrived at Theresienstadt by train transport on June 13, 1942. She was nineteen years old and would stay for three years. Today she makes her meager living by giving guided tours of the camp, a job she says she is able to endure only by shutting off her emotions when she goes to work each day.

10. Ravel, June 14, 1997; Berenbaum, *The World Must Know,* p. 69.

11. Bradley, *Czecho-Slovakia: A Short History,* p. 161; Gawdiak, *Czechoslovakia, A Country Study,* p. 47.

12. Berenbaum, *The World Must Know,* p. 87.

13. Jews were not allowed to leave the ghetto. The term *ghetto* was first used in Venice 1590.

14. Berenbaum, *The World Must Know,* p. 87.

15. Ctibor Rybár, "Jewish Prague," Prague, TV Spektrum, p. 120.

16. Berenbaum, *The World Must Know,* pp. 87–88.

17. Ibid., p. 87.

18. Ibid., p. 88.

19. Ibid.

20. Ibid.

21. Miroslava Karneho, ed., *Terezínská pamětní kniha* (Terezín Memorial Book) (Prague: Terezínská iniciatíva, 1995).

22. Tomáš Kraus, Nazi files collected by the Federation of Jewish Communities, Prague.

23. Ibid.

24. Ibid.

25. Michael Dobbs, "Out of the Past," p. 20.

26. Ibid., p. 18.

27. Korbel, *Twentieth-Century Czechoslovakia*, p. 214.

28. Ibid., pp. 214–15.

29. Stephen D. Kertesz, *The Fate of East Central Europe: Hopes and Failures of American Foreign Policy*, p. 202.

30. Korbel, *Twentieth-Century Czechoslovakia*, p. 215.

31. Gerhard L. Weinberg, *A World at Arms: A Global History of World War II* (New York: Cambridge University Press, 1994), p. 817; David Eisenhower, *Eisenhower: At War, 1943–1945* (New York: Vintage Books, 1986), pp. 771, 785.

32. Weinberg, *A World at Arms*, p. 826.

33. Korbel, *Twentieth-Century Czechoslovakia*, p. 215.

CHAPTER 5: LISTS THAT LIE

1. Interview with Dagmar Šímová, Prague, June 11, 1997.

2. Martin Gilbert, *Second World War* (London: Weidenfeld and Nicolson, 1989), pp. 640–41.

3. Šímová, June 11, 1997.

4. Interview with Jana Paříková, Prague, December 3, 1997. Paříková's family has owned the building for seventy-five years.

5. Josef Korbel is listed as Dagmar's guardian on her school records at the Berkhamsted School.

6. Blackman interview with Madeleine Albright, February 7, 1998.

7. Šímová, June 11, 1997.

8. Interview with Pavel Tigrid, June 13, 1997.

9. Albright, February 7, 1998.

10. Ihor Gawdiak, *Czechoslovakia, A Country Study*, p. 48.

11. J. F. N. Bradley, *Czecho-Slovakia: A Short History*, pp. 166–67.

12. Gawdiak, *Czechoslovakia, A Country Study*, p. 48.

13. Interview with Eduard Goldstücker, Prague, December 5, 1997.

14. Gawdiak, *Czechoslovakia, A Country Study*, p. 49.

15. Ibid., pp. 181–82.

16. Ibid., p. 55.

17. Bradley, *Czecho-Slovakia: A Short History*, p. 169.

18. Ibid.

19. Gawdiak, *Czechoslovakia, A Country Study*, p. 55.

20. Josef Korbel's University of Denver vitae.

21. Goldstücker, June 9, 1997.
22. Ibid.; Goldstücker repeated this December 5, 1997.
23. Josef Korbel's official file at the Czech Ministry of Foreign Affairs.
24. *Politika,* September 29, 1945.
25. Goldstücker, December 5, 1998.
26. Ibid., June 9, 1997.
27. Albright, February 13, 1998.

Chapter 6: Brutal Choices

1. Josef Korbel, *Tito's Communism,* p. 1.
2. Ibid., p. 2.
3. Ibid.
4. Michael Dobbs, "Out of the Past," pp. 21–22; interview with Eduard Goldstücker, Prague, December 5, 1997.
5. Korbel, *Tito's Communism,* p. 18.
6. Ibid., p. 19.
7. Ibid., p. 23.
8. Ibid.
9. Ibid., pp. 146–47.
10. Ibid., p. 76.
11. Dobbs, "Out of the Past," p. 22.
12. Years later, when Madeleine Albright visited in May 1997, she identified the bathroom where her father made her kneel on the cold tile for half an hour, a typical Czechoslovak punishment. Her bedroom, which had large windows looking out onto a courtyard, had been made into another apartment. Douglas Waller, *Time,* May 1997.
13. Blackman interview with Madeleine Albright, February 7, 1998.
14. Ibid.
15. Ibid.
16. Ibid.
17. Ibid.
18. Dobbs, "Out of the Past," p. 20.
19. Bradley, *Czecho-Slovakia: A Short History,* p. 171.
20. Gawdiak, *Czechoslovakia, A Country Study,* p. 56.
21. Albright, February 7, 1998.
22. Interview with Dagmar Šímová, Prague, February 19, 1998.
23. Ibid., December 3, 1997.
24. Albright, February 7, 1998.
25. *Paris Peace Conference, 1946: Selected Documents.* Department of State. Publication 2868. Conference Series 103. (Washington, D.C.: United States Government Printing Office), p. 11.
26. Ibid., p. iv.
27. Josef Korbel's University of Denver vitae.
28. Interview with Ctibor Rybár, Prague, December 5, 1997.

29. Ibid., June 13, 1997.

30. Josef Korbel's official file at the Czech Ministry of Foreign Affairs.

31. Gawdiak, *Czechoslovakia, A Country Study,* p. 56.

32. Josef Korbel, *The Communist Subversion of Czechoslovakia, 1938–1948: The Failure of Coexistence* (Princeton, N.J.: Princeton University Press, 1959), p. 198.

33. Ibid.

34. Ibid.

35. Ibid., p. 200.

36. Jan M. Stránský correspondence, October 14, 1997.

37. Gawdiak, *Czechoslovakia, A Country Study,* p. 56; Bradley, *Czecho-Slovakia: A Short History,* p. 177.

38. Gawdiak, *Czechoslovakia, A Country Study,* p. 57.

39. *Resolutions and Decisions of the Security Council, 1948.* "Resolution of 20 January 1948"; "Resolution of 21 April 1948."

40. Albright, February 7, 1998.

41. Josef Korbel, *Danger in Kashmir* (Princeton, N.J.: Princeton University Press, 1954), p. 118.

42. Press statement by Josef Korbel attached to his February 12, 1949, request for political asylum in the United States, National Archives.

43. Barry Paris, "Profiles: Unconquerable," p. 42.

44. Šímová, December 3, 1997.

45. Albright, February 7, 1998.

46. Korbel, *Danger in Kashmir,* p. 104.

47. Ibid., p. 118.

48. Gawdiak, *Czechoslovakia, A Country Study,* p. 57.

49. Interview with Eduard Goldstücker, Prague, June 9, 1997.

50. Due to slow and poor communication between the Czechoslovak government and its representatives at the United Nations, Korbel served on the U.N. Commission for India and Pakistan until February 1949 when the commission returned to the subcontinent. Korbel had been dismissed from the Foreign Ministry on December 12, 1948.

51. Goldstücker, June 9, 1997.

52. CIA reply to FOIA appeal, May 30, 1997.

53. Goldstücker, June 6, 1997.

54. Interview with Marcia Burick, Washington, July 29, 1997.

55. Waller, *Time* interview, February 1997.

56. Albright, February 7, 1998.

57. Goldstücker, June 9, 1997.

58. Twenty years later, when the Soviets occupied Czechoslovakia and Goldstücker was forced to flee to London as a refugee, Josef Korbel returned the favor. By then, happily ensconced at the University of Denver, Korbel wrote to his old friend and asked him to come to America. "He said he would find a place for me and that he had already spoken to his dean," Goldstücker says. While Goldstücker deeply appreciated the offer, he did not accept it and chose instead to remain in London.

59. Goldstücker, June 9, 1997.

CHAPTER 7: THE DEFECTION

1. Blackman interview with Madeleine Albright, February 7, 1998.
2. Josef Korbel, *Danger in Kashmir,* p. 120.
3. Ibid., p. 145.
4. Josef Korbel, *Tito's Communism,* p. 249; Josef Korbel's University of Denver vitae; Korbel, *Danger in Kashmir,* p. 150.
5. Albright, February 7, 1998.
6. Interview with Anna Sonnek, Canvey Island, England, May 26, 1997.
7. Jan M. Stránský correspondence, October 14, 1997.
8. Sonnek, May 26, 1997.
9. SS *America* manifest. National Archives and Records Administration of New York.
10. Josef Korbel's February 12, 1949, letter asking for political asylum in the United States, National Archives; SS *America* manifest.
11. Albright, February 7, 1998.
12. Ibid.
13. SS *America* manifest; Douglas Waller, *Time* interview, February 1997.
14. Albright, February 7, 1998.
15. Josef Korbel, "Memorandum on J. Korbel's conversation with V. Clementis." Written on April 5, 1949, less than four months after arriving in America, for J. Mosely of the Rockefeller Foundation. There is no evidence that Korbel wrote this for the benefit of the CIA, which was in the throes of recruiting Eastern Europeans to find what they knew about Communist activities in their homelands. But for a political dissident asking for asylum in America and needing a full-time job to support his family, it was certainly in Korbel's interest to make his feelings about communism known in clear, unmitigated terms. Also, while Korbel may not have been recruited by the CIA, it is likely the intelligence agency had sources at Columbia University who reported to them on Korbel's activities. Korbel transcribed this conversation with Clementis himself. At times, the English is somewhat awkward.
16. Ibid.
17. Ibid.
18. Ibid.
19. Interview with Jan Stránský, Prague, December 6, 1997.
20. Interview with Pavel Tigrid, Prague, June 13, 1997.
21. Interview with Zdeněk Mastník, London, May 25, 1997.
22. Press statement by Josef Korbel attached to his February 12, 1949, request for political asylum in the United States, National Archives. This quote, altered slightly, appeared in the *New York Times* on February 14.
23. Josef Korbel's official résumé at the Czech Ministry of Foreign Affairs.
24. SS *Queen Mary* manifest. Korbel's FBI file mistakenly has him arriving on the *Queen Elizabeth.*
25. Ministry of Foreign Affairs, the Czech Republic.

CHAPTER 8: STARTING OVER

1. Blackman interview with Madeleine Albright, February 7, 1998.
2. Blackman interview with John Korbel, *Time*, January 27, 1997.
3. When news stories appeared in early 1997 that Madeleine's parents had been born Jewish, several reporters jumped to the conclusion that Josef Korbel had moved his family to Great Neck because he wanted his family to live in a Jewish community. In fact, Great Neck has a large Jewish population today, but in the late 1940s, it was mostly Christian.
4. Albright, February 7, 1998.
5. Interview with Winifred Freund, Great Neck, N.Y., February 7, 1997.
6. Ibid.
7. Albright, February 7, 1998.
8. Ibid.
9. Ministry of Foreign Affairs, the Czech Republic, cable 7564/A/49.
10. Ministry of Foreign Affairs, the Czech Republic, cable 10241/A/49.
11. Ministry of Foreign Affairs, the Czech Republic, cable 19.
12. Josef Korbel's February 12, 1948, letter to Senator Warren R. Austin, U.S. Representative to the United Nations, requesting political asylum in the United States, National Archives.
13. Ibid.
14. Ibid.
15. Statesman's Yearbook, 1948. United Nations Archives.
16. Ministry of Foreign Affairs, the Czech Republic, cable 2756/B/1948.
17. Josef Korbel's official file at the Czech Ministry of Foreign Affairs; SS *Queen Mary* manifest. National Archives and Records Administration of New York; Jan Papánek papers, Library of Congress, pp. 343, 350, 351.
18. SS *America* manifest.
19. Interview with Eduard Goldstücker, Prague, December 5, 1997.
20. Masaryk was foreign minister.
21. Confidential memo from Thomas F. Power, Jr., March 14, 1949, National Archives.
22. University of Denver Archives; Allen D. Breck, *From the Rockies to the World* (Denver: Hirchfield Press, 1989), pp. 126–29.
23. Letter from Thomas F. Power, Jr., to Ambassador Jessup, U.S. Delegation to the Council of Foreign Ministers, titled "Dr. Korbel's status," June 9, 1949, National Archives.
24. George F. Simor, M.D., *Psychiatric Times*, vol. XIV, nos. 10, 42, 44 (October 1997). Simor is assistant chief of psychiatry service at the Samuel S. Stratton Veteran Affairs Medical Center in Albany, N.Y.
25. David Halberstam, *The Fifties* (New York: Villard Books, 1993), p. 55.
26. Ibid., p. 53.
27. November 25, 1997, letter from the CIA's Agency Release Panel turning down a FOIA appeal that it release any documents relating to Josef Korbel.
28. Interview with Zdeněk Mastník, London, June 20, 1997.
29. Interview with Dagmar Šímová, Prague, June 11, 1997.

30. Ibid., December 3, 1997.
31. Albright, March 1, 1998.
32. Šímová, June 11, 1997.
33. Ibid.
34. Ibid.
35. Albright, February 7, 1998.
36. Goldstücker, December 6, 1997.
37. Albright, February 7, 1998.
38. Ibid.
39. Arrandale Elementary School graduation program.

CHAPTER 9: THE TEENAGER

1. Blackman interview with Madeleine Albright, February 7, 1998.
2. Douglas Waller, *Time* interview, February 1, 1997.
3. Korbel letter with return address, December 20, 1950, National Archives.
4. Blackman interview with John Korbel, *Time,* January 27, 1997.
5. Waller, *Time* interview, February 1, 1997.
6. Memorial Service for Josef Korbel, July 20, 1977, *Personal Thoughts on Josef Korbel,* Graduate School of International Studies, University of Denver, Russ Porter, p. 3.
7. Albright, February 13, 1998.
8. Ibid.
9. Ibid.
10. Interview with Joseph Szyliowicz, May 12, 1997.
11. Memorial Service for Josef Korbel, Charlotte Read, pp. 2 and 3.
12. Letter from Korbel to Mr. John C. Campbell, December 20, 1950, National Archives.
13. Waller, *Time* interview, February 1997.
14. Interview with Marion Gottesfeld, May 12, 1997.
15. Waller, *Time* interview, February 1997.
16. Korbel, January 27, 1997.
17. Albright, February 13, 1998.
18. Ibid., February 7, 1998.
19. Waller, *Time* interview, February 1997.
20. Albright, February 7, 1998.
21. Ibid.
22. Interview with Stephanie Allen, May 13, 1997.
23. Fawn Germer, *Rocky Mountain News,* December 6, 1996.
24. Allen, May 13, 1997. Asked if there was any thought at the time that Madeleine was Jewish, Allen replied, "Oh Lord, no. Kent was a very non-Jewish place, but it wasn't anti-Jewish. We did have some Jewish people there but it wasn't something we ever thought about."
25. Interview with Julika Balajty Ambrose, May 15, 1997.
26. Ibid.
27. Albright, February 7, 1998.

28. Annie Hill, *Denver Post,* December 6, 1996, p. 16A.
29. Allen, May 13, 1997.
30. Germer, *Rocky Mountain News,* December 6, 1996.
31. Ambrose, May 15, 1997; Hill, *Denver Post,* December 6, 1996, p. 1A.
32. Allen, July 5, 1997.
33. Hill, *Denver Post,* December 6, 1996, p. 16A.
34. Waller, *Time* interview, February 1, 1997.
35. Albright, February 7, 1998.
36. Waller, *Time* interview, February 1, 1997.
37. Memorial Service for Josef Korbel, Russ Porter, p. 5.
38. "Speaking Engagements of Dr. Josef Korbel: January 30, 1951 to November 5, 1951."
39. Waller, *Time* interview, February 1, 1997.
40. Korbel's University of Denver vitae.
41. Ben M. Cherrington, *A Personal Reminiscence.* The Social Science Foundation of the University of Denver 1926–1951. Graduate School of International Studies, 1973, pp. 41, 42.
42. Memorial Service for Josef Korbel, Russ Porter, pp. 4, 5.
43. Memorial Service for Josef Korbel, Charlotte Read, p. 2.
44. Ibid., p. 3.
45. Waller, *Time* interview, February 1, 1997.
46. Ibid.
47. Waller, *Time* interview with Albright, February 6, 1997.
48. Waller, *Time* interview, February 1, 1997.
49. Ibid.
50. Albright, February 7, 1998.
51. Ibid.
52. Ibid.
53. Gottesfeld, May 12, 1997.
54. Hill, *Denver Post,* December 6, 1996, p. 1.

Chapter 10: Dust on Her Shoes

1. Interview with Mary Jane Durnford, January 23, 1998.
2. Wellesley College Archives.
3. Interview with Winifred Freund, Great Neck, N.Y., February 7, 1997.
4. Blackman interview with Madeleine Albright, February 7, 1998.
5. Interview with Edward Vose Gulick, December 10, 1997.
6. Albright, February 7, 1998.
7. Ibid.
8. Wilma Slaight, Wellesley College archivist, January 7, 1998.
9. Interview with Barbara LeWin Luton, Wellesley College, April 7, 1997.
10. Albright, February 7, 1998.
11. Wellesley College Archives.
12. Albright, February 7, 1998.

13. Interview with Emily MacFarquhar, Cambridge, Mass., March 31, 1997.

14. Barbara LeWin Luton, e-mail, October 24, 1997.

15. Albright, February 7, 1998.

16. Ibid.

17. Wellesley College archives; *Wellesley College News.*

18. MacFarquhar, March 31, 1997.

19. Albright, February 7, 1998.

20. Freund, March 22, 1997.

21. Ibid.

22. Wellesley College archives; Freund, March 22, 1997.

23. *Wellesley College News,* November 5, 1956, p. 9.

24. Ibid., November 21, 1957, p. 1.

25. Ibid., October 16, 1958.

26. Freund, March 22, 1997.

27. U.S. District Court, Denver.

28. Interview with Marcia Burick, June 3, 1997.

29. Albright, February 7, 1998.

30. Robert F. Keeler, *Newsday* (New York: Arbor House, 1990), pp. 275–76.

31. Ibid., p. 102.

32. Ibid., p. 278.

33. Joseph Medill Patterson Albright, *Joseph Medill Patterson: Right or Wrong, American.* May 1958. Williams College archives.

34. MacFarquhar, March 31, 1997.

35. Albright, February 7, 1998.

36. Burick, June 3, 1997.

37. Interview with Newton N. Minow, June 30, 1997.

38. *New York Times,* December 29, 1958.

39. Madeleine Jana Korbel, *Zdenek Fierlinger's Role in the Communization of Czechoslovakia: The Profile of a Fellow Traveler,* Wellesley College, May 1959, p. 146.

40. Ibid., p. 59.

41. Freund, February 7, 1997.

42. MacFarquhar, March 31, 1997. A *U.S. News & World Report* survey in 1994 shows that 61 percent of the Wellesley Class of '59 started, resumed work, or changed careers after age thirty-five. The Class of '59 entered the work force in greatest numbers in their forties.

CHAPTER 11: LOVE AND MARRIAGE

1. *Chicago Sun-Times,* May 23, 1959.

2. Blackman interview with Madeleine Albright, February 7, 1998.

3. Ibid.

4. Ibid.

5. Confidential source.

6. Confidential source.

7. Interview with Jan Stránský, Prague, December 6, 1997.

8. *Chicago Sun-Times,* June 16, 1959.

9. Robert F. Keeler, *Newsday,* p. 279; Wellesley Class of 1959 Record Book, 1974.

10. Albright, February 7, 1998.

11. Ibid.

12. CBS-TV, *60 Minutes,* February 9, 1997. Albright quoted the editor.

13. Albright, February 7, 1998.

14. According to family members, Stevenson was in love with Alicia Patterson, proposed to her when she was a young girl, and she rejected him. But they renewed their friendship years later.

15. Interview with Newton Minow, June 30, 1997.

16. Keeler, *Newsday,* p. 279.

17. Ibid.

18. Interview with Jim Toedtman, Washington, April 29, 1997.

19. Ibid.

20. Albright, February 7, 1998.

21. Ibid.

22. Laura Muha, *Newsday,* January 3, 1993.

23. Albright, February 7, 1998.

24. Ibid.

25. Interview with Danielle Gardner, September 15, 1997.

26. Interview with Richard Gardner, New York, November 7, 1997.

27. Albright, February 7, 1997.

28. D. Gardner, November 7, 1997.

29. Ibid.

30. Ibid.

31. Ibid.

32. *Sun-Times,* November 1, 1961.

33. Interview with James Hoge, New York, May 14, 1997.

34. James Reston, *Deadline: A Memoir* (New York: Random House, 1991), p. 291.

35. Ibid., pp. 291–92.

36. Albright, February 7, 1998.

37. Ibid.

38. Interview with Rebecca Beauchamb, September 10, 1997. Beauchamb is the registrar at Johns Hopkins.

39. Albright, February 7, 1998.

40. Doris Kearns Goodwin, *Wait 'Til Next Year, A Memoir* (New York: Simon & Schuster, 1997), p. 190.

41. *Time,* June 20, 1960, p. 16.

42. Betty Friedan, *The Feminine Mystique* (New York: W.W. Norton, 1963), p. 344.

43. Ibid., p. 378.

44. Albright, February 7, 1998.

45. Interview with Winifred Freund, March 22, 1997.

46. Adlai E. Stevenson Papers, Seeley G. Mudd Manuscript Library, Department of Rare Books and Special Collections, Princeton University. Published with permission of Princeton University Library.

47. Albright, February 7, 1998.

48. Columbia University's Graduate School of Arts and Sciences.

49. Hoge, May 14, 1997.

50. Freund, March 22, 1997.

51. Interview with Mort Abromowitz, Washington, D.C., April 29, 1997.

52. Interview with Marcia Burick, Washington, D.C., July 29, 1997.

53. Ibid.

54. Albright, February 7, 1998.

55. Ibid.

56. Keeler, *Newsday*, p. 381.

57. Toedtman, April 29, 1997.

58. Keeler, *Newsday*, p. 393.

59. Ibid.

60. Toedtman, April 29, 1997.

61. Alice Albright Hoge, *Cissy Patterson* (New York: Random House, 1966), p. 176.

62. Ibid., p. 177.

63. Hoge, *Cissy Patterson*, pp. 194–95.

64. Confidential source.

65. Confidential source.

66. Confidential source.

67. Burick, April 2, 1997.

CHAPTER 12: THE KORBEL

1. Asked if she had any inkling at the time that Madeleine's parents were Jewish, Burick replied, "With the knowledge I had, I would have known. She would have told me. I could swear she didn't know."

2. Interview with Marcia Burick, July 29, 1997.

3. Confidential source.

4. *New York Times*, August 16, 1967, p. 1.

5. Burick, July 29, 1997.

6. Albright, February 13, 1998. Albright discussed the cellist story with Burick the previous day. Most details come from Burick. Albright amended some facts in Burick's first account and added what details she could recall.

7. Trip details are from interviews with Burick, April 2 and July 29, 1997. Albright said in an interview on February 13, 1998, that she does remember the "korbel" story.

CHAPTER 13: THE DEMANDING PROFESSOR

1. Interview with Zbigniew Brzezinski, Washington, D.C., September 18, 1997.

2. Ibid.

3. Waller, *Time* interview, February 1997.

4. Brzezinski, September 18, 1997.

5. Ibid.

6. Waller, *Time* interview, February 1997.

7. David Detzer, *The Brink: Cuban Missile Crisis, 1962* (New York: Thomas Y. Crowell, 1979), p. 234.

8. Waller, *Time* interview, February 1997.

9. Waller interview with Albright, *Time,* February 6, 1997.

10. Interview with Fred Knubel, December 16, 1997.

11. *Time,* May 10, 1968, p. 77.

12. Blackman interview with Madeleine Albright, February 7, 1998.

13. Madeleine Albright, "The Soviet Diplomatic Service: Profile of an Elite." Russian Institute, Columbia University, p. 26.

14. Albright, February 13, 1998.

15. Interview with Winifred Freund, February 7, 1997.

16. Ibid.

17. Interview with Jiří Dienstbier, Prague, July 14, 1997.

CHAPTER 14: CROSSROADS

1. Interview with Winifred Freund, March 22, 1997.

2. Albright served on the board of directors from 1968 to 1976. She was chair from 1978 to 1983.

3. Interview with Harry McPherson, Washington, D.C., March 25, 1997.

4. Interview with Frances Borders, Chevy Chase, Md., July 31, 1997.

5. Dorothy G. Singer and Tracey A. Revenson, *A Piaget Primer: How a Child Thinks* (New York: A Plume Book, New American Library, 1978), p. 3.

6. Anne B. Putzel, *Piaget and Education,* November 2, 1979.

7. Borders, July 31, 1997.

8. McPherson, March 3, 1997.

9. Borders, July 31, 1997.

10. Interview with Jack Valenti, October 6, 1997.

11. Borders, July 31, 1997.

12. Robert F. Keeler, *Newsday,* p. 412.

13. Ibid., pp. 457–60.

14. Ibid., p. 459.

15. Ibid., p. 461.

16. Ibid., p. 466.

17. Ibid., p. 473.

18. Ibid., p. 474.

19. Ibid., p. 492.

20. Ibid., p. 496.

21. Interview with Eduard Goldstücker, Prague, June 9, 1997.

CHAPTER 15: A DEMANDING SENATOR

1. Interview with Harry McPherson, Washington, D.C., March 25, 1997.

2. Interview with Sheppie Abromowitz, Washington, D.C., August 14, 1997, and February 2, 1998.

3. Interview with Leon Billings, Washington, D.C., July 30, 1997.
4. Ibid.
5. Ibid.
6. Cohen was named secretary of defense when Albright was named secretary of state.
7. Interview with Anita Jensen, Gaithersburg, Md., September 9, 1997.
8. Waller, *Time* interview, February 1997.
9. Interview with Alan Platt, Washington, D.C., December 18, 1997.
10. Memorandum, August 16, 1976, Bates College, Edmund S. Muskie Archives.
11. Platt, December 18, 1997.
12. Waller, *Time* interview, February 1997.
13. Platt, February 16, 1998.
14. Billings, July 30, 1997.
15. Interview with Cokie Roberts, Washington, D.C., April 1, 1997.
16. Interview with Emily MacFarquhar, March 31, 1997.
17. Interview with Sally Shelton-Colby, Washington, D.C., April 29, 1997.
18. William Safire, "The New-Boy Network," *New York Times,* February 20, 1975.
19. Platt, December 18, 1997.
20. Waller interview with Albright, *Time,* February 6, 1997.
21. Ibid.
22. Ibid.
23. Billings, July 30, 1997.
24. Jensen, September 9, 1997.
25. Ibid.
26. Ibid.
27. Waller, *Time* interview, February 1997; Billings, July 30, 1997.
28. Platt, December 18, 1997.
29. Waller, *Time* interview, February 1997; Billings, July 30, 1997.
30. Platt, December 18, 1997.
31. Waller interview with Albright, *Time,* February 6, 1997.
32. Waller, *Time* interview, February 1997.
33. Platt, May 1, 1997.
34. Ibid., December 18, 1997.
35. Jensen, September 9, 1997.
36. Ibid.
37. Memorandum, September 15, 1977, Bates College, Edmund S. Muskie Archives.
38. Shelton-Colby, April 29, 1997.
39. Blackman interview with Madeleine Albright, February 7, 1998.
40. Ibid.
41. Interview with Milan Radovich, July 29, 1997. The time of the visit was confirmed on February 16, 1998. Radovich cannot recall if it was the spring of 1973 or 1974.
42. Memorial Service for Josef Korbel, Charlotte Read, p. 3.
43. Ibid., James Bruce, p. 2.
44. Ibid., Russ Porter, p. 4.
45. Ibid., p. 5.

CHAPTER 16: THE WHITE HOUSE

1. James T. Patterson, *America in the Twentieth Century: A History,* 3rd ed. (New York: Harcourt Brace Jovanovich, 1989), p. 472; *Time,* January 31, 1977, p. 10.
2. Patterson, *America in the Twentieth Century,* p. 473.
3. Established by the National Security Act of 1947, the NSC has four statutory members: the president, vice president, secretary of state, and secretary of defense. Others who attend NSC meetings include the director of the Central Intelligence Agency, the chairman of the Joint Chiefs of Staff, and the national security adviser, who serves as the council's day-to-day director.
4. Elizabeth Drew, *On the Edge: The Clinton Presidency* (New York: Simon & Schuster, 1994), p. 141.
5. Interview with Zbigniew Brzezinski, September 18, 1997.
6. Ibid.
7. Blackman interview with Madeleine Albright, February 7, 1998.
8. Interviews with Zbigniew Brzezinski, Madeleine Albright, Leslie Denend, and William Odom, Miller Center Interviews, Carter Presidency Project, vol. XV, February 18, 1982, p. 21, Jimmy Carter Library.
9. Miller Center Interviews, p. 12.
10. Interview with Christine Dodson, New York, October 8, 1997.
11. Ibid.
12. Ibid.
13. Lawrence X. Clifford, "An Examination of the Carter Administration's Selection of Secretary of State and National Security Adviser," in *Jimmy Carter: Foreign Policy and Post-Presidential Years,* edited by Herbert D. Rosenbaum and Alexej Ugrinsky (Westport, Conn.: Greenwood Press, Hofstra University, 1994), p. 6.
14. Ibid., p. 8; Burton I. Kaufman, *The Presidency of James Earl Carter, Jr.* (Lawrence: University Press of Kansas, 1993), pp. 37–38.
15. Kaufman, *The Presidency of James Earl Carter, Jr.,* pp. 37–38.
16. Clifford, "An Examination of the Carter Administration's Selection of Secretary of State and National Security Adviser," pp. 6–7.
17. Kaufman, *The Presidency of James Earl Carter, Jr.,* p. 37.
18. Brzezinski, September 18, 1997.
19. Clifford, "An Examination of the Carter Administration's Selection of Secretary of State and National Security Adviser," pp. 9, 12.
20. Sally Quinn, *Washington Post,* December 21, 1979.
21. Clifford, "An Examination of the Carter Administration's Selection of Secretary of State and National Security Adviser," p. 10.
22. Quinn, *Washington Post,* December 21, 1979.
23. Ibid.
24. Clifford, "An Examination of the Carter Administration's Selection of Secretary of State and National Security Adviser," pp. 10–11.
25. Interview with Alan Platt, February 16, 1998.
26. Miller Center Interviews, p. 10.
27. Memo, Madeleine Albright to Zbigniew Brzezinski, "Accomplishments and Set-

backs," February 22, 1979, "National Security Affairs, Staff Material, Press and Congressional Relations," Box 3, Madeleine Albright's chronological file, July 1978–March 1979, Jimmy Carter Library.

28. Miller Center Interviews, p. 19.

29. Ibid., p. 11.

30. Memo, Madeleine Albright to Zbigniew Brzezinski, "Accomplishments and Setbacks," February 22, 1979.

31. Kaufman, *The Presidency of James Earl Carter, Jr.*, pp. 88–89; *Facts on File: Weekly World News Digest*, vol. 38, no. 1958 (May 19, 1978), p. 357.

32. Patterson, *America in the Twentieth Century*, p. 474.

33. Kaufman, *The Presidency of James Earl Carter, Jr.*, p. 117.

34. Miller Center Interviews, p. 13.

35. Memo, Madeleine Albright to Zbigniew Brzezinski, "Weekly Legislative Report," April 15, 1978, "National Security Affairs, Staff Material, Press and Congressional Relations," Box 1, Weekly Legislative Reports, April 1977–May 1979, Jimmy Carter Library.

36. *Facts on File: Weekly World News Digest*, vol. 38, no. 1958 (May 19, 1978), p. 357.

37. Memo, Madeleine Albright to Zbigniew Brzezinski, "Overview of 95th Congress," October 20, 1978, "National Security Affairs, Staff Material, Press and Congressional Relations," Box 3, Madeleine Albright's chronological file, July 1978–March 1979, Jimmy Carter Library.

38. Memo, Albright to Brzezinski, "Accomplishments and Setbacks," February 22, 1979.

39. Strobe Talbott, *Deadly Gambits* (New York: Alfred A. Knopf, 1984), pp. 30, 33, 34, 215. Ground-launched cruise missiles and sea-launched cruise missiles.

40. Interview with Karl F. Inderfurth, February 3, 1998.

41. Miller Center Interviews, p. 11.

42. Memo, Albright to Brzezinski, "Accomplishments and Setbacks," February 22, 1979.

43. Miller Center Interviews, p. 11.

44. Ibid.

45. Memo, Madeleine Albright to Zbigniew Brzezinski, "Your Meeting with Senators Culver, Hart, and Leahy on Wednesday, April 26," April 27, 1978, Box FG-27, Jimmy Carter Library.

46. Memo, Madeleine Albright to Zbigniew Brzezinski, "Weekly Legislative Report," November 30, 1979, "National Security Affairs, Staff Material, Press and Congressional Relations," Box 2, Weekly Legislative Reports, June 1979–October 1980, Jimmy Carter Library.

47. Memo, Madeleine Albright to Zbigniew Brzezinski and David Aaron, "Briefing of Senator Hart's Colorado 30 Group," March 22, 1979, Box MC-7, Meetings-Conferences, Zbigniew Brzezinski's Files, Jimmy Carter Library.

48. Brzezinski, December 17, 1997.

49. Interview with Brian Atwood, Washington, D.C., September 17, 1997.

50. Platt, December 18, 1997.

51. Memo, Madeleine Albright to Zbigniew Brzezinski, "Briefing of New Members," November 30, 1978, Box FG-28, Zbigniew Brzezinski's Files, Jimmy Carter Library.

52. Memo, Madeleine Albright to Zbigniew Brzezinski, "Meeting with New Republican Senators," April 11, 1979, Box FO-41, Zbigniew Brzezinski's Files, Jimmy Carter Library.

53. Ibid.

54. Memo, Madeleine Albright to Zbigniew Brzezinski, "Your Lunch with Senator Sam Nunn," May 7, 1979, Box FG-28, Zbigniew Brzezinski's Files, Jimmy Carter Library.

55. Kaufman, *The Presidency of James Earl Carter, Jr.*, pp. 90–91.

56. Memo, Press/Congressional Liaison to Zbigniew Brzezinski, "Evening Report," July 12, 1978, "National Security Affairs, Staff Material, Press and Congressional Relations," Box 3, Madeleine Albright's chronological file, July 1978–March 1979, Jimmy Carter Library.

57. Patterson, *America in the Twentieth Century*, p. 475.

58. Kaufman, *The Presidency of James Earl Carter, Jr.*, p. 176.

59. Miller Center Interviews, p. 56.

60. Confidential source.

61. Confidential source.

62. Miller Center Interviews, p. 23.

63. Ibid., p. 20.

64. Ibid., p. 54.

65. Ibid., p. 50.

66. Interview with Richard Moe, Washington, D.C., July 22, 1997.

67. Memo, Albright to Brzezinski, "Accomplishments and Setbacks," February 22, 1979.

68. Moe, July 22, 1997.

69. Two confidential sources.

CHAPTER 17: DIVORCE

1. In a revelatory interview with the *New York Times Magazine* (Elaine Sciolino, "Madeleine Albright's Audition," September 22, 1996), Albright set the scene.

2. Ibid.

3. Interview with Christine Dodson, October 8, 1997.

4. Confidential source.

5. Two confidential sources.

6. Confidential source.

7. Confidential source.

8. Interview with Marcia Burick, July 29, 1997.

9. Confidential source.

10. Dodson, October 8, 1997.

11. Ibid.

12. Blackman interview with Madeleine Albright, March 1, 1998.

13. Confidential source.

14. Numerous confidential sources. In her book *The Hidden Children* (New York: Bantam, 1993), author Jane Marks interviewed twenty-two individuals who, as children growing up during the Holocaust, were hidden by their parents in hopes that they

would survive. Now adults, several discuss how the pain of divorce forced them to relive the abandonment they felt as children.

Childhood experiences affect everyone differently, so it would be presumptuous and undoubtedly wrong to speculate how the war years affected Albright's outlook as an adult. Yet without being prompted, virtually everyone interviewed for this book mentioned Albright's divorce, usually making the point that it seemed to affect her much more deeply and for much longer than it does most people; that while divorce is always painful, the blow to her self-confidence never really went away.

15. Two confidential sources.
16. Confidential source.
17. Superior Court of District of Columbia, February 2, 1983, *Joseph M. P. Albright v. Madeleine K. Albright.*
18. Interview with Winifred Freund, March 22, 1997.
19. Confidential source.
20. Confidential source.
21. Confidential source.
22. Confidential source.
23. Blackman interview with Madeleine Albright, February 7, 1998.

CHAPTER 18: ON HER OWN

1. Blackman interview with Madeleine Albright, February 7, 1998.
2. Ibid.
3. Interview with Peter Krogh, Washington, D.C., September 9, 1997.
4. Albright, February 7, 1998.
5. Krogh, September 9, 1997.
6. Interview with Nancy Soderberg, Washington, D.C., October 28, 1997.
7. Interview with Jan Kilicki, Washington, D.C., October 7, 1997.
8. Krogh, February 18, 1997.
9. Confidential source.
10. Confidential source.
11. Confidential source.
12. Confidential source.
13. Confidential source.
14. Krogh, September 9, 1997.
15. Interview with Rosemary Neahus, September 11, 1997; interview with Peter Rodman, September 11, 1997.
16. Krogh, September 9, 1997.
17. "Great Decisions 1990," Girard Video, Washington, D.C., the Foreign Policy Association and Georgetown University School of Foreign Service.
18. Ibid.
19. Douglas Waller, *Time,* February 3, 1997.
20. Krogh, September 9, 1997.
21. Waller, *Time,* February 3, 1997.
22. Ibid.

23. Albright, February 7, 1998.
24. Confidential source.
25. Krogh, September 9, 1997.
26. Waller, *Time,* February 3, 1997.
27. Ibid.
28. Interview with Christine Dodson, New York, October 8, 1997.
29. Ibid.

CHAPTER 19: THE GOLDEN GIRLS

1. Blackman interview with Geraldine Ferraro, March 25, 1997.
2. Confidential source.
3. The Fine Arts Committee, U.S. Department of State.
4. Blackman interview with Geraldine Ferraro, *Time,* December 19, 1996.
5. Interview with Gail Sheehy, February 16, 1998.
6. Walter Isaacson, *Kissinger: A Biography* (New York: Simon & Schuster, 1992), p. 700.
7. Interview with John Sasso, September 16, 1997.
8. Geraldine Ferraro, *Ferraro, My Story* (New York: Bantam Books, 1985), p. 118.
9. Ferraro, December 19, 1996.
10. Ibid., May 15, 1997.
11. Confidential source.
12. Ferraro, *Ferraro, My Story,* p. 272.
13. Ibid., pp. 273–74.
14. Ibid., p. 275.
15. Interview with Representative Barbara Kennelly, Washington, D.C., August 1, 1997.
16. Ferraro, March 25, 1997.
17. Ibid.
18. Interview with Senator Barbara Mikulski, Washington, D.C., April 24, 1997.
19. Ferraro, March 25, 1997.
20. Ibid.
21. Ibid.
22. Mikulski, April 24, 1997.
23. Ibid.
24. Ibid.
25. Ibid.
26. Carol Giacomo, "Connecticut's Next Governor," *Connecticut,* November 1983, p. 7.
27. Interview with Barbara Kennelly, August, 1, 1997.
28. Ibid.
29. Ferraro, March 25, 1997.
30. Kennelly, August, 1, 1997.
31. Ibid.
32. Ibid.
33. *New York Times,* September 23, 1997, p. A28.
34. Adam Nagourney, *New York Times,* January 6, 1998, p. A17.
35. *Washington Post,* February 24, 1998, p. B1.

CHAPTER 20: MOVING UP

1. Confidential source.
2. Interview with Christine Dodson, October 8, 1997.
3. Ibid.
4. Ibid.
5. Interview with Patricia O'Brien, February 1, 1998.
6. Christine M. Black and Thomas Oliphant, *All by Myself: The Unmaking of a Presidential Campaign* (Chester, Conn.: Globe Pequot Press, 1989), p. 322. It is a mark of Albright's relatively low profile in the campaign that there are only three references to her in the book, all minor.
7. Estrich was campaign manager, having replaced John Sasso when he resigned on September 30, 1987, for failing to tell Dukakis that he was responsible for sending reporters an attack video against fellow Democratic presidential candidate Joe Biden. Dukakis brought back Sasso just before Labor Day 1988.
8. Interview with Susan Estrich, October 30, 1997.
9. Interview with James Steinberg, Washington, D.C., October 3, 1997.
10. Confidential source.
11. Ibid.
12. Estrich, October 30, 1997.
13. Steinberg, October 3, 1997.
14. Robert Squier interview, April 2, 1998.
15. Black and Oliphant, *All by Myself,* pp. 221–22. Dukakis eventually toughened requirements for furlough eligibility before agreeing to eliminate it.
16. Estrich, October 30, 1997.
17. Ibid.

CHAPTER 21: TRAINING GROUND

1. Confidential source.
2. Interview with Barry Carter, September 18, 1997. On May 17, 1987, Carter married Kathleen Ambrose, a lawyer who had been a scheduler in the Mondale-Ferraro campaign.
3. Interview with Richard Moe, Washington, D.C., July 22, 1997.
4. Interview with Wendy Sherman, Washington, D.C., September 24, 1997.
5. Confidential source.
6. Interview with Maureen Steinbruner, Washington, D.C., September 2, 1997.
7. Sherman, July 23, 1997.
8. Elaine Sciolino, "Madeleine Albright's Audition," *New York Times Magazine,* September 22, 1996, p. 66.
9. Blackman interview with Madeleine Albright, February 7, 1998.

CHAPTER 22: MADAME AMBASSADOR

1. Confidential source.
2. Interview with Nancy Soderberg, the White House, October 28, 1997.
3. Jeffrey H. Birnbaum, *Madhouse: The Private Turmoil of Working for the President* (New York: Random House, 1996), p. 178.
4. Ibid., p. 175.
5. Soderberg, October 28, 1997.
6. Interview with Donna Shalala, Department of Health and Human Services, January 8, 1998.
7. Commerce Secretary Ron Brown and thirty-two other Americans died April 3, 1996, when a U.S. Air Force jet collided with a mountain near Dubrovnik, Croatia.
8. Elizabeth Drew, *On the Edge: The Clinton Presidency*, p. 28.
9. Confidential source.
10. James Walsh, "Flash of War," *Time*, Europe Edition, September 30, 1991.
11. Drew, *On the Edge*, p. 139.
12. Interview with James Rubin, the State Department, November 11, 1997.
13. Ibid.
14. Ibid., January 6, 1998.
15. Interview with Karl Inderfurth, February 3, 1998.
16. Interview with Yuli Vorontsov, embassy of the Russian Federation, Washington, D.C., November 18, 1997.
17. Inderfurth, November 2, 1997.
18. Stanley Meisler, *Los Angeles Times*, October 3, 1993, p. 26.
19. Jeane Kirkpatrick was both a member of Nixon's cabinet and the NSC, as well as the National Security Planning Group, but she did not get along with her boss as well as Albright did.
20. Confidential source.
21. Confidential source.
22. Confidential source.
23. Interview with Deborah Tannen, February 2, 1998.
24. Three confidential sources.
25. Blackman interview with Madeleine Albright, February 13, 1998.
26. The monthly rent went to $28,000 on November 1, 1997, according to the U.N. budget office.
27. Douglas Waller, *Time*, February 3, 1997.
28. Ibid.
29. Meisler, *Los Angeles Times*, October 3, 1993, p. 24.
30. Ibid.
31. Blackman interview with U.N. secretary-general Kofi Annan, United Nations, January 15, 1998.
32. Confidential source.
33. Confidential source.
34. Confidential source.

35. Interview with Sir John Weston, British Mission, New York, January 15, 1998.
36. When she became secretary of state, Albright negotiated a deal with Helms and Senate Republicans to pay the debt, but the bill was voted down by conservative House Republicans over an unrelated provision that funded family-planning programs overseas, which included abortion services.
37. Confidential source.
38. Vorontsov, November 18, 1997.
39. Ibid.
40. Ibid.
41. Confidential source.
42. The women's group included the ambassadors from the United States, Canada, Lichtenstein, Trinidad, Jamaica, Kazakhstan, and the Philippines.
43. Annan, January 15, 1998.
44. Confidential source.
45. Drew, *On the Edge,* p. 142.
46. Ibid., p. 141.
47. Interview with Anthony Lake, Georgetown University, November 20, 1997.
48. Colin Powell, and Joseph E. Persico, *My American Journey* (New York: Random House, 1995), p. 576.
49. Confidential source.
50. Confidential source.
51. Elaine Sciolino, "Madeleine Albright's Audition," *New York Times Magazine,* September 22, 1996, p. 67.
52. Blackman interview with President Bill Clinton, March 4, 1998.
53. Lake, November 20, 1997.
54. Confidential source.
55. Confidential source.
56. Sciolino, "Madeleine Albright's Audition," p. 68.
57. Suzy George, Albright office correspondence, February 3, 1998.
58. Barbara Crossette, *New York Times,* November 25, 1994, p. 1.
59. Waller, *Time,* February 3, 1997.
60. Dobbs, Michael, and John M. Goshko, *Washington Post,* December 6, 1996, p. A25.
61. Interview with David Scheffer, the State Department, October 27, 1997.
62. Waller, *Time,* February 3, 1997.
63. Ibid.
64. Ibid.
65. Two confidential sources.
66. Waller, *Time,* February 3, 1997.
67. Clinton, March 4, 1998.
68. Interview with Christine Dodson, October 8, 1997.
69. George J. Church, "Dropping the Ball?" *Time,* May 2, 1994.
70. Kevin Fedarko, "Policy at Sea," *Time,* July 18, 1994.
71. Sciolino, "Madeleine Albright's Audition," p. 87.
72. Vorontsov, November 18, 1997.
73. Interview with Strobe Talbott, December 22, 1997.

74. Vorontsov, November 18, 1997.
75. Ibid.
76. Ibid.
77. Thomas W. Lippman and John M. Goshko, *Washington Post*, January 7, 1997, p. A1.
78. Ibid.
79. Annan, January 15, 1998.
80. Confidential source.
81. Confidential source.
82. Confidential source.
83. Confidential source.
84. Confidential source.
85. Confidential source.
86. *Facts on File 1995*, vol. 55, no. 2860 (September 21, 1995), p. 687.
87. Confidential source.
88. Confidential source.
89. Interview with Anne Wexler, Washington, D.C., June 24, 1997.
90. Three confidential sources.
91. Confidential source.

CHAPTER 23: THE BRASS RING

1. Interview with Roman Bohuněk, Prague, June 12, 1997.
2. Interview with Melanne Verveer, the White House, September 9, 1997.
3. Interview with Michael McCurry, the White House, October 20, 1997.
4. Confidential source.
5. Confidential source.
6. Douglas Waller, *Time,* February 3, 1997.
7. Elaine Sciolino, *New York Times,* November 24, 1996, p. 1.
8. McCurry, October 20, 1997.
9. Ibid.
10. McCurry, January 19, 1998.
11. Blackman interview with President Bill Clinton, March 4, 1998.
12. Confidential source.
13. Waller, *Time,* February 3, 1997.
14. Confidential source.
15. Confidential source.
16. Confidential source.
17. McCurry, October 20, 1997.
18. Two confidential sources.
19. Interview with Erskine Bowles, the White House, November 14, 1997.
20. McCurry, October 20, 1997.
21. Confidential source.
22. Confidential source.
23. Waller, *Time,* February 3, 1997.
24. Ibid.

25. Interview with Geraldine Ferraro, December 19, 1996.
26. Interview with Marcia Hale, October 23, 1997.
27. Leslie H. Gelb, "Why Not the State Department?" *Washington Quarterly*, Autumn 1980, pp. 25–40.
28. Bowles, November 14, 1997.
29. Ferraro, December 19, 1996.
30. The White House, Office of the Curator.
31. Two confidential sources make the same point; one is quoted.
32. *Washington Post,* December 6, 1996, p. 1
33. Interview with Barbara Mikulski, January 30, 1997.
34. Ibid.
35. Interview with Barbara Kennelly, Washington, D.C., August 1, 1997.
36. Interview with Donna Shalala, January 30, 1997.
37. Confidential source.
38. Clinton, March 4, 1998.
39. Todd S. Purdum, *New York Times,* December 6, 1996, p. 7.
40. Clinton, March 4, 1998.
41. Ibid.

CHAPTER 24: MADAME SECRETARY

1. Interview with Erskine Bowles, November 14, 1997; interview with Elaine Shocas, the State Department, January 20, 1998.
2. Blackman interview with Madeleine Albright, February 7, 1998.
3. Shocas, January 20, 1998.
4. Confidential source.
5. Weston retired from his post in June 1998.
6. Albright press conference, January 24, 1997.
7. CNN-TV, *Larry King Live,* January 24, 1997.

CHAPTER 25: BOMBSHELL

1. Blackman interview with Madeleine Albright, February 7, 1998.
2. Ibid.
3. Interview with Michael Dobbs, June 29, 1997.
4. In an interview in Prague on December 3, 1997, and at the author's request, Dagmar Šímová reviewed the text of everything that she had discussed in previous interviews.
5. Interview with Dagmar Šímová, Prague, June 11, 1997.
6. Ibid.
7. Ibid.
8. Dobbs, June 29, 1997.
9. Two confidential sources; Albright, February 7, 1998.
10. Interview with Emily MacFarquhar, March 31, 1997.
11. Albright, February 7, 1998.

12. MacFarquhar, March 31, 1997.

13. Dobbs, June 29, 1997.

14. Albright, February 7, 1998.

15. Ibid.

16. Ibid.

17. Ibid.

18. Interview with Katharine Graham, January 27, 1998.

19. In 1993, Henry Leon Ritzenthaler wrote Bill Clinton that they are both the sons of William Jefferson Blythe, a traveling salesman who died before Clinton was born. *Newsweek,* February 24, 1997, p. 24. Albright confirmed Clinton's response on February 13, 1997.

20. Two confidential sources.

21. Interview with Barry Schweid, the State Department, May 9, 1997.

22. Ibid.

23. Transcript of the State Department interview.

24. Barry Schweid, Associated Press, April 10, 1997.

25. Šímová, June 11, 1997.

26. Interview with Eduard Goldstucker, Prague, June 9, 1997.

27. "Periscope," *Newsweek,* February 17, 1997.

28. CBS-TV, *60 Minutes,* February 9, 1997.

29. *Newsweek,* February 24, 1997, p. 30.

30. Remarks from the U.S.–Mexico Bilateral Meeting, Houston, Texas, February 8, 1997.

31. ABC-TV, *TheWeek,* February 23, 1997.

32. *Newsweek,* February 17, 1997; interview with James Rubin, January 26, 1998.

33. Albright, February 13, 1998.

34. Helen Epstein, *Children of the Holocaust* (NewYork: Putman's, 1979), p. 138.

35. Albright, February 13, 1998.

36. Walter Isaacson, *Kissinger, A Biography,* p. 26.

37. Ibid., p. 499.

38. *NewYork Times,* February 13, 1997, p. A27.

39. Associated Press, February 13, 1997.

40. Barton Gellman, *NewYork Times,* February 13, 1997, p. A27.

41. Steven Roberts and Cokie Roberts, *Daily News,* February 14, 1997.

42. Philip Taubman, *NewYork Times,* February 9, 1997.

43. Frank Rich, *NewYork Times,* February 19, 1997.

44. Ibid.

45. Ibid., February 26, 1997, p. A29.

46. Interview with Kati Marton, NewYork, April 22, 1997; *Newsweek* column, February 17, 1997.

47. *Newsweek,* February 17, 1997.

48. Ibid.

49. Marton, April 22, 1997.

50. Rubin, January 6, 1998.

51. Several confidential sources.

52. Šímová, June 11, 1997.
53. Ibid.
54. Ibid.
55. Interview with Petr Šilar, June 10, 1997.
56. Šímová, December 3, 1997.
57. Šilar, June 10, 1997; Šímová, June 11, 1997.
58. Interview with Věra Ruprechtová, June 10, 1997.
59. Šilar, June 10, 1997.
60. Ibid.
61. Ibid.
62. Ibid.
63. Interview with Tomáš Kraus, Prague, July 10, 1997.
64. Šímová, June 11, 1997.
65. Ibid.
66. Šímová, July 14, 1997.
67. Confidential source.
68. Gridiron notes.
69. Confidential source.
70. Two confidential sources; interview with Richard Cohen, July 25, 1997.
71. The "pool" is used when a newsmaker decides that there are too many members of the media to cover one event. For routine White House events, the "pool" generally consists of two wire service reporters and photographers, one newspaper reporter and photographer, one television reporter and cameraman, and a radio reporter.
72. Kraus, December 3, 1997.
73. Ibid., July 14, 1997.
74. Albright's remarks, July 13, 1997, Prague.

CHAPTER 26: CELEBRITY

1. Interview with Mark Gearan, November 5, 1997.
2. Walter Isaacson, *Kissinger, A Biography,* p. 356.
3. Interview with Erskine Bowles, November 14, 1997.
4. Blackman, conversation with Robert Rubin, the White House, January 28, 1997.
5. Confidential source.
6. Interview with Stuart Eizenstat, the State Department, January 3, 1997.
7. Ibid.
8. Blackman interview with Madeleine Albright, February 7, 1998.
9. Al Kamen, "In the Loop," *Washington Post,* April 2, 1997.
10. *New York Times,* April 3, 1997, p. D19.
11. Interview with Strobe Talbott, Washington, D.C., December 22, 1997.
12. Republicans took the House in the 1994 elections, giving them total control of Congress for the first time in forty-two years.
13. Douglas Waller, *Time,* June 14, 1997.
14. Thomas W. Lippman, *Washington Post,* March 26, 1997, pp. A1, A14.

15. Kevin Whitelaw and Thomas Omestad, *U.S. News & World Report,* January 19, 1998, p. 46.
16. Interview with Věra Ruprechtová, December 3, 1997.
17. Ibid.
18. Confidential source.
19. Albright, February 7, 1998.
20. Ibid.
21. Interview with James Rubin, January 6, 1997.
22. Talbott, December 22, 1997.
23. "Secretary Albright's First Tour," *Washington Post,* February 26, 1997, p. A18.
24. Waller, *Time,* June 4, 1997.
25. Ibid., May 30, 1997.
26. Confidential source; *South China Morning Post,* January 20, 1998; *The Mirror,* March 31, 1998.
27. Robert Burns, Associated Press, February 7, 1997, a0657.
28. Rubin, January 6, 1997.
29. Transcript of the town meeting, *New York Times,* February 19, 1998, p. 9.
30. Thomas W. Lippman, *Washington Post,* April 21, 1997, pp. A1, A11.
31. Rubin, January 26, 1998.
32. Steven Erlanger, *New York Times,* September 12, 1997, pp. A1, A7.
33. Thomas W. Lippman, *Washington Post,* November 21, 1997, p. A47.
34. Talbott, December 22, 1997.
35. Blackman interview with President Bill Clinton, March 4, 1998.
36. Talbott, December 22, 1997.
37. Strobe Talbott, *Deadly Gambits* (New York: Alfred A. Knopf, 1984), p. 125.
38. "Ms. Albright's Awkward African Tour," *New York Times,* December 17, 1997, p. A34.
39. Albright, February 7, 1998.
40. Thomas Lippman, *Washington Post,* March 25, 1997, pp. A1, A9.
41. Confidential source.
42. Jim Hoagland, *Washington Post,* June 4, 1998, A23.
43. Confidential source.
44. Interview with Jeane Kirkpatrick, Washington, D.C., December 10, 1997.
45. Census Bureau, March 1996 Current Population Survey. There are 7.9 million naturalized Americans.
46. *New York Times,* June 30, 1983.
47. Ibid.
48. Confidential source.
49. Albright, March 1, 1998.
50. Interview with Christine Dodson, October 8, 1997.
51. Ibid.
52. Confidential source.
53. At dinner at The Jefferson, Rubin ordered a fancy bottle of St. Julien, Château Gloria.
54. Rubin, January 6, 1998

55. Albright, February 7, 1998.
56. Ibid., February 13, 1998.
57. Ibid.
58. Confidential source.
59. Confidential source.
60. By law, the secretary of state is fourth in line to succeed the president, behind the vice president, speaker of the House of Representatives, and president pro tempore of the Senate. However, because she is not a "natural born" citizen, Albright is, under the Constitution, ineligible to be president.

Bibliography

BOOKS

Berenbaum, Michael. *The World Must Know*. Boston: Little, Brown and Company, 1993.

Birnbaum, Jeffrey H. *Madhouse: The Private Turmoil of Working for the President*. New York: Random House, 1996.

Black, Christine M., and Thomas Oliphant. *All by Myself: The Unmaking of a Presidential Campaign*. Chester, Conn.: Globe Pequot Press, 1989.

Bradley, J. F. N. *Czecho-Slovakia: A Short History*. Edinburgh: Edinburgh University Press, 1971.

Breck, Allen D. *From the Rockies to the World*. Denver: Hirschfield Press, 1989.

Detzer, David. *The Brink: Cuban Missle Crisis, 1962*. New York: Thomas Y. Crowell, 1979.

Drew, Elizabeth. *On the Edge: The Clinton Presidency*. New York: Simon & Schuster, 1994.

————. *Whatever It Takes*. New York: Viking, 1997.

Drtina, Prokop. *Memoirs*. Vydalo nakladatelstvi Sixty-Eight Publishers, Corp., 1982. Translation by Joe Monik.

Eisenhower, David. *Eisenhower: At War, 1943–1945*. New York: Vintage Books, 1986.

Epstein, Helen. *Children of the Holocaust*. New York: G. P. Putman's Sons, 1979.

Ferraro, Geraldine. *Ferraro, My Story*. New York: Bantam Books, 1985.

Friedan, Betty. *The Feminine Mystique*. New York: W. W. Norton & Company, Inc., 1963.

Gawdiak, Ihor, ed. *Czechoslovakia, A Country Study*, 3rd ed. Washington, D.C.: Library of Congress, Federal Research Division, 1989.

Gilbert, Martin. *Second World War*. London: Weidenfeld and Nicolson Ltd., 1989.

Goodwin, Doris Kearns. *Wait 'Til Next Year, A Memoir*. New York: Simon & Schuster, 1997.

Graham, Katharine. *Personal History.* New York: Alfred A. Knopf, 1997.

Halberstam, David. *The Fifties.* New York: Villard Books, 1993.

————. *The Unfinished Odyssey of Robert Kennedy.* New York: Bantam Books, 1968.

Hastings, Max. *Victory in Europe.* Boston: Little, Brown and Company, 1985.

Hoge, Alice Albright. *Cissy Patterson.* New York: Random House, 1966.

Inderfurth, Karl F., and Loch K. Johnson. *Decisions of the Highest Order: Perspectives on the National Security Council.* Pacific Grove, Calif.: Brooks/Cole Publishing Company, 1988.

Isaacson, Walter. *Kissinger: A Biography.* New York: Simon & Schuster, 1992.

Karneho, Miroslava, ed. *Terezininska pametni kniha.* (Terezin Memorial Book.) Prague: Terezinska iniciativa, 1995.

Kaufman, Burton I. *The Presidency of James Earl Carter, Jr.* Lawrence: University Press of Kansas, 1993.

Kee, Robert. *Munich: The Eleventh Hour.* London: Hamish Hamilton Ltd., 1988.

Keeler, Robert F. *Newsday.* New York: Arbor House, 1990.

Kennan, George. *From Prague After Munich, Diplomatic Papers 1938–1940.* Princeton, N.J.: Princeton University Press, 1968.

Kertesz, Stephen D. *The Fate of East Central Europe: Hopes and Failures of American Foreign Policy.* Notre Dame, Ind.: University of Notre Dame Press, 1956.

Lincoln Library of Essential Information, The, 34th ed., vol. 1. Columbus, Ohio: The Frontier Press Company, 1971.

Maraniss, David. *First in His Class.* New York: Simon & Schuster, 1995.

McCullough, David. *Truman.* New York: Simon & Schuster, 1992.

Mosley, Leonard. *Battle of Britain.* New York: Time-Life Books Inc., 1977.

Ogden, Christopher. *Life of the Party: The Biography of Pamela Digby Churchill Hayward Harriman.* New York: Little, Brown and Company, 1994.

Paris Peace Conference, 1946: Selected Documents. Department of State. Publication 2868. Conference Series 103. Washington, D.C.: U.S. Government Printing Office.

Patterson, James T. *America in the Twentieth Century: A History,* 3rd ed. New York: Harcourt Brace Jovanovich, Inc., 1989.

Powell, Colin, and Joseph E. Persico. *My American Journey.* New York: Random House, 1995.

Reston, James. *Deadline: A Memoir.* New York: Random House, 1991.

Rybar, Ctibor. *Jewish Prague.* Prague: TV Spektrum, 1991.

Seton-Watson, Hugh. *The East European Revolution.* London: Methuen & Co. Ltd., 1950.

Singer, Dorothy G., and Tracey A. Revenson. *A Piaget Primer: How a Child Thinks.* New York: A Plume Book, New American Library, 1978.

Stransky, Jan. *East Wind Over Prague.* New York: Random House, 1951.

Talbott, Strobe. *Deadly Gambits.* New York: Alfred A. Knopf, 1984.

Weinberg, Gerhard L. *A World At Arms: A Global History of World War II.* New York: Cambridge University Press, 1994.

Who's Who in America. Chicago: Marquis Who's Who Inc., 1984.

Wiesel, Elie. *Night.* New York: Hill & Wang, 1960.

Willmott, H. P. *The Great Crusade: A New Complete History of the Second World War.* New York: The Free Press, 1989.

Woodward, Bob. *The Agenda: Inside the Clinton White House.* New York: Simon & Schuster, 1994.

Zinner, Paul E. *Communist Strategy and Tactics in Czechoslovakia, 1918–1948.* New York: Frederick A. Praeger, 1963.

ARTICLES

Associated Press, February 3, 1997 and February 13, 1987.

Burns, Robert. Associated Press, February 7, 1997.

Chicago Sun-Times, May 23, 1959; June 16, 1959; and November 1, 1961.

Church, George J. "Dropping the Ball?" *Time,* May 2, 1994.

Clifford, Lawrence X. "An Examination of the Carter Administration's Selection of Secretary of State and National Security Adviser." In *Jimmy Carter: Foreign Policy and Post-Presidential Years,* edited by Herbert D. Rosenbaum and Alexej Ugrinsky. Westport, Conn.: Greenwood Press, Hofstra University, 1994.

Crossette, Barbara. *New York Times,* November 25, 1994.

Dobbs, Michael. "Out of the Past." *Washington Post Magazine,* February 9, 1997.

Erlanger, Steven. *New York Times,* September 12, 1997.

Fedarko, Kevin. "Policy at Sea." *Time,* July 18, 1994.

Gelb, Lesley H. "Why Not the State Department?" *Washington Quarterly,* Autumn 1980.

Gellman, Barton. *New York Times,* February 13, 1997.

Germer, Fawn. *Rocky Mountain News,* December 6, 1996.

Giacomo, Carol. "Connecticut's Next Governor." *Connecticut,* November 1987.

Goshko, John M. *Washington Post,* December 6, 1996.

Grimsley, Kirstin Downey. "Avon Calling . . . on a Man." *Washington Post,* December 12, 1997.

Henneberger, Melinda. *New York Times,* December 14, 1997.

Hill, Annie. *Denver Post,* December 6, 1996.

"Jan Masaryk of Czechoslovakia: Which Truth Will Prevail?" *Time,* March 27, 1944. Reproduced from the collections of the Manuscript Division, Library of Congress.

Kamen, Al. *Washington Post,* April 2, 1997.

Laqueur, Walter. "Madeleine Albright and Jewish Identity." *New Republic,* March 10, 1997.

Lippman, Thomas W., and John M. Goshko. *Washington Post,* January 7, 1997.

Lippman, Thomas W. *Washington Post,* March 25, 1997; March 26, 1997; April 21, 1997; and November 21, 1997.

Meisler, Stanley. *Los Angeles Times,* October 3, 1993.

Mitchell, Alison. *New York Times,* December 6, 1996.

"Ms. Albright's Awkward African Tour." *New York Times,* December 17, 1997.

Myers, Steven Lee. *New York Times,* March 26, 1997.

Nagourney, Adam. *New York Times,* January 6, 1997.

Newsweek, February 17, 1997 and February 24, 1997.

New York Times, December 29, 1958; June 30, 1983; February 13, 1997; April 3, 1997; August 16, 1997; and September 23, 1997

Paris, Barry. "Profiles: Unconquerable." *New Yorker,* April 22, 1991.

"Periscope," *Newsweek,* February 17, 1997.

Politika, September 29, 1945.

Purdum, Todd S. *New York Times,* December 6, 1996.

Putzel, Anne B. *Piaget and Education,* November 2, 1979.

Quinn, Sally. *Washington Post,* December 21, 1979.

Rich, Frank. *New York Times,* February 19, 1997 and February 26, 1997.

Roberts, Steven, and Cokie Roberts. *Daily News,* February 14, 1997.

Safire, William. "The New-Boy Network." *New York Times,* February 20, 1975.

Schweid, Barry. Associated Press, April 10, 1997.

Sciolino, Elaine. "Madeleine Albright's Audition." *New York Times Magazine,* September 22, 1996.

"Secretary Albright's First Tour." *Washington Post,* February 26, 1997.

Simor, George F., M.D. *Psychiatric Times,* vol. xiv, no. 10 (October 1997).

Sunday Mirror, February 28, 1988.

Taubman, Philip. *New York Times,* February 9, 1997.

Time, June 20, 1960; May 10, 1968; and January 31, 1977.

Walsh, James. "Flash of War." *Time,* Europe Edition, September 30, 1991.

Wellesley College News.

Whitelaw, Kevin, and Thomas Omestad. *U.S. News & World Report,* January 19, 1998.

ARCHIVES

Albright, Joseph Medill Patterson. *Joseph Medill Patterson: Right or Wrong, American.* May 1958. Williams College archives.

Albright, Madeleine, memo to Zbigniew Brzezinski and David Aaron. "Briefing of Senator Hart's Colorado 30 Group," March 22, 1979. Box MC-7, Meetings-Conferences. Zbigniew Brzezinski's Files, Jimmy Carter Library.

Albright, Madeleine, memo to Zbigniew Brzezinski. "Accomplishments and Setbacks," February 22, 1979. "National Security Affairs, Staff Material, Press and Congressional Relations," Box 3, Madeleine Albright's chronological file, July 1978–March 1979, Jimmy Carter Library.

Albright, Madeleine, memo to Zbigniew Brzezinski. "Briefing of New Members," November 30, 1978. Box FG-28, Zbigniew Brzezinski's Files, Jimmy Carter Library.

Albright, Madeleine, memo to Zbigniew Brzezinski. "Overview of 95th Congress," October 20, 1978. "National Security Affairs, Staff Material, Press and Congressional Relations," Box 3, Madeleine Albright's chronological file, July 1978–March 1979, Jimmy Carter Library.

Albright, Madeleine, memo to Zbigniew Brzezinski. "Weekly Legislative Report," April 15, 1978. "National Security Affairs, Staff Material, Press and Congressional Relations," Box 1, Weekly Legislative Reports, April 1977–May 1979, Jimmy Carter Library.

Albright, Madeleine, memo to Zbigniew Brzezinski. "Weekly Legislative Report," November 30, 1979. "National Security Affairs, Staff Material, Press and Congressional Relations," Box 2, Weekly Legislative Reports, June 1979–October 1980, Jimmy Carter Library.

Albright, Madeleine, memo to Zbigniew Brzezinski. "Your Lunch with Senator Sam Nunn," May 7, 1979, Box FG-28, Zbigniew Brzezinski's Files, Jimmy Carter Library.

Albright, Madeleine, memo to Zbigniew Brzezinski. "Your Meeting with Senators Culver, Hart, and Leahy on Wednesday, April 26," April 27, 1978, Box FG-27, Jimmy Carter Library.

BBC Archives: *Use of Gas Against the Jews.*

Brusak, Karel. *Notes on the Czechoslovak Section.* BBC Written Archives Centre.

Brzezinski, Zbigniew, interview with Madeleine Albright, Leslie Denend, and William Odom. Miller Center Interviews, Carter Presidency Project, vol. XV, February 18, 1982, Jimmy Carter Library.

Cherrington, Ben M. *A Personal Reminiscence.* The Social Science Foundation of the University of Denver 1926–1951. Graduate School of International Studies, 1973.

Columbia University's Graduate School of Arts and Sciences.

Czech Republic, Ministry of Foreign Affairs.

Czech Republic, Ministry of Foreign Affairs, cable 10241/A/49.

Czech Republic, Ministry of Foreign Affairs, cable 19.

Czech Republic, Ministry of Foreign Affairs, cable 7564/A/49.

"Documents from the History of Czechoslovak Politics, 1939–1943: Relations of International Diplomacy to Czechoslovak Exiles in the West." Prague: Czechoslovak National Academy Publishers, 1966.

Edmund S. Muskie Archives, Bates College, Lewiston, Maine.

Imperial War Museum brochure on the Morrison "Table" Shelter.

Imperial War Museum data.

Korbel, Josef, letter with return address, December 20, 1950. National Archives.

Korbel, Josef, February 12, 1948, letter to Warren R. Austin, U.S. Rep. to the United Nations, requesting political asylum in the United States. National Archives.

Korbel, Josef, press statement attached to his February 12, 1949, request for political asylum in the United States. National Archives.

Korbel, Josef, *Memorandum on J. Korbel's Conversation with Mr. V. Clementis.* Columbia University Rare Book and Manuscript Library, Bakhmeteff Archives, April 5, 1949.

Korbel, Josef, official file at the Czech Ministry of Foreign Affairs, Prague.

Korbel, Josef, official résumé from the University of Denver, Denver, Colorado.

Korbel, Josef, letter to Mr. John C. Campbell, December 20, 1950. National Archives.

Korbel, Josef, personal letter to Secretary of State Dean Acheson. National Archives.

Korbel, Mandula. Personal essay.

Kraus, Tomas, Nazi files collected by the Federation of Jewish Communities, Prague.

News & Mail Series, February 19, 1997.

Papánek, Jan, papers, Library of Congress.

Power, Thomas F., Jr., confidential memo, March 14, 1949. National Archives.

Power, Thomas F., Jr., letter to Ambassador Jessup, U.S. Delegation to the Council of Foreign Ministers, titled "Dr. Korbel's Status," June 9, 1949. National Archives.

Press/Congressional Liaison, memo to Zbigniew Brzezinski. "Evening Report," July 12, 1978. "National Security Affairs, Staff Material, Press and Congressional Relations," Box 3, Madeleine Albright's chronological file, July 1978–March 1979, Jimmy Carter Library.

Resolutions and Decisions of the Security Council, 1948. "Resolution of 20 January 1948"; "Resolution of 21 April 1948."

Ripka, Hubert. *We Think of You.* Library of Congress, Manuscript Division. Published by the Czechoslovak Maccabi, London, 1941.

"Speaking Engagements of Dr. Josef Korbel, January 30, 1951 to November 5, 1951."The Social Science Foundation of the University of Denver, Graduate School of International Studies, 1973.

SS *America* manifest. National Archives and Records Administration of New York.

SS *Queen Mary* manifest. National Archives and Records Administration of New York.

Stevenson, Adlai, letter. Seeley G. Mudd Library, Princeton University.

Superior Court of District of Columbia, February 2, 1983, *Joseph M. P. Albright* v *Madeleine K. Albright.*

University of Denver Archives.

U.S. District Court, Denver.

Wellesley Alumnae Report.

Wellesley Class of 1959 Record Book, 1974.

Wellesley College Archives.

MISCELLANEOUS

Arrandale Elementary School graduation program.

Census Bureau. March 1996 Current Population Survey.

CIA reply to FOIA appeal, May 30, 1997.

Facts on File:Weekly World News Digest. New York: Facts on File, Inc.

Gridiron notes, 1998.

Memorial Service for Josef Korbel, July 20, 1977. "Personal Thoughts on Josef Korbel," Graduate School of International Studies, University of Denver.

Stránský, Jan M., correspondence, October 14, 1997.

The Fine Arts Committee, U.S. Department of State.

The White House. Office of the Curator.

TELEVISION AND VIDEO

ABC-TV, *The Week,* February 23, 1997.

CBS-TV, *60 Minutes,* February 9, 1997.

CNN-TV, *Larry King Live,* January 24, 1997.

Great Decisions, 1990. Girard Video, Washington, D.C., Foreign Policy Association and Georgetown School of Foreign Service.

NPR, *Car Talk,* March 28, 1997.

MADELEINE ALBRIGHT PUBLIC SPEECHES AND COMMENTS

Comments in Prague, July 13, 1997.

Press Conference, January 24, 1997.

Remarks at swearing-in ceremony, The White House, January 23, 1997.

Remarks from the U.S.–Mexico Bilateral Meeting, Houston, Texas, February 8, 1997.

MADELEINE ALBRIGHT CORRESPONDENCE

Response to written questions, January 13, 1998.

WORKS BY MADELEINE KORBEL ALBRIGHT

Albright, Madeleine Korbel. *The Role of the Press in Political Change: Czechoslovakia 1968.* Columbia University, Ph.D. dissertation, 1976, Political Science, International Law and Relations.

Albright, Madeleine. *The Soviet Diplomatic Service: Profile of an Elite.* Russian Institute, Columbia University.

Korbel, Madeleine Jana. *Zdenek Fierlinger's Role in the Communization of Czechoslovakia: The Profile of a Fellow Traveler.* Wellesley College, Wellesley Massachusetts, 1959.

WORKS BY JOSEF KORBEL

Korbel, Josef. *Tito's Communism.* Denver, Colo.: University of Denver Press, 1951.

Korbel, Josef. *Danger In Kashmir.* Princeton, N.J.: Princeton University Press, 1954.

Korbel, Josef. *The Communist Subversion of Czechoslovakia, 1938–1948: The Failure of Coexistence.* Princeton, N.J.: Princeton University Press, 1959.

Korbel, Josef. *Poland Between East and West: Soviet and German Diplomacy Toward Poland, 1919–1933.* Princeton, N.J.: Princeton University Press, 1963.

Korbel, Josef. *Detente in Europe: Real or Imaginary?* Princeton, N.J.: Princeton University Press, 1972.

Korbel, Josef. *Twentieth-Century Czechoslovakia, The Meaning of Its History.* New York: Columbia University Press, 1977.

——*Documents*

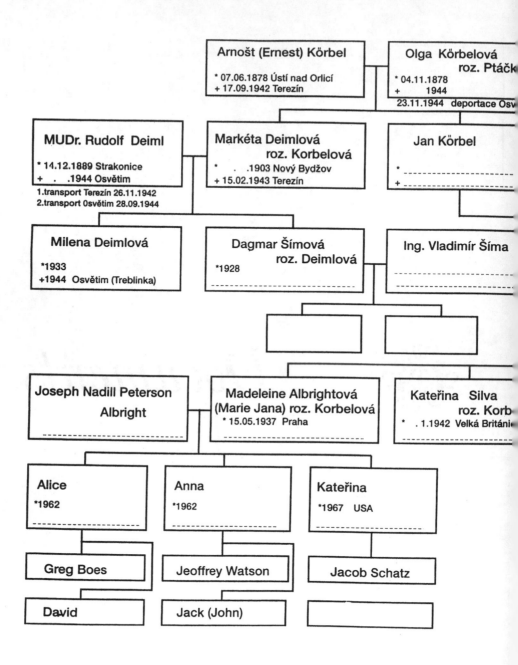

Arnošt (Ernest) Körbel

* 07.06.1878 Ústí nad Orlicí
\+ 17.09.1942 Terezín

**Olga Körbelová
roz. Ptáčk**

* 04.11.1878
\+   1944
23.11.1944 deportace Osv

MUDr. Rudolf Deiml

* 14.12.1889 Strakonice
\+   .   .1944 Osvětim
1.transport Terezín 26.11.1942
2.transport Osvětim 28.09.1944

**Markéta Deimlová
roz. Korbelová**

*   .   .1903 Nový Bydžov
\+ 15.02.1943 Terezín

Jan Körbel

* _____
\+ _____

Milena Deimlová

*1933
\+1944 Osvětim (Treblinka)

**Dagmar Šímová
roz. Deimlová**

*1928

Ing. Vladimír Šíma

**Joseph Nadill Peterson
Albright**

**Madeleine Albrightová
(Marie Jana) roz. Korbelová**
* 15.05.1937 Praha

**Kateřina Silva
roz. Korb**

*   . 1.1942 Velká Británi

Alice

*1962

Anna

*1962

Kateřina

*1967   USA

Greg Boes

Jeoffrey Watson

Jacob Schatz

David

Jack (John)

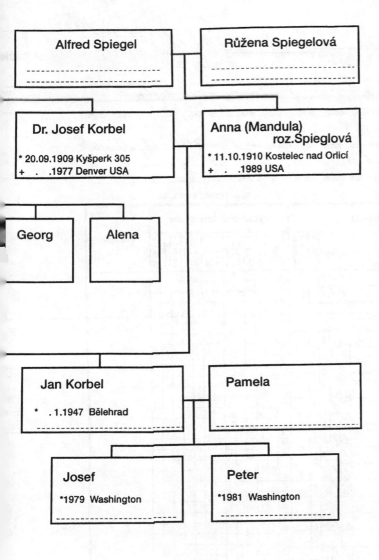

Madeleine Korbel Albright's family tree, as supplied by Letohrad mayor Petr Šilar.

Str. *14.*

oddělení.

Jméno a příjmení dítěte __*Josef Körbel*__

Číslo řadné *14.*

narozen(a) dne __*20. září*__ 19*09* v __*Kyšperku*__,

náboženství __*židovského*__, příslušný(á) domovem do

__*Kyšperka*__ v okresu __*žamberském*__ v __*Čechách*__

*pře*očkovaný(á), začal(a) choditi do školy vůbec dne __*16. září 1915*__, do školy zdejší

dne __*16. září 1915*__

Jméno, stav a bydliště (číslo domu) otce (nebo matky) __*Arnošt Körbel, obchodník*__

v Kyšperku č. 305.

Jméno, stav a bydliště (čís. domu) poručníka (nebo stravovatele) __*týž*__

Opatrovnický soud:

Klasifikace						Výkaz docházky školní													Poznámky
ve čtvrtletí	I.	II.	III.	IV.	Vysvědčení propouštěcí	dne	září	říjen	listopadu	prosince	ledna	února	března	dubna	května	června	července	srpna	
Mravy	1	1	1	1		1.														
						2.														
Pilnost	1	1	1	1		3.														
						4.	⌀													
Prospěch:						5.								⌀						
						6.														
v náboženství	2	1	1			7.														
						8.														
v jazyce vyučovacím	ve čtení	1	1	1	1		9.													
	v mluvnici a pravopise	2	2	2	1		10.													
						11.														
	ve slohu	1	1	1	1		12.													
ve vlastivědě	1	1	1	1		13.	⌀													
						14.	⌀													
v počtech s měřictvím	1	1	1	1		15.														
v kreslení	2	2	2	2		16.	⌀													
						17.														
v psaní	2	2	3	2		18.														
						19.														
ve zpěvu	2	1	1	1		20.														
v tělocviku	1	1	1	1		21.														
						22.														
v ženských ručních pracích	-	-				23.														
v jazyce německém	3	2	1	1		24.														
						25.														
						26.														
Vnější úprava písemných prací	2	2	2	2		27.														
						28.														
Za- meškal(a) půldnů	omluvených	8			2		29.													
	neomluvených						30.													
						31.														
Měsíční součet půldnů zameškaných	omluvených							8								2			
	neomluvených																		

Jest ∼ způsobilý(á) postoupiti do vyšší třídy (vyššího oddělení).

Přesídlil(a) dne _____ do _____

Josef Körbel's fifth-grade report card from his elementary school in Letohrad. It covers the school year 1919–20 and shows that he was a good student, getting all 1s and 2s in his subjects, on a scale of 5. His best subjects that year were religion, the Czech language, civics, math, and music. He was also a conscientious student. The report card shows he missed only two days of school. It lists his religion as Jewish.

Anno 19*1*0 die *11* mensis *Maii* nat *9* et anno 19*41* die *31* mensis *Maii*
baptizat a est *Anna Körbelová*
fili a *Alfredi Spiegel* et *Rosa Sadu-sova* (olim ,) conjugum:
a me *Anselmo Spaček, delegato* a Parocho vel Vicario
Patrinus fuit
Matrina fuit *Cisařová Antonie*

Anno 19*37* die *15* mensis *Maii* nat *9* et anno 19*41* die *31* mensis *Maii*
baptizat a est *Maria Joanna Körbelova*
fili a *Josephi Körbel* et *Annae Spieglová* (olim) conjugum:
a me *Anselmo Spaček, delegato* a Parocho vel Vicario
Patrinus fuit
Matrina fuit *Cisařová Antonie*

Anno 19*06* die *25* mensis *Augustus* nat *mo* et anno 19*42* die *15* mensis *Junii*
baptizat us est *Joannes Körbel*
fili us *Arnošt* et *Olga* (olim *Pták̄ova*) conjugum:
a me *P. Anselmo Spaček, delegato* a Parocho vel Vicario
Patrinus fuit *Prof. Jaroslavus Stránský*
Matrina fuit

Photocopy of the baptism registrations of Anna (Mandula) Körbel, Madeleine Körbel (Maria Joanna Körbelova), and Joannes (*sic*) Körbel, who was Madeleine's uncle, known to the family as Jan. *(Courtesy of Jan M. Stránský and the Catholic Church of Berkhamsted)*

MRS. M. F. E. PALMER-MOREWOOD

-to-

J. KORBEL ESQ.

C O N V E Y A N C E

of freehold land and premises known
as The Old Cottage, Bank Mill Lane,
Berkhamsted in the County of Herts.

xd.

Deed to The Old Cottage on Bank Mill Lane,
the Berkhamsted house purchased in 1942
for £5,000 by John Korbel, Madeleine's
uncle, who was known to the family as Jan.
(Courtesy of Inge Woolf, the current owner)

THIS CONVEYANCE is made the ~~tich~~ day
of ~~February~~ One thousand nine hundred and forty two BETWEEN MARY
FORBES ELEANOR PALMER-MOREWOOD of Lower Kings Road Berkhamsted in the
County of Herts formerly of "Two Oaks" Bushfield Road Bovingdon in the
same County Married Woman (hereinafter called "the Vendor") of the one
part and JOHN KORBEL of 20 Vivian Way Finchley in the County of Middlesex
(hereinafter called "the Purchaser") of the other part
WHEREAS the Vendor is seised of the property hereinafter described for
an estate in fee simple in possession and has agreed to sell the same to
the Purchaser free from incumbrances for the sum of One thousand six
hundred and fifty pounds NOW THIS DEED WITNESSETH that in consideration of the sum of One thousand six hundred and fifty pounds paid to the
Vendor by the Purchaser (the receipt whereof the Vendor hereby acknowledges) the Vendor as Beneficial Owner HEREBY CONVEYS unto the Purchaser FIRST ALL THAT piece or parcel of land situate opposite the gate
of New Lodge Bank Mill Lane Berkhamsted in the County of Herts TOGETHER
with the Cottage erected and standing thereon or on part thereof and known
as The Old Cottage (formerly known as The Rustic Cottage) and the barn
garden and orchard thereto belonging all which said premises contain an
area of half an acre and are more particularly delineated and described
(by way of identification only and not by way of limitation or otherwise)
in the map or plan annexed to a Conveyance dated the twelfth day of
August One thousand nine hundred and thirty three and made between the
said Lancelot Desmond Fellows of the one part and the Vendor of the other
part and thereon coloured green SECONDLY ALL THAT piece or parcel of
land containing an area of one acre and twenty five perches situate adjoining the premises first hereinbefore described on the East or southeast being the piece or parcel of land numbered 52 on the Ordnance map
(old issue) for the Parish of Northchurch and more particularly delineated and described (by way of identification only) on the said map or plan
annexed to the said Conveyance and thereon coloured pink TO HOLD unto
the Purchaser in fee simple.

IN WITNESS whereof the parties hereto have hereunto set their hands
and seals the day and year first above written.

SEALED AND DELIVERED by the
said MARY FORBES ELEANOR
MOREWOOD in the presence of:-

E. F. E. Palmer-Morewood

R. J. Baylin.
25. Castle Street
Berkhamsted. Herts.

DATED 15ᵗʰ April 1954.

J. KORBEL ESQ.

— to —

M. G. DIXON ESQ.

C O N V E Y A N C E

- of -

The Old Cottage, Bank Mill Lane, Berkhamsted, Herts.

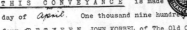

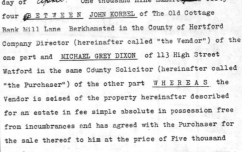

T H I S   C O N V E Y A N C E   is made   day of April. One thousand nine hundred and fifty-four B E T W E E N   JOHN KORBEL of The Old Cottage Bank Mill Lane Berkhamsted in the County of Hertford Company Director (hereinafter called "the Vendor") of the one part and MICHAEL GREY DIXON of 113 High Street Watford in the same County Solicitor (hereinafter called "the Purchaser") of the other part W H E R E A S the Vendor is seised of the property hereinafter described for an estate in fee simple absolute in possession free from incumbrances and has agreed with the Purchaser for the sale thereof to him at the price of Five thousand pounds ——————————————————————

N O W   THIS DEED   W I T N E S S E T H   that in consideration of FIVE THOUSAND POUNDS paid by the Purchaser to the Vendor (the receipt whereof the Vendor hereby acknowledges) the Vendor as Beneficial Owner hereby conveys unto the Purchaser FIRST ALL THAT piece of land situate opposite the gate of New Lodge Bank Mill Lane Berkhamsted in the County of Hertford TOGETHER with the messuage and premises erected thereon and known as The Old Cottage All which premises contain an area of half an acre or thereabouts and are more particularly delineated and described (by way of identification only and not by way of limitation or otherwise) on the plan annexed to a Conveyance dated the Twelfth day of August One thousand nine hundred and thirty-three and made between Lancelot

Desmond Fellows of the one part and Mary Forbes Eleanor Palmer-Morewood of the other part and thereon coloured green AND SECONDLY ALL THAT piece of land containing an area of one acre twenty-five perches or thereabouts situate adjoining the premises first hereinbefore described on the East or South East as the same is more particularly delineated and described (by way of ident-ification) on the said plan and thereon coloured pink TO HOLD the same unto the Purchaser in fee simple ————

IN WITNESS whereof the parties hereto have hereunto set their hands and seals the day and year first above written ——————————————————————

SIGNED SEALED and DELIVERED by   }
the said JOHN KORBEL in the
presence of :-

Witness   Name A S Craig
                "Bookbinn"
                55 Victoria Rd
                Holywood Co Down N J
          Occupation Secretary Director

Berkhamsted School for Girls S

DEIMLOVA' Christian Names } Daša

of Father } Dr. Joseph Korbel Postal Address at
Guardian

Birth	
Year	28

Admission	
Year	40

of Last Attendance	
Year	44

on Admission

U. III . A .

Position on Leaving

U v B .

Boarder or Day-Scholar

Day Girl
Boarder Spring 1944

7. Terms kept

Autumn	Spring	Summer
'40	41	41
41	42	42
42	43	43
43	44	44

8. **Place of Residence**

1. County Borough or

2. Borough, Urban District or Parish ... **Berkhamsted**

County in which situate ... **Herts.**

9. Occupation late occupation deceased or

Dr. Josep

Official of

Czechoslov

Office.

11. **Particulars of any Special Place held or of any Exemption from Tuition Fees**

(a) Particulars of SPECIAL PLACE AWARD (whether carrying any remission of fees or not)	(b) Particulars of any exemption from Tuition fees other than a Special Place award		N.
		Total Exemption	Partial Exemption
(i) Granted from (Date)	(i) Granted from (Date)		
(ii) Granted by (i.e. Body financially responsible)	(ii) Granted by (i.e. Body financially responsible)		
(iii) Extent of remission of fees. Enter "Total" "Partial" or "None"	(iii) If Art. 15 award enter "Art. 15"		
	(iv) Tenable for		

14. **Particulars of any Scholarship or Exhibition for further education to be held elsewhere.**

Name of Scholarship

Name of Body awarding

1. If no entry in Head employment taken up, or ho occupied.

left to Czecho
School.

Sex	B. or D.	Status	P.E.	Father's Occup'n	Stat. Year	Age on Admn.	Transfer in

No. 2307

Sex....*Female*....

Cottage, Bank Mill, Berkhamsted.

, or
is

10. Previous Education

el

1. Is this the first Secondary School attended....~~Date~~ *No.*
   (*enter "yes" or "no"*)

2. If so, did the pupil attend a Public Elementary School(s) in England
   or Wales for at least two years immediately preceding admission.... *No.*
   (*enter "yes" or "no"*)

gn

3. If not, give names of all
   schools previously attended,
   whether Elementary,
   Secondary or other, with dates .... *Danesfield Girls School, Walton-on-Thames.*

ticulars of Public Examinations taken.

in this space should be confined to the exam-
below, and when taken as a whole. Passes in
ects or in other examinations may be recorded
the form.

13. If proceeding to an Institution for full-time further
    education enter, in the appropriate space below, the
    name of the Institution.

Date of Examination.	Did the pupil pass the examination as a whole. (State Yes or No.)
ificate or Matriculation.	
ificate or Intermediate for a University Degree.	

University ....

University Training Dept. ....

*Training College recognised under the Regulations for the
Training of Teachers* ....

Secondary School ....

e   16. Remarks

Public Elementary School ....

Any other type of full-time Institution .....

Period of Exit	Transfer out	Sch. Cert.	Age at Leaving	Sch. Life	Occup'n	Sch'p	Hr. Cert.	

Dagmar Deimlová's report card from the Berkhamsted School for Girls. It lists
her guardian as Joseph (*sic*) Korbel. (*Courtesy of the Berkhamsted Collegiate School,
Berkhamsted, Herts, England*)

```
P r a h a  XIII.

Körbel Arnošt  7.6.1878
           30.7.1942 AAv 452 Terezín
           18.9.1942 zemřel        "

         Olga    4.11.1878
           30.7.1942 AAv 451 Terezín
          ,23.10.1944 Et 55 Osvětím
```

Nazi card file showing transport of Madeleine Albright's grandparents, Olga and Arnošt Körbel.

srpen 16. Londýn. — *Dopis E. Beneše poslanci Fr. Schwartzovi v Londýně, v němž formuloval své zásady zahraniční akce politické, diplomatické a vojenské.*

51/39/A

Dne 16. srpna 1939.

poslanec Ing. Schwartz,

Londýn.

Vážený pane poslanče,[1])

Na Váš včerejší dopis Vám sděluji, že pro nějaké další účelné rozhodnutí potřebuji míti nové zprávy z Varšavy, o které jsme společně s gen. Ingrem žádali v pondělí. Proto jsem Vás žádal o odložení rozmluvy. — Jsem rád, že jste poradil gen. Prchalovi, aby přijel do Londýna.

Sděluji Vám také to, oč ve svém dopise žádáte:

1) Věci krajanské.

Po objektivní úvaze soudím, že zdejší ústředí dá našim krajanům v Polsku vysvětlení, jak věci se od počátku měly v Americe, že naši krajané organisují výlučně *svou* akci *krajanskou* sociální, kulturní a propagační, kdežto ve vedení věcí vojenských, politických a diplomatických účasti nemají a účasti míti nemohou. To musí býti reservováno centrálnímu vedení vojensko-politickému. Ukáže se tím, že se tím nikomu v Polsku nekřivdí, protože je to všude stejné — ve Francii, v Anglii i v Americe.

2) Zásady, jimiž se naše práce řídí[2]) a jež jsem Vám přečetl ze svých poznámek a slíbil, že Vám je dám písemně, jsou tyto:

a) Musí býti jednotné vedení politické a vojenské, jemuž bude všecka naše práce ve všech zemích podléhat. To si přeje každý také doma ve vlasti.

[1]) J. Smutný použil dopisu ke své nedokončené studii „Utvoření, práce i konec Národního výboru," z níž byl citovaný dokument rekonstruován. Viz také dokument č. 128.

[2]) Ve snaze vytvořit na západě kádrovou platformu pro zahraniční akci, sestavili na jaře 1939 Benešovi stoupenci v Paříži tzv. listinu ohrožených lidí, kterým mělo být umožněno odejít do emigrace. Seznam byl zaslán J. Smutnému do Istambulu, který dne 29. března 1939 potvrdil jeho příjem: „...ohledně našich lidí, jichž listinu jsi mi poslal, udělám opatření u vlád jihoslovanské, rumunské a bulharské (event.), aby jejich vyslanci v Praze dali jim visa a byli jim nápomocni." Viz AÚD KSČ, 37—50/1/115—116. Dne 31. března 1939 sdělil J. Smutný dopisem vyslanci J. Lípovi do Bělehradu, že má vzkaz od E. Beneše, aby se odebral na západ. K dopisu přiložil kopii seznamu „některých našich lidí. Mnozí z nich jsou ohroženi, z nich by byli potřebí za hranicemi. Myslíš-li, že by jihoslovanská vláda dala pokyn vyslanci v Praze, aby udělil visa ke vstupu do Jihoslavie alespoň některým z nich, máš-li možnost v tomto smyslu to projednat ještě aniž by tím byla porušena diskretnost a lidé tito v důsledku toho ještě více ohroženi, udělej co uznáš za vhodné a možné". Viz AÚD KSČ, 37—50/1/30. V „Listině ohrožených lidí" jsou uvedena tato jména: „Pešl Antonín, Praha XII., Na Folimance 2119. Drtina Prokop JUDr, bývalý sekretář presidenta republiky. Jína Jan, Praha-Smíchov, Nábřeží Legií 30. Papoušek Jaroslav JUDr, ministerský rada MZV, Praha-Bubeneč, Jiráskova 27. Rašín Ladislav, poslanec, Praha II., Žitná 6. Klíma Vlastimil JUDr, poslanec. Sychrava Lev, Národní osvobození. Chmelař Josef, ministerský rada MZV. Hoffman Kamil, ministerský rada MZV. Körbel Josef JUDr, ministerský rada MZV, Kraus, odborový rada MZV (býval na vyslanectví v Londýně). Opočenský Jan, konsul, MZV. Kopačka, podplukovník, Hlavní štáb. Štábní kapitán Fárek, Hlavní štáb. Štábní kapitán Kukula, Hlavní štáb. Podplukovník Růžek, Hlavní štáb. Podplukovník Houška, Hlavní štáb. Budík Jan Ing., Praha-Smíchov, Plzeňská tř., Meissner Alfred JUDr, bývalý ministr. Fischer Josef PhDr, Vydavatel Nové Svobody, Pha II., Hybernská 7. Patzak Václav, ministerstvo školství, vydavatel Nové Svobody, Hybernská ul. 7. Stránský Jaroslav JUDr, poslanec, Brno, Česká 6. Smetáček Zdeněk, redaktor Lidových novin. Dérer Ivan, býv. ministr. Slánský, poslanec. Clementis, poslanec, Bratislava. Dolanský, sekretář poslaneckého klubu komunistického. Dölling, poslanec. Zenkl Petr, býv. primátor. Vrbenský Bohumil. Dr. Sekanina Ivan. Dr. Richter Ferdinand, poslanec, Brno, Královo Pole. Dohalský Zdeněk, Praha III., Nerudova 8. Jaksch Wenzel, poslanec. Elsner MUDr, Praha II., Mikulanská 4. Generálové: Inger, Eliáš, Fiala. Podplukovník Moravec. Hála, generální tajemník katolické lidové strany. Macek, profesor, poslanec. Fiala Josef, redaktor, Orbis. Heidrich, vyslanec MZV. Karvaš (Slovák), býv. ministr. Kunoši JUDr, Exportní ústav. Kozák J. B. PhDr, profesor, poslanec. Schejnost, šéfredaktor Lidových listů. Hoffmeister Adolf JUDr. Peroutka Ferdinand, redaktor Přítomnosti. Jíše Karel, redaktor Českého slova. Kavan Pavel (České slovo). Nezval Vítězslav. Haas Hugo, herec. Dostál Karel, režisér. Kladivo, redaktor Lidových novin. Gottlieb (býval v propagačním oddělení Hlavního štábu)." Viz AÚD KSČ, 37/50/1/117.

Endangered Person's List of forty-eight people who stood a good chance of being fingered by the Nazis. It includes the name of Josef Körbel.

V Praze, 22. září 1945.

R/1945.

Vážený pane doktore,

                 pan náměstek předsedy vlády J. D a v i d
mně uložil,abych Vás požádala o laskavé odeslání dopisu
paní Emilii V a š a t o v é   do Londýna kurýrní cestou.
           Děkuji Vám za Vaší laskavost předem a

znamenám

              s projevem úcty   ÚŘAD PŘEDSEDNICTVA VLÁDY

                                    osobní tajemník
                                nám .předsedy vlády

Pan Dr.Josef K o r b e l ,
   přednosta kabinetu min,zahr.věcí
        v Praze IV.Černín.

Letter, dated May 22, 1945, from Josef Korbel on official Czech government stationery, suggesting that for a brief period, he was *chef de cabinet* to Jan Masaryk. It was the only document the current Czech government could find that had any reference to Korbel being *chef de cabinet,* a position he frequently referred to in his later years. (*Courtesy of the Ministry of Foreign Affairs, the Czech Republic*)

Z a m i n d e l e   N e w   Y o r k

Houdkovi. — Notifikuj Trygve Lie—u dr. Jozefa
Korbela, teraz veľvyslanca v Belehrade do kašmírskej
komisie s tým, že nemôže z Belehradu odísť pred
15. májom. Informuj ihneď, či zástupca, poradca a
pomocný personál tiež na útraty UNO.

                                    Clementis   92.347

Cable, dated May 3, 1948, from Czechoslovak minister Vladimír Clementis, a
Communist, to Vladimír Houdek, the Czechoslovak representative to the United
Nations, saying that Korbel cannot leave his post as ambassador to Belgrade
before May 15, 1948. Korbel had accepted a posting as Czech representative to
the United Nation's Kashmir Commission. Clementis asks Houdek for information about whether Korbel would have a deputy, adviser, and assistants, billable
to the U.N. *(Courtesy of the Ministry of Foreign Affairs, the Czech Republic)*

13.I.1949

7564/A/49
Korbel – Kašmírska komisia.

Ihneď

Z a m i n i   N e w   Y o r k

Houdkovi – Korbel od decembra nie je viac úradníkom MZV.
Oznám, či podľa názoru Trygve Lieho bude notifikovanie
tohto faktu automaticky znamenať, že stráca členstvo v
kašmírskej komisii. Vzhľadom na to, že na veci je zain-
teresovaná aj India, nemožno riskovať novú papánkiádu.

Clementis 7564/A/49.

Odd. „B": telegram prevzat
dne 3. I. 1949 hod./

Cable, dated January 13, 1949, from Clementis to Houdek saying that Korbel has defected from the Czechoslovak government and asking whether this means that the United Nations will automatically take him off the Kashmir Commission. It shows that Clementis did not know Korbel's plans once he arrived in the United States. *(Courtesy of the Ministry of Foreign Affairs, the Czech Republic)*

17.I.1949

1o241/A/49
Korbel - Kašmírska komisia.

Z a m i n i   N e w   Y o r k

Houdkovi - Tvoje 1o5 - Zisti u Soboleva, či notifikácia
odvolania Korbela a nahradenie inou osobou bude bez ďal-
ších prieťahov prevedené.

Clementis 1o241/A/49.

17. I. 1949

Odd. „B": telegram prevzať
dne 13,45   hod.
17-1-

Cable, dated January 17, 1949, from Clementis to Houdek concerning Korbel's dismissal and asking whether he will be replaced right away. *(Courtesy of the Ministry of Foreign Affairs, the Czech Republic)*

Došlé č. 2756/B/1948

Věc: Kašmírská komise,

Na vědomí: PV, A-ST, KPR, GS, P, I, II, III, IV, V, VI.

Odesílá: N e w D e l h i kdy 17.7.48
12.20
Došlo: 18.VII.48 v 08.30 hodin
Referent: Hanušová 19.VII.48 v 10 hodin
K vyřízení: A č. Sekce: Fla

Pro pana ministra Clementise,

K Vašemu čís.145,942 sděluje Korbel toto: Komise rozvinula plnou činnost. Zasedá 2x denně. Utvořila vojenskou subkomisi a posílá právě některé členy do Karajhi. Jejím prvým cílem je zastavení palby. Na oficielních místech mně řekli, že uvítají cestu do Kašmíru. Komise byla velice pěkně přijata indickou vládou a je stále ve styku s úřadujícím ministrem zahraničních věcí Bajpaiem. (PEIPERA) přítomnost nutná. Jinak nemohu plně dělat svou povinnost. Prosím odpověď. Korbel.

30   Sejnoha 1450

Podle sdělení p. generálního sekretáře sdělil mu pan ministr před odjezdem do Bukurešti, že vyslání Pecha do Kašm. Komise nepřichází v úvahu. Dlužno tudíž vyčkati názoru pana ministra.

Poznámka oddělení B: Podtržené místo zkomolené.

19. VII. 48

Pecha?

Albrecht

Odd.B.1

Cable from Josef Korbel to Clementis saying that the Kashmir Commission had developed its activities in full, that it meets twice a day, had established a military subcommission, and is sending some members to Karachi. He says its first goal is to stop the open fire and that they would welcome a trip to Kashmir. The cable is signed by Sejnoha. In his letter asking for asylum in the United States, Korbel states that he never transmitted information about the commission to the Czechoslovak government because it was run by Communists. However, he seems to have provided information through the Czechoslovak ambassador to India Jaroslav Sejnoha. (Courtesy of the Ministry of Foreign Affairs, the Czech Republic)

JUDr. Josef Korbel

(pův. Körbel - změna jména v červenci 1945)
nar. 20. 9. 1909 v Kyšperku, okr. Žamberk ve východních Čechách

Vzdělání: čsl. státní reálka v Kostelci nad Orlicí,
maturita 21. 6. 1927;
Právnická fakulta v Praze, doktorát 31. 3. 1933

Znalost jazyků: němčina, francouzština, angličtina

Vojenská prezenční služba: 17. 7. 1933 - 17. 9. 1934

Profesní dráha:
Od 5. 5. 1933 do 16. 7. 1933 a od 4. 10. 1934
do 21. 11. 1934 advokátní koncipient u dvou právnických kanceláří
v Praze. Od 22. 11. 1934 ve službách MZV, nejprve v ústředí
v Praze, od 1. 1. 1937 do 30. 11. 1938 na čsl. vyslanectví
v Bělehradě jako legační attaché tiskové služby. 25. 3. 1939
opustil obsazenou vlast a přes Jugoslávii, Řecko a Francii
se dostal do Londýna, kde se zapojil do čsl. odboje. Byl členem
informační kanceláře prezidenta E. Beneše organizované zprvu
neoficiálně, po vypuknutí II. sv. války a uznání čsl. národního
výboru pod vedením tohoto výboru. Po uznání čsl. londýnské vlády
pracoval na MZV, kde byl pověřen vedením rozhlasového oddělení.
Po skončení II. sv. války opět na MZV. 1. 9. 1945 byl pověřen
správou vyslanectví ČSR v Bělehradě, od 11. 10. 1945 zde působil
jako vyslanec a po povýšení diplomatického zastoupení na úroveň
velvyslanectví v r. 1946 se stal 1. čsl. velvyslancem
v Jugoslávii. V listopadu 1947 byl jmenován rovněž vyslancem
pro Albánii rezidujícím v Bělehradě. 13. 5. 1948 byl jmenován
čsl. členem v mezinárodní komisi k projednání sporu mezi
Pákistánem a Hindustánem o Kašmír. Změněné politické poměry
po únoru 1948 však brzy znamenaly konec diplomatické kariéry
dr. Korbela. Rozhodnutím prezidenta Gottwalda z 19. 5. 1948 byl
zproštěn funkcí v zahraničí, přeložen do ústředí a 6. 12. 1948
byl propuštěn ze služeb MZV. Pro nelegální opuštění republiky byl
zbaven čsl. státního občanství a byl mu zabaven veškerý majetek.

Vyznamenání: 17. 6. 1947 obdržel čsl. vojenskou medaili I. stupně
jako uznání vynikajících zásluh o osvobození ČSR

Rodina: manželka: Anna, roz. Spieglová,
nar. 11. 5. 1910 v Kostelci nad Orlicí,
sňatek uzavřen 20. 4. 1935

děti: Marie Jana, nar. 15. 5. 1937
Anna Kateřina, nar. 7. 10. 1942
Jan, nar. 15. 1. 1947

Korbel's official curricula vita from the Czech Ministry of Foreign Affairs, showing promotions, awards, and listing his defection on December 12, 1948. *(Courtesy of the Ministry of Foreign Affairs, the Czech Republic)*

Form 5118
TREASURY DEPARTMENT
UNITED STATES CUSTOMS SERVICE

UNITED STATES DEPARTMENT OF JUSTICE
IMMIGRATION AND NATURALIZATION SERVICE
(Rev. 1-6-48)

Form approved.
Budget Bureau No. 42-R019-2.

MANIFEST NO. 30

MANIFEST OF IN-BOUND PASSENGERS (ALIENS) TEMPORARY

Class FIRST from SOUTHAMPTON , NOV. 5th, 1948
(Port of embarkation)

on S.S. "A M E R I C A" arriving at port of NEW YORK - NOV. 11th, 1948
(Name of vessel)

LINE No.	FAMILY NAME—GIVEN NAME DESTINATION IN UNITED STATES	AGE (Years)	SEX (F-M)	MARRIED OR SINGLE	TRAVEL DOC. No. NATIONALITY	NUMBER AND DESCRIPTION OF PIECES OF BAGGAGE	HEAD TAX COLLECTED	THIS COLUMN FOR USE OF MASTER, SURGEON, AND U.S. OFFICERS
1	ANDERSON, Suzanne Plaza Hotel New York, N.Y.	42	F	Wd.	V-736510 British	3	(c) No	EXEMPT
2	ASPREY, Charles E.C. c/o British Consulate New York, N.Y.	40	M	M	V-736457 British	11	No	EXEMPT
3	ASPREY, Doris E. do	42	F	M	V-736459 British		No	EXEMPT
4	ASPREY, Caroline E. do	12	F	S	V-736539 British		No	EXEMPT
5	ASPREY, Charles P. do	10	M	S	V-736434 British		No	EXEMPT
6	BEDUS, Emil Shoreham Hotel Washington, D.C.	53	M	M	V-872136 Austrian	3	No	EXEMPT
7	BRICKMAN, Eda 161 Westchester Ave., Crestwood, N.Y.	42	F	M	I-94 T-947358 British	4	Yes	
8	COLEMAN, Margaret M. 1674 Macombs Rd., New York, N.Y.	30	F	S	V-725061 Irish	2	no	EXEMPT
9	CROSLEY, Nina 700 Poppy Ave., Corona del Mar, Calif.	45	F	S	V-717450 British	3	yes	
10	DE CRANE D'HEYSSELAER, Jan c/o P.H. Barrus, 2 Stone St., New York, N.Y.	48	M	M	V-902301 Belgian	9	YES	
11	DE CRANE D'HEYSSELAER, Christiene do	53	F	M	V-902302 Belgian		YES	
12	DREXLER, Oscar 1674 Macombs Rd., New York, N.Y.	43	M	M	"USC" 119 New York	6	NO USC	U.S. CIT.
13	DREXLER, Marjorie M. do	30	F	M	V-740840 British		(c) no	EXEMPT
14	DREXLER, Carole V. do	3	F	S	"USC" 2073 England		NO USC	U.S. CIT.
15	DREXLER, David J. do	2	M	S	"USC" 2073 England		NO USC	U.S. CIT.
16	FEJTEK, Vladimir. 38 Pearl St., New York, N.Y.	42	M	Wd.	V-379908 Czech.	7	yes	EXEMPT
17	FISCHER, Rudolf Hotel Roosevelt New York, N.Y.	40	M	M	V-760370 Austrian	3	no	EXEMPT
18	FLEMING, Eric M. 246 Summer St., Boston, Mass.	44	M	M	V-735053 British	6	no	EXEMPT
19	FLEMING, Marjorie P. do	39	F	M	V-735058 British		no	EXEMPT
20	FRICKEL, Gerardus Van Leer Metal Prod., 33 W.42nd St., New York, N.Y.	56	M	M	V-724301 Holland	3	no	EXEMPT
21	GODIN DE LUPE, Andre Plaza Hotel New York, N.Y.	74	M	S	V-917538 French	3	no	EXEMPT
22	GOLDBERG, Alexander Seagram Distillers Corp. Chrysler Bldg., N.Y.	51	M	M	I-94 T-447140 Canadian	4	no	EXEMPT
23	GRUENSEIS, Franz Shoreham Hotel Washington, D.C.	53	M	M	V-872131 Austrian	3	no	EXEMPT
24	KAPNEK, Pita Partwood Manor, Upper Darby, Pa.	52	F	Wd.	I-94 T-947341 SOUTH AFRICA British	5	yes	
25	KORBEL, Anna 149 Station Rd., Great Neck, N.Y.	38	F	M	V-274411 Czech.	21	no	EXEMPT

17

0300-271660

0300-299062

30

11/11/48 - (10:10 AM) -

Form I-418
TREASURY DEPARTMENT
United States Customs Service

Form approved.
Budget Bureau No. 42-R019-2.

UNITED STATES DEPARTMENT OF JUSTICE
IMMIGRATION AND NATURALIZATION SERVICE
(Rev. 1-6-48)

MANIFEST OF IN-BOUND PASSENGERS (ALIENS) TEMPORARY

Class FIRST from SOUTHAMPTON NOV. 5th, 19 48
(Port of embarkation)

on S.S. "A M E R I C A" arriving at port of NEW YORK - NOV. 11th, 19 48
(Name of vessel)

LINE No.	FAMILY NAME—GIVEN NAME DESTINATION IN UNITED STATES	AGE (Years)	SEX (F-M)	MAR-RIED OR SINGLE	TRAVEL DOC. NO. NATIONALITY	NUMBER AND DESCRIPTION OF PIECES OF BAGGAGE	HEAD TAX COL-LECTED	THIS COLUMN FOR USE OF MASTER, SURGEON, AND U.S. OFFICERS
1	KORBEL, Marie - 149 Station Road Great Neck, N.Y.	11	F	S	V-274411 CZECH.	0300-299060	(A) no	EXEMPT 18
2	KORBEL, Jan-Josef - do	2	M	S	V-274411 Czech.	0300-299063	(A) no	EXEMPT
3	KORBEL, Anna-Katherine do	6	F	S	V-274411 British	0300-299062	(A) no	EXEMPT
4	KURK, Pamela J. 713 DeGraw Ave., Newark, N.J.	24	F	S	V-736904 Egyptian I-94	3	yes	
5	LINDQUIST, Harry M. Savoy Plaza, New York, N.Y.	35	M	M	T-747342 Swedish	3	(C) ne	EXEMPT
6	MENCINGER, Tanci S. 149 Station Road, Great Neck, N.Y.	18	F	S	V-274413 Yougoslav.	0300-298960 -	(A) no	EXEMPT
7	MOORE, Ethel M. Barclay Hotel New York, N.Y.	36	F	M	V-736787 British	0300-275 / 13	(C) no	EXEMPT
8	MOORE, Edward L. do	40	M	M	V-724466 British	-	(C) no	EXEMPT
9	MOORE, Mary V. do	1	F	S	V-736787 British	-	(C) ne	EXEMPT
10	PERKINS, Ralph McQ. c/o Export Mgr.,Pittsburgh Glass Co.-Pitts.Pa.	33	M	M	V-142268 Austral.	7	(C) yes	I 755 refund EXEMPT
11	PERKINS, Jean M. do	33	F	M	V-142269 Austral.	-	(C) yes	I 755 refund EXEMPT
12	PERLOWSKI, Michael American Automobile Assoc., Washington, D.C.	45	M	M	V-736450 Polish	3	(C) ne	EXEMPT
13	PHILIPP, Rudolf Hotel Roosevelt, New York, N.Y.	61	M	M	V-872135 Austrian	-	(A) no	EXEMPT
14	SAGMEISTER, Otto Hotel Roosevelt New York, N.Y.	42	M	M	V-872137 Austrian	2	(A) no	EXEMPT
15	SMITH, Joseph 7322 Bay Parkway, Brooklyn, N.Y.	49	M	M	V-769863 British	2	(C) no	EXEMPT
16	SOTHERLAND, Thomas S. Henry Hudson Hotel, New York, N.Y.	49	M	S	V-737182 British	3	(C) no	EXEMPT
17								
18								
19								
20								
21								
22								

USC
ALIEN 16

SS *America* manifest showing Anna Korbel, Marie Korbelova (Madeleine), Jan-Josef Korbel (Madeleine's brother), Anna-Katherine Korbelova (Madeleine's sister), and their Yugoslavian maid, Tanci (*sic*) Mencinger. They sailed from Southampton, traveled First Class, and arrived in New York on November 11, 1948. The maid's address in Great Neck, Long Island, is the same as that listed for the Korbels. (*Courtesy of the National Archives and Records Administration, New York*)

.19-2.

MANIFEST OF IN-BOUND PASSEN...

Class ....FIRST.... from ....SOUTHAMPTON........
(Port of embarkation)

on ...."QUEEN MARY"....... arriving at port of ....NEW YORK.. 22n.
(Name of vessel)

Line No.	Family Name—Given Name Destination in United States	Age (Years)	Sex (F-M)	Married or Single	Travel Doc. No. Nationality	Number and Description of Pieces of Baggage	Head Tax Collected	This Column for Use of Master, Surgeon, and U. S. Officers
	(1)		(2)		(3)	(4)	(5)	
1	KORBEL Josef 149, Station Rd. Gt.Neck, N.Y. 0300-298961	39	M	M	V.274410 CZECHO.	6	(C) No	EXEMPT
2	SINGH SAHNEY Bant c/o Hong Kong,Shanghai Bank, New York.	51	M	M	V.722279 BRIT.INDIA	4	(C) No	EXEMPT
3	SINGH SAHNEY Basantkaur add. as above.	39	F	M	V.722280 BRIT.INDIA	–	(C) No	EXEMPT
4	WHETTON JOHN Houston Labs.Shell Oil,Texas, TRNS. TO VENEZUELA.	54	M	M	V.735117 BRITAIN	2	C No	EXEMPT
5	PHELAN VINCENT Dept. of Labour,Ottawa. TRANS. TO CANADA.	49	M	S	V.719154 CANADIAN	10	C) No	EXEMPT
6								
7								
8								
9								

Form approved.
Budget Bureau No. 43-R019-2.   Cherbourg

MANIFEST OF IN-BOUND PASSENGERS (ALIENS)

MANIFEST NO. .....

NON-QUOTA.

Class ....FIRST.... from ....CHERBOURG.. 17 DEC.. 19 48
(Port of embarkation)

on ...."QUEEN MARY"....... arriving at port of ....NEW YORK.. 22 DEC.. 19 48
(Name of vessel)

Line No.	Family Name—Given Name Destination in United States	Age (Years)	Sex (F-M)	Married or Single	Travel Doc. No. Nationality	Number and Description of Pieces of Baggage	Head Tax Collected	This Column for Use of Master, Surgeon, and U. S. Officers
	(1)		(2)		(3)	(4)	(5)	(6)
1	CAMPBELL Winifred E 668 W.T.T. Naperville, New	53	F	S	V.694208 BRITAIN	8	755 YES	EXEMPT
2	PAPANEK Jan 395 Riverside Drive, N.Y.	52	M	M	I.662805 C.S.R.	11	YES	
3	PAPANEK Betka Address as above. (U.S.C)	48	F	M	264719 U.S.A.	–	No	U S CIT.
4	MONIQUE DE GUNZBURG Hotel Carlisle, 76th St. New York.	40	F	M	V.112437 FRENCH	6	YES	
5	LEVEN HUBERT as above De GUNZBURG	9	M	S	V.147329 FRENCH	–	3 No	EXEMPT
6	LEVEN SOLANGE as above.	13	F	S	V.147328 FRENCH	–	3 No	EXEMPT
7	ESMOND FERNANDE 237 E. 61 Str. New York.	64	F	M	7-662646 RP.176661 BRITISH	6	YES	Med cut 68
8	DELEPINE JOSEPHINE 22, E.47th Str. New York.	54	F	M	V.124862 FRENCH	4	No	EXEMPT
9	DELEPINE NELLY as above.	17	F	S	V.124861 FRENCH	–	No	EXEMPT
10	DE MAUKE CESAR Hotel Pensylvania, N.Y.C.	48	M	S	RP.150581B FRENCH	10	YES	

RMS *Queen Mary* manifest showing Josef Korbel sailing from Cherbourg to New York, traveling First Class and arriving December 22, 1948. Also listed on the manifest are fellow Czechoslovak official Jan Papánek and his wife, Betka.

EUR - Mr. C. Heyden Raynor   March 14, 1949
USUN - Thomas F. Power, Jr.   *CONFIDENTIAL*

Reliability of Korbel

As requested, I asked Dr. Papanek on March 11 for his opinion of Korbel.

Dr. Papanek said that he was not entirely sure what to think
about him. He said that his firsthand acquaintanceship with Korbel had been rather brief. He knew that he had been of great
assistance in making Clementis' political fortune by placing him
on BBC during the war when Korbel was in charge of this work for
the Czech Government-in-Exile.

Papanek said that there were some people who had a very
strong opinion against Korbel for reasons with which Papanek was
not familiar. He said that other persons had alleged to him that
Korbel as Ambassador to Belgrade had sent some of the best
information regarding the real nature of Titoism to President
Benes and Prime Minister Masaryk through private channels.
Papanek's understanding was that this information had been quite
different from that which was being sent back officially along
the party line. Papanek had also heard it said that Noel-Baker
had expressed the opinion in London last winter that Korbel had
been very helpful to "our side" both while at Belgrade and while
on the UNCIP.

Perhaps you could make a check with the British about Korbel
in view of the quotation from Noel-Baker.

TFPower:ka

Letter from Thomas F. Power, Jr., a career diplomat at the United Nations, explaining that
he asked Jan Papánek, a Czechoslovak diplomat who represented the Czechoslovak government-in-exile in the United States during the war, for his opinion of Korbel. Papánek, who
had sailed to America with Korbel on the *Queen Mary,* replied that he was not sure what to
think about him, that he knew there were some people who had very strong opinions about
Korbel, but Papánek did not know what they were.

Josef Korbel's official curriculum vitae from the University of Denver, with the last date listed as 1974.

VITA

JOSEPH KORBEL, Professor

University of Denver

Born: 1909 in Czechoslovakia

Education: Secondary school, gymnasium at Kostelec n., Orl, 1920–27
Student at Paris Sorbonne University, 1928–29
Law at Charles University in Prague, 1929–33 with special studies in international law and national economic theories
Promoted to Doctor of Law in spring, 1933.

Military Service: 14 months of military service, July 1933 to September 1934. Lieutenant of the Czechoslovak army.

Diplomatic Service: Entered the Czechoslovak diplomatic service in November 1934. Worked in the Department of Information until 1936 and wrote many articles on international affairs. From January 1937 until December 1938 was Press Attache to the Czechoslovak Legation in Belgrade, Yugoslavia. Participated in the Conference of the Little Entente. Became well acquainted with the Yugoslav history and political life. Was recalled from Belgrade after Munich when attacked by Prague fascist papers as a man of Benes.

After the occupation of Czechoslovakia, in March 1939, he escaped and went to London as correspondent of the Yugoslav papers OBZOR and JUTRO. After the outbreak of war he took part in the organization of the information service of the Czechoslovak government-in-exile in London and was for one year the secretary to Mr. Jan Masaryk. From 1940 until the end of the war he was the head of the broadcasting department of the Czechoslovak government in London and delivered several hundreds of broadcasts about international affairs as "diplomatic correspondent". During the whole time of war he was one of the closest collaborators of President Benes and Minister Jan Masaryk.

After the war he went to Prague by the first plane which flew from London to liberated Czechoslovakia. He was appointed Chef de Cabinet to Mr. Masaryk in the newly-formed Ministry of Foreign Affairs and took part in the organization of this office with its Secretary General Mr. A. Hedirich.

In September 1945 he was accredited as Czechoslovak Minister Plenipotentiary in Belgrade and when the Legation there was raised to the rank of Embassy, he became Ambassador.

At the Peace Conference in Paris in the summer of 1946 he was a member of the Czechoslovak delegation and presided at the Economic Commission for Roumania, Hungary, Bulgaria and Finland. As Ambassador he negotiated several commercial and financial agreements with the Yugoslav government.

At the beginning of February 1948, before the Communist putch in Czechoslovakia, he was appointed member of the United Nations Commission for India and Pakistan. He left Belgrade in May 1948, started to work with the Commission in Geneva, then proceeded to India and Pakistan and returned to Paris with the Commission which prepared the Interim Report for the Security Council.

Other Activities: After the Communist coup, Dr. Korbel came to the United States to write and lecture on the inside workings of the Communist threat to world peace. He came to the University of Denver in 1949 as professor of International Relations and a member of the staff of DU's famed Social Science Foundation.

Dr. Korbel was elected University Lecturer for the University of Denver for 1958.

Books by Dr. Korbel include *Tito's Communism*, published in 1951 by the Denver University Press, *Danger in Kashmir*, published in 1954 by the Princeton University Press, and *A Study of the Impact of the Soviet-German Relations upon Poland*, now in preparation.

Dr. Korbel is married and has three children: Madeline, 21, Katherine, 16, and John, 11. The Korbels live at 2314 So. Madison, Denver.

CURRICULUM VITAE

JOSEF KORBEL
    Andrew W. Mellon Professor of International Studies
    Graduate School of International Studies
    University of Denver
    Denver, Colorado 80210

    Home address
    2335 South Madison Street
    Denver, Colorado 80210

I. *Personal*:
    Born in Czechoslovakia, September 20, 1909; American citi-
    zen since 1957. Married, three children.

II. *Education*:
    Doctor of Law Degree, Charles University, Prague, 1933,
    with emphasis on International Relations. At the Sorbonne,
    Paris, 1928-1929.

III. *Professional positions*:
    a) In the Czechoslovak diplomatic service, 1934-1948; Min-
       istry of Foreign Affairs, Prague, 1934-1936; Press and
       Cultural Attaché, Czechoslovak Legation, Belgrade,
       1937-1938; with the Czechoslovak government in exile, Lon-
       don—Jan Masaryk's personal secretary, 1939-1940; head of
       broadcasting department 1940-1945; Jan Masaryk's Chef de
       Cabinet, 1945; Ambassador to Yugoslavia, September
       1945-May 1948.

       Czechoslovak Delegate to the Paris Peace Conference and
       Chairman of its Economic Committee for the Balkan coun-
       tries and Finland, summer 1946.

       Chairman of the United Nations Kashmir Commission,
       1948-1949.

       Participant at many international conferences on Eastern
       Europe before and after World War II. Close associate of
       E. Beneš and Jan Masaryk.

    b) *Academic—at the University of Denver*:
       Andrew W. Mellon Professor of International Studies, Uni-
       versity of Denver, July 1969-

       Dean, Graduate School of International Studies, and Direc-
       tor, Social Science Foundation, University of Denver,
       November 1959-July 1969.

Professor of International Relations and staff member of
the Social Science Foundation, University of Denver, June
1949–July 1969.

Visiting Appointments:
Visiting Professor at the University of Washington, Seattle, summer 1950.

Research Fellow at the Center of International Studies,
MIT, Cambridge, Massachusetts, summer 1953.

Research Associate, Russian Research Center, Harvard University, Cambridge, Massachusetts, Spring 1957.

Senior Fellow, St. Antony's College, Oxford, England, Fall
1962.

Senior Research Fellow, European Institute, Columbia University, Spring 1968.

IV. *Publications*:
(List attached).

V. *Grants and Honors*:
Rockefeller Foundation, 1949–1950
Rockefeller Foundation, 1952–1953
Guggenheim Foundation Fellow, 1956–1957
Social Science Research Council, 1956 (declined)
Columbia University European Institute, 1968
National Endowment for the Humanities, 1973–1974
ACLS, 1973
Graduate School of International Studies, University of
    Denver, 1970
University of Denver Lecturer, 1957–1958 (award for
    achievements in scholarship)
Phi Beta Kappa (honorary)
Omicron Delta Kappa (honorary)

VI. *Professional Associations and Recognitions*:
Member, Council on Foreign Relations, New York
Member, American Association for the Advancement of Slavic
    Studies
Member and former President, Western Slavic Conference
Member and former President, Rocky Mountain Association
    for Slavic Studies
Member, Atlantic Studies Committee

Member of the Executive Committee and former Vice-
President, Czechoslovak Society for Arts and Sciences
in America
Selected as an "Outstanding Educator of America" for 1971
Listed in: Who Is Who in America; National Faculty Direc-
tory; Who Is Who in American College Administration;
American Men of Science—Social and Behavioral Sciences;
Who Is Who in Colorado; International Scholars Direc-
tory; Personalities of the West and Midwest; National
Register of Prominent Americans.

VII. *Field of specialization*:

Soviet foreign policy, East Europe, East-West European
relations

VIII. *Travel*:

Six years in England, five years in Yugoslavia, two years
in France, shorter visits in almost all other European
countries, in India, Pakistan and Kashmir.

IX. *Languages*:

English, Czech, Serbo-Croat, French fluently; Russian, German good; reading knowledge in Polish and Bulgarian good.

Index